MUSIC AT THE CROSSROADS
LIVES & LEGACIES OF BALTIMORE JAZZ

EDITED BY
MARK OSTEEN
&
FRANK J. GRAZIANO

MUSIC AT THE CROSSROADS

LIVES & LEGACIES
OF BALTIMORE JAZZ

EDITED BY
MARK OSTEEN
&
FRANK J. GRAZIANO

CONTRIBUTING EDITORS
MATTHEW BLACKBURN
ERIN BOWMAN
CATHLEEN CARRIS
BENJAMIN DiFRANCO
JENNIFER MARGARET NORDMARK
KATHERINE R. RYNONE
ANDREW ZALESKI

Baltimore, MD
www.apprenticehouse.com

ISBN 978-1-934074-51-0

Printed in the United States of America

Commemorative Edition

Published by Apprentice House
The Future of Publishing...Today!

Book Design: Jesse DeFlorio

Apprentice House
Communication Department
Loyola University Maryland
4501 N. Charles Street
Baltimore, MD 21210

410.617.5265
410.617.5040 (fax)
www.ApprenticeHouse.com
info@ApprenticeHouse.com

COMMEMORATIVE EDITION

——— / ———

About the Aperio Series

Aperio: *I uncover, disclose, make accessible*

Through "Aperio Series: Loyola Humane Texts," Loyola University Maryland's Apprentice House publishes important and illuminating texts in the Humanities that have been edited, annotated, and/or translated by the University's students in collaboration with faculty. Students also work with faculty to design and publish the texts. The texts are intended for all readers but should be of particular interest and use to college students and in undergraduate classes.

Table of Contents

Introduction
Mark Osteen

I. PIONEERS

II. INNOVATORS

III. LEGACIES

IV. APPENDICES

Introduction
by Mark Osteen

Baltimore possesses a rich jazz history that began even before the music had a name. Buddy Bolden, the legendary originator of jazz, became famous for playing cornet in New Orleans during the first decade of the twentieth century, yet Eubie Blake, born in 1883, was composing and performing ragtime piano pieces in Baltimore as early as 1898. In the years that followed, the city produced three more jazz legends—singer/bandleader Cab Calloway, big band drummer Chick Webb, vocalist Billie Holiday—and gave birth to an impressive constellation of national and regional stars, including saxophonists Gary Bartz, Mickey Fields, Andy Ennis, and Antonio Hart; pianists Albert Dailey, Ellis Larkins, and Cyrus Chestnut; composer/arranger Hank Levy; and vocalists Ruby Glover and Ethel Ennis, among others.

Yet despite this impressive legacy, Baltimore's singular contributions to jazz history have been largely neglected. Blake, for example, endured a long eclipse in the 1940s and '50s, resurfacing only in the '60s and '70s as an elderly purveyor of the ragtime and stride styles that he had mastered and helped to invent decades earlier. Because his major contributions occurred so early in jazz history, much of his music went unrecorded, and by the time he died in 1983, his few recordings were mostly out of print. Chick Webb, though often mentioned in passing as a significant Swing Era band leader, has never been allotted a book-length biography and seldom even granted a comprehensive critical essay. Although many pages have been written about Cab Calloway and Billie Holiday, never have they been presented as sharing a Baltimore heritage. Gary Bartz, Ellis Larkins, and Andy and Ethel Ennis, all four of whom owe their musical education to Baltimore clubs and institutions, have been denied the attention their work merits: Bartz experienced a lengthy recording drought in the 1980s; Larkins made only a few records under his own name, appearing primarily as an accompanist and duo performer; Andy Ennis, though serving as Ray Charles's musical director for many years, was seldom in the spotlight during "The Genius'"s performances; Ethel Ennis, after recording several albums and touring widely, returned to Baltimore and kept a relatively low profile. Other artists who elected to remain in Baltimore never received the level of media attention trained on New York-based artists, despite their high-caliber musicianship or, in Levy's case, a canon of compositions performed across the nation. This book aims to right those wrongs by locating each artist within the Baltimore firmament, as well as by honoring and analyzing each artist's contribution to jazz as a whole.

A second important tradition lies in the Baltimore jazz community: on Pennsylvania Avenue, where a strip of jazz clubs and theaters featured national artists and nurtured home grown talent; and in organizations such as the Left Bank Jazz Society, which sponsored concerts by regional and national jazz artists for more than two decades, thereby sustaining the local jazz audience and connecting it to the national scene. Though local elders fondly remember these gatherings, they have been eclipsed with the passing of years. This volume also examines and celebrates these significant, but underappreciated, legacies.

The Baltimore Buzz

While growing up in Baltimore, Eubie Blake made a name playing in the city's brothels and luxury hotels. After he left Maryland, he used his compositional skills to create, with Noble Sissle, the music for the pathfinding all-black musical *Shuffle Along*, which premiered on Broadway in 1921. Though the show was somewhat constrained by the residue of minstrel conventions, *Shuffle Along* nonetheless broke new ground with its music, which synthesized diverse ingredients—including ragtime, blues, Latin rhythms, and vaudeville—into a satisfying stew. In his later career, Blake became a living embodiment of jazz elegance, showcasing his courtly manner along with his piano skills in a career that endured into his nineties.

Despite his lifelong physical disability (a form of dwarfism caused by tuberculosis of the spine), Chick Webb became a powerful and charismatic drummer and Swing bandleader. One of the highlights of his career was his orchestra's legendary Battle of the Bands against Benny Goodman's group in May, 1937; by most accounts Webb's group won. The Goodman drummer—a young Gene Krupa—was forever afterward in awe of Webb and cited him as his mentor and idol. After Webb's early death, an impressive roster of other jazz drummers professed admiration for his innovative work.

Cab Calloway took advantage of the thriving jazz scene in 1920s Baltimore, learning there how to win an audience, lead a band and hustle for gigs. By the early 1930s his band's shows were being broadcast nationally on the radio, and in 1931 he recorded his signature tune, "Minnie the Moocher." Later in life he made movies, and played important roles in revivals of *Porgy and Bess* and *Hello,*

Dolly. Calloway's contributions are myriad: not only did he lead one of the top bands of the Swing Era, but along with Louis Armstrong, he helped to popularize scat singing and make it an integral part of the jazz repertoire. Perhaps most importantly, his joyous engagement with audiences—his insistence that they participate in the show and leave the theater energized—set a new standard for jazz performance, and enabled him to serve as a disseminator and global ambassador for the music.

Though born in Philadelphia, Billie Holiday was raised in Baltimore, where she endured a difficult childhood with an absent father and a mother who struggled to make a living and find a stable relationship. Holiday not only confronted the racism that oppressed virtually every black jazz artist of the day, but also coped with sexism in both her personal and professional lives. Yet despite a limited range and quiet voice, she carved out a niche as one of the greatest singers in the history of jazz, cultivating a distinctive style that favored emotional authenticity and rhythmic suppleness over technique, meanwhile protesting against racism with the anti-lynching song "Strange Fruit," and lending lyrics to such classic tunes as "Don't Explain," and "God Bless the Child."

Before becoming famous, each of these artists faced a personal crossroads that required a decision: uproot from Baltimore to woo fame and perform with the country's top musicians; or remain at home, thereby staying true to his/her heart but sacrificing a chance at national recognition. All four of these jazz legends chose the former option. Many of the younger artists discussed in this volume—including Bartz, Larkins, Chestnut—followed their lead. This pattern exposes a major reason for the neglect of Baltimore's jazz heritage: its greatest jazz artists left town. How, then, can Baltimore claim them? The essays that follow provide an answer: these artists' inspiration and styles grew from Baltimore roots, and likely would not have flourished elsewhere.

From sneaking out at night to play in Baltimore's brothels, and later by performing at the luxurious Goldfield Hotel, Blake learned early on how to tailor his music to diverse audiences—a skill he perfected in *Shuffle Along*, as Jennifer Margaret Nordmark argues in her essay. He also cultivated a sophisticated manner that both lifted him above racial stereotypes and helped to demolish them. Calloway acquired much of the determination and drive that enabled him to forge a successful career from his early experiences in Baltimore. As Matthew Blackburn writes, "young Cab spent his days as a 'hustler,' selling newspapers, shoes, and working at the nearby Pimlico racetrack. This hard work ethic was likely instilled in him by the family's financial struggles and inspired by his stepfather John Nelson Fortune's devotion to earning money for the family." After a year's stay at the Downingtown reform school at around age 13, Calloway recalls, "I knew, from then on, I'd have to make it on my own" (Calloway 28). Webb devised a performance style that minimized his weaknesses and exploited his early experiences as a street-wise paper boy who learned how to drum by beating on garbage cans. Thus, although he left Maryland in his teens, Webb's indomitable spirit—as well as his innovative drumming—derived from his upbringing in East Baltimore. "Webb was a character who frequently took it on the chin and refused to be marginalized," Frank J. Graziano notes, because he came from a city that existed "in the shadow of other East Coast metropolises" and thus had a "history of doing the same thing." Webb, indeed, embodies in miniature the story and spirit of Baltimore jazz. According to Erin Bowman, Eleanora Fagan/Gough's turbulent, unstable childhood of rotating homes and parent surrogates (along with at least one stay at an institution for female delinquents) contributed to the restless adulthood, traumatic relationships and drug abuse that characterized her life as Billie Holiday. If some of her lyrics express passivity and sadness, the words to her signature song imply that Lady Day wasn't merely a victim, but a resilient woman who learned early on that she could depend upon no one but herself: "God bless the child," she declares, "that's got his own." Baltimore may have torn her down, but it also built her up.

Though the other musicians discussed herein experienced less difficult childhoods than Holiday, Baltimore nonetheless left its mark upon them. For example, like Calloway and Webb, Ellis Larkins received his early training from W. Llewellyn Wilson, music director at Frederick Douglass High School, as well as formal schooling from Baltimore's finest private teachers and, eventually, at Peabody Conservatory. Bob Jacobson suggests in his chapter that Larkins, as the first African-American admitted to the school, learned to cultivate the self-effacing manner and flexible style that fueled his career as a coveted accompanist. It was in Baltimore that Gary Bartz first forged his love affair with jazz by attending shows at Pennsylvania Avenue's jazz clubs, one of which was owned by his parents. Despite an ambivalent relationship to the city, Geoffrey Himes notes, Bartz has returned frequently, for a time holding down a house gig at a local club, where he mentored and encouraged many younger musicians. As Himes also demonstrates in his chapter on Cyrus Chestnut, the pianist grew up playing—and still occasionally returns to play—in Baltimore churches, and has habitually celebrated and elaborated upon those gospel roots in his recordings and performances. In short, although these musicians left Baltimore, Baltimore never left them. Indeed, it provided a certain jolt—a Baltimore buzz, to borrow the title of one of Blake's tunes—that prepared them for their lives in jazz.

Despite the departure of many of its most talented musical children, Baltimore also maintained its own local jazz buzz from the 1950s through the '70s. The lilt in this sound, Liz Fixsen's chapter reveals, was engendered by Baltimore's talented female vocalists, particularly Ruby Glover, who served as godmother for aspiring singers for three decades, and Ethel Ennis, who had sung with Benny Goodman and courted national fame before growing weary of being asked to sound like other singers and returning to Baltimore. If Glover and Ennis were the soul of Baltimore jazz, its beating heart was located on Pennsylvania Avenue, where a line of jazz clubs (including the North End Lounge, owned by Bartz's parents, and the Red Fox, where Ennis performed regularly, as well as the Club Casino, Comedy Club and many others) featured jazz shows almost nightly, and the elegant Royal Theatre showcased national artists of various genres. Mary Zajac's chapter pays tribute to this historic jazz hub. Another indispensable tone in Baltimore's jazz buzz issued from the city's saxophone players; this legacy is the subject of Eliot Caroom's chapter, "Passing the Axe." At the center of the chain of influence was Mickey Fields, a powerful, versatile tenor player who could have achieved international recognition but instead chose to stay in Baltimore, where he served as inspiration and mentor for two generations of sax players, including Bartz and Hart. A chameleonic player equally capable of delivering lightning bursts of bebop or blowing gutbucket blues, Fields epitomizes the meeting of forces that characterizes Baltimore jazz.

Covering the Waterfront

This meeting of forces derives in part from the city's unique character as a port and regional crossroads. Its identity as a port made it a destination for a wide array of ethnic groups, each of which brought along its own music; in this regard, Baltimore resembles jazz's original home, New Orleans. In addition, Baltimore's location as a border state and crossroads between North and South also exposed its musicians to a confluence of traditions. Thus, Baltimore jazz is heavily inflected with gospel and blues—southern idioms—as indicated by the style that dominated the city's jazz scene from the '50s through the '70s, and even later: hard bop, with its strong rhythmic pulse and distinct gospel/blues flavor. Yet the city's music also manifests some of the sophistication and avant garde impulses of New York and the Northeast, as Geoffrey Himes points out in his chapter on Gary Bartz. Thus, for example, Bartz's and Chestnut's experiments in amalgamating styles— Chestnut's forays into sources as divergent as Elvis Presley and the rock group Pavement, as well as his more familiar blues and gospel; Bartz's endeavors to blend jazz, R & B and funk—typify the mix of genres that has fed Baltimore jazz.

But the experimental strain in Baltimore jazz is perhaps best represented by saxophonist/arranger/composer Hank Levy. At the same time that Mickey Fields was holding court in city clubs, Levy was building a national name in a far different setting. While working as director of the jazz program at Towson State College (now Towson University) just north of Baltimore city, Levy created a canon of challenging charts for the nation's collegiate bands as well as for orchestras such as those of Stan Kenton and Don Ellis. Levy's signature innovation was the deployment of meters—5/4, 9/4, 13/8, and the like—that had seldom before been used in jazz. If these charts presented great difficulties for players schooled in Kansas City-style riff charts, the blues, or even bebop, they nevertheless possessed that indefinable thing called swing. Levy's music thus reveals a rare ability to synthesize jazz's modernist strains—its aspirations to be art—with its history as dance music, as well as the capacity to make a national mark while remaining in Baltimore.

The city's crossroads status has also permitted Baltimore-bred artists to develop an unusual ability to adapt to variety of audiences. Just as Eubie Blake's penchant for drawing from divergent genres may stem from the flexibility he learned in Baltimore, a similar flexibility also enabled Ellis Larkins to hone his prowess as an accompanist, and eventually to compile a list of credits that reads like a Hall of Fame roster of jazz vocalists and to record a series of highly regarded duets with cornetist Ruby Braff. If Larkins's adaptability and unassuming nature paradoxically vaulted him to the forefront of jazz, the same qualities may also have prevented him from becoming as well known as he deserves. In that regard Larkins resembles Baltimore itself, long overshadowed by nearby Washington and Philadelphia.

Yet because of its proximity to those cities, Baltimore became a destination for virtually every major jazz artist, in large part through the work of the Left Bank Jazz Society (LBJS), a nonprofit interracial alliance of jazz lovers which sponsored weekly concerts from the 1960s through the '80s, mostly at the Famous Ballroom on North Charles Street. Though shrewd negotiation certainly helped to bring artists to LBJS concerts for a fraction of their usual salary, location mattered as well: because Baltimore was not far from New York or Philadelphia or Washington, bands who had played in these towns on Saturday could easily make the short jaunt to Charm City and perform for an appreciative crowd on a Sunday, when they would otherwise be idle. The LBJS not only kept the Baltimore jazz community buzzing; it also ensured that local audiences remained linked to the national jazz scene. Indeed, as Cathleen Carris's chapter demonstrates, the organization also made important contributions to interracial collegiality and to prisoner rehabilitation. And once in a while, the LBJS made history: thus, as Ms. Carris documents, the final live performance of legendary saxophonist John Coltrane took place not at an April, 1967 benefit in Harlem, as some histories assert, but on May 7th, 1967, at an LBJS concert in Baltimore.[1]

Close to the south but not truly southern, near the north but not exactly northern, Baltimore tapped into both the rural and urban, traditional and modernist currents in jazz. The city's mixing of regions and ethnicities, then, has enabled its artists to cover the entire waterfront of jazz styles.

Getting Their Own

As its border state location would also suggest, Baltimore has not been immune from the racial prejudices and tensions that have so long divided this nation and stymied its social progress. Baltimore's jazz history, like that of jazz in general, provides numerous disturbing examples of these problems and of Americans' attempts to overcome them. Blake and Sissle, for example, rejected promoters' suggestions that they resort to racial caricatures in their performances; even so, Flournoy Miller and Aubrey Lyles, *Shuffle Along*'s male leads (also the authors of the original libretto), performed in blackface. Thus the show's advance in presenting an all-African-American cast was partly negated by the stereotypes it was forced to promulgate. Cab Calloway was brought face-to-face with the realities of racism when his band toured the south, where they were subject to hostility and treatment as second-class citizens. In his autobiography he recalls one Easter Sunday when he and his men were in Raleigh, NC, and he realized that, although each of them had "two or three hundred dollars in his pocket, [they] couldn't buy anything to eat or drink because we were Negroes. . . . [I]t took something out of us to accept that kind of crap" (126). Chick Webb was never honored as the King of Swing because a white leader, Benny Goodman, had been awarded the title by white critics. Yet his group defeated Goodman's orchestra in at least one epic Battle of the Bands. Billie Holiday endured appallingly dehumanizing treatment when fronting Artie Shaw's all-white orchestra in the late 1930s: barred from hotels and restaurants, sleeping on the tour bus, eventually she grew tired of "having a federal case over breakfast, lunch and dinner" (Holiday/Dufty 75) and quit the band. Even on New York's 52nd St., she notes, "we were not allowed to mingle in any kind of way. The minute we were finished . . . we had to scoot out back to the alley or go out and sit in the street" (97). Gary Bartz, disgusted by the racist culture of Baltimore in the 1950s—though a member of one of the first desegregated classes at City College High School, he was not allowed to attend his own prom—felt he simply must get out of town as soon as possible. Unable to enter Peabody Conservatory as a regular student, Ellis Larkins instead took private lessons from Peabody instructors until his singular talent forced the institution to admit him as its first African-American student.

Yet Baltimore's jazz musicians and organizations also defied racial lines. For example, the clubs on Pennsylvania Avenue were frequented by both white and black, straight and gay jazz fans, despite the segregation and prejudices that prevailed in many parts of the city; the LBJS, which emerged from an organization called the Interracial Jazz Society, welcomed all races into its governing body and its concerts. Cab Calloway, with his "hep" lingo and risque lyrics, gave white jazz fans "an entree into the black ghetto," write Scott DeVeaux and Gary Giddins, and its "alluring world of illicit drugs and sex." To other African Americans, however, he "offered hope," showing how "a man with talent and ambition could rise to the top of the music business," by appealing both to Harlem cats and to the stodgier black middle class (191). Like Calloway, Webb won both white and black audiences, and performed regularly at the Savoy Ballroom, one of the few integrated venues of the era. Lady Day fought back with "Strange Fruit," the haunting anti-lynching song that she debuted at Café Society (another integrated venue) in 1939; though the pain in her voice testifies to her personal encounters with the dehumanization that the song so horribly describes, merely singing such a song made a powerful statement against racism.

Racial prejudice was also complicated by other factors: Holiday's gender made her the subject of abuse from male promoters and lovers; Webb waged a lifelong battle with his painful physical disability. Yet both artists found ways not only to prevail over these challenges but to use them to their advantage, Holiday by cultivating an elegant persona—Lady Day—that combined vulnerability and strength and captivated audiences everywhere; Webb by tailoring his drum kit to his size and by devising an idiosyncratic style. Indeed, according to Giddins, Webb not only "overcame staggering obstacles," but "did it with élan, never asking for or requiring handicap points" (138).

Many of Baltimore's jazz artists also found themselves at another crossroads, one reached by virtually every musician who desires success: whether to devote him/herself to achieving the highest artistic standards, or instead to please audiences, even if it means compromising those standards. Thus Webb, frustrated by his inability to break through to national fame even though his bands were admired by cognoscenti, decided to add a vocalist—finally settling on a chubby street urchin named Ella Fitzgerald—and with her earned the recognition that had previously eluded him. If the addition of Fitzgerald sometimes seemed to satisfy both impulses (with her fronting the group, Webb's orchestra won a Battle of the Bands against Count Basie in 1938), his music became increasingly dominated by novelty tunes such as "A-Tisket, A-Tasket," which scarcely showed his band in its best light. As jazz styles changed, Blake failed to equal the success of *Shuffle Along* with his later shows; his career thus went into a long decline before its revival in his old age. Bartz temporarily abandoned the straight-ahead jazz that he had mastered in his early career to make a series of R&B-oriented albums in the 1970s. Ethel Ennis's career embodies a constant battle between the desire to forge a distinctive identity and the efforts of promoters and mentors to turn her into someone else; eventually, she found a more comfortable home back in Baltimore, mixing local performances with other appearances, including singing the national anthem at Richard Nixon's inauguration.

Though some artists were able to satisfy both their musical ambitions and the tastes of the masses, their balancing acts were usually temporary and fragile: Billie Holiday never changed her style, and though she maintained a high level of popularity, her best-selling record came in the 1950s, after her voice had become frayed and worn. Though Calloway's bands featured topnotch musicians such as Milt Hinton, Chu Berry, and Dizzy Gillespie, the groups played mostly novelty tunes, and after the demise of the big band era, Calloway struggled to find work, until accepting the role of Sportin' Life in a revival of *Porgy and Bess.* In negotiating between the demands of art and commerce, Baltimore's jazz artists typify the transience of fame, the evolution of styles, and the unforgiving nature of the entertainment business. As the vagaries of the musician's lifestyle and the fickleness of audiences took their toll on the musicians, no matter whether they stayed in Baltimore or left town, each one had to learn the lesson conveyed in "God Bless the Child": that wealth and fame come and go, so one must learn to take care of him- or herself—as Bartz did by founding his own label, fittingly titled "OYO," or "on your own." Strength and resilience, the essays in this volume suggest, emerge from the adversity that seems to be a defining characteristic of Baltimore jazz.

But what of today's local jazz scene? Are contemporary Baltimore jazz musicians getting their own, or merely earning the "crust of bread" so disdainfully described in Holiday's lyrics? Though jazz will never be as popular as it was 50 years ago, echoes of the original Baltimore buzz still ring through local clubs and concert halls. Investigating the current jazz scene in Baltimore, Andrew Zaleski finds musicians struggling with changing demographics and tastes and experiencing intense competition for dwindling gigs, as the once-unified Baltimore jazz community becomes riven by generational and racial divides. Nevertheless, after a period of darkness in the 1990s, Baltimore jazz is undergoing a minor renaissance, largely due to the rise of nonprofit organizations such as the Baltimore Jazz Alliance, Be Mo Jazz, the Chamber Jazz Society, and to educational institutions such as the Peabody Institute. This trend reflects conditions throughout the United States: whereas jazz musicians once obtained their musical education by working on their chops, showing up at jam sessions, and finding out what they still didn't know, today they enroll in college courses or conservatories and earn degrees in music performance or education, after which they often become educators themselves.

Even so, jazz remains in what seems to be a state of permanent crisis. Its survival both nationally and locally will require the emergence of new, younger audiences for the music; the maintenance and growth of school music programs and the emergence of nonprofit organizations dedicated to preserving and promoting the music; and, perhaps most importantly, the cultivation of new attitudes by musicians themselves.

The long-standing individualist ethos of jazz musicians—hiring themselves out as sidemen with little or no commitment to any group or community—is no longer a viable approach. In other words, just getting one's own is not enough; instead, musicians, music lovers, promoters, and venue owners must create alliances, come together to restore a sense of community, and in so doing make that Baltimore buzz ring loudly once more.

:::::

This volume is the fourth in the Aperio Series: Loyola Humane

Texts, a unique endeavor sponsored by Loyola University Maryland, in which students work under faculty guidance to produce an original work of scholarship published by Apprentice House, a student-run press housed in Loyola's Department of Communication. We would like to acknowledge the sponsors and supporters who have helped to bring this project to fruition. First, kudos go to my co-editor, Frank Graziano, who initiated the project. We have also benefitted enormously from the contributions of our non-student authors, as well as from the guidance and support of Loyola's faculty and administrators, including Professors Joseph Walsh, Jack Breihan, and Matthew Mulcahy; Dean James Buckley, and Nancy Dufau, Director of Loyola's Office of Research and Sponsored Programs. Indispensable funding for this project was supplied by grants from the Loyola Center for the Humanities and from the Gladys Krieble Delmas Foundation. We also extend our gratitude to Desiree Mundell Collins for generously allowing us access to the Benny Kearse Collection of Left Bank Jazz Society memorabilia; to the Maryland Historical Society, the Sojourner-Douglass College library, the Enoch Pratt Library, and to the many jazz musicians and fans whose words we have quoted herein.

NOTES

1. See, for example, Nisenson 216, and Woideck 222 and 245. Even the original edition of Lewis Porter's highly regarded biography states that Coltrane's last performance took place on April 23rd, 1967, at the Olatunji Center in New York City; Porter has corrected this error in recent editions (Porter 289). Coltrane died on July 17th of that year.

Works Cited

Calloway, Cab, and Bryant Rollins. *Of Minnie the Moocher and Me*. New York: Crowell, 1976.

DeVeaux, Scott, and Gary Giddins. *Jazz*. New York: Norton, 2009.

Giddins, Gary. *Visions of Jazz: The First Century*. New York: Oxford UP, 1998.

Holiday, Billie, with William Dufty. *Lady Sings the Blues*. 1956. Rev. Ed. New York: Penguin, 1992.

—., and Arthur Herzog, Jr. "God Bless the Child." 1941. *The Real Vocal Book*. 2nd ed. Milwaukee: Hal Leonard, n.d. 108.

Nisenson, Eric. *Ascension: John Coltrane and His Quest*. New York: St. Martin's, 1993.

Porter, Lewis. *John Coltrane: His Life and Music*. Ann Arbor: U of Michigan P, 1998.

Woideck, Carl. "Chronology." *The John Coltrane Companion: Five Decades of Commentary*. Ed. Carl Woideck. New York: Schirmer, 1998. 239-45.

—. "Later Critical Reception." *The John Coltrane Companion: Five Decades of Commentary*. Ed. Carl Woideck. New York: Schirmer, 1998. 221-22.

I. PIONEERS

1. Eubie Blake: From Baltimore's Bordellos to Broadway's Bigshot
  Jennifer Margaret Nordmark

2. Chick Webb: Coup in the Kingdom of Swing
  Frank J. Graziano

3. The Singin', Swingin' Life and Times of Cab Calloway
  Matthew Blackburn

4. Billie Holiday: A Story of Sorrow and Success
  Erin Bowman

Eubie Blake

"A catalyst for the Harlem Renaissance, Eubie Blake's Shuffle Along would not have been possible without his Baltimore upbringing and musical training."

1 From Baltimore's Bordellos to Broadway's Bigshot

by Jennifer Margaret Nordmark

Musician, composer, visionary—many words can be used to describe the legendary pianist James Hubert Blake, whose best-known work, *Shuffle Along,* paved an unprecedented path in African-American theater. Despite his many achievements, perhaps the best word to describe "Eubie" Blake is "Baltimorean." Although he is typically associated with musical theater, Blake's diverse body of work has its roots in his humble but prolific beginnings as a ragtime pianist. The heavy bass lines, syncopated melodies, and upbeat tempos for which he is known are all traits of the ragtime compositions he wrote in the saloons and bordellos of his native Baltimore.

James Hubert Blake, known to most as Eubie, was born in Baltimore in 1883 to John Sumner Blake and Emily Johnston Blake, both former slaves. John worked as a stevedore, or longshoreman, in the Inner Harbor. From the very beginning of their marriage, John and Emily had wanted to start a family, but Eubie was the only child of 11 to live past infancy (Rose 4). Though frail at birth, he surpassed all expectations and lived to be 100 years old.

Eubie attended Primary School No. 2 at 200 East Street, an "all-Negro" school near Lexington (Rose 5). His father also took an active role in his child's education. In addition to making Eubie read the Baltimore *Sun* newspaper, John shared with his son his experiences as a slave, emphasizing the immorality of racist attitudes. Eubie's father

1

insisted that "there were good and bad white people just as there were good and bad Negros" (Rose 8). Eubie Blake retained the lessons his father taught him for his entire life. In his biography of Blake, author Al Rose writes,

> Irrespective of the philosophical merits of John Sumner Blake's attitudes, Eubie never shook them. In later years they helped him to control his inevitable rage at obvious inequity and injustice. It's doubtful that he could have had all of the success in show business that he ultimately achieved had some of his father's guidance not remained in his personality. (9)

Blake obviously took his father's words to heart. Throughout his successful career, Blake challenged racial stereotypes and advanced the perception of African Americans through his accomplishments and actions. Instead of openly accusing his racist detractors, he smiled and proved them wrong with his undeniable talent.

Blake's parents discovered that musical talent when he was only four or five years old. He recounts, "I was shopping with my mother in the market at night, and I must have got away from her. I wandered across this wide street and I found a music store. I climbed up on the bench of an organ and I fooled around with it until it made a sound" (qtd. in Rose 11). The store manager told Emily Blake that her son had a God-given talent. Emily, who was deeply religious, felt she couldn't stand in the way of the Lord. She and John decided to make 25-cent weekly payments on a 75-dollar pump organ. The one stipulation was that their son was allowed to play only music that "was doing the Lord's work" (Rose 13). If Emily caught young Eubie syncopating the notes or "ragging" a hymn, she would shout at him to "Take that ragtime out of my house!" (Rose 12).

2

Despite her protests, Blake was drawn by the irresistible pull of ragtime. At age 12, he learned to play the cornet and joined a band, in which he began adding his own flair to the less-than-exciting arrangements given to the musicians. The bandleader, Captain Harris, didn't allow ragtime in his band and promptly fired Blake. "I figured I worked as hard as the other guys and that I played as much as they did, but Cap Harris just didn't care for the kind of music I cared about," recalled Blake (qtd. in Rose 15).

Across the United States, jazz evolved in the brothels of major cities. Baltimore was no exception. At the age of 15 Blake was playing piano at Aggie Shelton's, one of the classiest establishments in town. "You know, those fellows and those girls used to just sit and talk together like a church social or something, no rough stuff at all. Of course, the scagmo happened one flight up. I made a lot of tips. The more tunes you'd know, the more money you'd make" (Blake, qtd. in Rose 22). Blake learned quite a lot of tunes and in time began composing a few of his own. He started with folk classics like "The Beautiful Blue Danube" and "Rustle of Spring." To spice up the music he played, Blake took older classics and added his signature stride style.

The stride piano style of playing is characterized by a heavy rhythmic pulse from the left hand, which covers the piano's lower register. While the left hand plays a four-beat pulse that alternates notes (think "oom-pa, oom-pa"), the right hand ornaments the melody of the song with syncopation and contrapuntal lines. Many of Blake's fans referred to his sound as a "wobble-wobble bass," describing the alternation in the lower notes (Rose 21). Strong, audible bass lines help to give ragtime its jaunty, playful sound. To achieve this distinctive style, Blake took advantage of a physical gift: one look at Blake's hands and it is clear that he was built to play the piano. His oversized hands made it possible for him to play complex chords and rhythms with his left hand while ornamenting and syncopating with the right. The span of his hands could cover many more keys than most piano players', and he took advantage of this ability when composing. Many of his pieces require more dexterity and range than most musicians possess.

Blake heard a few ragtime songs like "Hello, Ma Ragtime Gal" and "After the Ball" and learned to play them just by remembering what he had heard (Rose 22). He also learned to "rag" more classical songs. By adding the prominent bass lines and syncopation to well-known classical pieces, Blake brought a distinctively African-American sound to European standards. This conflux of cultures is a constant theme in almost all types of jazz music, including ragtime.

Every bit of musical knowledge Blake picked up in Baltimore influenced his later compositions. For example, many of Blake's pieces roughly follow the structure of a march. Blake would have learned march form while playing in Cap Harris's band and listening to the Sousa tunes that were popular at the time. Eventually, Blake began writing his own music. While working in Aggie Shelton's bordello in 1899, he wrote his first hit, "The Charleston Rag" (though its first title was "Sounds of Africa"). The piece has a consistent descending bass line that gives it a sense of urgency. While the left hand plays the bass line and Blake's signature "wobble-wobble," the right hand plays a highly syncopated and lively melody that loosely follows the compositional structure of a march. After a short, scalar introduction, there is an A melody that repeats itself. Then a second melody, B, is introduced

4

and also repeated. However, instead of the trio section, which usually occurs in this part of a traditional march, Blake repeats the A and B melodies once again. Next, a short bridge leads into the last repetition of the B melody. In short, though this tune deviates slightly in its lack of a trio section, it does, like many of Blake's ragtime pieces, follow a modified march structure.

In order to work at Aggie's, 15 year-old Blake had to escape the watchful eye of his God-fearing mother. Blake waited until his parents went to bed, and then sneaked out of the house. His first stop every night was Rabb Walker's pool hall, where he rented a pair of long pants to wear to work. Then he would go to Aggie's, play all night, and be back in bed before his parents even knew he was missing (Rose 22). He must have known that he wouldn't be able to fool his mother forever, but he probably did not think that he would be the one to betray his own secret. One night, the minister's wife at Emily Blake's church happened to walk by Aggie's and hear Eubie playing his wobble-wobble bass. Soon after, she went to Emily to inform her of her son's nighttime whereabouts. The minister's wife told Emily that she was absolutely sure it was him playing in Aggie Shelton's because "Nobody plays with that wobble-wobble bass but Hubie [Eubie]. Anyone can tell it" (Rose 25).

When Eubie's father learned about his son's night job, he asked him what he did with all of his earnings. Eubie compliantly showed his father all of his money, neatly laid under the carpet in his bedroom. Despite Emily's moral objections, John allowed Eubie to keep his job.

Al Rose writes, "Emily never did come to terms with Blake's calling, though she couldn't fail to note a consistently improving standard of living in the Blake household from that day on" (26).

After his careers in various "hookshops," as Blake liked to call them, he moved on to touring musical shows. The first gig that brought Blake—now 18 years old—out of Baltimore was *Dr. Frazier's Medicine Show*, in which Blake played piano. His talents in buck dancing (rhythmic tapping on a sandy surface) were also employed. But the biggest town Dr. Frazier's show ever played was Fairfield, Pennsylvania to a crowd of 50 at most (Rose 28). Understandably dissatisfied, Blake returned to Baltimore and joined a touring cast of *In Old Kentucky*, a famous traveling show. The show was booked in New York, where they played at the Academy of Music on Fourteenth Street. His first New York experience was short lived. "They backed the truck up to the stage door and we went into the theater and did the show. Then we got back in the truck and they took us to this little boarding house on Bleeker Street. . . . Then we go to bed, and the next day the same thing. I only stayed three days. My mother made me go home" (Blake, qtd. in Rose 30). Blake did not get to see Broadway on his first trip to New York, but he would become very familiar with it in just a few short years.

Once he returned to Baltimore, he began working as the relief pianist for the well-known Big Head Wilbur at Alfred Greenfield's saloon, located at the intersection of Chestnut and Low. It was here in 1903 that he composed the piece "Chestnut and Low (In Baltimo')." The piece showcases his signature "wobble wobble" bass. The left hand keeps time with a steady, scalar line while the right hand plays a complex and also scalar melody that explores a wide range of the piano keys.

Blake's mother allowed him to work, but she still controlled everything that went on in her house. "She just had to learn to put up with all that what I was doing. She used to stay up till I got home at night so to make sure I'd get all the sawdust off my shoes before I came into the house." Blake's father had a different opinion of his son's occupation. "The old man never said anything more about it. He knew when he had a good thing going. I'm glad I was able to make their lives easier. They worked hard for me and they deserved it" (qtd. in Rose 31).

His next gig was at Annie Gilly's bordello, which shared little with classy Aggie Shelton's. Blake recounts his experience: "They had all kinds of fights in there. Customers came in with brass knuckles and knives and sharp razors—just lookin' for fight, see?" (qtd. in Rose 32). Blake goes on to describe the establishment as one large dance hall with bedrooms off to the side. The girls who worked at Annie Gilly's were as tough as the customers. Often, the men had to watch their wallets.

Though the atmosphere was dangerous and Blake could never "sit with [his] back to the door" (Rose 32), the difficult crowd helped him improve his skills as an entertainer. He quickly learned how to read a crowd to determine what he would play. The customers at Annie Gilly's would dance rowdily to fast-paced, ragtime tunes and would completely drown out soft-spoken ballads. This skill of catering to the needs of the audience, learned in the hookshops of Baltimore, would serve him well in his upcoming theatrical career.

Between 1905 and 1906, Blake spent most of each year playing piano at the Middle Section Assembly Club. In pre-air-conditioning Baltimore, the sweltering summer heat seldom fostered a lively entertainment industry; Blake spent those summers in Atlantic City.

One of Blake's memories from the Middle Section Club explains why he didn't copyright his compositions for another 15 years. On one Sunday while working at the club, a lady asked Blake's friend and fellow pianist Hughie Wolford to play "Holy City." Since the woman hadn't specified how she wanted the piece played, Hughie decided to "rag" it so dramatically that the woman couldn't tell he was playing her request. Seeing her confusion, Blake played "Holy City" straight, without "ragging." Blake remarked to his co-worker, "If someone told you to play the scale, you'd rag it too" (qtd. in Rose 41). The next day Wolford came to work and played a new "ragged" scale. Blake one-upped Hughie by "ragging" the scale in five keys. When Wolford accused Blake of copying his idea, Blake responded, "I copped that from you? I didn't have to cop that from nobody. Don't you understand? That's the scale. Nobody owns the scale" (qtd. in Rose 41). Years later, when Ed Claypoole copyrighted his ragged scale in five keys, Blake did not complain or accuse him of stealing, since he believed everyone had a right to the scale. For a long time he copyrighted none of his tunes because he believed music was for everyone. When recording became more popular, however, copyrighting became necessary.[1]

In 1906, Baltimore native Joe Gans won the lightweight boxing championship in Goldfield, Nevada. The following year, he returned to Baltimore and used his winnings to construct the Goldfield Hotel, an elegant establishment on Lexington and Chestnut, at the center of Baltimore's red-light district. Gans had been a childhood idol for young Blake. He and his childhood friend Hop used to run errands for Gans when they were children, and Gans never forgot. Soon Blake was playing piano at the Goldfield.

The three years he spent there were among the most musically productive of his career. During this time he wrote "The Baltimore Todolo," "Kitchen Tom," "Tricky Fingers," "Novelty Rag," and "Poor Katie Redd," among countless other unpublished pieces. Few recordings of these pieces survive today. There are likely some piano roll versions scattered around America, but only a handful were transfered onto records and CDs.[2] Nevertheless, one look at the original sheet music is enough to reveal the difficulty of these pieces. The bass lines show wide chord ranges that most pianists cannot play because their hands are not large enough. The right-hand parts are equally challenging because of their quick, intricate melodies. The pages of "Tricky Fingers," for example, are almost entirely covered in little black dots and the tempo is labeled *vivace* (extremely fast) (Blake, Box 007-01-001). What makes the music even more daunting is that in ragtime, pianists often improvise over the melody to "rag" the tune. Therefore, the notes on the sheet music most likely represent only its basic structure. Blake's time at the Goldfield thus gave him invaluable composing experience that would help him throughout his career, especially in his most famous endeavor, *Shuffle Along*.

In addition to composing, he learned how to accompany the many famous singers who came to stay at the Goldfield, including Mary Stafford, Lottie Dempsey, and Alberta Hunter (Rose 47). Accompanying singers on the piano is quite a change from playing solo. Jazz and ragtime vocalists rarely sing exactly what is written on the sheet music. Often they embellish the melody or sing behind the beat to make the tune more interesting and swinging. These variations can cause problems for a pianist, who can never quite predict what the vocalist will do. An accompanist needs to pay very close attention to what he is playing as well as to how the vocalist is singing. Later, in his vaudeville career with Noble Sissle, Blake's skills as an accompanist would come in handy. Later still, when he began conducting pit orchestras for musicals including *Shuffle Along*, he would need his accompanist talents to keep the orchestra and vocalists harmonious and synchronized.

The Goldfield went under in 1910 after Joe Gans's death. During the following five years, Blake alternated between living in Baltimore and in Atlantic City with his new bride, Avis Lee Blake. Though many of Blake's tunes from this period have been lost to time, two of his most famous tunes from 1911, "Chevy Chase" and "Fizz Water," were recorded onto piano rolls and have been preserved in CD format. "Chevy Chase" is a lively piece that has almost as many scale runs in the left hand as in the right hand. The tune showcases Blake's talent for using the wide range of the piano to write complex pieces, one of his most identifiable compositional characteristics. When listening to "Fizz Water," it is impossible to sit still. Blake classifies the tune as a one-step, a spirited dance number that moves along rather quickly. His compositional genius and knack for dance tunes would prove to be valuable skills when he entered the world of musical comedy.

In May of 1915, Eubie Blake met the man who would change the direction of his life forever. Booked to play piano at the Riverview Park in Baltimore with Joe Porter's band, he met a singer from Indianapolis named Noble Sissle. Without much of an introduction, Blake asked Sissle if he would be willing to write lyrics for his piano pieces, and so their historical partnership began.

Their first tune together, written that same year, was "It's All Your Fault" (Rose 56). Sissle was so confident about their song that the pair brought it to celebrity vocalist Sophie Tucker during her stint at the Maryland Theater in downtown Baltimore. After seeing the piece on a Monday, she had a fully orchestrated arrangement written for her show on Thursday. "It's All Your Fault" became an instant Baltimore hit. Soon Sissle and Blake were a performing duo for high society. "It was inevitable that young buddies Sissle and Blake should become well-known society entertainers along the Eastern seaboard. They played for Goulds, Dodges, Schwabs, Wanamakers—anybody who was anybody in the haut monde," writes Rose (58). Noble charmed audiences with his smooth voice and sophisticated lyrics while Blake dazzled listeners with his prodigious piano skills. Both dressed to the nines and never resorted to degrading minstrelsy humor.

With the outbreak of the First World War, Noble enlisted with James Reese Europe's 369th Infantry Army Band. Europe, a friend of both Blake and Sissle, revolutionized the music scene for blacks. Blake reverently recalls, "To colored musicians he was as important—he did as much for them as Martin Luther King did for the rest of the Negro people. He set up a way to get them jobs—The Clef Club—and he made them get paid more" (qtd. in Rose 57). Europe founded New York's Clef Club and led the Clef Club Symphony Orchestra (Bolcom and Kimball 59). Prior to the Clef Club, blacks had little power to stand up to booking agents or even headwaiters when they performed. Their salaries were low and non-negotiable. But in Europe's Clef Club, the performers' salaries and hours were fixed by contract. Soon many other establishments in New York began to follow suit (Bolcom and Kimball 59).

Blake and Europe remained good friends even while Europe was overseas during the war. Europe made sure the two kept in touch by sending friendly and encouraging letters from the battleground. In one letter, Europe, deployed in France, instructs Blake, safe at home, to "Just stay on the job and take your medicine" (Europe, Box 001). His concern and love for his friend Blake is clear. Europe writes hopefully of the pair's (his and Blake's) eventual musical success after the war. He even promises Blake, "When I go up I will take you with me. You can be sure of that" (Europe, Box 001). Upon the band's return home, they embarked on a concert tour across their home country. During the intermission of their concert in Boston, Europe was stabbed to death by one of his own musicians. But neither Blake nor Sissle would ever forget the impact James Reese Europe had on their lives.

When Sissle was no longer on tour with the deceased Europe's band in 1919 (Rose 62), he and Blake put a vaudeville routine together and embarked on a vaudeville circuit as the Dixie Duo.[3] Vaudeville circuits are corporations of theaters in different locations. Acts would travel from theater to theater within the same circuit to bring their act to the greatest number of cities. Sissle and Blake were booked in the Keith Circuit and toured all over the Northeast.

Conditions were discouraging for black musicians during this time. Al Rose describes the realities of vaudeville in his biography:

> They got the worst dressing rooms in the worst locations. They performed, as they knew, for far less pay than white entertainers received. They were expected to black up and do low "darky" comedy. And they always were second on the program. That was because the representatives of the press— the all-powerful critics—didn't arrive until the third act. (62)

Though the performing conditions mirrored the racial attitudes of the time, Sissle and Blake resisted the minstrel stereotypes. The duo was one of the first black acts to perform without the blackface makeup that was then expected. Blake recounts the derogatory expectations of theater agents:

> "Some agent had a smart idea for an act for us. We were supposed to shuffle on stage in blackface and patched-up overalls. In the middle of the stage there is this big black box with a piano in it. The idea was to look at it as if it were from the moon and I'd say, 'What's dat?' and Noble would say 'Dat's a py-anner!' and then we'd do our act. Well, Pat Casey would have none of that. He told the agents that Sissle and Blake had played in the houses of the millionaires and the social elite and they dressed in tuxedos and he'd be damned if he'd let us go on the stage in old overalls and act like a couple of ignoramuses." (Bolcom and Kimball 80)

Instead of complying with the offensive demands of theater agents, Sissle and Blake dressed elegantly for every show. Additionally, Sissle prided himself on writing lyrics that were among the cleanest in vaudeville among either black or white acts (Sissle, Box 012-01). Coming from a deeply religious background as he had, Sissle's personal decorum matched the innocence of his lyrics. Despite the humiliating stereotypes associated with black vaudeville acts, Sissle and Blake made a respectable name for themselves in theater.

Most black acts appeared early in vaudeville shows, but before long, Sissle and Blake gained popularity and became quite a difficult act to follow. "Finally, by the end of a week's run their act would be next to last because the head-liners refused to follow them" (Bolcom and Kimball 81).

Since most vaudeville circuits would book only one black act on a bill, Sissle and Blake had little contact with any other African-American performers on the road. It wasn't until they performed at an NAACP benefit in Philadelphia in 1920 that they met other black vaudevillians (Bolcom and Kimball 86). The comedy team of Flournoy E. Miller and Aubrey Lyles were among the many performers they met that day.

Miller and Lyles had toured England and the Keith Circuit with their blackface comedy act, which consisted of "Southern small town humor, dance sequences, and a famous fight scene which was imitated by many other vaudevillians for years afterward" (Bolcom and Kimball 86). When the four performers met, Miller and Lyles expressed their desire to join forces to create a Broadway show. The plan was to expand a comedy sketch they had written called "The Mayor of Dixie", about a small town mayoral race. The newly formed group quickly used all their talents to piece together a complete musical. "Drawing on their songs and comedy routines, the four assembled a rough sketch of a show that was, in some respects, the fusion of two vaudeville acts—with dancing numbers, a sort of continuous plot, and thrown-in love interest" (Bolcom and Kimball 88). The result was the legendary show eventually titled *Shuffle Along*.

Everything seemed to be working against the production of *Shuffle Along*. Most Broadway shows in the early 1900s began by touring in different cities. If the show did well, it could settle down in New York. *Shuffle Along*'s tour route primarily included "town, hamlet, theater, auditorium, barn, and movie house" venues throughout Pennsylvania and New Jersey (Bolcom and Kimball 89). Most engagements lasted a single night. Blake recalls in an interview with Bolcom and Kimball,

"No one knew us, so they'd only book us for a short time. We'd get good reviews in one town, but before they could do us any good we'd be on to another town—that is, if we had the money" (89). The cast wore used costumes from older shows that had closed and the scenery was bare. By the end of the tour, the cast and crew had scarcely enough money to cover the train fare back to New York. Given this inauspicious tour, *Shuffle Along*'s enthusiastic reception in the city was a huge surprise.

The story takes place in the fictitious African-American city of Jimtown. Two corrupt co-owners of the local grocery store, Sam Peck and Steve Jenkins, decide to run against each other in the upcoming mayoral election. Idealistic and virtuous Harry Walton also enters the race, though clearly the underdog. Both Peck and Jenkins steal from the grocery store's cash register to fund their campaigns. Their respective wives independently convince the men to hire a private eye to prove the other man is stealing.

The comedic premise is balanced by the love story between Walton and Jessie Williams, whose father will not permit the lovers to marry unless Walton becomes the new mayor. Jessie sings about her love in the tune "I'm Just Wild about Harry," later revived for Harry Truman's presidential campaign.

When asked about Harry, Jessie gushes,
> *The heavn'ly blisses of his kisses*
> *Fill me with ecstasy*
> *He's sweet just like choc'late candy*
> *And just like the honey bee.* (Sissle and Blake)

Though these lyrics are not terribly fitting for a presidential election, they are remarkably clean and innocent compared to those of most other black musicals of the time.

While Peck and Jenkins spend their stolen money to buy the votes of the townspeople, Walton refuses to compromise his integrity, even if it means he will never marry the woman he loves. Walton then sings "Love will Find a Way," one of the first serious love songs in a black musical. The tune, a hopeful ballad, presents a stark contrast from the provocative burlesque songs of many previous black musicals. The melody is soft and flowing, with many piano flourishes that add to the romantic tone. Though this piece is much slower than Blake's earlier ragtime compositions, the melody encompasses the right and left hand parts, showcasing Blake's dexterous left hand. The lyrics match the soothing melody with encouraging verses.

> *Dry each tear-dimmed eye*
> *Clouds will soon roll by*
> *Though fate leads us astray*
> *My dearie, mark what I say*
> *Love will find a way.* (Sissle and Blake)

Eventually, Peck and Jenkins are exposed as crooks, and Walton is awarded the mayoral office and marries Jessie. The show ends with an upbeat dance tune called "Baltimore Buzz," which then leads into the grand finale with fast-dancing chorus girls and big orchestrations.

While the script of *Shuffle Along* is heavy with fractured dialect and stereotypes, the music shows an undeniable forward progression. *Shuffle Along's* score has Blake's trademarks all over it. Every song harkens back to Blake's piano compositions from the start of the century. For example, in "Baltimore Buzz" the tuba part mimics Blake's signature "wobble-wobble" bass by playing a walking, rhythmic line. Just as Blake's left hand kept the beat of his tunes while also providing a chordal structure, the tuba moves from the first note of the chord to the fifth. This has almost the same effect as Blake's intricate chord alternations. The melody of "Baltimore Buzz" is also reminiscent of Blake's ragtime melody lines. Further, the vocalist and higher instruments use the same ragtime elements of syncopation and ornamentation that Blake uses in his earlier songs such as "Charleston Rag."

"I'm Just Wild About Harry" is incontestably the most famous number from *Shuffle Along*. Even before Harry Truman used the song for his presidential campaign,[4] people all over America who saw the show were whistling the tune. "I'm Just Wild About Harry" also exemplifies Blake's Baltimore musical roots. For example, the instrumental version of the song on the *Shuffle Along* album features a contrapuntal piano melody that is not only a characteristic of ragtime in general, but particularly of Blake's complex melodies. Moreover, the melodic low brass lines are a result of Blake's agile left hand, which often played parts as complicated as did the right hand. Without the ability to compose these tunes on the piano first, he would not have been able to expand the arrangement for the entire pit orchestra.

The musical arrived on the Broadway scene after more than a decade had passed with no African-American shows (Bolcom and Kimball 101). Therefore, on opening night in New York, Sissle was most concerned about how the audience would receive "Love Will Find a Way." Until then, it was unconventional for African-American theater to portray an un-burlesqued love story. He recalls that during the number,

> Miller, Lyles, and I were standing near the exit door with one foot inside the theater and the other pointed north toward Harlem. We thought of Blake, stuck out there in front,

leading the orchestra—his bald head would bear the brunt of the tomatoes and the rotten eggs. Imagine our amazement when the song was not only beautifully received but encored.

(Bolcom and Kimball 93)

Shuffle Along had one of the longest New York runs of any play in its time, running for 504 performances, followed by a successful year-long tour. Why was it so successful? Perhaps because *Shuffle Along* tactfully incorporated groundbreaking new conventions for African-American theater while also pandering just enough to mainstream white audiences. Theater historian David Krasner explains the two extremes presented in the musical:

> *Shuffle Along* was one of the first shows to provide the right mixture of primitivism and satire, enticement and respectability, blackface humor and romance, to satisfy its customers. Many critics praised *Shuffle Along* as an advance in musical theater and a critical turn away from the minstrel tradition. Yet, *Shuffle Along* complicated minstrelsy. Its blackfaced comedians, fractured dialect, malapropisms, and post-ragtime jazz music were refashioned minstrel theater. . . . This mixture of blackface denigration and progressive change, mockery and pride, pandering and resistance created a paradox of competing urges. (264)

What Krasner fails to point out is that if *Shuffle Along* had not contained elements such as blackfaced comedy, it would never have lasted in theaters. White audiences would have been outraged and the production would quickly have gone out of business. By thoughtfully combining progressive changes with nostalgic conventions, *Shuffle Along* satisfied a broad audience and served as a monumental stepping-stone for blacks in theater.

Musical theater was just emerging from the light operas popularized by the team of Gilbert and Sullivan. The tunes in most musicals still relied much more heavily on European musical techniques than on American jazz and ragtime. But when Eubie Blake composed the score to *Shuffle Along*, he combined the popular ragtime music of vaudeville with the older conventions of musical theater. For decades afterward, composers like Richard Rodgers, Jerome Kern, George Gershwin, and Irving Berlin would also use jazz elements in their compositions. But *Shuffle Along* broke new ground, as perhaps the first complete musical to blend different musical styles in this way.

After the success of *Shuffle Along*, Blake and Sissle continued their partnership and wrote the music to several other hit shows. *In Bamville*, later to be renamed *The Chocolate Dandies*, was their first production after *Shuffle Along*. It was a polished, opulent production that didn't conform to common stereotypes and conventions of black minstrelsy. As a result, many critics dismissed the show. Blake recalled, "Friends had encouraged us, and so Sissle and I felt that after *Shuffle Along* we could write any show we wanted. We were wrong. People who went to a colored show—most people, not all people expected only fast dancing and Negroid humor, and when they got something else they put it down" (qtd. in Bolcom and Kimball 181).

Blake's next endeavor was a tour with Sissle on the European vaudeville circuit. They advertised themselves as the "American Ambassadors of Syncopation" and left for France in September of 1925 (Rose 95). The tour was a great success, but Blake was glad to return to Baltimore when the tour ended. Sissle, on the other hand, decided to move to Europe permanently only two years after their tour. Blake recounts the conversation that changed the course of his career:

Sissle says, "I'm goin" to the American Legion convention in Paris." He was a soldier, remember. I say, "When you comin' back?" He don't say nothin". I ask him, "You gonna stay over there?" No answer. I tell him, "You know we still got eleven weeks of bookings left on our contracts." He still don't say nothin". So I say, "Well, I guess this is the end of Sissle and Blake." He never takes his eyes off the floor. In a minute he gets up and leaves. And that was the end of Sissle and Blake. (Rose 98)

After Sissle's departure, Blake worked in a variety of other successful partnerships. He composed floor shows with Henry Creamer, went on a vaudeville tour with Broadway Jones, toured with the USO, and wrote musicals with both Andy Razaf, with whom he composed *Tan Manhattan* and *Blackbirds of 1930*, and with Milton Reddie, his collaborator on *Swing It*. Blake had been introduced to Andy Razaf during the creation of *Blackbirds of 1930*. Lew Leslie, the show's producer, put them together as the musical team. Though the show was a hit at Brooklyn's Majestic Theater, Leslie mysteriously abandoned the show, forcing it to close. *Tan Manhattan* enjoyed a long and successful run in New York's Ubangi Theater, despite the depression. *Swing It* was one of many musicals co-written by Blake and Reddie, but it was the only one to be produced. Though all three shows were praised by critics, none garnered the acclaim achieved by *Shuffle Along*.

In 1946 at the age of 63, after marrying his second wife Marion, Blake decided to retire. Taking a break from performing, he enrolled in New York University (Rose 122). But less than two years after graduating, in 1950, he decided he was not suited to the retired lifestyle. A short-lived revival of *Shuffle Along* took place in 1952. The script was changed entirely to sound more modern, and only a few songs remained from the original production. The effect was disastrous. Blake was disappointed by the outcome of the show, and remarked, "If you been in show business all your life, it hurts more than anything to see an audience that's not gettin' what it paid to see" (qtd. in Rose 124).

Blake's subsequent career mostly consisted of concerts at ragtime festivals, including the St. Louis Ragfest in 1966, where he performed in his first actual concert. Until that point, Blake had performed vaudeville acts or conducted pit orchestras, but had never headlined an entire performance by himself (Rose 132). The concert was a success, and was followed by many similar performances at festivals throughout the country for years to come.

Blake's later years were filled with honorary degrees from prestigious universities, concert performances, and appearances on the *Tonight Show* with Johnny Carson. On February 7th, 1983, Blake was unable to attend his 100th birthday celebration due to a serious case of pneumonia. He watched the two-hour concert, featuring selections from *Shuffle Along* and performances by a variety of talented pianists, via closed-circuit television. Five days later, the ragtime legend died.

Shuffle Along, Blake's best-known musical accomplishment, is touted by many Harlem Renaissance leading lights as a catalyst for that unforgettable artistic movement. James Weldon Johnson, for example, notes the ability of *Shuffle Along* to adhere to African-American theatrical conventions of the time while showing remarkable progress in the musical score. "*Shuffle Along* was cast in the form of the best Williams and Walker, Cole and Johnson tradition; but the music did not hark back at all; it was up to the minute" (39). In his autobiography, *The Big Sea*, Langston Hughes writes of *Shuffle Along*:

"It gave just the proper push—a pre-Charleston kick—to that Negro vogue of the 20's, that spread to books, African sculpture, music, and dancing" (77). Joel A. Rogers also recognized the significance of Sissle and Blake's music, listing the pair among many great jazz artists whose music had "none of the vulgarities and crudities of the lowly origin or the only too prevalent cheap imitations" (55). Yet Blake's work on *Shuffle Along* would not have been possible without his Baltimore upbringing and musical training.

In Baltimore, Blake learned to compose texturally rich pieces that involved the right and left hands equally. Though Blake primarily composed and performed ragtime pieces, his technique and style inspired pianists of all musical genres. Blake's talent and enthusiasm influenced Dr. Anthony Villa, jazz pianist, music professor, and director of the Loyola University Maryland Jazz Ensemble. "While he was a ragtime and stride player and I am not, his vibrant use of rhythm was always an intriguing element to me. The left hand was steady but never rigid and the right hand floated above in a delightfully musical manner." Though ragtime has long since been displaced as America's favorite type of music, Villa agrees that Blake's techniques "are still important elements in playing solo jazz piano."

Blake also acquired the skill of playing piano for vocalists, which requires a strong degree of concentration and musical ability, while working in Baltimore's hotels and lounges. These compositional characteristics and highly developed ability as an accompanist led directly to the success of *Shuffle Along*. Though Blake's life after *Shuffle Along* was successful and always filled with performances, *Shuffle Along* is undoubtedly his best-known work. With three separate tours spanning from 1922 to 1952 (MDHS 22) and a soundtrack released in 1976, the music of *Shuffle Along* has clearly passed the test of time. Blake's catchy, lively compositions, stemming from his musical development in Baltimore, are a strong element of *Shuffle Along*'s timeless appeal.

NOTES

1. Thankfully, since Blake never cared much for the business aspects of the music industry, his second wife, Marion, kept careful records of all his copyrights and correspondences.

2. Piano rolls are a recording medium that are inserted into player pianos. The rolls record exactly what the pianist plays, and were mass-produced and sold to the public. People inserted a piano roll into their player pianos at home, and the piano played exactly what the pianist played, but no one had to be seated at the instrument.

3. Vaudeville shows typically consisted of a group of unrelated acts by separate performers or groups who performed one after the other to create an entire show.

4. In 1967, President Truman sent a letter to Blake thanking Blake for giving him permission to use "I'm Just Wild About Harry" in his campaign.

Works Cited

Blake, Eubie. "The Baltimore Todolo." Maryland Historical Society, Eubie Blake Collection, Baltimore MD. Sheet Music. Box 35. 1908.

---. "The Charleston Rag." Maryland Historical Society, Eubie Blake Collection, Baltimore MD. Sheet Music. Box 1. 1899.

---. "Chestnut and Low (In Baltimo')." Maryland Historical Society, Eubie Blake Collection, Baltimore MD. Sheet Music. Box 1. 1903.

---. "Kitchen Tom." Maryland Historical Society, Eubie Blake Collection, Baltimore MD. Sheet Music. Box 8. 1907.

---. "Memories of You". Shout! Factory, 2003. CD.

---. "Novelty Rag." Maryland Historical Society, Eubie Blake Collection, Baltimore MD. Sheet Music. Box 69. 1910.

---. "Poor Katie Redd." Maryland Historical Society, Eubie Blake Collection, Baltimore MD. Sheet Music. Box 4. 1910.

---. "Tricky Fingers." Maryland Historical Society, Eubie Blake Collection, Baltimore MD. Sheet Music. Box 7. 1908.

--- and Noble Sissle. *Shuffle Along*, A Musical Comedy. n.p., 1922. Print.

Hughes, Langston. "The Big Sea." *The Portable Harlem Renaissance Reader*. Ed. David Levering Lewis. New York: Penguin, 1995. Print. 77-91.

Johnson, James Weldon. "Black Manhattan." *The Portable Harlem Renaissance Reader*. Ed. David Levering Lewis. New York: Penguin, 1995. Print. 34-45.

Kimball, Robert, and William Bolcom. *Reminiscing with Noble Sissle and Eubie Blake*. New York: Cooper Square, 2000. Print.

Krasner, David. *A Beautiful Pageant: African American Theatre, Drama, and Performance in the Harlem Renaissance, 1910-1927*. New York: Palgrave Macmillan, 2002. Print.

Rogers, Joel A. "Jazz at Home." *The Portable Harlem Renaissance Reader*. Ed. David Levering Lewis. New York: Penguin, 1995. 52-57.

Rose, Al. *Eubie Blake*. New York: Schirmer, 1979. Print.

Sissle, Noble. Letter to Eubie Blake. MS. Maryland Historical Society, Eubie Blake Collection, Baltimore, MD. Box 12. Undated.

Sissle, Noble and Eubie Blake. *Sissle & Blake's Shuffle Along*. Rec. 1976. New World Records, 1976. LP.

Truman, Harry S. Letter to Eubie Blake. 25 July 1967. MS. Maryland Historical Society, Eubie Blake Collection, Baltimore, MD. Box 12.

Discography

Over the course of his 100 years, Eubie Blake made countless recordings of his many compositions. This discography concentrates on Blake's early compositions from his time in Baltimore and pieces Blake composed with Noble Sissle for Shuffle Along. *Tunes from Blake's collaboration with Sissle and Europe are also included. Blake plays piano on all recordings, unless otherwise specified, and all compositions are by Eubie Blake, unless otherwised specified.*

Recordings: Piano Rolls

"Fizz Water," played by Steve Williams. Perfection 86393, August, 1915..
Compilation 4.

"Chevy Chase," played by Gertrude Baum. Artempo 2227, September, 1915.
Compilation 4.

"Charleston Rag," played by Eubie Blake. Ampico 5417E, August, 1917.
Compilation 4.

"Memories of You," (Blake and Razaf), played by Eubie Blake. QRS
Cel 126, May, 1973. Compilation 4.

Recordings: 78 RPM

"Good Night, Angeline" (Sissle, Blake, and Europe). Noble Sissle, Eubie Blake
and the Pathé orchestra. Pathé 20226, 1917-18.

Sissle, Blake and Europe began a promising collaboration before the outbreak of World War II. Europe's 369th Infantry Band performed many of the songs composed by the trio, including "Good Night, Angeline," overseas during the war.

"Mirandy" (Sissle, Blake, and Europe). Noble Sissle and Lt. Jim Europe's
369th Infantry Band.Pathé 22089, March, 1919. Compilation 1.

"On Patrol in No Man's Land" (Sissle, Blake, and Europe). Noble
Sissle and Lt. Jim Europe's 369th Infantry Band. Pathé 22089,
March, 1919. Compilation 1.

"I'm Just Simply Full of Jazz" (Sissle and Blake). Noble Sissle, Eubie
Blake and the Pathé Orchestra. Pathé 22284, April, 1920.

"In Honeysuckle Time" (Sissle and Blake). Noble Sissle and his
Sizzling Syncopators. Emerson 10385, April or May, 1921.
Compilation 1.

"Daddy Won't You Please Come Home" (Sissle and Blake). Gertrude
     Saunders and Tim Brynn and His Black Devil Orchestra.
     Okeh 8004, May, 1921. Compilation 1.

"I'm Craving For That Kind of Love" (Sissle and Blake). Gertrude
     Saunders and Tim Brynn and His Black Devil Orchestra.
     Okeh 8004, May, 1921. Compilation 1.

"Love Will Find a Way" (Sissle and Blake). Noble Sissle and Eubie
     Blake. Emerson 10396, June, 1921. Compilation 1.

"Baltimore Buzz" (Sissle and Blake). "Shuffle Along" Orchestra.
     Victor 18791, July, 1921. Compilation 1.

"Bandana Days; I'm Just Wild about Harry" (Sissle and Blake). Eubie Blake
     and the "Shuffle Along" Orchestra. Victor 18791-B, 15 July
     1921. Compilation 1.
     *"I'm Just Wild about Harry" is undoubtedly Blake's most renowned
composition. Long after it became a hit in* Shuffle Along's *first run on Broadway,
President Harry Truman used the tune for his presidential campaign.*

"Sounds of Africa [Charleston Rag]." Emerson 10434, 1921.
     *Blake's first big hit was written in 1899 while he worked in Aggie Shelton's
bordello. Since, at the time, music was only distributed through piano rolls and
sheet music, it was difficult for a song to become popular. The fact that Blake
managed to have a hit without records or radios speaks to his undeniable talent.*

Long-Playing Records

The Wizard of Ragtime Piano. Noble Sissle, Eubie Blake and Orchestra.
     Twentieth Century-Fox 3003, 1958.
     *This album contains an assortment of tunes written over the years by Sissle
and Blake. In addition to Blake on piano and Sissle on vocals, the rest of the
orchestra includes Buster Bailey, clarinet; Bernard Addison, guitar; Milton
Hinton, George Duvivier, bass; and Panama Francis, Charles Persip, drums. A
few tunes on the album, like "Eubie's Boogie," were composed by Blake during
the years he worked as a brothel pianist. Others were written while he and
Sissle were on tour with their vaudeville routine, and many, including "I'm Just
Wild about Harry," are from Sissle and Blake musicals.*

The Eighty-six Years of Eubie Blake. Noble Sissle and Eubie Blake.
     Columbia C2S 847, March, 1969.
     *This two-LP collection took almost four months to record. The albums
include compositions from Eubie's earlier years as a ragtime composer, a medley*

26

from Shuffle Along *and another medley of songs composed by James P. Johnson, a fellow legendary ragtime pianist. Many of Blake's earliest compositions have been lost in the transition from piano rolls to 78s and from 78s to LPs. Here, however, Blake plays "Baltimore Todolo," "Tricky Fingers," "Kitchen Tom," and "Poor Katie Redd," which all number among his early hits.*

Compilations: Long-Playing Records

1. Sissle & Blake's *Shuffle Along.* New World Records, 1976.

Many numbers from Shuffle Along *were recorded before the invention of the LP. However, many individual recordings of tunes from the famous musical were made around the time it first played on Broadway. This LP compiles a selection of tunes from* Shuffle Along *featuring many of the original cast members, including Gertrude Saunders, Flournoy Miller, and Aubrey Lyles. In addition to numbers from the musical, the album includes selections from Europe's 369th Infantry Band. Most tunes in the compilation feature only Blake on piano and Sissle on vocals.*

2. Sissle and Blake: *Early Rare Recordings*, Vol. 1. Noble Sissle and Eubie Blake. Eubie Blake Music-4.

3. Sissle and Blake: *Early Rare Recordings*, Vol. 2. Noble Sissle and Eubie Blake. Eubie Blake Music-7.

Compilations: Compact Discs

4. Eubie Blake. *Memories of You.* Eubie Blake, Gertrude Baum, and Steve Williams Biograph Records, 1990.

This disc compiles songs composed by Blake and originally played on piano rolls. Though most of the rolls are played by Blake himself, "Chevy Chase" is played by Baum and "Fizz Water" is played by Williams.

5. Eubie Blake. *Tricky Fingers.* Eubie Blake. Quicksilver, 2003.

This CD primarily contains songs composed by Blake but also includes classics like "Stars and Stripes Forever" by John Philip Sousa.

6. Eubie Blake. *That's Ragtime!* Aei, 12 July 2005.

Chick Webb

"Although he was the heart of the group, pumping swinging rhythm that drove crowds into frenzies, he was also the brain. "

2 Coup in the Kingdom of Swing
by Frank J. Graziano

Gene Krupa was crying. The legendary drummer sat at the side of a polished brass casket in a little brick house in East Baltimore. The early morning light came through the window of the flower-packed room as mourners shuffled in and out of the doorway, but Krupa was fixated, devastated by the stunted, caramel-skinned body in the white dinner jacket before him. His idol and mentor—a man who had been like a father to him—was dead at 30. Krupa stayed there most of the day, until the body was moved to the packed Waters AME Church a few blocks away for the funeral, where Ella Fitzgerald sang the eulogy, a version of "My Buddy," through her tears, to a silent crowd of an estimated 15,000. The diminutive man with the unbreakable smile had bought her first dress. The next day, in honor of her fallen son, Baltimore stopped all traffic for a few minutes. His death marked the end of a short life of battling chronic illness, fighting conniving music industry sharks, and leading legendary bands, all to break into the national spotlight for just a few months. But by his demise at age 30, Chick Webb had redirected the course of jazz drumming and impacted the lives of the Swing Era's greatest.

Despite his fame and impact, Webb is a contemporary ghost. The clubs where he played have been demolished, and his complete recordings total fewer than 200 songs. Only a handful of photographs of him exist, and he was never captured on film. There are no books about him, only sections and chapters, and though countless articles have been written about him, the most complete biography is broken up over two chapters in Stuart Nicholson's *Ella Fitzgerald*. Nicholson cites personal interviews with band members (not with Webb, as these too seem not to exist) and disparate primary documents.

Webb is the Ozymandias of jazz. Like the forgotten king, his grandiose efforts to make himself memorable instead merely made him a withering symbol of their futility. Webb's fate derived from a combination of his desire to succeed and his developing understanding of what success meant in jazz during the peak of its commercialization in the 1930s.

From 1931 to 1939 Chick Webb's big band was the monster at the gates of Harlem. For those eight years they defended their periodic spots as house band at the Savoy, challenging national acts—bands led by the likes of Duke Ellington, Count Basie, Fletcher Henderson, Jimmy Lunceford, and Benny Goodman. Their well-known weapon— the dynamo, the small man with the heart of a giant—sat behind his drums on a riser: William Henry "Chick" Webb.

As with most legendary jazz figures, he was unique in physicality and talent. Dwarfed by tuberculosis of the spine since birth, he had a head that was too big for his body, a grin that was too big for his face, and a soul that wasn't content merely sitting between his broad shoulders, but had to make itself known in fiery, flailing, precise bursts of his arms. Elevated at the center of the band, Chick directed through his drums. Although he was the heart of the group, pumping swinging rhythm that drove crowds into frenzies, he was also the brain. He could never read music, but led every number by memory, and was storied to sing well-played solos note-for-note back to his musicians after the show. He was crowned "King of Swing" in Harlem, but Chick's charm and work ethic were learned in East Baltimore. Webb was a character who frequently took it on the chin and refused to be marginalized, and was from a city, in the shadow of other East Coast metropolises, with a history of doing the same thing.

Indomitable Pluck

According to the municipal handbook of the year, Baltimore in 1909 was a city that had "risen from its ashes in an astonishing way" (Coyle 8). Five years earlier, a fire that had begun in a dry goods warehouse had spread to become a veritable inferno. It burned for over 24 hours, swelled to cover 140 acres, and leveled 46 blocks in the center of the city. Among other areas, the financial district and a large section of the harbor front had been destroyed. Fifteen hundred buildings had been reduced to rubble or left as smoldering frames. Damage was estimated at between $125 million and $150 million. On February 8th, as the city still burned, the *Sun* reported, "Many spectators saw their all go up in flames before their eyes, and there were men with hopeless faces and despairing expressions on every hand" (Williams).

But the city did not die, and thanks to the "indomitable pluck and ingenuity of Baltimoreans," had begun a reconstruction effort (Williams n.p.). The first few years were slow, but by 1909 new sewers were being built, modern docks had replaced the gutted ones, parks had been extended, schools reconstructed, and city streets opened and widened. Sixty percent of streets were cobbled then, and on those stones, in the center of the badly damaged but fertile area, a young Chick Webb walked, drumming as he went (Coyle 8-10).

He was born the youngest of three to a poor family living on Ashland Avenue in 1909. He was called "Chick" because he was small, and kept the nickname despite a powerful drive to become something more than a human fleck. When the Webb family made its way to church on Sundays, Chick would run off and follow a parade band. A 1937 biography in *DownBeat* reports, "There was one drummer in particular, and Chick will tell you today that this boy was his greatest inspiration" ("Rise" Dec. 1937, 14). On days when his tuberculosis kept him from school he would drum on pots and pans lent to him by a neighbor. On days when he delivered the *Afro-American* he would step with tiny strides down Gay and Aisquith, drumming on fences, stoops, and garbage cans along his route, probably with his iconic smile spread across his face. He quit school at nine, and eventually afforded a ten-dollar drum set bought from a shop on Gay Street. In his early teens he played weekend gigs and performed on steamships in the Sheepshead Bay. Before he was 15 he was playing in the Jazzola band, which entertained the passengers of pleasure boats in the Chesapeake Bay. This was semi-steady work, and provided Chick his first taste of the money a career in music could offer. In 1925, at 16, he and a friend from the Jazzola band, guitar player John Trueheart, left for the Harlem scene. Although Chick departed Baltimore in his teens he had stayed there for half his life, and the sounds he had made in that city influenced his playing for the rest of his career ('Rise' Dec. 1937; Nicholson 25).

First Swing

During Chick's time in New York, the Swing Era was emerging, and drummers were playing an integral part in the artistic development of the style. For the first few months he played with small-time bands in spotty jobs, but with a salary of 60 dollars a week, "Webb had never had so much money in his life" ("Rise" Dec. 1937). His drumming impressed up-and-coming musicians, most notably Duke Ellington, who influenced him at many integral points in his career.

By age 17, Chick was leading a five-piece band filling in for Ellington's at $200 a week. He had been reluctant to jump from musician to bandleader and did so only at Ellington's urging. Duke also helped him get booked for a steady gig at the Paddock Club, where Chick's drumming caused a "minor sensation" (Nicholson 26), and was noticed by more celebrities. The band was now an eight-piece group known as "Chick Webb and His Orchestra." The gamble move to New York was paying off, until Chick suffered what would be the first episode in a long series of mishaps and trickeries that dotted and shaped his career: near the end of 1926 the Paddock Club burned down during a show, and the band was out of work.

Chick was still young, naïve, inexperienced at managing a band, and frequently taken advantage of. In 1927 he was offered work at the Savoy Ballroom in Harlem at a price of $67.50 a week for his band and $70 for himself. When he showed surprise at the raise, the management exploited his greenness by telling him to not be such a wise guy. Humbled, Chick signed for the band rate. A few months later, while enjoying a stint as the house band at Rose Danceland, Chick agreed to a phony offer to tour with a vaudeville troupe. Despite

Danceland's management's begging him to stay, he left for the road. But the act was a sham: the band was soon out of work and banned from returning to Danceland.

During this period of unemployment, rival bandleader Fletcher Henderson asked to borrow Chick's premier trumpeter, Bobby Stark. Chick agreed as long as Stark would be back for a later audition. When the audition date came, Stark stuck with Henderson, and Chick failed to secure the gig. This was a low point for the band, and after the incident employment was sparse. To deepen the slump, trumpet player Cootie Williams publicly berated the resident band at the Alhambra in a moment of hot-headedness. The bandleader brought Chick and Williams before the musicians union, which then banned the two from working together (Nicholson 25-28).

Chick retreated. By the end of 1928 he had gathered what was left of his band and hooked up with other desperate musicians'. They became bound to Chick's work ethic, rehearsing constantly, playing only occasional gigs to pay the rent. Fighting starvation, they would "hole up in one room and refuse to separate" (Nicholson 28). Chick turned down offers from Ellington and Henderson to join their bands, but "though he was literally hungry still he would not give in" ("Rise," Jan. 1938). He was no longer reluctant to lead his own ensemble. The forces he had been battling his whole life had come to a head against him, but he did not falter. Chick Webb was determined to become a successful bandleader.

Rising from the Ashes

By 1929 Chick was 20 years old and more mature than when he had first arrived in Harlem. He stood less than five feet tall and kept his hair tightly cropped. When he smiled his eyes were a bit squinty and his bottom lip lay parallel to his square chin while his top angled in a slight snarl—a face easily caricatured on the front of his bass drum. When he played he wore snug double-breasted suits that made him look like some sort of doll king. He was self-conscious about his twisted stature, and when the curtain rose at a show he was usually already seated behind his drums.

Chick's custom set was a departure from the norm. He played a booming 28-inch bass drum that was half his height, fitted with extensions on the pedals so his feet could reach them. His style was powerful. He constantly kept time on a high hat with strokes so forceful he could use brushes even on loud, upbeat songs. Legend holds that the drums needed to be nailed down to weather his kicks. A collection of cowbell and wood and temple blocks added to Chick's distinct sound. Until this time, drummers used these pieces as novelties, playing them consistently through an entire piece. But Chick would pepper these colors into solos and fills in numerous songs, producing rapid pops, clops, and dings that doubled and tripled the meter and recalled the things he drummed on as a boy in Baltimore.

On the most representative recordings that exist, such as "Harlem Congo" and "Liza (All the Clouds'll Roll Away)" the drums sound like a crooked spine jerkily cracking into place. On these tracks Chick accentuates transitions with big splashes on cymbals and firm kicks. "Harlem Congo" shows his ability to add snare rolls at blistering speed while still making the drum pop. His solo at the beginning of "Liza, All the Clouds'll Roll Away" sets the tempo and swing for the rest of the band, showing how Chick led from behind his set. The band follows in an upbeat fashion, mirroring Chick's dynamics through different sections. With this sound and swagger came a fortification of the self-assurance that powered Chick from the beginning. He was ready, once again, to take on the world, and proceeded to do so with a fervor that suggested knowledge of his limited time. Chick had only 10 years to live and wasted not a day, with small exaggeration, playing himself to death.

That same year Chick signed with Moe Gale, a talent agent, who added business guidance to his now-practiced act. Gale was also a stakeholder in the Savoy Ballroom. Later in 1929, Gale booked Chick Webb and His Orchestra for a weekly gig in the Roseland Ballroom on 52nd Street. The club was swanky, paid $1,500 a week, and exposed the band to its all-white clientele for nearly two years. Chick had finally tasted the crumbs of success he was searching for. Although playing a set weekly at Roseland, he still frequently returned to Harlem to battle, and by 1930 Gale had Chick booked for a steady gig at the Savoy.

On May 14th, 1930, Webb's band played for "The Battle of 1812" at the Savoy, which featured some of the top black bands in New York. He shared a bill with the bands of Duke Ellington, Fletcher Henderson, Cab Calloway, Cecil Scott, and Lockwood Lewis. In 1932, after a brief setback and the loss of a couple members, the band reformed at the Savoy to play to a record-breaking crowd of 4,600 with Henderson and Calloway.

Chick was the King of Swing in New York, but dreamed of national attention. His band's recordings had always lacked a musical identity, largely failing to replicate the locomotion present in its live performances. Aware of the lukewarm nature of his sides, Chick made sweeping adjustments to change it. Thus, by 1933, the band's line-up was at its peak with Taft Jordan and Mario Bauzá on trumpets, Sandy Williams on trombone, and Edgar Sampson on alto sax. It was around this time that Chick was also spending his rent money on higher quality arrangements and experimenting with various male and female singers.

In 1934 the Chick Webb Orchestra recorded with Decca, producing some of its most representative tracks. These, writes Nicholson, proved to be "perhaps only a dozen or so sides from the whole Webb discography that captured the coiled-spring intensity that must have been so riveting in live performance" (32). Among the songs recorded are ones arranged by Edgar Sampson, including "Blue Lou," "Blue Minor," "What a Shuffle," and "Don't Be That Way." The sides showcase the band's energetic ability and Sampson's arrangements, but archaic recording technology does little for Chick's drumming, which is barely audible except on bombs and rolls. Chick's legacy was finally preserved, however primitively, on wax and it was about time—his funeral was less than half a decade away. Chick's waning years were filled with signs of his foreshadowed death, as well as his apparent recognition of it, and his grind to complete the mysterious personal mission that had been driving him since childhood.

The King of Swing vs. The King of Swing

In 1937 Chick saw his defining moment within his grasp. On the night of May 11th, during their engagement at the Savoy, his band was slated to battle Benny Goodman's. Goodman was white, and boasted hit records by the score and the national fame that Chick had sought. Success in the world of Swing was measured by the new standard of record sales. Jazz was beginning to be commercialized, and catchy, danceable tunes were in demand for radio and home record players. Goodman's clarinetting over his swinging band was the sound America wanted from jazz. For the first time, the music was becoming widely popular, and with teens and college students—and a larger audience of white people—buying up records, Benny Goodman had become the celebrity "King of Swing." Mere months after the Savoy Battle, in an event that would represent a huge step toward legitimacy for jazz in the eyes of the country, Goodman would play his legendary concert at Carnegie Hall (Sandler).

Goodman had the best intentions with regard to musical integrity, but the popularity of his songs, it could be argued, came from their approachability. His recordings are marked by a more relaxed swing that allowed new jazz fans to ease into the style (Gioia 137-145). They have the personality that Webb's band had been seeking on its sides, but without the raw, electric edge of Chick's live performances. Regardless, when the two names were illuminated on the marquee of the Savoy, the feeling in Harlem was palpable. The King of Swing was going to battle the King of Swing.

The Savoy was located between 140th and 141st Streets on Lenox Avenue in Harlem, on the second floor of a block-long building with a huge marquee hanging over the street. It was such a center of dance that fads rippled from it semi-annually, and the wooden, spring-loaded dance floor had to be replaced every three years. It had two band stands so that one group could set up while the other finished to avoid gaps in the lindy hopping and jitterbugging. It was also one of the first places in the country to be racially integrated in both staff and clientele.

The attendance record was shattered on May 11th. John Hammond wrote in *DownBeat*, "About four thousand people actually managed to jam their way into the Savoy, where four or five cops were stationed on the Goodman bandstand to maintain law and order." Another article reports, "Traffic was held up for hours in that vicinity and several thousand people jammed the pavement outside the Savoy until the early hours of the morning" (Oakley 1). Out in the spring evening mounted police, fire marshals, police reserves, and the riot squad worked to control an integrated crowd as large and excitable as you would find anywhere in the U.S. during the era. Chick was ready to win them.

It is hard to imagine what Chick felt, but he must have known he was about to touch greatness. Trumpeter Mario Bauzá remembered, "Chick told everyone the night before, 'Fellas, tomorrow is my hour. Anybody that misses notes, don't look for notice—don't come back to work" (qtd. in Nicholson 51). Chick's notoriety had been growing, but this was the chance he had been looking for: a way to make up for all the flat tires and bumps in the road, a shot at legitimizing his title.

Goodman played first, opening with Harry James's arrangement of "Peckin.'" The crowd applauded generously but "when Chick gave them that first beat on the bass drum, the crowds went absolutely mad" (Oakley 1). Goodman's band was out of its element, and "Benny's band was obviously flustered by the proceedings. The noise level was so high that none but the brass soloist was even audible" (Hammond). The Savoy was a dancing venue, and Chick's band was full of veterans who were practiced in front of Harlem's crowd. Edgar Sampson, who had played sax for Chick, was now playing for Goodman and as a result both bands played Sampson's arrangement. Ken Burns's jazz documentary compares the two bands' takes on the songs. Juxtaposing both bands' recordings of "Stomping at the Savoy," the film reveals the advantage of Chick's group. His drums push the track forward, with heavy kicks and fills between sections to keep the feel boiling. "Chick placed himself and his drums right in front of his band, while poor Gene [Krupa, who was drumming for Goodman] was buried in a back row, invisible to the audience because of the formidable cops who stood up in front of him" (Hammond). At the time, the young Krupa played in the standard, toned-down swing style, using a cymbal or high hat to keep the song moving. But he was out-classed by Chick's frontal assault, and remembered of Webb, "he cut me to ribbons" (Sandler).

The climax of the night was when Chick's band followed Goodman's with their own hit, "Jam Session" and "blew the roof off the house with it" (Oakley 3). As it is summed up by Helen Oakley in *DownBeat*, "Chick had the edge on Benny in the fact that he provided the dancers with 'those right tempos' and due to previous experience in battling bands, he knew just how to call his sets and what to feed those people" (1).

Bauzá recalled, "That was a big night. Everybody in Benny's band, they were congratulating Chick." *Metronome*'s headline read, "Chick Webb Defeats Benny Goodman!" (qtd. in Nicholson 51). Oakley wrote in *DownBeat*, "Benny Goodman who without a doubt is the supreme 'King of Swing' among white bands, was forced in this instance to relinquish his title to Chick Webb, who satisfactorily proved that in this, his very own field, he is absolutely unbeatable" (3). In one night, using the skills he had been arduously polishing for most of his life, Chick had cemented his reputation as the "King of Swing" in Harlem and, more importantly, brought his name the national attention he had been seeking. But this event seemed merely a beneficial psychological victory and Chick didn't bask in his success. *DownBeat* wrote, "Up until this time [1938] he had always had astoundingly good bands about which there was certainly nothing commercial. He had a style, but it was a purely musical style and not one which would be easily recognizable by the public" (qtd. in Nicholson 32). This situation would soon change, and the Chick Webb Orchestra would be transformed into a hit machine, with Chick, usually the hard-edged musician, uncharacteristically pushing for a more commercialized sound.

Chick and Ella

In fact, as early as 1933 Chick was looking to build upon his success. As *DownBeat* noted in January, 1938, "He began to understand that it was the finished product that mattered both to the booker and to the public, that it did not matter very much whether the band was good or mediocre as long as it had something about it to which the public could relate." Then in 1935 Chick's singer, Charles Linton, introduced him to a possible female replacement. She was the shy, 16-year-old winner of a talent contest at the Apollo in Harlem (not an uncommon title for aspiring black songstresses) named Ella Fitzgerald. She owned only the clothes on her back and looked in need of a good scrubbing. She was an orphan, and like many early jazz figures, a street person. One account of the story is that Chick resisted Linton's idea of putting this urchin in front of his polished band. "You're not puttin' that on my bandstand," he whispered to Linton while Ella waited at the other end of his room during their introduction (Nicholson 35). Another version is that Chick's manager wouldn't give her a chance, and Chick bought her some frocks out of his own paycheck and adopted her out of an orphanage to make her acceptable. Whatever the murky origins of their relationship, it was only months later, after she wooed crowds and demonstrated a knack for memorization, that Chick began to accept Ella as the potential heir to his throne. Chick had learned what it took to be a dynamic bandleader, and saw that Ella was a deserving successor: she was empathetic on stage, personable on a record, and wrote hit songs.

She had sung for the Goodman battle, and after a few months, on January 16th, 1938, Chick and Ella faced the Count Basie band from Kansas City at the Savoy. It was the same night as Goodman's Carnegie Hall concert, and many celebrities in that crowd, including Goodman, were also in the club that night. If ever there was a test of Ella's fortitude it was here, as the already legendary Billie Holiday was singing for Basie at the time. The crowd, as well as *DownBeat* and *Metronome*, was split on which band had won, but all three agreed that Ella was the more engaging singer. By 1938 Chick was allowing Ella Fitzgerald to take more responsibility for choosing what songs the band would play. His goals, whether they were now money or fame, were being achieved. In February of 1938, *DownBeat* wrote:

> Having seen through his own experience that good music did
> not really pay, Chick decided that in order to make a living,
> he would be forced to compromise. He therefore set about to
> prove that his band could play commercial music in a very
> creditable fashion. ("Rise")

On May 2nd, the band recorded with Decca what would become its most popular track. "A-Tisket, A-Tasket," which Ella had adapted from a nursery rhyme about a yellow basket, debuted at number 10 on the hit parade on June 18th, 1938. Two weeks later it rose to number one, and stayed on the parade for 19 weeks. The song was simple, and Decca was hesitant to use it, but Ella's vocals drove the track to popularity. Chick's drumming took a backseat, as did the rest of the band and any hard jazz style, in favor of a safe, mid-tempo, commercialized formula that was easy for all audiences to get ahold of. After Ella joined the band, the large majority of Chick's sides followed this formula (Nicholson 53-55).

Jazz writer Helen Oakley-Dance remembers, "After he got Ella, it was different because his point of view had changed. He began to see that there could be a commercial future for the band" (qtd. in Nicholson 39). On November 11th Chick and Ella followed up again, releasing three records. "I Found My Yellow Basket" debuted at number three and "Wacky Dust" and "MacPherson Is Rehearsin' (to Swing)" came in at numbers 13 and 14 respectively. The songs lack the sectional complexity of earlier recordings but give space for Ella's trademark vocals and lyrical hooks. By all commercial measures the band was a success. Their shows were swarmed, especially in Baltimore, and they broke attendance records in Chicago, New York, and New Jersey. By January, 1939 they were booked for a steady gig at the swanky, all-white Cocoanut Grove of the Park Central Hotel, where black bands were almost never billed (Nicholson 58-59). The songs they were playing were popular standards, but they performed them in an energetic manner, fueled by Ella's personality and Chick's increasingly selective drumming. He was toning down his style to fit the songs, but he was also losing the fight to tuberculosis.

"To struggle so hard as he did . . ."

Long stints of one-nighters and exhausting performances are not beneficial to a case of TB. Beginning on April 4th, 1938, Chick spent two weeks in the hospital, then returned to the stage for an engagement at the Roseland. Tenor saxophone player Teddy McRae remembered, "Every time we closed a stage down at Roseland, the valet had to go and pick him up and bring him off the stage" (Nicholson 53). By 1939, Chick was dealing with bouts of debilitating pain, and played only a few songs per set, with someone else filling in on the others. In April, 1939 he underwent a surgery at Johns Hopkins Hospital in Baltimore to have fluid drained from his back. But he never fully recovered. In June he was back in Johns Hopkins, but before he went he could sense something was wrong. McRae remembered Chick, before he went to the hospital, repeatedly telling him to "take care of Ella" (Nicholson 61). On June 16th, 1939, tuberculosis and kidney complications finally overcame Chick after a lifetime of fighting. Ella was leading the band in Alabama to a crowd who already knew about his death, and when they finished playing, the room was silent (Nicholson 60-62).

To interpret Chick Webb's commercialization of his music as a tendency of the worst element of the Swing Era is a mistake. This was not the period of bebop or free jazz, when jazz forms had strong audiences dedicated to the aesthetic aspects of the music; there was scant room for experimentation. The idea of success in Swing was ambiguous, and in a struggle between commercial popularity and artistic development, the former often won. Unfortunately for Chick, his late style regressed to a more popular sound and he is remembered, and perhaps unjustly neglected, because of those late recordings. There is no denying that in the last years of his career Chick sought mass appeal, but commercial sides like "A-Tisket, A-Tasket" are not representative of Chick's drumming style and work against his legacy.

Starting in late 1937, *DownBeat* ran a serial feature on Chick Webb entitled "The Rise of a Crippled Genius" that was divided over the issues of several months. Although it contains a complete biography that seems to be derived from an interview with Chick, among many valid points of analysis, it also contains opinions that have the potential to gain prevalence and need to be debunked. For example, when handling Chick's decision to play a more commercial style, "The Rise of a Crippled Genius" suggests, "His major fault is a natural laziness. . . . There is the inclination not to work hard . . . but only when the occasion calls for it."

Chick didn't "sell out" because of laziness. He was from East Baltimore, where you succeeded with what you were given and when the neighborhood burned down, you rebuilt. Chick inherited this attitude, working out of poverty and taking hiatuses only when his health didn't permit him to play. While it fueled his drive, this blue-collar attitude also contributed to Chick's stylistic regression: he had no reason to take risks as he would make more money and draw bigger crowds playing popular material.

It is hard to say if drumming for him was an art or an occupation, and in terms of Chick's goals it may have been the latter. But it is unfair to judge his mind with no record of his defense—especially with his life cut short so abruptly—and it may be hasty to infer that he didn't push his drumming and music in a more stylistically adventurous direction because he had found a comfortable place in the spotlight. The tuberculosis and frailty he was born with held him back where poverty, segregation, and occasional naiveté couldn't.

Only with this consideration does the tragedy contemplated by Krupa at coffin-side come into full light. Chick's illness allowed us only a glimpse of his potential. As "The Rise of a Crippled Genius" declares, "It is unfortunate that so comparatively little is known by musicians and swing enthusiasts about the capabilities of Chick Webb himself and of his band." But the world met only one Chick Webb—the one who died at 30; the one who never broke free of the East Baltimore paperboy mindset; the one whose biography will probably never be written—and when considering his story, his potential is a vital chapter.

In February, 1940, six months after Chick's death, over 50 famous black entertainers put on a memorial show at Baltimore's Fifth Regiment Armory. Artists included Duke Ellington, Billie Holiday, Peg Leg Bates, Teddy Hill, Taps Miller, the Ink Spots, Jackie Mabley, the Nicholas Brothers, and Claude Hopkins. The highlight was Ella leading Chick's band—now her band—in "Royal Garden Blues" and "Oh Johnny." In attendance were the governor of Maryland, a state senator, and most importantly heavyweight champion Joe Louis (whose appearance caused a commotion), along with a crowd of 8,000. The concert was to benefit the Chick Webb Recreation Center Memorial

Fund, to create a community center for the poor kids of East Baltimore. The *Sun* reported, "[Chick] wanted to build them a recreational center such as he never had when he was a little boy peddling papers. He wanted to make things easier for other youths so they wouldn't have to struggle so hard as he did" (Rasmussen).

Despite his artistic shortcomings, and although only newspaper clippings, grainy photographs, and tinny recordings of Chick Webb remain and chronic illness left him destined to live a short life, the work ethic he had learned from a devastated Baltimore that rebuilt itself, combined with the dedication to live performance he had learned from its parades and pleasure boats, allowed him to carve a legacy that rips through jazz in the twentieth century. He laid a foundation for all subsequent jazz drumming, and without his polishing, Ella's development and success would have been impossible. It takes strong-willed characters to keep an art form alive, and while some may be overlooked it would be a grave injustice to do that to Chick Webb: the disabled East Baltimore paper boy who battled despite physical and material limitations to perform a thunderous coup in the Kingdom of Swing.

Works Cited

Some of the newspaper and magazine articles cited below derive from a vertical file at the Enoch Pratt Library. These clippings do not include page numbers.

"Chick Webb, Swing King, Dies Near Old Home Here." Baltimore

Evening *Sun*, 17 June 1939. N.p. Print.

Chick Webb and his Orchestra "Stomping at the Savoy." Booklet.

Proper 2006. CD.

Coyle, Wilbur F. *Municipal Hand-Book City of Baltimore* 1909.

Baltimore: Lowenthal Wolfe, 1909. Print.

Gioia, Ted. *The History of Jazz*. New York: Oxford UP, 1997. Print.

Hammond, John. "Thousands of Show Folks out in New York –

Goodman Dance an Incredible Sight" *DownBeat* (4.6), June 1937: 3. Print.

Johnson, J. Wilfred. *Ella Fitzgerald: An Annotated Discography; Including Complete Discography of Chick Webb*. Jefferson, NC: McFarland, 2001.

Print.

Nicholson, Stuart. *Ella Fitzgerald*. New York: Macmillan, 1994. Print.

Oakley, Helen. "Call Out Riot Squad to Handle Mob at Goodman-Webb

Battle" *DownBeat* (4.6), June 1937: 1,3-4. Print.

Rasmussen, Fred. "The band played on . . .". Baltimore *Sun*. 28 July

1996. N.p. Print.

"The Rise of a Crippled Genius." *DownBeat* December, 1937- March,

1938. N.p. Print.

Sandler, Gilbert. "Webb Won the Battle of the Bands." Baltimore

Evening *Sun* April 28, 1992. N.p. Print.

"Swing: The Velocity of Celebration." *Jazz*. Dir. Ken Burns. PBS,

2001. DVD.

"Swing Music's Leaders Give King of the Drums a Stirring Funeral."

Baltimore Evening *Sun* Jun 20, 1939. N.p Print.

"Will Ella Take Over Webb Ork?" *DownBeat* (4.7) July, 1939: 1,19. Print.

Williams, Harold A. *Baltimore Afire*. Baltimore: Schneidereith &

Sons, 1979. Print.

Discography

A complete discography of Chick Webb's recorded work is available in J. Wilfred Johnson's Ella Fitzgerald: An Annotated Discography. *The list below uses that and other resources to provide a guide to some of Chick's important and representative sessions.*

The Jungle Band. "Dog Bottom." *Chick Webb: 1929-1939*
   Chronological Classics, 2006. CD.
   This is Chick's first release, recorded in 1929, while leading The Jungle Band. Band members included musicians who would play with Chick for years, including John Trueheart on guitar. Chick is around 20 years old on this recording, and shows his style through some fills.

(The following tracks, all by Chick Webb and His Orchestra, are collected on the CD *Stomping at the Savoy.* Proper, 2006.)

"Heebie Jeebies." Arr. Benny Carter.
"Blues in My Heart." Arr. Benny Carter.
"Soft and Sweet." Arr. Benny Carter.
"Stompin' At The Savoy." Rec. 18 May 1934. Arr. Edgar Sampson.
"Blue Minor." Rec. 6 July 1934. Arr. Edgar Sampson
   Recorded early in the band's career, these tracks are solid examples of Benny Carter and Edgar Sampson arrangements the group frequently played. The recording technology is so obsolete it's unclear if Chick is even on any of these tracks.

"What a Shuffle." Rec. 19 November 1934. Arr. Don Kirkpatrick.
"Don't Be That Way." Rec. 19 Nov. 1934. Arr. Edgar Sampson.
"Blue Lou." Rec. 19 Nov 1934. Arr. Edgar Sampson.
   These recordings come from the Decca session of 1934. The orchestra's synergy and musicianship are represented through Edgar Sampson's arrangements and the tasteful soloing. Chick's drumming is heard predominantly as a high hat keeping time. Occasionally he has a hard hit or a cymbal crash, but not much else.

"Harlem Congo." Rec. 1 Nov. 1937. Arr. Charlie Dixon.
   "Harlem Congo" is a great example of the band playing at a fast tempo and of Chick's drumming style. His high hat work is furious and constant and his snare hits are loud. The band has an excellent line up here with Mario Bauzá, Bobby Stark, and Taft Jordan on trumpets, Sandy Williams on trombone, and Teddy McRae on tenor. The energy the band puts into a quality arrangement here shows why they drove audiences wild. Chick's solo is very representative, as he keeps a loud roll going on the snare while hitting the blocks and bells, and then brings the band into a new section.

"A-Tisket, A-Tasket." Rec. 2 May 1938. Arr. Van Alexander.
"Heart of Mine" Rec. 2 May 1938. Arr. Van Alexander.
"I'm Just a Jitterbug." Rec. 2 May 1938. Arr. Van Alexander.
"Azure." Rec. 2 May 1938. Arr. Van Alexander.

These sides show how the band took a backseat to Ella's vocals (except on the instrumental ballad "Azure"). "A-Tisket, A-Tasket," the band's biggest hit, in particular focuses on Ella's nursery-rhyme lyrics. The rest are catchy, with melodies and solos that follow and accentuate the vocals. Chick enjoys a solo at Ella's request in "I'm Just a Jitterbug," but it is only a few seconds long, and nothing like those of his earlier recordings.

"Liza (All the Clouds'll Roll Away)." Rec. 3 May 1938. Arr. Benny Carter.

Recorded only a day after the previous session, "Liza (All the Clouds'll Roll Away)" shows some vicious drumming by Chick and some hard swinging by the band. It's a fine contrast to the hits and shows that the band was recording quality material right up until Chick's death in 1939.

"MacPherson is Rehearsin' (to Swing)." Rec. 9 June 1938.

This song retains some hard swing style while still allowing room for Ella's vocals. It is a meeting place between the commercial hits and the band's jazzier songs. A hit in its own right, it reached number 14 on the hit parade, but never matched the success of "A-Tisket, A-Tasket."

"Wacky Dust" Rec. 17 August 1938.

What substance "Wacky Dust" is referring to is debatable, but the song reached number 13 on the hit parade, and Ella is hopelessly loveable on it.

"F.D.R. Jones." Rec. 6 Oct. 1938.
"I Found My Yellow Basket" Rec. 6 Oct. 1938.

Two more tracks dominated by Ella: "I Found My Yellow Basket" is the follow up to the band's big hit, and "F.D.R. Jones" is cutesy. The tracks resort to call-and-response vocals from the band and abandon hard-swinging style, but show Ella's potential for band-leading, scatting, and popularity.

Cab Calloway

"If the music is right, the people will appreciate it."

3 The Singin', Swingin' Life and Times of Cab Calloway
by Matthew Blackburn

Hi-de-hi-de-hi-de-ho,
Wah-de-doo-de-way-de-ho,
Wah-de-wah-de-wah-de-doo,
Bee-de-doo-de-dee-de-dow,
Teedle-do-de-dee rah-de-dah-de-dah.
Hi-de-hi-de-hi-de-ho.
Now here's a story 'bout Minnie the Moocher . . .

The year was 1931, and though America was in the thick of the Great Depression it was making the transition easily from the Jazz Age to the Swing Era, and the music and entertainment industries were thriving just as they had been for the past three decades. Quite appropriately, it was in this year that Cabell "Cab" Calloway made the mistake that would forever change his style and ultimately make his career as a singer and bandleader: he forgot the lyrics to a song during a performance at one of the premier sites of New York City night life—the Cotton Club. Cab recalls the incident in his autobiography *Of Minnie the Moocher and Me*:

> During one show that was being broadcast over nationwide radio in the spring of 1931, not long after we started using "Minnie the Moocher" as our theme song, I was singing, and in the middle of a verse, . . . the damned lyrics went right out of my head. I forgot them completely. I couldn't leave a blank there as I might have done if we weren't on the air. I had to fill the space, so I just started to scat-sing the first thing that

came into my mind. . . . "Hi-de-ho-de-ho-de-hee." The crowd
went crazy. And I went on with it—right over live radio—
like it was written that way. Then I asked the band to follow
it with me and I sang, "Hi-de-hi-de-hi-de-ho." And the band
responded. And I sang, "Dwaa-de-dwaa-de-dwaa-de-doo."
And the band responded. By this time, whenever the band
responded some of the people in the audience were beginning
to chime in as well. So I motioned for the band to hold up and
I asked the audience to join in. And I sang and the audience
responded; they hollered back and nearly brought the roof
down. We went on and on for I don't know how long, and by
the end the rafters were rocking and people were standing up
and cheering. . . . From that night on, "Minnie the Moocher"
and "hi-de-ho" have been one and the same as far as most
people are concerned. (112)

From then on, scatting became an important element of Cab's
charismatic musicianship, and he eventually earned the trademark
nickname "the Hi-Dee-Ho Man" as he became identified with the
uniquely wild and energetically improvisational style that he brought
to jazz[1]. Cab Calloway's role as a bandleader likewise had enormous
significance for the jazz world, as his musical outfits served as the
professional crossroads for many great jazz musicians.

Ironically, Cab's passionate and intense showmanship, rooted
largely in his love of entertaining his audiences and simply "making
people feel good" (Calloway 2), contrasted sharply with his private
life. In his own words as well as in the testimonies of his close friends
and loved ones, Cab was a surprisingly introverted individual on the
personal level.[2] Though unable to express himself in this mode, the
reticent singer seemed to find in entertainment a ready outlet for the
emotions he contained offstage and launched an enormously successful

career that accelerated the spread of jazz across the nation, molded the careers of numerous great jazz figures, and demolished racial barriers in the entertainment industry (234).

Cabell "Cab" Calloway was born in 1907 in Rochester, New York to Martha Eulalia Reed and Cabell Calloway, Sr., a relatively nonmusical family (although his mother regularly served as organist during the Sunday services at their local church). Though it was in Rochester that he spent his early childhood, Cab's musical roots lie in Baltimore, where the family relocated in 1918; Cab resided there, on Druid Hill Avenue, for the next four years (13). But Cab's musical interests were not piqued until the age of 14, when he began singing with the local church choir and taking voice lessons from Ruth Macabee, a close family friend and grade school music teacher (35). Until that time, young Cab spent his days as a "hustler," selling newspapers, shoes, and working at the nearby Pimlico racetrack. This hard work ethic was likely instilled in him by the family's financial struggles and inspired by his stepfather John Nelson Fortune's devotion to earning money for the family (15-26). After spending a year's stint at a Downingtown reform school at around age 13 (his parents were worried about his proclivity for the streets and lack of interest in school), Cab recalls, his drive for success was solidified.

> That year in Downingtown made a big difference. . . . Being away from home and having to make it on my own. . . .
> [I]n Downingtown, if I made a mistake, there was nobody to look after me but myself. It was me who would have to miss supper. It was me who would have to work after everyone else was finished. Suddenly there was no one to bail me out. . . . I knew, from then on, I had to make it on my own. (28)

Thus, upon his return home, young Cab began working diligently in school and applying himself musically when he began his vocal training with Macabee. When he entered Frederick Douglass High School in 1924, after the family had moved to Madison Avenue (near their first Baltimore home at Druid Hill), Cab began expanding his musical activity. Even as he became strongly involved in his studies and athletics, he continued working odd jobs as he had done in his younger days. "In high school I began to play drums and to sing with a small group and even do vaudeville with some kids from school. And best of all," writes Cab, "I found out that I could get paid for entertaining. I could do two of the things most important to me at the same time— make people happy and make money" (32). It was not long before young Cab's industrious nature led him from his church's choir loft to the stages of Baltimore's nightclubs, where he expanded his repertoire and took his first major step toward a robust career as an entertainer.

Always on the lookout for an opportunity to perform, Cab began plying the instrumentalists at the local clubs for a chance to sing along to their tunes, and gradually earned some repute as a regular performer at places like the Gaiety and the Arabian Tent Club (36). He soon immersed himself in working with a local startup band, assuming the dual role of drummer and vocalist.[3] During this period, Baltimore played host to a thriving jazz community rife with opportunities for the aspiring musician. Thus Cab took it upon himself to lead and arrange gigs for the little group—important, precocious managerial functions that foreshadowed his later career as a singer and bandleader (37). Charm City's jazz culture launched the careers of other great artists, many of whom Cab encountered during his own exploration of the city's entertainment. "Baltimore was at that time one of those centers of jazz," writes Cab. He recalls:

> Some great musicians came out of there. Johnny Jones and
> his Arabian Tent Orchestra was one of the best in the city. .
> . . And Chick Webb was from Baltimore, and he had a little
> band around there. In fact, [they] were my inspirations. . .
> . The pianist Ulysses Chambers was around Baltimore in
> those years and so was Harold Steptoe. . . . I used to sing with
> all those guys in the Baltimore nightclubs. (37-38)

However, before long, Cab expanded his entertainment interests beyond the nightclubs and began performing at the Regent Theatre, participating in its revues while simultaneously maintaining his work with the band, as a student-athlete at school, and at his part-time job at a local catering company (40, 51). Though his parents disapproved (but looked the other way), he relished the nightclub and revue-oriented aspects of his life; they in turn sparked his aspirations as an entertainer and bandleader (38-40). He sustained this work pace throughout his high school career. Then, in his senior year, just as he came to realize that "in my heart . . . entertainment was my world" (40), his elder sister Blanche returned to Baltimore playing one of the major roles in the traveling musical *Plantation Days*.[4]

Inspired by the professionalism of the show and enthralled with his sister's talent, Cab attended the performances religiously. He then encountered what would be the first of several big breaks in his life as a performer-to-be: one of the singers in the show fell ill and a replacement was needed. After much cajoling, he managed to convince Blanche to secure him an audition for the part, which he won (52). Remaining with the show for the remainder of the tour, Cab traveled to and performed in Pennsylvania, Michigan, Ohio, and finally in

Chicago, where the show closed in 1927. He enrolled at Crane College in the autumn of that same year, honoring the promise he had made to his mother before leaving Baltimore (54).

But his experiences with the revue had permanently aroused his interest in show business and so, months later, Cab resumed his nightclub activities (helped by Blanche's boyfriend's connections[5]) with a greater fervor than he had in Baltimore (57). "What a city!" expounds Cab. "What a world I had been missing. . . . And the music. Chicago was just full of music. In those days the South Side in Chicago was to jazz what Harlem came to be a few years later" (55). His first gigs took place in an unassuming little place known as the Dreamland Café, where he was booked to sing three times a week. The unpolished reputation of the club was of little consequence to Cab; all that mattered was that he was doing what he loved in one of the jazziest cities in the country (57). Of course, he did not confine himself to the Dreamland, but wandered around Chicago as he had in Baltimore, looking for the opportunity to earn some money on the side—a behavior that, Cab notes, was common among musicians of the day and which helped catalyze the spread of jazz culture throughout America (82).

Only months later, Cab's connections through his sister brought him still closer to a full-time career in entertainment. He once again managed to secure a position at a nightclub, but this time it was much more strongly associated with Chicago's mainstream jazz scene. The place was the Sunset Café, "the most popular club on the South Side," and incidentally also the locale where he and Louis Armstrong first crossed paths—the latter at the time was playing with Joe "King" Oliver's band at the café (58; Cook and Morton 1131). Before long Cab's talent and persistence led to his hiring as the café's emcee. Just as he had done in Baltimore, Cab was soon playing multiple roles: by 1928, he was the Sunset Café's house singer, master of ceremonies, and the leader of its house band (58-59). "All of a sudden I had a band of my own," remembers Cab, "and I went stone crazy. I worked with these guys day and night. . . . It was a lot of work, but it was easy because it seemed so natural. It was exactly what I wanted to be doing" (63). Exactly what he wanted, indeed: under his direction, the Alabamians developed an innovative, vocalized call-and-response style that incorporated the entire band in Cab's performances, something he exploited (as scatting) regularly as his career matured. Yet the Alabamians' act was not unusual for its time, and Cab's earlier style of interacting with his instrumentalists was strongly influenced by other contemporary groups. He recalls,

> There had been a guy in Chicago named Benny Meroff who had a heck of a presentation band, as we called novelty bands in those days. Benny would run back and forth across the stage with a megaphone and carry on a kind of call-and-response with the band, directing, singing, hollering, bringing the whole dixieland [sic] thing to life. . . . Paul Ash was another white bandleader who I dug. . . . Both guys had something going with their bands; they would really turn the audiences on. . . . [T]hey taught me how to get a band moving and how to stimulate an audience. (65)

The Alabamians became extremely popular with the Sunset's regulars and soon caught the attention of the Music Corporation of America (64). The company booked the band; Cab and his Alabamians would soon be on their way to New York—they would play at the Savoy Ballroom the coming November after a brief period of touring (66).

Unfortunately, though the Alabamians had a significant following in Chicago, they were unable to adapt to the expectations of the Savoy audience, molded by a predominance of Swing in the New York scene (71). At the conclusion of a short-lived contract with the club, which culminated in the band's defeat in a contest with the Savoy's house band, the Missourians, Cab broke ties with the Alabamians.

He remained in New York, but without his band or a nightclub to call home, he was without work. Using his connections with Louis Armstrong, Cab won a role in the popular Broadway show *Connie's Hot Chocolates*, in which he encountered some of the musicians he would later incorporate into his band (76). As the show reached the end of its tour, Cab learned that the Savoy was interested in hiring him as the leader of the Missourians: Cab's charisma as master of ceremonies, singer, and bandleader had shone through, and the Savoy's management recognized the advantage of pairing his entertainment skill with the strong musicianship of its house band (76-78).

So, by 1930 Cab Calloway was once again at the helm of his own band, but this time the musicians were skilled professionals and Cab was officially under contract. Upon the construction of the new Plantation Club in Harlem, Cab and his band were booked to travel back to New York and perform for the new club's opening night. With prestige to rival that of the famed Cotton Club, the Plantation Club represented a major career opportunity for Cab and the Missourians, but it was never to be. It was the era of Prohibition, and the illegality of alcohol distribution had encouraged the formation of the speakeasies and nightclubs where Cab performed. Inevitably, many of the more successful clubs were tied to organized crime, and such was the case with the Plantation and Cotton Clubs. Thus, before that fateful opening night, the Plantation Club was ransacked, utterly destroyed. "In typical gangland style, the owners of the Cotton Club had made sure that they wouldn't have the Plantation Club for competition after all," writes Cab. "And they were successful. The club never opened" (83). Without other major bookings, Cab, his band, and their management were forced to return to the Savoy part-time and find other gigs at the other New York nightclubs.

Come spring of that year, Cab and his Missourians were playing regularly at another club: the Crazy Cat. This club presented another chance for success for the group, as it had a reputation for drawing patrons from celebrity circles. Additionally, its ties to radio allowed the band to go on air nightly, and through Cab's rigorous band-leading and energetic performances the group attained some notoriety. The on-stage interaction he had so strongly emphasized in his performances with the Alabamians he now incorporated into his shows with the Missourians, priming him for the development of the unique scat singing that would typify his performing style (and win him the hearts of his audiences) for the rest of his career (86).

In time, the success of Cab and his Missourians attracted the attention of the management of the Cotton Club. Ironically, the same mobsters who had destroyed the opportunity of a lifetime for the group in 1930 now presented it with a new one barely a year later. The management wanted Cab and his band to perform at the Cotton Club as a periodic replacement for Duke Ellington and his group, who were often on tour. Cab recalls, "The Cotton Club mob had just bought out my contract and the Missourians' contract the easy way. Pure muscle"

(87). But this employer turnover was more than welcome; the Cotton Club was one of the premier sites of the American nightlife and jazz scene in the nation (*Hi-Dee-Ho Man* 8).

Roughly a year into the group's contract with the Cotton Club, Cab and his band had performed so well and so frequently that their reputation began to match that of Ellington's orchestra (Calloway 108). Naturally, the change of settings demanded a change of name, and so Cab Calloway and his Missourians became Cab Calloway and his Orchestra, a moniker far more suitable to the wide-ranging entertainment functions that the group would perform in this new residency, which Cab summed up in one short statement: "record contracts, network radio, publicity, national tours" (88). At the time of the 1931 recording of "Minnie the Moocher" (only weeks after Cab and his band were contracted by the Cotton Club), Cab, heavily influenced by the improvisational singing style of Louis Armstrong (59), supposedly averted what could have been a disastrous performance and scatted. The audience's response was immediate and explosive, and when Cab invited them to join his singing he created the paradigm of audience-entertainer interactivity that would shape his entire career. By that time, Cab had already partnered with his agent, Irving Mills, to form a separate corporation, Cab Calloway, Inc.; now the two began writing and recording on a much larger scale (110).

Following the enormous success of "Minnie the Moocher," Cab adapted his style to the form that would earn him fame for decades to come, all the while employing a unique jive dialect (McRae 581). Given that jazz grew largely out of African-American culture and that, simultaneously, the development of the slang that eventually became jive language represented a source of pride within African-American communities as a unique form of cultural expression, it was only natural that jive talk and jazz music became inseparable (Leonard 158). With the soaring popularity of jazz, jive rapidly became the vernacular among jazz aficionados and musicians alike; there was a certain measure of pride associated with the ability to communicate in the language of jazz (McRae 580-581). Indeed, scatting arose as a form of improvisation that incorporated jive, and as many musicians used it Cab added it as a permanent part of his repertoire after 1931, inspired, as the story goes, by its successful use in "Minnie the Moocher" (McRae 581). Cab's commercial success, coupled with his unique talent as a scatter, won him great acclaim as an artist, and he later published (with the help of his associates) several editions of *The New Cab Calloway's Hepsters Dictionary*, a compendium of jive terminology, along with a supplementary piece entitled *Prof. Cab Calloway's Swingformation Burea* (Calloway 176). In short, Cab popularized jive language as a dialect of its own (McRae 581). Because scatting and jiving would become such major aspects of jazz at the peak of Cab's career, they ultimately provided him with a powerful tool in popularizing and disseminating jazz throughout America and the globe.

With Cab fully integrating scat singing with his music and his call-and-response oriented band leading, the nature of his business dealings evolved. As the band recorded and toured with greater regularity, Cab began to change the membership of the band. With increased expectations came the need for better musicians, some of them relatively new faces on the jazz scene who had earned great repute for their instrumental virtuosity: Benny Payne on piano, Ed Swayzee, Eddie

Barefield, Walter Thomas on saxophone, Doc Cheatham on trumpet, Al Morgan on bass, and Leroy Maxey (retained from the Missourians) on drums. "At every stage of the band's development I was satisfied that I had the best men behind me that I could find for the money," Cab noted; "as the money got better I could afford better musicians" (170).[6] In every case Cab greatly improved the band from its original cast of Missourians, and though he mainly occupied the spotlight he ensured that the musical prowess of each member was on display (Papa 4). In the end, what gave the group the force to break from the Cotton Club and independently operate under its own corporate contract was the renown reaped by excellent musicianship and the charisma of their singing, jiving bandleader (*Hi-Dee-Ho Man* 11). Years of honing his nascent skills in the Baltimore scene in his youth had paid off—Cab was his own agent, and the band was truly his own.

With the formation of the new corporation in 1931, the band continued to perform at the Cotton Club but no longer restricted itself to that venue. With Mills acting as the driving force, the group signed a number of contracts for a variety of tours (Calloway 120-121). Indeed, that year marked a period of unprecedented fame and success for Cab Calloway and his Orchestra, during which the group played at the Cotton Club over the radio throughout the week. "All of a sudden Cab Calloway was famous," Cab recalls.

> We were on the radio from the Cotton Club three nights a week, Monday, Wednesday, and Friday, with the new Columbia Broadcasting System, National Broadcasting, and Mutual Broadcasting. Each of them had us for thirty minutes one night a week. . . .We had built up a hell of a following around New York, and although I didn't know it then, across the country. (121)

Given this national acclaim, it was to be expected that Mills would approach Cab with the proposition of publicly touring the South—a significant move for the group, because the South was still plagued with racial laws and extremist groups like the Knights of the White Camellia. Segregation was still enforced per state policy, and though jazz had its roots in the South, notes Cab, it survived outside of the public sphere, confined mostly to small, discreet clubs (122). Thus, Cab remembers, when Mills approached him with this proposition, "Well, I really had to think about that some" (122). But he had always known when to seize an opportunity and confront a challenge, and decided to follow through with it, against the wishes of several of his instrumentalists.

Cab and his band were excluded from some concert halls and the more posh nightclubs in the cities they toured, which included Durham, Virginia Beach, Norfolk, Savannah, and Raleigh (122-126). Nevertheless, the tour ultimately met with great success, although as expected at various shows the group was not well received and in some cases was even threatened. In one particularly telling point of the journey down to Virginia, the buses carrying the musicians were stopped by Virginia state troopers, who were responding to a report that a white woman (Mrs. Knowles, who had contracted their sponsorship) was traveling with the all-black band. Although she owned the buses and was the group's primary employer for this tour, the troopers forced her to leave her buses behind on account of a law mandating that "nigras cannot be on the same bus together like this with no white woman" (123). During the same trip, which was taking the band to the upscale white resort town Virginia Beach, a number of the buses broke down and most of the band was delayed for about an hour. When Cab and pianist Benny Payne arrived and attempted to appease the already irate crowd with some ad hoc arrangements, threats were hurled. Cab recalls that stressful night:

> Well, half the damned people there thought it was a trick. They were sure that we were trying to cheat them out of their money, so they started hollering again, and raised a whole boatful of hell. Benny and I went out there, and I started singing show tunes and pop tunes. . . . People were hollering and stomping and somebody shouted, "Let's take this nigger out and lynch him." All of this was going on while I was trying to sing, and I could see Benny sweating and I was sweating like hell, too. I was just waiting for somebody to jump up on the stage and start something. (124)

Fortunately, with the arrival of the rest of the musicians the show proceeded without incident, though Cab did have to convince his band to remain on the tour (125).

Of course, it was still only 1931; the Civil Rights Movement would not begin for decades, and the retrogressive "separate but equal" ruling of Plessy vs. Fergusson was still the law of the land. Yet Cab Calloway and his Orchestra, an all African-American group, was touring the South; in most cases, they were the first African-American band to hold public concerts in the cities they visited (125). But even when crowds were not threatening the group, the revolutionary nature of their tour caused some resistance from certain audiences and hosts. Cab recalls a number of particularly bitter, frustrating reminders of the South's traditional misgivings about African Americans:

> State troopers in the South at that time could give a Negro hell—especially a Negro of any status. I've known colored physicians in the deep South who owned their own cars; in

order to travel safely on state highways from one town to the next, they put on a chauffeur's cap so the troopers would figure the car was owned by a white man and not some uppity Negro. . . . [While traveling together] Benny used to tell me, "Hell, Cab, you may think Maryland is the North, but as far as I'm concerned, it might as well be Alabama. They've got us coming in and leaving from the backs of theaters, dressing in toilets, and eating while we sit on potato sacks in the kitchen. You know damned well they don't treat white bands like this." . . . [I]t took something out of us to accept that kind of crap (123, 126).

In the end, the majority of the tour was relatively calm, disturbed only during gigs in particularly racist locales and at various points on the road. In fact, at Tybee Beach in Savannah, Georgia, the group was greeted with fanfare and a police escort, and were able to sign into rooms in the resort itself (125). Upon their return to New York Cab and his Orchestra reentered the New York circuit and the Cotton Club. In light of their incredible success in New York and the successful official opening of the South to African-American bands, Cab decided to take the group beyond their standard touring and the Cotton Club revues and into the film industry.

Using his friendship with the Cotton Club's management, Cab secured an appearance in the new film, *The Singing Kid*, in 1936, though he had already begun dabbling in theater earlier with *The Big Broadcast* of 1932 (Calloway 131; Gale Reference Team). Film quickly became a significant part of Cab's entertainment agenda, and the years between 1931 and 1941 marked the busiest period for Cab Calloway and his Orchestra. The group was now performing its regular Cotton Club revues, touring the New York circuit, and performing in a variety of films, while also producing and broadcasting a large number of new songs and tunes. His film and songwriting activity during that stretch of time was extensive: Cab Calloway's Cotton Club Orchestra was featured in films such as *Stormy Weather* and *International House* (Gale Reference Team). Additionally, the group's continued involvement with the Cotton Club revues led to the creation of several hit songs written for the revues themselves (not by Cab, though he made them famous by his singing), including "Wail of the Reefer Man," "The Reefer Man," "I've Got the World on a String," and an original, interesting piece designed as a sequel to Cab's own "Minnie the Moocher"—"Minnie the Moocher's Wedding Day" (Calloway 131). The group even began performing at fundraising events for a wide variety of causes (131-135).

Soon the group experienced what Cab later recognized as the peak of their career: the group's tour abroad in Europe in 1934 (135). A number of factors caused this sojourn to be an enormous success— the band was outfitted with the best musicians Cab could find, as always (including Cheatham and Swayzee on trumpet, saxophonist Garvin Bushell, bassist Al Morgan, Walter "Foots" Thomas, De Priest Wheeler, Benny Payne on piano as usual, and Harry White [135]); Europe was as yet still catching on to jazz (making their performances vastly popular); and racism was virtually nonexistent, allowing for a peaceful, uneventful tour (135-137). The group toured England, France, Holland, and Belgium, among other countries (Papa). Now, other African-American bands had traveled the European circuit previously, but Europe still had not had extensive jazz exposure; for that reason, not only was Cab and his Orchestra an instant hit with the European audiences (138), but they served as musical ambassadors. Already household names in the United States, Cab Calloway and his group helped to introduce jazz to Europe, effectively internationalizing the music's culture (*Hi-Dee-Ho Man* 12).

Cab credited their success to his musicians—an outfit that was transformed from what it had once been back in the late '20s. It would be pointless to argue whether it was Cab himself who was the highlight of every show or his musicians, because they performed as a single, streamlined unit, a collective instrument. Cab certainly did dominate the stage as a showman, garbed in a garish zoot suit and large hat, strutting to the beat of the tune. Yet this act was always part of a larger whole, and the call-and-response scatting he carried out with his band during performances was just one aspect of the interactivity he had with his musicians. The group had perfected a new type of jazz musicality: if Cab's scatting gave voice to the sound of his musicians, his musicians' playing gave sound to Cab's movements onstage. The result was an innovative approach to jazz, and although critics sometimes belittled this novelty approach the audience begged to differ (Murphy). "If the music is right," argued Cab, "the people will appreciate it" (Calloway 143). He truly knew how to communicate with the audience, and the result was the lively, flamboyantly interactive performances that drew fans wherever they performed. People simply loved hearing and seeing Cab Calloway and his Orchestra live, after having had to rely on national radio prior to the tours; there was never a shortage of avid listeners (139-140).

With the relocation of the Cotton Club in 1936 and its ultimate closing in 1940, Cab moved to another club. At that stage, jazz as a pure musical form (as distinct from the dance-oriented music that characterized the Swing Era) was coming to dominate America's musical landscape (152). This shift in musical demand was largely responsible for Cab's assimilation of the nation's best musicians into what would become the most musically accomplished band of his career; the 1941 outfit that was composed of such greats as Dizzy Gillespie, Chu Berry, Walter Thomas, Lammar Wright, Keg Johnson, Milt Hinton, Benny Payne, Danny Barker, and Cozy Cole, among many others (152-162, 170). The year 1943 saw the arrival of another inspired set of arrangements; nevertheless, as one appropriately titled piece suggested, "The Jive's Been Here and Gone". Swing's popularity had begun to wane with the emergence of bebop (185), and this fact, coupled with the recording ban enforced by the American Federation of Musicians from 1942-1943, spelled the demise of the big band in the late 1940s. By 1948, Cab's band-leading career was all but gone, and he was forced to terminate his Orchestra (*Hi-Dee-Ho Man* 15).

Ever undaunted, Cab found new avenues in show business. His experience in movie acting gave him access to filmmaking as a career option, and by 1952 he was also fully involved in theater (16). Though theater would occupy a significant chunk of his professional time until his death in 1994, he intermittently mingled band leading with appearances in a wide array of films, musicals, and shows that included the 1950s revival of *Porgy and Bess*,[7] a biography of W.C. Handy, and *The Blues Brothers* (1980), among others (16).

Cab Calloway's contributions to jazz culture at large are not to be underestimated. Though they are manifested primarily in the stylistic elements and dynamic improvisational innovations he brought, they also reside in broader cultural and racial terrain. Oddly, his fair countenance seemed to belie his ethnicity, which often opened him to fire from his fellow African Americans. Yet his pale complexion was not enough to shield him from the racist assumptions of some whites (Murphy). This uniquely difficult position presented Cab with enormous pressure, and catering separately to white and African-American audiences left him without much of a break from either community. Yet it also gave him the opportunity to reach out to both audiences, to show whites that African-American entertainers could be elegant and sophisticated while still swinging, and to stand as a role model for aspiring black singers. Hence, Cab's persona enabled him to craft a unique genre of jazz performance, achieve enormous popularity, and encourage the dissemination of jazz throughout the nation.

Using his most powerful weapon (next to his genius as a vocalist), his devotion to professionalism, Cab was also indispensable to his musicians' development into excellent instrumentalists and showmen. In every aspect of musicality and showmanship, Cab was a staunch disciplinarian with his musicians, who came to refer to him as "the General" (Calloway 158). Cab made sure that his musicians were dressed in fresh tuxedos for every show and that instruments were always cleaned; anyone not ready to play a quarter of an hour ahead of time was fined (159; Murphy). "The singer is sort of an extension of the band," explains his daughter, Camay Calloway Murphy. "You sing as if you were an instrument." In that regard, though he was not an instrumentalist himself, Cab was a source of invaluable musical knowledge, which he had garnered over years of training while growing up in Baltimore—training for which he remained grateful throughout his career.[8] He understood the importance of each instrument in the band, and was adamant that every musician play to the best of his ability. To that end, though he cultivated a familial relationship with band members, his expectations always remained astronomically high (Murphy).

Artistically speaking, Cab's greatest contribution lay in the context in which he employed his scatting and jiving—that unique fusion of instrumentation with movements and vocals, a style of performance that "broke the mold" of mainstream jazz (Murphy). His career as a band leader, singer, and all-around entertainer was revolutionary not only in the destruction of color barriers (whether in network and national broadcast radio, in his tours of the South with his band, in film, or even at the racetracks he had loved since his childhood hustling days) (Calloway 99, 125, 235), but in its incredible musical innovation as well.

NOTES

1. This story was probably fabricated by Cab; according to his daughter Camay Murphy, he was far too disciplined to have simply forgotten the lyrics to his band's theme song. She suggests that he had likely been developing his scatting well in advance of the session with the intention of incorporating it into his performances. Calloway rehearsed his band constantly, and the high standards of professionalism to which he held himself and his musicians earned him the nickname "The General." It therefore would have been very uncharacteristic of him to forget an entire set of lyrics, especially during a recording session on radio. Ms. Murphy's suspicion is corroborated by the sequence of Cab's own recordings. In the 1930 recording of "St. Louis Blues" he incorporates scat into the bulk of the lyrics—and this precedes that infamous 1931 "Minnie the Moocher" recording during which he allegedly first began scatting.

2. All quotations to follow are from *Of Minnie the Moocher and Me* unless otherwise specified.

3. Cab never identified these musicians by name.

4. Blanche Calloway was the first in the family to pursue show business as a career, although talent was clearly evident in the Calloway bloodline—her first musical strides in New York landed her among the cast and crew of *Shuffle Along* (Calloway 38).

5. Cab only knew him by the nickname "Watty."

6. By 1941, trumpeter Dizzy Gillespie, bassist Milt Hinton, and saxophonist Leon "Chu" Berry had been added to Cab's band; he esteemed this particular lineup above all his previous bands (170).

7. *Porgy and Bess* represented significant recognition for him; Gershwin and company had originally crafted the character that Cab eventually played in the revival—Sportin' Life—after Calloway's own likeness.

8. Cab strongly attributed his own musical prowess to this early Baltimore training. Camay Murphy recalls that on the night she saw Cab perform in *Porgy and Bess* some of his original vocal instructors attended. He wanted to know what they thought of his performance, and they offered critiques as if he was still the young student they had instructed decades ago. "He was very humble to them, beholden to suggestions" (Murphy).

Works Cited and Consulted

Calloway, Cabell & Bryant Rollins. *Of Minnie the Moocher and Me.* New York: Crowell, 1976. Print.
This is the primary source of many details of Cab Calloway's life and career (as told by Cab himself). Though filled with valuable anecdotal insight and instrospection by the Hi-Dee-Ho-Man, Of Minnie *contains some stories that must be viewed with skepticism and need cross-referencing.*

The Hi-Dee-Ho-Man. Booklet. Cab Calloway and his Orchestra.
Included in the Classic Jazz Archive's compilation of Cab's best-known work (entitled The Hi-Dee-Ho-Man*), this source provides an objective overview of the major points in Cab's life and career.*

Cook, Richard and Brian Morton. "Joe 'King' Oliver." *The Penguin Dictionary of Jazz.* 5th ed. 2000. Print.

Dempsey, Travis. "Chicago's Jazz Trail, 1893-1950." *Black Music Research Journal 10* (1990): 82-85. Jstor. Loyola Notre Dame Library, Baltimore, MD. Web. 6 Jan. 2010.
This essay ties Cab's musical success back to the growing jazz movement across the nation.

Gale Reference Team. "Biography—Calloway, Cab(ell) (III) (1907-1994)." *Contemporary Authors.* Web. 6 Jan. 2010.
Like the Classic Jazz Archive piece, this article supplies an objective overview of the key points in Cab's life. It also helps to cross-reference details from Cab's own account for accuracy.

Leonard, Neil. "The Jazzman's Verbal Usage." *Black American Literature Forum* 20 (1986): 151- 160. Jstor. Loyola Notre Dame Library, Baltimore, MD. Web. 6 Jan. 2010.
One of two scholarly articles that focuses on the origins of "jive language."

McRae, Rick. "'What Is Hip?' and Other Inquiries in Jazz Slang Lexicography." *Notes, Second Series 57 (2001)*: 574-584. Jstor. Loyola Notre Dame Library, Baltimore, MD. Web. 6 Jan. 2010.
This article explains the origin of jive language and shows why it became important for scat singing. It also connects the success of jazz in America with the popularization of jiving and scatting.

Murphy, Camay Calloway. Personal interview. 29 Jan. 2010.

Papa, Christopher. *CabCallowLLC*. Web. <http://www.cabcallowayllc.com/>
    Still under construction, this website is devoted completely to Cab and his legacy. It furnishes another source of biographical material to clarify and cross-reference certain details of Cab's life.

Additional Information

http://www.youtube.com/watch?v=lBOgH5f36cQ&feature=related
    This links to footage of Cab Calloway performing "It Ain't Necessarily So" (while conducting the band), the famous song delivered by the character Sportin' Life in Porgy and Bess. The role of Sportin' Life was modeled after Cab himself.

http://www.youtube.com/watch?v=JZEmJ_XEAoQ
    This is a link to a video of Louis Armstrong's rendition of "St. Louis Blues" for comparison to the performance by Cab Calloway and his Orchestra.

http://www.youtube.com/watch?v=fvr7nkd_IJM
    This is Armstrong's version of "St. James Infirmary"; notice the striking difference in style between Armstrong's rendition and that of Cab Calloway and his Orchestra.

http://www.cabcalloway.cc/calloway_lyrics.htm
    This site contains the lyrics to a number of Cab's well-known works.

Discography

All recordings are by Cab Calloway and His Orchestra

"St. Louis Blues" (W. C. Handy), 1930. *The Hi-Dee-Ho-Man.*
 Among the traditional jazz classics of the early twentieth century, "St. Louis Blues" was one of Cab's first recordings during his time at the Cotton Club before he began creating original pieces. Nevertheless, Cab's innovative, explosive style shines through in this time-tested classic—within the first few measures he sustains a long, high note and rapidly begins incorporating multiple elements of scat, which then occurs regularly throughout the piece.

"St. James Infirmary," 1930. *The Hi-Dee-Ho-Man.*
 "St. James Infirmary" was notable for its somber tones and lyrics. It is ironic to consider how this melancholy chart served as the signature piece of an artist like Cab Calloway, but it showcases his unusual ability to sing up and down the scale with relative ease, as he sings many of the lyrics in the upper register. This piece is also important to the development of Cab as an entertainer because it precedes "Minnie the Moocher" as the identifying chart of Cab and his Orchestra.

"Sweet Jenny Lee" (Donaldson), 1930. *The Hi-Dee-Ho-Man.*
 This early piece has an intriguing underlying theme produced by a bass progression on the upbeats and piano on the downbeats and built upon by the other instrumentalists, creating an effect reminiscent of a carnival. In the vocal section, Cab demonstrates his versatility as he moves throughout the scale, often jumping rapidly between the upper and lower registers with remarkable control.

"Between the Devil and the Deep Blue Sea" (Arlen/Koehler), 1931.
 The Hi-Dee-Ho-Man.
 This is one of Cab's love songs, and notable as one of the few pieces he performed with an unbroken vocal section. Beginning in the style of a gentle ballad, his vocals soon proceed to a light scat that remains loyal to the overall theme and constitutes a significant chunk of the piece, only yielding to his Orchestra in the last fourth of the song for the resolution.

"Minnie the Moocher" (Calloway/Mills/Gaskill), 1931, 1942. *The Hi-De-Ho Man* (1931). *Are You Hep to the Jive?* (1942 recording).
 The iconic tune that launched Cab's recording career, "Minnie the Moocher" replaced "St. James Infirmary" as the official theme of Cab Calloway and his Orchestra. The 1931 recording is the original recording of the piece and is more subdued than the comparatively explosive 1942 rendition. The scat lines in each recording are completely different, as are the vocalizations that Cab employs. Both recordings are fine demonstrations of Cab's impressive improvisational and tonal versatility.

"Minnie the Moocher's Wedding Day" (Koehler/Arlen), 1932. *The Hi-De-Ho Man.*

Written only a year after the recording and subsequent success of "Minnie the Moocher," this piece is the sequel to the original tale of Minnie. Despite the strikingly distinct melodic qualities of the piece, which include noticeable key changes, there are many familiar vocal motifs. The call-and-response scatting between Cab and his instrumentalists and recurrence of phraseology like "kicking the gong around [in Chinatown]" are recognizable flashbacks to this piece's predecessor.

"Farewell Blues" (Mares/Rapplo/Schoebel),1932. *The Hi-Dee-Ho-Man.*

In this compelling tune the melody opens with muted trumpets repeating a theme over a growing crescendo and sudden decrescendo, giving an almost airy quality to the music. Cab's vocal part is quite brief, and mostly constitutes very rapid scatting that climbs up and down the scale. Once again, Cab's improvisational ability and vocal skill are showcased as he creates an unexpected, unique echoing yodel effect.

"The Scat Song" (Perkins/Calloway/Parrish), 1932. *The Hi-Dee-Ho-Man.*

This appropriately-named tune epitomizes the spontaneity of scat, and seems to have been built almost solely on improvisation. Cab opens with a few scatted lines, and the instruments progress through a series of seemingly unrelated melodies broken by large chunks of scatting by Cab. It has the sense of being a turn-based improvisation session between Cab and his musicians; by the end it becomes a call-and-response. The song highlights Cab's musicality at its most experimental.

"Twee-Twee-Tweet" (Maxwell/Myrow), 1939. *Are You Hep to the Jive?.*

This is another unusual piece that is unique among Cab's various productions, yet does not appear on most compilations. The tune is dotted by whistled melodies intended to mimic birdsong; the whole Orchestra participates on several occasions, harmonizing this "birdsong" with Cab, who at one point scats in a way that mimics the whistling itself. Musically, the piece is rapid and the playing heavy, with emphasis on repeated brass motifs. Towards the end, Cab singles out Jonah Jones, Dizzy Gillespie and Chu Berry as soloists.

"Are You All Reet?" (Calloway/Clark/Palmer), 1941. *Are You Hep to the Jive?*

One of many pieces that incorporate jive language, this piece is unique in that it is dominated by vocals—not only Cab's, but shared vocals between himself and his Orchestra—that produce a slight tension as Cab and his instrumentalists issue the challenge to each other: "Are you all reet?" After an instrumental interlude, the call-and-response is reinitiated and the piece is brought to a close.

"What's Buzzin,' Cousin?" (Gordon/Owens), 1942. *Are You Hep to the Jive?*

Displaying the more humorous aspect of Cab's singing, "What's Buzzin', Cousin?" is a cheery song with a lightly swung melody and an upbeat tempo. Opening with a brief solo by bassist Milt Hinton, the song rapidly progresses to the vocal part. Here, Cab initiates a series of rhymes that builds as the instrumentalists begin joining in; it soon becomes a call and response in which the rhyming falls to the musicians, where the lyrics become steadily more humorous. The piece closes with a strong, clean finish.

"Hey Now, Hey Now" (Calloway/Hill), 1946. *Are You Hep to the Jive?*

This is yet another showcase of Cab's consistent vocal flexibility at different registers as well as his thematic creativity. Against an impressive instrumental background, Cab belts out repeated a "Hey, now" to a developing melody. At various points the instrumentation becomes subdued and an echoing call-and-response begins with Cab and proceeds through different sections of his group. The overall effect is quite humorous.

"Don't Falter at the Altar" (Calloway/Seeger/Harding), 1947. *Are You Hep to the Jive?*

One of Cab's more humorous pieces, "Don't Falter" stands out among his recordings for the conversational dialogue that takes place between Cab and his instrumentalists at the beginning and end of the tune, a theme that is continuous throughout as the entire group harmonizes with Cab, supported by a subdued melody composed entirely of the bass and percussion sections. "Don't Falter" exemplifies the high degree of interaction that took place between Cab and his musicians.

"The Calloway Boogie" (Calloway/Gibson), 1947. *Are You Hep to the Jive?*

Opening with heavy instrumentation that proceeds throughout, this exciting number is strongly swung and syncopated. Cab's strong vocal part incorporates growls and sharp scoops, techniques reflective of the changing musical trends of the late '40s that he did not usually employ in the previous decade. His archetypal "hi-de-ho" call-and-response survives in its original basic form, however. This recording demonstrates the musical adaptability of Cab and his different bands.

Compilations

Cab Calloway. *Are You Hep to the Jive?*: Rhythm and Soul. Legacy, 1994. CD.

Cab Calloway. *The Hi-Dee-Ho-Man.* Classic Jazz Archive, 2004. CD.

Billie Holiday

"She was a successful jazz musician, a woman who had fallen in love many times, a person who had dared to ignore society's mores, a child who had escaped the poverty that plagued her early years"

4 A Story of Sorrow and Success
by Erin Bowman

For the everyday music listener, Billie Holiday is best known for her performances of Lewis Allan's "Strange Fruit," a song which depicts the tragedy of lynchings in the South. She is typecast by many as simply a troubled woman who grew up in Baltimore and faced a lifetime of struggles with drugs. Though that image is not completely incorrect, it is based largely on the book *Lady Sings the Blues* and the myths about her that it perpetuated and is therefore missing much of her life's depth.

Lady Sings the Blues, formally authored by both Billie Holiday and William Dufty, was first published in 1956. However, after the book's release Holiday told others that she had never even read the book, much less contributed to its writing (Griffin 46). Instead the book likely developed out of informal conversations between Dufty and Holiday, to which Dufty applied his own creativity. Julia Blackburn points out that Dufty "added whatever extra spice he felt was needed, particularly in relation to Billie's lesbian experiences and her history of drug addiction. . . . It didn't matter that the voice was not hers" (Blackburn 201). Nevertheless, reviewers at the time focused on the story, not on its questionable provenance. R. G. Peck from the Chicago Sunday *Tribune* wrote, "The book gives every indication of telling the sincere and unpretty truth about what it's like to grow up in a Negro slum" (qtd. in Griffin 47). *The New York Times* review similarly applauds, "William Dufty . . . has displayed a remarkable virtuosity in so effacing himself as to make Miss Holiday emerge whole—colloquial, bitter, generous, loving, foolish, and tragic" (qtd. in Griffin 47). The reviewers' acceptance of the book's story allowed for its lies and half-truths to gain a following. It was not until later that her life was more thoroughly researched and statements such as "Mom and Pop were only a couple of kids when they got married. She was thirteen, he was sixteen and I was three" were proven false (Dufty 3).

Countless people have written about Billie since her death, not only because of her contributions to the jazz world but also because of her personality and past. The intrigue lies in comments such as those in Tallulah Bankhead's letter to J. Edgar Hoover, requesting that a narcotics charge against her be dropped: "Although my intention is not to condone her weaknesses I certainly understand the eccentricities of her behavior because she is essentially a child at heart whose troubles have made her psychologically unable to cope with the world in which she finds herself" (FBI document, Tallulah's letter). Pianist Mal Waldron also recognized the reality of Billie's tragic life when he said, "Faults? Well of course she drank too much. . . . She wouldn't stop drinking and she never did really stick the dope habit. But Lady Day had an awful lot to forget. . . . Don't forget, if you are treated like a common criminal, after a while you begin to act like one" (qtd. in Blackburn 203). As contemporaries of Billie who knew her well, they had an insider's perspective; however, even their comments do not give her the credit she deserves.

A more accurate entry point to her life is through the song, "God Bless the Child," for which she wrote the lyrics. Through this song she reveals the heartbreak of her own past: "Rich relations give / Crust of bread and such / You can help yourself / But don't take too much / Mama may have, Papa may have / But God bless the child that's got his own" (*Billie Holiday Songs*). The lyrics are borne out by her experiences: throughout Billie's life, people came and went, even the family members who were supposed to support her; as a result, she carved her path virtually by herself. While these struggles were without a doubt a part of her life, the song is not an attempt to wallow in the pain of her past but rather to emphasize that she made it through. In the end, she was a successful jazz musician, a woman who had fallen in love many times, a person who had dared to ignore society's mores, a child who had escaped the poverty that plagued her early years. Her legacy is in the memory that remains: through her sorrows and successes, she "got [her] own."

As memories fade, and the majority of the people who knew her have passed away, she moves from a figure present in the public's awareness to the realm of a storybook character. Billie Holiday was a woman who suffered incredibly and the intensity in her songs came from that pain. While it is difficult to pin down many specifics about her childhood in Baltimore and even some of her adult life, it was clearly her fragmented and challenging lifestyle that made her. Without her experiences, both the good and the bad, she would not have been the same artist. After all, in her song "Lady Sings the Blues" she describes her own past, singing: "The blues ain't nothing but a pain in your heart / When you get a bad start" (*Billie Holiday Songs; Billie Holiday Discography*). Similarly, in "Glad To Be Unhappy," she sings, "I can't win but here I am / More than glad to be unhappy" (*Billie Holiday*

Songs; Billie Holiday Discography). Though she did not write the lyrics to the latter, it rings true nonetheless. Her pain was so fundamental to her being that she could not comprehend a life without it, and her contribution to jazz would have been impossible if she had not been singing from her own experiences. Perhaps this is why she allowed the dark side of her life to be captured by the media, and why she perpetuated some of the misunderstandings regarding her past.

"Rich relations give crust of bread and such": Cast of Characters

Billie Holiday was born Elinore Harris on April 7th, 1915, but was also known as Eleanor, Eleanora Fagan, Eleanora Gough, Madge and Theresa (at the House of the Good Shepherd) Eleanora Monroe, Eleanora McKay, Eleanora Gough McKay (Nicholson 18, 284; Clarke 10, 18). Though all of her name changes are significant in that they allude to important people in her life, the name she created for herself and the one people remember her by is Billie Holiday. Nothing in Eleanora's life lasted very long, not the people she knew nor the places she lived; her many name changes testify to this fluid lifestyle. Nonetheless, in order to understand Eleanora, one must consider the many people who raised her.

Eleanora's mother, Sadie Harris (1895-1945), was also known by a variety of names at different times, including Sadie Fagan, Julia Harris, Sara Gough, Sadie Gough, and Sadie Holiday. Sadie's mother and father, Sussie Harris and Charles Fagan, later separated and Charles ceased to actively play a role in Sadie's life (Nicholson 284). Throughout her life, Sadie tried to maintain a sense of family and though at times Charles showed his love for her, he generally maintained his distance at the urging of his second wife (Clarke 38). Sadie allowed for this pattern of uninvolved parents and hurt children to be inherited by Eleanora by carving for her a difficult childhood. Unstable employment, frequent absences from her daughter, and rocky relationships with men marked Sadie's adult life.

Her biological father, Clarence Holiday (1898-1937), sometimes known as Holliday, also had a great impact on her, though he never lived with either Sadie or Eleanora. One of the most striking examples of his impact on his daughter is seen in her name change to Billie Holiday. This decision was partly inspired by the actress Billie Dove but was primarily derived from Clarence's childhood nickname for her, Bill, and his last name. Changing her name was an attempt to build a relationship with her father, if only on a superficial level. In addition to contributing to her name, her father helped to set her on the path toward jazz. His own connections—he played with Fletcher Henderson, Don Redman, McKinney's Cotton Pickers, Elmer Snowden, and Billy Fowler—gave her a foot in the door. But even though he helped to get her a gig with Fletcher Henderson, their relationship was principally marked by his absence. Finally, after he returned from WWI in 1918 he soon left Baltimore altogether and began a new family (Greene 7).

Despite Clarence's weak relationships with both Sadie and Eleanora, it is universally accepted that he is her father and not Frank DeViese, the man listed on Eleanora's birth certificate (Nicholson 18; Blackburn 13). As far as records show, DeViese had no further contact with either Sadie or Eleanora after they left Philadelphia, where Sadie had escaped to avoid her parents' disapproval at her having a child so young and out of wedlock. Though DeViese may have been present at her birth, Eleanora likely had no memory of him.

Robert, Eva, and Martha Miller were also important relatives because Eleanora and Sadie lived with them at varying points throughout their time in Baltimore. Eva Miller was Sadie's half sister, Robert her husband, and Martha his mother. Despite the fact that she had already raised her own children, Martha continued to help out anyone in need of a home, including Sadie and Eleanora. Her role in the child's life was so great that Martha Miller, technically only distantly related to Eleanora, was known to her as a grandmother (Nicholson 19). Throughout Eleanora's time in Baltimore, Robert and Eva often filled in for Sadie and Clarence as her parents, which meant everything from Robert's picking her up at the hospital in Philadelphia to Eva's being on school records as her mother (Blackburn 14; Nicholson 19).

Another potentially formative figure in her life, Philip Gough, born in 1893, married Sadie when Eleanora was either five or seven (Nicholson 21; Clarke 13). During their marriage, Sadie lived with Philip, though Eleanora continued to live with Eva Miller. However, after only a few years Sadie and Philip split up; Sadie went back to living with Martha Miller and Philip disappeared. The next father figure who entered Eleanora's life was Wee Wee Hill. In an interview he recognized that he was not a good role model: "I was gambling, running around, running different women" (qtd. in Clarke 24). Though Sadie may have wanted to marry Wee Wee, he had no intention of marrying her. Even so, it was in the midst of their affair that Sadie first went to New York and he soon followed. Their romance ended, though, when his mother fell ill and he returned to Baltimore (Clarke 25).

Other people, such as Miss Viola Green, Miss Lou Hill, Alice Dean, and Ethel Moore, are known to have been involved in Eleanora's early life, although there are few details about them available today. Eleanora lived with both Miss Green and Miss Hill for periods, and spent time at the "good time" houses of Alice Dean and Ethel Moore (1906-1968) (Clarke 16). Johnny Fagan, Eleanora's uncle, said of Moore's house, "You didn't have to worry about running out the back door; she paid for protection. All the years she run her house, she never went to jail. You could say she run it like some people run Wall Street" (qtd. in Clarke 15). Depending on the source, we learn that Eleanora became involved with Dean and Moore doing errands, working as a prostitute, or simply singing. Dean and Moore each had a gramophone, which, regardless of Eleanora's reason for being at their houses, attracted her because they gave her the opportunity to listen to music. While music may have provoked her involvement with Dean and Moore, her time at their houses also set her on the path toward prostitution (Blackburn 77).

Given that cast of characters, her early life begins to take shape. Because her mother needed to work, others stepped in, and each person who knew and raised her uniquely affected her. She is a classic example of someone whose unsteady childhood resulted in her wild adult life.

"Mama may have, Papa may have": Controversies and Milestones of Her Early Life

With an understanding of the major players in her childhood, one can more easily piece together different milestones. However, as a comparison of her major biographies—Donald Clarke's *Wishing on the*

Moon, Meg Greene's *Billie Holiday*, Robert O'Meally's *Lady Day*, Julia Blackburn's *With Billie*, and Stuart Nicholson's *Billie Holiday*—shows, even those milestones are difficult to pin down. Though the biographers attempted to illuminate Billie's character, the scarcity of primary sources leads to further contradictions, which have then propagated many of the misunderstandings about her life. While at different points they all provide varying accounts, to a certain extent the books can be grouped: Greene's and O'Meally's accounts both provide basic sketches, while Clarke's, Blackburn's, and Nicholson's demonstrate more substantial research. Another layer of comparison comes from the the authors' reliance on the Linda Kuehl archives, a series of interviews conducted but never published by Kuehl. For this reason, Blackburn's account of her life, presented simply as a compilation of Kuehl's archives, at times overlaps with O'Meally's and Clarke's, the two other biographies that most heavily rely on those interviews. Despite some overlaps, each account has a different perspective, which is able to shine unique light light on the reality of her childhood.

To begin with, all the major biographies agree that Eleanora spent time at the House of the Good Shepherd, which was opened in 1864 by the Sisters of the Good Shepherd to provide a home for girls and women who needed a safe space ("Good Shepherd Center: Our History"). However, sources disagree on the frequency of and reasons for her stays. Her time there—whether for rape, truancy, or both—speaks to her troubled childhood.

According to *Lady Sings the Blues*, she went to the House of the Good Shepherd only once, in 1925, because she had been raped by a neighbor, Mr. Dick, and was released after her grandfather hired a lawyer (Dufty 15, 16, 18). This account is widely viewed as a fabrication; however, even her major biographers do not reach the same conclusions about her time there. Robert O'Meally and Meg Greene, for example, agree that she went into the facility in 1925 for truancy, not because of rape, and that she was baptized in March of that year by Father Edward Casserly (O'Meally 79, Greene 8). Their biographies clash directly with Dufty's account of rape.

Julia Blackburn's, Stuart Nicholson's, and Donald Clarke's books provide more extensive accounts of her time at the House of the Good Shepherd, seeming to offer a sort of compromise between the O'Meally-Greene account and Dufty's. According to these sources, Eleanora was in the House of the Good Shepherd twice: once in 1925 for truancy and once in 1926 as a state witness against the man who had raped her, Wilbert Rich (Blackburn 25, 26; Nicholson 24; Clarke 18, 34). Blackburn and Nicholson also agree that after her second stay at the House of the Good Shepherd, her grandfather did contribute to her release by hiring a lawyer, which matches an aspect of Dufty's account (Blackburn 25; Nicholson 25). Though being there may have seemed like punishment, both times the courts ordered her to go they were attempting to protect her from her negligent family.

Though Blackburn and Nicholson agree on what happened and when regarding Eleanora's time at the House of the Good Shepherd, they disagree about her living situation preceding her first arrest in 1925. According to Blackburn's biography, in 1924 Sadie had her own house on Dallas and Caroline Street and moved there with Eleanora (14). However, according to Nicholson, Eleanora had been living with Martha Miller at the 600 block of North Barnes Street in 1924

(Nicholson 22). O'Meally, on the other hand, has her living with Wee Wee Hill on Durham Street around this time (O'Meally 81). No matter with whom or where she had been living, the major adults in her life were too busy trying to earn an income or watch over other children to think of Eleanora as a priority.

Lady Sings the Blues, regarding this part of her life, does not seem to be entirely false, but rather to have condensed her experiences at the House. Because her records cannot be accessed without permission of next of kin (and her next-of-kin being impossible to determine), the truth will likely remain forever uncertain. Nevertheless, her time at the House of the Good Shepherd conclusively reveals the extent of her struggles as a child and may have also prepared her for her later sentence at Alderson Federal Reformatory for Women and at Welfare Island, where she was sent for being a "vagrant and dissipated adult" (Blackburn 62).

Though she had many adult figures in her life, none was consistent, including her mother. Eleanora lived with different combinations of people, in many different places. Her experiences in 1920 serve as a representative sample of the inconsistency in and uncertainty about her living situation. Nicholson provides a few specifics about that year: Sadie and Philip Gough married, Eva Miller registered as her mother at school and listed her address as 609 Bond Street with Viola Green, and that Eleanora and Sadie later moved to 432 Colvin Street with the Millers (Nicholson 20, 21). Blackburn affirms the move to Colvin Street, but says that Philip Gough and Sadie did not marry until October of 1922 (Blackburn 14). O'Meally confirms Nicholson's dating of the marriage between Sadie and Philip but does not elaborate beyond that (O'Meally 72). Clarke presents a different story altogether, saying that

Gough and Harris were indeed married on October 20th, 1920, but that instead of living on either Colvin or Bond Street, Charles Fagan bought them a place at 1421 North Fremont Avenue (Clarke 13). Nineteen-twenty is just one year of the many she spent in Baltimore, and just one example of the many discrepancies in accounts of Eleanora's addresses and relationships.

Another source of controversy regarding her childhood concerns her departure from Baltimore. According to *Lady Sings the Blues*, her mother left in search of an easier and more comfortable life—a lifestyle she did not believe was attainable in Baltimore—and Eleanora followed in 1927, after the death of her Cousin Ida (Dufty 20). None of the other major biographies mentions a family member named Ida, or a time when she was living with her grandparents, as is depicted in *Lady Sings the Blues*. Instead, Blackburn writes that Sadie did not leave for New York until 1928 and that Eleanora did not leave until 1929. In an interview, Mary "Pony" Kane, an old friend of Eleanora, recalls that she went to New York after Miss Lou Hill no longer felt able to care for her (Blackburn 15, 44). Clarke's biography accounts for the discrepancies by comparing different sources: Diesel Haskins said that it must have been after 1928, while Elmer Snowden and Wee Wee Hill both recall her leaving in 1927 (Clarke 36). Nicholson's account supports the story that she left Baltimore in 1929, at age 14, but argues that she was living with Martha Miller, not Miss Lou Hill, prior to her departure (Nicholson 32). Nicholson and Blackburn agree, though, that with her mother gone, she explored the city even further and consorted with unsavory company. Regardless of when she left Baltimore, by 1930 census data places Eleanora and Sadie together in Manhattan (Census 1930).

"Money, you've got lots of friends":
Controversies and Milestones of Her Adult Life

Part of Billie's infamy comes from her drug abuse and the scandals that surrounded it, which some sources cite as beginning during her time in Baltimore. In an interview with Linda Kuehl, Skinny Davenport said, "Take her to Ethel Moore. That's where she start in smoking reefers" (Clarke 33). But her involvement with drugs did not become a matter of public knowledge or truly begin to interfere with her life until she was in New York. In *Lady Sings the Blues*, Billie fully admits to her drug use but also calls for pity. She says, "People on drugs are sick people," and goes on to compare the relationship between a drug addict and drugs to that of a person with diabetes and insulin (Dufty 152). In 1947 she was sent to the Alderson Reformatory for Women to recover from her addiction, but she did not manage to stay clean for very long (Clarke 261).

Two years later she was again brought to court on narcotics charges; her attempted recovery had failed. A declassified FBI document dated January 25th, 1949 reveals that three days prior, Holiday and John Levy had been arrested during a raid on their hotel room. The report claims that "Holiday was intercepted by supervisor . . . as she attempted to destroy makeshift opium pipe and bindle of opium in toilet bowl of her room" (FBI document 1). This arrest and the scandal that resulted made the national news, largely because Holiday claimed that Levy had framed her, even though the same declassified FBI memo claims that Holiday lied to draw attention away from her arrest (FBI document 1). A newspaper article included in the FBI file on Holiday reports Levy as saying, "We both deny everything. . . . [s]he didn't even sleep in her bed that night"(FBI file, "BILLY HOLIDAY HELD"). However, that account conflicts with the summary of the trial presented in another article in the file, which cites her claiming that "John Levy thrust a package of narcotics into her hand just before her hotel room was raided by federal agents. The defense contended Levy warned informer on Miss Holiday to avoid marriage" (FBI file, "Billie Holiday cleared of opium possession"). These versions do not come from Dufty's book or from personal testimonies taken decades after the events; they are dated from the time of her arrest and trial, yet still cannot project a single perspective or confirm a simple fact.

The successive tragedies of her life culminated in her death. All sources agree that Holiday died on July 17th, 1959. *The New York Times* obituary published the day after her death explains, "the immediate cause of death was given as congestion of the lungs complicated by heart failure" ("Billie Holiday Dies Here"). But coming as it did at the age of 44, Holiday's early death was likely brought on by her history of substance abuse, which she continued even into this final hospital stay ("BILLIE HOLIDAY HELD" 12).

In an interview, Dufty tells of seeing Holiday in the hospital, where she was malnourished and very much alone. He recalled that on "12 June she was arrested and charged with possession of narcotics; her radio, record player, flowers and telephone were taken away, and two guards were posted on her door to protect the public from her" (qtd. in Clarke 437). The guards eventually left after protests from both Dufty and the general public. Though the prosecution tried to get her to court, it was an impossible task, given her health. Many visited her at her bedside, but, according to Clarke, Dufty was there through it all. Indeed, regardless of the questionable reliability of Dufty's book, it is clear that the two were close. On the day before her death, she recognized that her time was drawing near and attempted to give him all the money she had with her, which supports Clarke's story that Louis McKay had no real presence in the hospital, and only wanted to take advantage of her. Dufty refused, but her premonition was correct: she died at three the next morning (Clarke 444).

Even her death is not without a myriad of renditions. In her biography, Greene claims that it was Louis McKay who was there through it all and at her deathbed (Greene 107). In Blackburn's presentation of Kuehl's interviews, other perspectives are introduced; Holiday's close friend Alice Vrbsky recounted: "[McKay] was playing dutiful husband who had lost his loving wife, but from what she told me there had long since been no love between them any more" (Blackburn 321). Blackburn also points out the number of articles that Dufty wrote about Holiday leading up to her death, which supports the likelihood that he was present throughout this final hospitalization. O'Meally's book tries to have it both ways: he states that McKay was there daily, but also that Dufty was a regular (O'Meally 190). Yet Nicholson's account of her final stay in the hospital includes no mention of Dufty, and only notes that McKay was there the day she died, but had left to make a phone call when she actually passed. Though each account tells a different story, they similarly describe the difference between Dufty and McKay: Dufty seemed to have genuinely cared about Holiday whereas McKay was simply doing as he thought he should and simultaneously trying to scam her.

Why was she enshrined in so many myths, many of which she perpetrated? Were they an intentional ploy to increase her audience? Though the link between the lore and myths surrounding her and her record sales is undeniable, she did not necessarily promote them intentionally for that purpose. Rather, the unknowns and discrepancies in her story were inevitable given the time and the mystique which surrounded jazz musicians, and represented attempts at coping with her loneliness. Given her talent and the intensity of her presence, even without her myths she would have made an impact on those who helped to make her a star.

"Yes the strong gets more, while the weak ones fade": Billie's Baltimore

Though part of the confusion surrounding Billie Holiday derives from her role—or lack thereof—in writing *Lady Sings the Blues*, a significant portion likely also developed out of her itinerant and casual lifestyle. Even so, one can better understand her perspective by acquiring a better understanding of the typical lifestyle of someone from her socio-economic background in that time. With that context in mind, her path from child drop-out to famous jazz artist becomes clearer.

Given today's federal legislation on child labor, which prohibits people younger than 14 from having a job, the stories about Eleanora's childhood jobs, whether they were prostitution or running errands, are somewhat shocking ("Child Labor Public Education Project: U.S. Laws"). As early as the mid-nineteenth century, child labor and its connection to education began garnering attention; however, no comprehensive legislation was passed ("Child Labor Public Education Project: Child Labor in U.S. History"). The first state child labor law passed in 1836 in Massachusetts, but not until 1904 did child labor became a national issue. Finally, in 1938 the Fair Labor Standards Act and its 1949 amendment explicitly outlawed child labor and enacted genuine change ("Selected US Labor Laws and Regulations Timeline"). By that time, however, Eleanora was well beyond an age at which it was applicable ("Child Labor Public Education Project: Child Labor in U.S. History"). In short, her independence and early jobs were far from abnormal at the time.

Education, like child labor, was not as regulated or monitored as it is today, but when she was first sent to the House of the Good Shepherd (allegedly for truancy) some legislation was in place. By 1918 all states had compulsory education laws, but only through elementary school. When Eleanora was first brought to court in 1925, she was nine years old and therefore still in elementary school. But only a few years later, during the fifth grade, she unofficially dropped out without anyone taking notice (Nicholson 25). Speaking about that period of her life, she said she was "always working at some job or other, [and] never had a chance to play with dolls like other kids. . . . About the only thing I learnt in school was how to play hooky" (qtd. in Nicholson 25). If she had received a more thorough childhood education her life would doubtless have unfolded differently. As an adult, she acknowledged her lack of education in a letter she wrote to William Dufty in 1956 which she closed by saying, "PS . . . Now you know why I don't write i can't" (qtd. inClarke 399). Whether she meant her handwriting or her literacy, she seemed aware of the disadvantage with which her lack of education had left her.

Throughout her life her gender also played a significant role. As a child it affected not only all of her personal relationships but the way that society as a whole responded to her. If women were as respected as men, would her father have made more of an effort to be part of her life? Would she have gotten into the same sorts of trouble with men: alleged rape, prostitution, and so forth? Would her mother have abandoned her at so many points? Though it is impossible to know how her life would have unfolded otherwise, one can understand more about her life by understanding more about women in the early twentieth century. Though one cannot know for sure if she would have gotten involved with Alice Dean and Ethel Moore had women's role in society been different, it is possible to hypothesize about the potential impact of her gender on her life.

In 1920, when Eleanora was five years old, the Nineteenth Amendment giving women the right to vote was ratified ("One Hundred Years toward Suffrage: An Overview"). Despite this milestone, popular thought held that women voted as their husbands did, meaning that even though they theoretically had been granted political rights to their own beliefs, many women did not choose to actualize them (Alpern and Baum 44).[1] Feminist circles existed at the time, but Eleanora was generally not exposed to them. Therefore, her alleged involvement in prostitution expressed not liberation but her low self-confidence and lack of skills. That lack of self-esteem is portrayed in her 1944 recording of "Don't Explain," when she sings, "Quiet, don't explain / You mixed with some dame. . . . And I know you cheat / Right or wrong, don't matter. . . . My life's yours, love" (*Billie Holiday Songs*; *Billie Holiday Discography*). Had she cared more for herself, either because her mother taught her to or because society demonstrated the importance of doing so, she likely would not have ended up in the abusive relationships in which she often found herself.

However, women like Ethel Moore and Alice Dean seemed to have had no problem taking advantage of women's newfound self-respect by running their own houses of prostitution, an enterprise that simultaneously expressed both their initiative and an indifference to the experience of the women working for them. Skinny Davenport recalled in an interview with Kuehl that Moore had "been like a mother to [Eleanora]"(Blackburn 31). It was in part from these women that she learned the importance of being strong and self-reliant. Their influence, though, was countered by that of her mother, who spent her entire life trying to please the men she loved. From her mother's childhood with a father who was not allowed to see her, to her teenage love affair with Eleanora's father and his subsequent marriages to other women, to her later love affairs and subsequent break ups, Sadie essentially allowed men to dictate her direction.

The suffrage movement did not directly affect Holiday but the energy of her generation did. She grew up and died in a time when women were urged simultaneously to be independent and to be submissive. The internal conflict this created no doubt compounded the other stressors with which she was dealing. In the 1944 recording of her song "Billie's Blues," she acknowledges in these lyrics her lack of autonomy and self-worth: "I've been your slave baby / Ever since I've been your babe" (*Billie Holiday Songs; Billie Holiday Discography*). The lyrics, unfortunately, are not fictional. According to Greene's biography, in 1940 she began an affair with her future first husband, James Monroe, who ran a night club. Greene contends that he first hit her within days of meeting her and implies that the abuse continued throughout their relationship (Greene 68). In Blackburn's interviews, Monroe's negative influence resurfaces in an interview with Ruby Helena, a friend of Billie's and Sadie's in New York. Helena claims that Monroe introduced Billie to drugs, and though she does not mention any physical abuse she does allude to psychological abuse, based on the fact that Monroe regularly maintained relationships with more than one woman at once and, left in financial ruin, abandoned Billie and went to California (Blackburn 106).

Just as her age and gender affected her life, so did her race. Though her mother's father's family had an Irish last name, Fagan, Eleanora and her mother received none of the benefits that the Irish had earned in US society by that time (Clarke 2). The Ku Klux Klan began its revival the same year that Eleanora was born (Chalmers 29). According to David Chalmers's book on the topic, the Klan already had thousands of members by the time Eleanora was four years old, and as it grew so did the instances of violence committed by its members (31, 35). The 1915 racist film *The Birth of a Nation* included attempted rapes of white women by black men, and argued that after Lincoln's assassination the nation was reborn through the Klan (Rogin 150).[2] Though the Klan was regaining support and prominence throughout the South, which meant riots and tar-and-featherings, the Republican candidate for Senate in 1926 was publicly anti-Klan, which limited its success in Maryland (Chalmers 161). Nonetheless, its revival implies that racial tensions and prejudices were ever-present just below the surface in the period.

How did the nation's racist tendencies affect Eleanora? Though it is hard to pinpoint exact moments, its influence was palpable throughout her life. If her mother had been white would she have had a similarly hard time as an unmarried pregnant teenager? Would she have had a larger support system? Some things can concretely be established: she would have lived in different neighborhoods, gone to different schools, attended a different House of the Good Shepherd, and likely never have sung jazz music. Racial problems continued through her adulthood, because Jim Crow legislation perpetuated the separate-but-equal mentality. During a tour in the South with Artie Shaw's band, for example, Holiday would not always be served in restaurants with the white band members, and she was often told to take a different elevator than the rest of the band (Nicholson 103-105). Her brief stint in Hollywood was similarly tainted by racial prejudice: in a film about jazz called *New Orleans Holiday* was given the role of a maid, while a less qualified white woman played the lead (Nicholson 152-53). Greene points out in her book that, "Jazz arose in the United States not by chance, but because of a unique set of social, economic, intellectual, and spiritual conditions that existed nowhere else" (Greene 5). Thus, it was out of the struggles experienced by the African-American community in the United States that jazz was born; without them, Billie Holiday would not have become Billie Holiday.

"Them that's got shall get / Them that's not shall lose": Billie the Singer

Was it necessary for her to have had all her hardships to be the singer she was? The simple answer is yes. Yes, because she sang of genuine suffering; her presence could not have been as impactful if she had not felt each lyric. Though many of the songs she performed, notably "Strange Fruit," were not written by her, her recordings and live performances tangibly demonstrated that she only sang songs that resonated with her.

Her issues with men began with her father's abandonment and became more deeply rooted after her rape and involvement with prostitution. Thus, in July of 1936 she first recorded "Billie's Blues" (a.k.a "I love my man"), which includes lyrics such as "I love my man tell the world I do / But when he mistreats me / Makes me feel so blue" (*Billie Holiday Discography; Billie Holiday Songs*). Eight years later she again recorded a song that she co-wrote with Arthur Herzog called "Don't Explain" (*Billie Holiday Discography; Billie Holiday Songs*). This song reveals a pattern in her relationships: "I'm glad you're back. . . . And I know you cheat / But right or wrong, don't matter / When you're with me" (*Billie Holiday Discography; Billie Holiday Songs*). These lyrics again point to her pattern of loving men whom she knew were bad for her and her inability to leave them even after they treated her poorly. Even the song "Everything Happens for the Best," recorded in 1939, which one would assume to be uplifting, expresses the deep pain she lived with: "You're so mean to me / But everything happens for the best" (*Billie Holiday Discography; Billie Holiday Songs*). The song that gave its name to her ghost-written autobiography also broadcasts her sorrow: "Lady sings the blues / She's got them bad / She feels so sad" (*Billie Holiday Discography; Billie Holiday Songs*). "Lady Day" was a well-known nickname given to her by Lester Young, and so this song without question refers to herself (Greene 44).

One can understand the ways in which Billie's life affected her music not only through her lyrics to her songs, but also through her performance style. Just as her life consisted of a series of improvised arrangements, she improvised her singing. Holiday said,

> I don't think I ever sang the same way twice and I don't think
> I ever sang the same tempo. One night is a little bit slower
> the next is a little bit brighter, it's cause of how I feel. I know
> the blues sort of a mixed up thing, you just have to feel it.
> Anything I do sing it's part of my life. (*The Sound of Jazz*)

Holiday is known for her distinctively slow singing. Instead of using volume or technical musical expertise to express herself as many artists do, Billie's performances were more like conversations. She meandered through the lyrics, allowing time for her subtle presence and lyrics to resonate with the listener. Though her substance abuse may have contributed to her meandering tempo, it was her style that appealed to listeners who had never touched a needle. In 1958, Frank Sinatra commented: "Lady Day is unquestionably the most important influence on American popular signing in the last twenty years" (qtd. in Giddins 368). Gary Giddins, who examines and reviews different types of jazz in his book *Visions of Jazz*, writes: "Despite a thin voice and a range of about fifteen notes, she seduced listeners with her multilayered nuances. . . . Holiday combined those achievements [of Bessie Smith, Louis Armstrong, and Bing Crosby], pushing song into the realm of unmitigated intimacy" (369). In short, it was her atypical approach that made her so iconic, drew audiences to her, and set the stage for her legacy.

Toward the end of her life, there is a marked change in her performances and recordings because she was no longer physically able to sing in same way; years of not caring for herself were finally taking a toll. In her 1957 live recording session of "Fine and Mellow" on CBS, Holiday's vocal limitations are evident. However, her decreased range does not negatively affect her style: to the contrary—it contributes to it. The emphatic pauses she takes between lines simply grow longer and more dramatic, and though her range has deteriorated she still conveys the intensity she always brought to her music (*Billie Holiday Discography*). In many ways, as in the CBS broadcast of "Fine and Mellow," the pain she always carried with her was even more tangible, more evocative. She still engages in the familiar musical dialogue with her old friend Lester Young on tenor saxophone, and when she sings she still captures every listener's attention. Ironically, her small range and simple style, unintentionally exaggerated toward the end of her career, made her performances more powerful and are a large part of the reason she remains an iconic figure in jazz.

The sorrow evident in her lyrics and performances most directly derives from her romantic involvements, but that does not mean that she forgot about or ignored the pain from the rest of her life. Her songs and performances were a culmination of her experiences and the people who had touched her. However, she was not entirely consumed by her pain. In "God Bless the Child" she asserts her independence from hangers-on and her ability to transcend hard times. Ultimately, she offers an image of resilience and the power of self-invention, by creating herself as Lady Day, the singer of painful ballads. In that way, perhaps, she also transcended the pain that plagued her. Though she started with nothing, she fought her way to the top and became, as the lyrics proclaim, "a child that got [her] own."

NOTES

1. It has only been since 1959, the year of Billie's death, that the government officially made it law that women receive equal pay and eliminated various other forms of discrimination. (*One Hundred Years toward Suffrage: An Overview*).

2. Interestingly, both Griffith and Thomas Dixon, author of the book The Clansman, on which the movie was based, were graduates of Johns Hopkins, one of Baltimore's own universities (Rogin 151).

Works Cited

Alpern, Sara, and Dale Baum. "Female Ballots: The Impact of the Nineteenth Amendment." *Journal of Interdisciplinary History* 16.1 (1985): 44. JSTOR. Web. 29 Nov. 2009.

Bankhead, Tallulah. Letter to J. Edgar Hoover. 9 Feb. 1949. *FBI Freedom of Information / Privacy Acts Section: Billie Holiday*. Print.

"Billie Holiday Cleared of Opium Possession." [San Francisco]. *FBI Freedom of Information / Privacy Acts Section: Billie Holiday*. Web. 5 Aug. 2009.

"Billie Holiday Dies Here at 44; Jazz Singer Had Wide Influence." *New York Times* [New York City] 18 July 1959. Web. 27 Nov. 2009.

Billie Holiday Discography. Web. 07 Jan. 2010. <http://www.billieholiday.be/>.

"BILLIE HOLIDAY HELD; Narcotics Squad Says Singer Had Heroin in Hospital." *New York Times* [New York City] 13 June 1959: 12. Web. 27 Nov. 2009.

"Billie Holiday, Singer, Held in Coast Dope Raid." [San Francisco]. *FBI Freedom of Information Acts Section: Billie Holiday*. Web. 5 Aug. 2009.

Billie Holiday Songs. Web. 27 Nov. 2009. <http://www.billieholidaysongs.com>.

Blackburn, Julia. *With Billie*. New York: Pantheon, 2005. Print.
 Blackburn was personally inspired by Holiday's life and compiled the biography largely because of the connection she felt with her. Her source is unique because of her access to Linda Kuehl's archives. Kuehl conducted a number of interviews with people who knew Billie best, but died before she was able to publish them. They are an extremely valuable resource because the major people in Holiday's life are deceased, and only through the interviews can one truly understand her character. Even so, the interviews are not always factually correct because they depend on individuals' memories.

Chalmers, David Mark. *Hooded Americanism: The History of the Ku Klux Klan*. Durham: Duke UP, 1987. *Googlebooks*. Web. 27 Nov. 2009.
 This source provides a good background on racial relations during Holiday's life. The book includes a discussion of the Klu Klux Klan and its revival, which directly relates to Holiday because it corresponded so directly with her childhood.

"Child Labor in U.S. History - The Child Labor Education Project." *Division of Continuing Education - The University of Iowa*. Web. 07 Nov. 2009.

Clarke, Donald. *Wishing on the Moon: The Life and Times of Billie Holiday.* New York: Viking, 1994. Print.

Clarke's biography is a well-researched account of her life that skeptically assesses the assertions in Lady Sings the Blues. *He too depends on Linda Kuehl's archives to provide first-hand accounts of Holiday's life; however, he organizes them by topic instead of by interview as Blackburn does. Though he doubtless used other sources, they are not cited. Instead, he first provides accounts or other information and then follows them with commentary and analysis. He explains in his introduction the inaccuracies and pieces missing from Kuehl's notes that he was able to identify.*

Giddins, Gary. *Visions of Jazz: the First Century.* New York: Oxford UP, 1998. Print.

"Good Shepherd Center: Our History." *Good Shepherd Center Homepage.* Web. 27 Nov. 2009.

Greene, Meg. *Billie Holiday A Biography (Greenwood Biographies).* New York: Greenwood, 2006. Print.

Greene has written a number of biographies, including those on Jane Goodall, Mother Teresa, and Pope John Paul II. However, though her biography includes valuable information about Holiday, it also does not reevaluate the information included in Dufty's book. She includes a basic timeline of Holiday's life in the beginning of the book and from there continues with a chronological account of her life.

Griffin, Farah. *If You Can't Be Free, Be a Mystery: In Search of Billie Holiday.* New York: Free, 2001. Print.

This book is not a biography, but a resource for general information about Holiday. Griffin warns the reader that she is first and foremost a fan who is analyzing the connection between Holiday and the reality for black girls today. When her work is read within that context, it proves to be a reliable resource.

Holiday, Billie, with William Dufty. *Lady Sings the Blues.* 1956. Rev. Ed. New York: Penguin, 1992.

Letter to Director. 25 Jan. 1949. *FBI Freedom of Information/Privacy Acts Section: Billie Holiday.* Print.

Nicholson, Stuart. *Billie Holiday.* New York: Northeastern UP, 1997. Print.

Nicholson is a jazz journalist who has also written biographies of Ella Fitzgerald and Duke Ellington. This book is a valuable source because not only does it include photocopies of some primary sources, but it also incorporates extensive references to other primary sources such as the US Census, and the Baltimore City Directory. These resources set his biography apart from the others, which rely heavily on first-hand accounts. His appendices are also extremely valuable, as they contain a family tree and extensive discography, among other things.

O'Meally, Robert G. *Lady Day: The Many Faces of Billie Holiday*. New York: Arcade, 1991. Print.
O'Meally, a professor at Columbia University and founder of the Center for Jazz Studies there, has also written on Ralph Ellison. His book on Holiday demonstrates the many sides she showed of herself. Though it appears that O'Meally used many sources, in addition to the Linda Kuehl archives, he does not cite them specifically; he does not contradict all accounts in Dufty's book as some of the other sources do.

"One Hundred Years toward Suffrage: An Overview." *American Memory from the Library of Congress - Home Page*. Web. 07 Jan. 2010.

Rogin, Michael. "'The Sword Became a Flashing Vision'": D. W. Griffith's The Birth of a Nation." *Representations* 9 (1985): 150-95. JSTOR. Web. 5 Dec. 2009.

"Selected US Labor Laws and Regulations Timeline." *The Network News* 6 (July 2004): 3. The Network News Timeline. Sloan Work and Family Research Network, Boston College. Web. 29 Nov. 2009.

The Sound of Jazz. CBS Television. New York City, New York, Dec. 1957.

United States of America. The Census Bureau. *Ancestry Library Edition*. Web. 30 Sept. 2009.

"U.S. Laws - The Child Labor Education Project." *Division of Continuing Education - The University of Iowa*. Web. 07 Nov. 2009.

Discography

Exhaustive discographies on Billie Holiday can be found both in Stuart Nicholson's Billie Holiday *and on the website www.billieholiday.be. For that reason, I have chosen to include here a discography of only selected songs—those that best portray her musical style throughout the years, and those that are significant because of what the lyrics reveal about her life and her historical context. Furthermore, the majority of her songs were recorded many times and so I have included here only the best-known recordings.*

Songs written or co-written by Holiday:

"Billie's Blues" (Holiday). First recorded with her Orchestra (Columbia Records [now SONY/CBS]; July 10th, 1936) (Compilation 1).
    Bass, Pete Peterson; clarinet, Artie Shaw; drums, Cozy Cole; guitar, Dick McDonough; piano, Joe Bushkin; trumpet, Bunny Berigan.

"Everything Happens for the Best" (Holiday/Smith). Recorded with her Orchestra (Columbia Records; March 21, 1939) (Compilation 1).

"God Bless the Child" (Holiday/Arthur Herzog, Jr.). Recorded with Eddie Heywood and his Orchestra (Columbia Records; May 9th, 1941) (Compilations 1, 6).

"Don't Explain" (Holiday/Herzog). Accompanied by Bob Haggart Orchestra (Decca [now GRP/MCA]; August 14th, 1945) (Compilation 2, 8).

"Lady Sings the Blues" (Holiday/Nichols). Recorded with Tony Scott and his Orchestra (Verve; June 6th, 1956) (Compilation 3).

"Fine and Mellow" (Holiday). Recorded with Mal Waldron and All Stars (Columbia Records; December 8th, 1957) (Compilation 4).
    Bass, Milton Hinton; drums, Osie Johnson; guitar, Danny Barker; piano, Mal Waldron; baritone saxophone, Gerry Mulligan; tenor saxophone, Coleman Hawkins, Ben Webster, Lester Young; trombone, Vic Dickenson; trumpet, Doc Cheatham, Roy Eldridge.
    This song is notable for the interactions between Holiday and the instrumentalists, especially Lester Young. In the video of this recording, Holiday can be seen nodding her head and smiling to Young's playing. The ease with which the song transitions from Holiday's vocals to instrumental solos seems almost casual, allowing each aspect of the music to be available to the audience. Though the instrumental solos are a huge part of this song and there were 11 people playing, Holiday's simple vocals keep the audience's attention.

Other notable songs:

"Your Mother's Son-in-Law" (Holiner/Nichols). Recorded with Benny Goodman and his Orchestra (Columbia Records; November 27th, 1933) (Compilation 5).

"The Way You Look Tonight" (Dorothy Fields/Jerome Kern). Recorded with Teddy Wilson Orchestra (Columbia Records; October 21st, 1936) (Compilation 6).

"I Must Have That Man" (Fields/McHugh). Recorded with Teddy Wilson Orchestra (Columbia Records; January 25th 1937) (Compilation 6).
   Bass, Walter Page; clarinet, Benny Goodman; drums, Jo Jones; guitar, Freddy Green; piano, Teddy Wilson; tenor saxophone, Lester Young; trumpet, Buck Clayton.

"When a Woman Loves a Man" (Hanighen, Jenkins, and Mercer). Recorded with her Orchestra (Columbia Records; January 12th, 1938) (Compilation 7).
   Bass, Walter Page; drums, Jo Jones; guitar, Freddy Green; piano, Teddy Wilson; tenor saxophone, Lester Young; trombone, Benny Morton; trumpet, Buck Clayton.

"Strange Fruit" (Allan/Marks). Recorded with Frank Newton and his Café Society Orchestra (Columbia Records; April 20th, 1939) (Compilations 1, 4, 5, 8).
   She will be forever remembered for her performances and recordings of this song, even though she was not even the first person to perform it, much less write it. Holiday did not typically explicitly deal with racism in her lyrics, but as it was a definite part of her life she is therefore able to bring the same intensity to the song that she does her others. Her understated style allows the listener to dwell more on the lyrics and realize the reality they are revealing. Not only does she sing slowly but she allows for ample breaks between the lines, which provide time for the lyrics to sink in.

"I Cover the Waterfront" (Green/Heyman). Recorded with Teddy Wilson Orchestra (Columbia Records; August 7th, 1941) (Compilation 4).
   This song calls to mind Baltimore's harbor and the ever-present theme of heartache and heartbreak in Holiday's lyrics. Relative to her other songs, her voice in this recording sounds hopeful or at least nonchalant. As opposed to parts of her recordings with Lester Young, the orchestra in this piece lies in the background. As this is in the middle of her recording career, her voice is still strong and as always her presence as a performer commands attention.

"Gloomy Sunday" (Lewis/Seress). Recorded with Teddy Wilson Orchestra (Columbia Records; August 7th, 1941) (Compilation 4, 6).

"I'll Be Seeing You" (Sammy Fain/Irving Kahal). Recorded with Eddie Heywood and his Orchestra (Commodore; April 1ˢᵗ, 1944) (Compilation 8).

"Good Morning Heartache" (Drake, Fisher, and Higginbotham). Recorded with Bill Stegmeyer Orchestra (Decca; January 22ⁿᵈ, 1946) (Compilation 8).

"Glad to Be Unhappy" (Lorenz Hart and Richard Rodgers). Recorded with Ray Ellis and his Orchestra (Columbia, February 21ˢᵗ, 1958) (Compilation 9).

"You've Changed" (Bill Carey and Carl Fischer). Recorded with Art Ford Jazz Party TV (Baltimore, Maryland; May 29ᵗʰ, 1958) (Compilation 2).
Bass, Joe Benjamin; drums, Jo Jones; guitar, Mundell Lowe; piano, Mal Waldron; vibraphone, Tyree Glenn.
This recording was made just over a year before her death and not only is the general tone markedly less hopeful than "I'll Cover the Waterfront" but her range has greatly decreased—the effect of years of substance abuse on her body. Yet she manages to maintain her casual style that conveys overwhelming emotion in a voice that embodies the song's lyrics about the ravages of time.

Album
Lady in Satin. Recorded from February 19ᵗʰ, 1958-February 21ˢᵗ, 1958, with Ray Ellis and his Orchestra.
Eighteen months before her death she recorded the songs for this album. Her vulnerability is obvious. Not only has her range shrunk greatly but her voice is notably raspier than in her earlier recordings. The album includes a variety of compelling tracks and aptly closes with "The End of a Love Affair." Its lyrics—"I'm reckless it's true . . . the smile on my face / Isn't really a smile at all. . . . So I smoke a little too much"—seem strikingly relevant not only to the love affair within in the song, but also to the fact that her health was beginning to fail and she was approaching the end of her career and life.

Compilations
1. *Billie Holiday: The Classic Decade 1935-1945.* Verve, 1998.
2. *Billie Holiday: Best Hits.* 1990 (Out of Print)..
3. *Billie Holiday: Complete on Verve 45-59, Vol. 7/10.* Verve, 1992.
4. *The Definitive Billie Holiday: Ken Burns Jazz.* Polygram, 2000.
5. *Billie Holiday: Lady Day's 25 Greatest 1933-1944.* ASV Living Era, 1996.
6. *Billie Holiday: 16 Most Requested Songs.* Sony, 1993.
7. *Complete Billie Holiday Lester Young 1937-1946.* 3 discs. Fremeaux and Assoc., 2000.
8. *Billie Holiday Ballads,* 1992 (Out of Print).
9. *Billie Holiday with Ray Ellis and his Orchestra,* 1991 (Out of Print).

II. INNOVATORS

Ellis Larkins

"I think of Ellis Larkins as a musical rainbow. He's an impressionist, constantly weaving extremely colorful textures."

5 Poet of the Piano
by Bob Jacobson

While browsing in a used book store in the mid-1970s, I was stopped in my tracks by beautiful sounds coming from loud speakers. I knew the voice was Ella's. I knew the music was Gershwin's. But who was the one-person orchestra on piano? After buying the LP, *Ella Sings Gershwin*, I saw the name Ellis Larkins for the first time. Later I was proud to learn that my adopted home of Baltimore was the training ground where Larkins developed the skills and self-assurance that suffused that classic album. I learned that Larkins, whose career spanned over half a century and included a wide variety of achievements—dozens of albums, night club and festival performances, critical acclaim—was seriously under-recognized. In fact, on National Public Radio (NPR), Nancy Wilson says that Larkins "has never commanded a wide listening audience," adding, "Well, after hearing this *Jazz Profiles* tribute, you'll be wondering, 'How did I ever miss him?'" ("Ellis Larkins"). By looking at the pianist's early years and initial success, I'll deal with that complex question and the reasons why Larkins deserves wider recognition.

Ellis Larkins's life of 79 years began and ended on Baltimore's West Side. Born on May 15th, 1923, he grew up at 1519 W. Lanvale St. in Harlem Park, the oldest of John and Clara Larkins's six children. "I heard so much music in that house. I grew up with music as a natural part of my life, so it isn't as if it was forced on me. I was just pleasantly stuck with it," Larkins told a reporter in 1985 (Guiliano C1). In the surrounding neighborhood, "You had singers for days. Piano players. Those that couldn't read the notes could still play. There was always music around." In fact, among the laborers, domestic workers and storekeepers of his block, the 1930 census listed Oscar Jones, "musician," three houses away. John Larkins was listed as a servant for a private family, homeowner, and veteran of the World War. The following year he became a violinist with Baltimore's new City Colored Orchestra. Clara Larkins played piano; one of Ellis's grandfathers and one uncle played organ; another uncle sang. His father had started teaching him violin when Ellis was somewhere between the ages of two-and-a-half and four. At age four or five he was taught piano by both parents.

Piano lessons with a teacher from the next block followed, but after six months she made it clear that Ellis was ready for the next level. John Larkins, while serving dinner at the home of his employer, Dr. Bloodgood, brought six-year-old Ellis to the attention of dinner guest Frederick Huber, Baltimore's Municipal Director of Music. After hearing the youngster play, Huber arranged for lessons with Josef Privette, who taught at Gilman, a private school for boys. Huber soon arranged for the cost of lessons (60 cents per week) to be waived and provided tickets for Ellis to attend concerts at Peabody Conservatory and the Lyric Opera House, where he heard Rachmaninoff perform (Larkins interview).

During his last year of lessons with Privette, Ellis performed for an audience of 2,000 at Frederick Douglass High School, where W. Llewellyn Wilson, conductor of the City Colored Orchestra, was head of the music department. "Young Prodigy Acclaimed at City Concert," declared the *Afro-American* on June 16th, 1934. "Playing the piano with all the assurance of a matured artist. . .[t]he youthful artist so aroused the audience that he was forced against custom to respond with an encore, Brahms Rhapsody in G Minor, Opus 79" (1). Nearly 51 years later Larkins told Mike Guiliano, "I was an innocent bystander to the planning on all this, but was happy about it." The practice regimen set by his father was strict, between two and four hours per day.

As Ellis's de facto manager, John Larkins arranged frequent concert appearances throughout the mid-to-late 1930s at hospitals, schools, churches, benefits, and private functions. For the dedication of Arbutus Memorial Park, the boy prodigy played Schumann and Rachmaninoff, sharing the bill with Anne Wiggins Brown, the Douglass High School graduate who starred in *Porgy and Bess*. In 1936 Ellis was one of 14 finalists out of 350 entrants competing in the Steinway Piano competition sponsored by Hecht Brothers department store ("Finalist").

Larkins's most publicized performance of the decade was the December 12th, 1935 concert celebrating the 25th anniversary of the National Urban League, with First Lady Eleanor Roosevelt as the featured speaker. Four thousand people attended the event, 2,000 of them inside Douglass High's auditorium, another 2,000 outside listening to loud speakers. "You might say I was nervous until I sat down at the keyboard," Larkins recalled. After performances by the City Colored Orchestra and the 100-member City Colored Chorus, Ellis played Moszkowsi's "Waltz in E-major," then an encore. Mrs. Roosevelt called him back for another ovation. "She told me I'd be a great musician and then she shook my hand. It meant a lot to me. After all, she was the first lady of the land," he told a reporter in 1999 (Thompson E-2). Encouragement also came from world-renowned concert pianist Shura Cherkassky, who had heard Ellis at the invitation of Frederick Huber.

Occasionally he ventured into forbidden musical territory. At Booker T. Washington Junior High, a teacher caught him playing the blues with friends. Amazingly, she didn't try to stop him, saying that such music was fine, "as long as you don't lose your touch." Larkins said much later that his elders "all thought jazz was banging. . . . I wasn't allowed to play jazz in the house until I got to a certain age, say 17. I'd sneak in the house with the boys" (Thompson E-2). But soon after a 1937 recital of Josef Privette's students, he was also listening to jazz on the radio—Fats Waller, Count Basie, Teddy Wilson and Earl Hines. At the Royal Theatre he heard the big bands of Cab Calloway, Jimmie Lunceford and Chick Webb, with Ella Fitzgerald.

In the 1930s, Peabody Conservatory still did not admit black students. However, some Peabody faculty circumvented this policy by teaching black students off-campus. Ellis Larkins was to follow in this "tradition," first with Josef Privette's own teacher, Austin Conradi, whom former Peabody archivist Elizabeth Schaaf calls "the Leon Fleisher of his day" (Schaaf), then with Pasquale Tallarico. At first Ellis took lessons at Tallarico's home in the Pimlico section of Baltimore. In 1939, his last year at Douglass High School, Larkins became the first African-American student officially enrolled at Peabody Conservatory, attending on full scholarship. "It wasn't under the radar. It was fairly open and done with the director's blessings. His talent was so considerable that all considerations just went on hold for him," says Schaaf. Nevertheless, he was registered as "Larkins, Ellis L. (colored)."

"People ask me how it was to be the first black pupil at the Peabody. All I know is that I said hello to people here and they said hello to me. I never heard anything derogatory said about me. I took my lessons and that's about the size of it. If I was different from other students I never was made to feel that way," Larkins told a reporter in 1985 (Guiliano C-1). In 1984, Crystal Larkins wrote about her husband to Peabody director Robert Pierce, "When asked if he received most of his knowledge from Julliard, he replies, 'No, from Peabody. Julliard was simply icing on the cake'" (C. Larkins letter).

After graduating from Douglass High in 1940, Larkins entered Juilliard School of Music on a full, three-year scholarship, buoyed by the support of W. Llewellyn Wilson, his Peabody teachers and members of his church. While studying at Juilliard, Larkins began listening to jazz at its epicenter, 52nd Street. To support himself, he began playing jazz in studios and at Gallagher's Steak House.

Record producer and impresario John Hammond, who played a key role in the careers of artists from Benny Goodman to Bruce Springsteen, became an early advocate of Larkins, helping him get into the musicians' union. Hammond, who booked talent for Barney Josephson's Café Society, recommended guitarist Billy Moore on the condition that his trio include Larkins at the piano.

An oft-repeated anecdote of his Juilliard years shows that Larkins had acquired the ability to improvise in more ways than one. "I had to give a little dissertation before I graduated, but I knew I couldn't get up there and talk. I was standing on a corner of Madison Avenue, on my way to the event, when what I'd do came to me [hits his right temple with his right hand]: demonstrate the similarities between the melodic lines of Bach and boogie-woogie. The teacher told me afterward that he knew that I'd made up the whole thing on the spot [pulls an object out of the air and shapes it into a ball], but that I'd done it very well" (Balliett, "Touch" 20).

Larkins began playing with Billy Moore in September, 1942. Three months later, when Moore got sick, Larkins took over the lead for his trio, with Bill Coleman on trumpet and Al Hall on bass. At Café Society Uptown the trio alternated with a sextet led by the pianist he credited as his main influence, Teddy Wilson. Wilson would later recommend Larkins as his replacement at the club (Larkins interview).

Graduation from Juilliard, however, was not to be. "I started on the fourth year, and I'd intended to stay with classical music but, well, I had to eat," Larkins recalled in 1979. "The classical thing was a long road. I didn't exactly switch, I just deviated and never deviated back" (Saal).

A recording career spanning over 50 years began in December, 1943, when Larkins recorded with the two reigning giants of the tenor saxophone, Coleman Hawkins and Lester Young. Six tunes with Hawkins and four with Young were later included in the two volumes of the LPs *Classic Tenors*. On these tracks Larkins plays with some of the brightest lights of jazz at that time—bassist Oscar Pettiford, drummers Jo Jones, Max Roach and Shelly Manne, guitarist Freddie Green, and trombonist Dickie Wells. Consider that in the same time period, 1941–1944, Coleman Hawkins's pianists included most of Larkins's early influences—Count Basie, Art Tatum, Teddy Wilson, and Earl Hines.

Through the rest of the 1940s, Larkins played some of New York's best jazz clubs—Café Society Uptown, the Blue Angel and the Village Vanguard. In addition to leading his own small groups, he played under the leadership of clarinetist Edmond Hall and trombonist Dickie Wells. Café Society, where pianists had to play for singers and dancers from a wide range of genres, was a great training ground for accompanists. Larkins was soon accompanying and acting as musical director for vocalists, notably Mildred Bailey, and substituting for Eddie Heywood, Jr. on Billie Holiday's recording of "No More."

The pivotal moment in Larkins's career occurred in 1950 when Decca Records producers Milt Gabler and John Hammond recruited him as accompanist for Ella Fitzgerald's first long-playing album, eight songs by George and Ira Gershwin. Asked what other instruments he wanted to bring into the studio, Larkins insisted on going it alone. The recording involved no rehearsal and the singer had laryngitis at the time. Yet this album is widely recognized as a classic. Ira Gershwin said, "I never knew how good our songs were until I heard Ella Fitzgerald sing them" (Gavin, *Pure Ella*). *The Penguin Guide to Jazz* refers to the album as "a masterpiece, all of it with Larkins's gentle, persuasive accompaniments" (Cook, Morton 490). Gary Giddins says that *Ella Sings Gershwin* is "one of the great records of that decade, and proof that she never needed all that fancy-dan arranging" (Gourse 150). Introducing Ella and Ellis at the 1973 Newport Jazz Festival in New York, impresario George Wein spoke of *Ella Sings Gershwin* as "one of the classic albums I remember in my life" (Fitzgerald). The LP also had a profound effect on Roulette Records producer Teddy Reig, who recalled, "I always remembered an album Ella Fitzgerald did with only the backing of pianist Ellis Larkins" (Gavin, *Sarah +2*), adding that he approached Sarah Vaughan in 1961 with the suggestion to do her next album with simple background. That album, *After Hours*, had just piano and bass accompaniment. The next one, *Sarah + 2*, had only guitar and bass.

Ella and Ellis were again paired for the 1954 Decca album *Songs in a Mellow Mood*, twelve selections from some of the greatest composers and lyricists of the golden age of American popular song. "It's a song recital that is one of the most rewarding in the history of jazz recording," Nat Hentoff writes in *DownBeat* (Gavin, *Pure Ella*). Cornetist Ruby Braff was so impressed that he wrote to Ella, "In the early '50s, I was asked to make another quartet record, but I told John Hammond that I wanted to make one with Ellis Larkins because of his recording with you" (Dance). Harmonica virtuoso Larry Adler, similarly taken with the Ella-Ellis recordings, asked Larkins to accompany him at the Village Gate.

Other effects of his recordings with Ella rippled throughout the 1950s—club dates, recordings as a soloist and small ensemble leader, even a Decca album with string quartet, oboe, and percussion—but demand for Larkins's services came mostly from singers. He began a decades-long working relationship with Anita Ellis. In the 1953 movie *The Joe Louis Story*, Larkins leads a trio accompanying Ellis on Alec Wilder's "I'll Be Around." Twenty-five years later the singer told *New Yorker* writer Whitney Balliett, "The most remarkable thing about Ellis is that he has such Einfuhlung—such in-feeling, or sympathy. He really feels with you. I can change my way of doing a song and he will catch it immediately. . . . If he finds what he considers a weak chord in a song, he changes it. He listens and invents" (Balliett, *American* 325).

Chris Connor, whom Larkins backed with a trio on her first album in 1954, recalled after Larkins's death: "Ellis was my absolute favorite pianist in the world. He just lifted you up into the clouds. . . . He was so easy and inspiring to work with. He just wrote out fast chord changes, and we took care of business. . . . Ellis had his own magic style, soft and sensitive . . . he just enhanced you" (qtd. in Dilts 26). Consider that after Larkins, Connor's piano accompanists included Fred Hersch, Ralph Sharon, and Hank Jones.

Larkins greatly enjoyed the role of accompanist. "I like the interplay of playing for people. . . . I can play by myself anytime, but it is a great challenge to play off someone else. . . . I think I like it more than playing solo. If you're a good accompanist you're going to be heard anyhow. I never had the urge to 'cut' anybody" (Voce). On NPR's *Jazz Profiles*, Dr. Billy Taylor sums up Larkins's role as an accompanist: "There was a feeling of completeness. He left nothing to be desired, in my opinion, when he played for a singer. All things necessary melodically, harmonically and rhythmically are there." No wonder Larkins is considered by many to be the top accompanist in jazz, with Jimmy Rowles sometimes mentioned as his equal. Ironically, herein may lie part of the reason for Larkins's under-recognition. His excellence as an accompanist may have led to his being pigeon-holed, while his talents as soloist, sideman, and leader of small ensembles were viewed as secondary by fans, musicians, and record producers.

During the 1950s, Larkins withdrew from performing, moving into vocal coaching, accompanying singers auditioning for the Gary Moore television show, studio work, and occasional teaching. In later years he mused, "I got disgusted. Something happened to the clubs in the '50s. They became joints. The audience listened, but they were strung out. I liked some of what was being played: Dizzy, Thelonious, Miles,

Charlie Mingus. But a lot of guys, I think, didn't know where they were going. I guess maybe the way I played was too tame for that time" (qtd. in Saal). Larkins's musical language is what Dr. Billy Taylor calls "pre-bop," while bop, post-bop, cool, hard-bop, and modal jazz now dominated the jazz landscape. The rising popularity of other genres— rock, R&B and blues—also took its toll on the jazz scene. While the 1950s were a fruitful recording period for Larkins, the '60s were dry. In 1966, Larkins played on the Sonny Stitt album *Stardust*, which received tepid reviews. *Pousse Café*, the Broadway show in which he performed Duke Ellington's compositions, closed within one week.

In 1968, Larkins's jazz career was revived with a phone call from John Levy, manager for Joe Williams, the singer who'd made his name with Count Basie's band. Levy says, "Things weren't going well for Ellis at the time, for either of them" (Levy). Larkins accepted Levy's invitation to "help Joe for a while," touring this country and Europe with Williams for the next four years (including playing a concert for Baltimore's Left Bank Jazz Society).

While appearing with Joe Williams at the Tropicana in Las Vegas in 1971, Larkins married Crystal Brown. They'd known each other since elementary school, when both appeared in *The Pied Piper*. As students at Douglass High School, they had worked together on radio commercials for National Bohemian beer. Crystal, much more assertive than her husband, would play a key role in reinvigorating his career.

Four years of visibility with Joe Williams enabled Larkins to join in the revival of Manhattan's jazz scene. In April, 1972, he and bassist Al Hall started a two-week engagement at Gregory's, an Upper East Side bar, that stretched into two years, six nights per week. Larkins's return was hailed in *Newsweek* (Saal); *The New York Times* ("Larkins Weaves Keyboard Moods"); New York *Post* (Mancini) and *DownBeat* (Wilder). An Editor's Note in the *DownBeat* article lamented that his "remarkable series of albums for Decca between 1951 and '59," his 1950s LPs for George Wein's Storyville label, and his duet albums with Ruby Braff were all off the market. Larkins's only available album was *Lost in the Wood*, on the non-jazz label, Stanyan. It was "mood music," mostly Rod McKuen compositions. The Editor's Note ends with the plea, "How about it, record producers?"

In fact, John Hammond had brought Larkins and Braff into the studio earlier that month to record *The Grand Reunion*, their first album together in 17 years. Larkins was also recorded accompanying Ella at the 1973 Newport Jazz Festival and again on a 1974 tour of Latin America with Marian McPartland, Teddy Wilson, and Earl Hines, all of them playing solo. But not until 1977 was Larkins recorded again as a leader on the album, *A Smooth One*, made in France after his appearance at the jazz festival in Nice. A modest Larkins renaissance was taking place, with a great steady gig in Manhattan and international touring. But he remained, in the words of Terry Teachout, "the most scandalously underrecorded of great jazz pianists."

Sometimes jazz musicians are not recognized due to lack of a distinctive style. This was certainly not the issue with Larkins. Marian McPartland, who hosted Larkins during her first year on NPR's *Piano Jazz*, says, "Stylistically he was one of a kind. . . . He was very deliberate and smooth with a wonderful sense of rhythm, an inner feeling of perfect time. He was elegant and very melodic" (Dilts 25-26). One hallmark of his style is a soft touch, in the style of his greatest inspiration, Teddy

Wilson, as well as the result of his early training. As bassist Keeter Betts told *Jazz Profiles*, "He takes the classical touch and puts it into a very, very warm jazz sound." Larkins plays the full keyboard, aided by hands that stretch an octave and a quarter. When asked about his unique harmonic conception by Nat Hentoff, Larkins replied, "I have 88 keys. I give them love and they give it back to me" (Hentoff). Ed Goldstein, leader of the Peabody Ragtime Ensemble, says, "I think of Ellis Larkins as a musical rainbow. He's an impressionist, constantly weaving extremely colorful textures" (*Jazz Profiles*). In many of his performances one hears the stride style of his early jazz mentors and flowing arpeggios that probably date back to his adolescence.

Larkins's style received much critical attention in the 1970s, especially from *New Yorker* jazz writer Whitney Balliett. The pianist told Balliett,

> "When I first recorded at Decca, there was a sign on the wall—it said, WHERE'S THE MELODY? I never forgot that. . . . Three things go on in my head when I solo: the melody, the lyrics, which I say to myself as I go along; and a kind of imaginary big band, which directs the voicings—the chords I play—so that some will resemble the reed section and some the brass. The word 'shimmering' in 'Autumn in New York' makes me see shimmering leaves and shimmering lights, and the light lyrics of 'Bidin' My Time' makes me see life just rocking along" (qtd. in *American Musicians* 328).

That was a major address for Larkins, a notoriously quiet man. Numerous writers, particularly Balliett, have commented on his use of hand gestures in place of words. My own two encounters with him in the 1990s included a concert during which he uttered not one word. For many years he began his sets with the tune "What's New?" as his non-verbal way of starting a conversation with his audience. On *Jazz Profiles*, bassist Keeter Betts describes Larkins as "a laid-back, withdrawn type person." Continuing with the adage about the squeaky wheel getting the oil, Betts says of the pianist, "He doesn't believe in squeaking." In a field where one must often trumpet himself in order to attract notice, Larkins's quietness, humility, and selflessness may well have forestalled greater recognition. But while Larkins may not have chased or created opportunities for himself, he excelled whenever opportunity came his way. His talents were so prodigious that they attracted many who provided him with those opportunities—John Hammond, George Wein, club owners, vocalists who sought the perfect accompanist. A band-leader since age 19, Larkins was confident and authoritative in all kinds of musical situations.

The upward arc of Larkins's career continued into the '80s, including a seven-year engagement at Manhattan's Carnegie Tavern and a Smithsonian series of solo jazz pianists (with Jimmy Rowles and Tommy Flanagan). In 1985, Peabody Conservatory awarded Larkins an honorary Bachelor of Music degree, with his wife Crystal calling out from the audience of 800, "It took all these years, Ellis, but you made it!" ("Larry Adler"). Three years later the couple returned to their home town and semi-retirement.

Larkins performed around Baltimore as the spirit moved him—alternating with local pianist Mel Spears at downtown restaurants, playing concerts or private parties. He enjoyed family gatherings and taught piano to his great-nephew. Larkins left Baltimore as opportunities arose, such as recording a Christmas album with Joe Williams, club dates with singers, and performing at the 1991 JVC

Jazz Festival in New York. Most significantly, in 1992, Larkins became the 22nd jazz pianist to record a solo album at Berkeley, California's Maybeck Recital Hall, right after fellow Baltimorean Jessica Williams. In liner notes for that album, Grover Sales calls Ellis Larkins "a venerable member of that exalted breed that Basie dubbed 'the Poets of the Piano.' . . . They are sometimes known as 'pianist's pianists,' that polite way of describing a towering but inadequately recognized talent." Dan Morgenstern raises an essential point when he says of Larkins, "His artistry is so subtle and understated that it sometimes eludes people who are looking for fireworks, but if you listen you'll be rewarded with some of the finest piano playing this side of Mozart" (qtd. in Dilts 20). Do we jazz listeners veer toward fireworks to the exclusion of those whose art is more subtle?

I believe that Dr. Billy Taylor best sums up the contribution of one of the greatest musicians to come out of Baltimore. "Ellis Larkins epitomizes the few musicians, and their number is much too small, who just on the strength of musicality, originality and certainly just creativity, have won over audiences. . . . Whenever they sat down at the piano you heard something very personal and you heard something unique" (*Jazz Profiles*).

NOTES

The author would like to thank, in addition to those quoted above, Edward Bailey, Jr., *Afro-American* archivist John Gartrell, Crystal Brown Larkins, Peabody Institute archivist Tracey Melhuish, and Enoch Pratt Free Library's African-American Department staff.

Works Cited

Balliett, Whitney. *American Musicians II: Seventy-One Portraits in Jazz*. New York: Oxford UP, 1966. Print.

---, "The Touch." *New Yorker* 6 Jan. 1973: 20. Print.

Cook, Richard and Brian Morton. *The Penguin Guide to Jazz Recordings: Ninth Edition*. New York: Penguin, 2008. Print.

Dance, Stanley. Liner notes. *Calling Berlin*, vol. 1. Arbors, 1995. CD.

Dilts, James. "The Quiet Piano Man." Baltimore *City Paper* 9 Oct. 2002: 25+. Print.

"Ellis Larkins." Narr. Nancy Wilson. *Jazz Profiles*. National Public Radio. 2 Feb. 1999. Radio.

"Finalist." Baltimore *Afro-American*. 21 Mar.1936: n. pag. Print.

Fitzgerald, Ella. *Newport Jazz Festival, Live at Carnegie Hall*. Legacy, 1995. CD.

Gavin, James. Liner notes. Ella Fitzgerald. *Pure Ella*. Decca Jazz, 1994. CD.

---. Liner notes. Sarah Vaughan. *Sarah + 2*. Blue Note, 2006. CD.

Giuliano, Mike. "Peabody pioneer returns for school jubilee." Baltimore *News American*. 18 Apr. 1985: C1. Print.

Gourse, Leslie. *The Ella Fitzgerald Companion*. New York: Schirmer, 1998. Print.

Hentoff, Nat. Liner notes. *A Smooth One*. Classic Jazz, 1977. LP.

Larkins, Crystal. Letter to Robert Pierce. 20 Aug. 1984. Peabody Institute Archives, Baltimore.

Larkins, Ellis. Interview by Elizabeth Schaaf. Peabody Institute Archives, Baltimore, 1998. TS.

---. Registration Card. Peabody Institute Archives. Print.

"Larkins Weaves Keyboard Moods." *New York Times* 24 Jun. 1972: n. pag. Print.

"Larry Adler and Friends Pay the Peabody a Visit." *New York Times.* 22 Apr. 1985: n. pag. Print.

Levy, John. Telephone interview. 8 Feb. 2010.

Mancini, Anthony. "Survival of the Softest." New York *Post* 2 Sept. 1972: n. pag. Print.

Saal, Hubert. "The Prodigy Returns." *Newsweek* 5 June 1972: n. pag. Print.

Sales, Grover. Liner notes. *Live at Maybeck Recital Hall, Vol. 22.* Concord, 1992. CD.

Schaaf, Elizabeth. Telephone interview. 10 Jan. 2010.

Teachout, Terry. Liner notes. *The Grand Reunion.* Chiaroscuro, 1999. CD.

Thompson, M. Dion. "Classical Jazz." The Baltimore *Sun* 3 February 1999: E-2. Print.

Voce, Steve. "Ellis Larkins: Coveted Jazz Pianist." *The Independent* 3 Oct. 2002. n. pag. Print.

Wilder, Alec. "Ellis Larkins: an appreciation." *DownBeat* 26 Oct. 1972: n. pag. Print.

"Young Prodigy Acclaimed at City Concert." *Afro-American* 16 Jun. 1934: 1. Print.

Discography

Many of Ellis Larkins's recordings are out of print or difficult to access, including some of those listed below. Fortunately, several have been re-issued. Many of Larkins's recordings may be heard and/or downloaded from sites such as iTunes (149 as of this writing). A small number are currently available on YouTube. Unless otherwise indicated, all recordings are in compact disc format.

Solo Piano

Blues in the Night: Melodies of Harold Arlen (LP), Decca, 1952. Duologue, Black
  Lion, 1/1/89.
Album headliner is vocalist Lee Wiley, but she and Larkins do not play together; he plays on four tracks. Originally recorded in 1954.

Perfume and Rain, remastered/import, Tokuma Records, 12/21/01. Originally
  on Storyville, 1954.

In an Ellington Mood, remastered/import, Story, 6/23/99. Originally titled *Do
  Nothin' 'Til You Hear From Me* (LP), 1955, Storyville

Concert in Argentina. The Jazz Alliance, 1992.
Earl Hines, Larkins, Marian McPartland and Teddy Wilson all appear as soloists. Omits 1-2 tunes per artist from original double LP, Concord Jazz, *1974*

Live at Maybeck Recital Hall, Vol. 22, Concord, 7/26/04. Recorded 3/29/92.
Most of Larkins's stylistic hallmarks are on full display. Eleven tracks feature mainly tunes by Great American Songbook composers, but the disc includes Larkins's own "Perfume and Rain," the album's gem, with a long, flowing rubato introduction and bluesy, impressionistic solo.

Duos with Ruby Braff

Duets, vol. 1, Vanguard, 10/26/99. Originally recorded in 1955.

Duets, vol. 2, Vanguard, 2/22/00. Originally recorded in 1955.

Two by Two: Ruby and Ellis Play Rodgers and Hart, Vanguard, 6/27/93.
  Originally recorded 10/14/55.

The Complete Duets, Definitive, 2/20/06. Two discs. Compiles the three discs
  listed above.

The Grand Reunion, Chiaroscuro, 5/25/99. Originally recorded 10/14/72.
A true collaboration, with Larkins soloing throughout and Braff marvelously fluid and expressive. Most tunes are ballad standards. Larkins makes some wonderfully surprising rhythmic contributions.

Calling Berlin, Vol. 1, Arbors, 10/31/95. Recorded 6/28 – 7/1/94.

Calling Berlin, Vol. 2, Arbors, 2/18/97. Recorded 6/28 – 7/1/94.

As a leader

Manhattan at Midnight, remastered/import, Universal, 11/3/03; or Lone Hill Records, 1/18/05.
Originally recorded in 1956.

Blue and Sentimental, remastered/import, Universal, 11/3/03.
Originally recorded in 1958.

Manhattan at Midnight, Lone Hill, 2/26/08, compiles the two discs above.

Penthouse Hideaway (LP), Decca, 1959 or 1960.

A Smooth One, import, Black and Blue, 1/1/90; originally released 7/21/77.
George Duvivier on bass and J.C. Heard on drums (just brushes and minimal kit). Three seasoned veterans, all former sidemen for Coleman Hawkins, team up for a great session of six swing and blues tunes. Larkins plays impeccable, authoritative, creative piano. Mainstream trio jazz rarely tops this.

As a sideman

Coleman Hawkins and Lester Young, *Classic Tenors*, Vol. 1, Sony, 8/7/89.
Recorded in December, 1943. Larkins plays on four tracks each with Hawkins and Young; the Teddy Wilson influence is very evident. Larkins plays short, sparkling introductions on most and nice extended solos on half the tunes, including light boogie woogie at bright tempo on "I'm Fer It Too." The Hawkins tracks also appear on the box set Coleman Hawkins, The Bebop Years, Proper, 2000.

Dickie Wells, 1927 – 1943, Classics, 1997.

Lucky Millinder & His Orchestra, 1943 – 1947, Classics, 1999.

Edmond Hall, Petite Fleur, Mighty Quinn, 11/15/05. Originally recorded in 1958.

Sonny Stitt, *Stardust* (alternate title: *What's New? Sonny Stitt Plays the Varitone*) (LP), Roulette, 1966.

Larry Adler, *Live at the Ballroom*, Newport Classics, 1994

With vocalists

Bea Wain, *That's How I Love the Blues, The Complete Recordings*, Vol. 2, Baldwin Street Music, 2/5/03.
Includes four V-Discs (World War II era) with the Ellis Larkins Trio.

Maxine Sullivan, *Ruban Bleu Years: Recordings*, 1944 – 1949, Baldwin Street Music, 5/5/98.

Mildred Bailey, *The Blue Angel Years*, 1945 – 1947, Baldwin Street Music, 12/7/99.

Ella Fitzgerald, *Pure Ella, Decca Jazz*, 2/15/94.
   Combines Ella Sings Gershwin, *recorded 9/11- 12/50 and* Songs in a Mellow Mood, *recorded 4/29-30/54. These are the albums that demonstrate vividly why Larkins's accompaniment was in such high demand. Providing brief introductions that sound at times like a big band, at others like Ravel or Debussy, echoing Ella or filling in the spaces with beautiful phrases, Larkins can do no wrong. He solos much more on the first eight tracks, the Gershwin album, than on the following 12 songs.*

Chris Connor Sings Lullabys of Birdland, Toshiba/EMI, 7/25/01. Original recordings 8/9-11/54.
   Includes five tracks with Ellis Larkins Trio.

Joyce Carr with Bob Vigoda and Ellis Larkins, Audiophile, 12/2/95. Original recordings 1957–1967.

Beverly Kenney Sings for Playboys, MSI, 9/25/06. Originally recorded in 1958

Aretha Franklin, Queen in Waiting: The Columbia Years, 1960–1965. Legacy, 9/24/02. Two discs.

Ella Fitzgerald, *Newport Jazz Festival, Live at Carnegie Hall*, July 5, 1973, Legacy, 7/18/95. Two discs.

Helen Humes, *Talk of the Town* (LP), Columbia, 2/18/75.

Anita Ellis with Ellis Larkins*: A Legend Sings* (LP), Orion Master Recordings, 1979.

Tony Middleton, *Swingin' for Hamp*, Concord Jazz, 1979.

Joe Williams, *That Holiday Feeling*, Verve, 11/6/90.

Barbara Lea, *Marshall Barer*, Pousse Café, import, Audiophile, 12/5/06.
   Previous release in 1992.

Thelma Carpenter, *Souvenir*, Audiophile, 12/25/99.

Sylvia Syms, *Lovingly*, Collectables, 8/14/01.

Joe Williams, *Having the Blues Under a European Sky*, Lester Recording Catalog, 12/25/01.

The Definitive Joe Williams, Verve, 9/24/02.

PHOTO: Ruby Glover

Ruby Glover & Ethel Ennis

"Both have performed with the greatest of American jazz musicians, but neither ever lost her humility or her integrity."

6 The Queens of Baltimore Jazz
by Liz Fixsen

Though Billie Holiday and Cab Calloway were two Baltimore-born stars who shone brightly on a national stage, the city also boasts two other singers whose exceptional talents were recognized internationally, but who spent decades of their performing careers at home in Charm City. Ruby Glover was often called Baltimore's "Godmother of Jazz," and Ethel Ennis, Baltimore's "First Lady of Jazz." In reality, we could call them the "Queens of Baltimore Jazz." Both were popular and familiar figures on Pennsylvania Avenue during its years as a jazz mecca. Ruby Glover was performing in Baltimore right to the day of her death in 2007, and Ethel Ennis, still among us, will no doubt be doing the same until she departs this life. Both women expressed a strong affection for the city and have served it in many ways besides as performers. Both have played with the greatest American jazz musicians but neither ever lost her humility or her integrity.

Ruby Glover: Baltimore's "Godmother of Jazz"
A Song Must Tell a Story

Sometime in 2003, I began taking voice lessons from Ruby Glover. Before we first met for a lesson, I was expecting to learn technical skills of vocal production, breath control, etc. In our first session, at her cluttered but cozy little row house on Sterling Street in Oldtown, I sang through "How High the Moon" while she listened intently.

When I finished, she had no comments on pitch, phrasing, or anything technical. Instead, she told me, "Now sing it again—and tell the story." Ruby wanted me to understand that before anything else, a song had to tell a story—and it had to be my story.

In October of 2004, I heard her in a concert at An Die Musik (with Tom Reyes's band, Lovecraft). As the band softly played a rubato introduction to the first song, Ruby started by telling a story. With her large, expressive hands, her brown, wizened face crinkled by decades of smiling, this tiny white-haired woman was like an African griot, holding her audience in a spell. She talked about a boy and a girl who grew up next door to one another, how as young teens, they naturally fell in love, but how time and circumstances came between them. Then, almost without a transition, she slipped into the lyrics of "Just Friends." In her voice I could feel all the wistfulness of memory and the sorrow of a love affair that has died. Although time had taken its toll on her voice, and although a cold that night had roughened it around the edges a bit more than usual, Ruby Glover's voice was still a powerful storytelling instrument.

Baltimore Born and Bred

When I visited Ruby's home, she enthusiastically pointed to the memorabilia and artifacts of her decades in the jazz world. The walls were covered with her awards, degrees, and certificates, and with pictures of musicians and other notables she had known over the years. She spent most of her life as a singer in Baltimore, right up until her death in 2007. Born on December 6th, 1929, on Dallas Street in Baltimore, Ruby spent her childhood at 1309 Monument Street,

East Baltimore. Her father was accidently shot dead at the scene of a robbery when she was two years old, so she was raised by her mother. As a child, she was immersed in jazz: her mother Inez was a vocalist, and would bring Ruby to work with her. There, she would sit Ruby on the bar and let her sing to the patrons ("Ruby Inez"). Inez would sometimes bring home her musician friends, such as Ernie Washington and Johnny Sparrow, late at night after gigs, where they would keep singing and playing music.

At age six, little Ruby was singing for family funerals. While she was at elementary school—a school now part of Sojourner-Douglass College—Ruby played Dorothy in a production of *The Wizard of Oz*. In middle school, her music teachers helped her form the Parrish Sextet, with James Parrish (piano), McKevett Seymour (bass), James Tillery (guitar), and James Brown (drums). (She did not recall the name of the saxophonist). The sextet carried on through to high school; as a teenager at Dunbar High School, Ruby sang at dances and in talent contests, and recalled that when her sextet entered a contest, none of the other kids would want to enter, because the Parrish Sextet was so sure to win (Schaaf).

As Ruby and her combo gained local fame, her mother received requests from big band leaders like Doug McArthur and his Blue Notes and King Draper to permit Ruby to sing with them. Permission was granted—as long as Ruby, still a teen, was chaperoned. So, the band leader's wife would chaperone. She would pick Ruby up from the shows—at the Biddle Hall, the Odd Fellows, and the Amsterdam, for example, and bring her home afterwards (Schaaf).

Finding Her Voice

With her own talent and with the influence of her mother and her mother's friends, Ruby moved into the heart of the lively scene of Pennsylvania Avenue in its heyday in the 1940s and 1950s. Ruby acknowledges that she was much influenced by the great jazz singers of the day, including Billie Holiday and Ella Fitzgerald. She particularly admired Sarah Vaughan, and devotedly studied and imitated Sass's style. When Ruby was 22, she made a recording at Columbia studios; later, listening to the playback, she thought they were playing a Sarah Vaughan recording. The pianist, Ray Chambers, told her, no, Ruby, that's you singing. She said, "Wow, I'll never go anywhere sounding like her. She's already alive and, well, I've got to find me" (qtd. in Schaaf).

She began behaving more assertively with her accompanists, asking them to try different approaches to song endings, for example. She also started listening more intently to other singers, such as Betty Carter and Carmen McRae. She liked Carter's "drive," her ability to sing like a horn; she liked McRae's sense of humor, but not her brashness. She adored Billie Holiday, but didn't want her singing to be as sad as Billie's (Schaaf).

But it was pianist Albert Dailey who taught her what she really needed to do. One day Ruby dropped in at the house where Dailey was playing Miles Davis's new tune, "Milestones," with Jimmy Wells on vibes, Donald Bailey on bass, and Purnell Rice on drums. Wells brought up Ruby's search for her own style, as she had been asking for guidance. Then Dailey weighed in:

> He said, "Man, you need to listen to horns." I looked at him
> and I said, "Why?" Like that. And he said, "A singer cannot
> learn from a singer without duplication. Her bad marks or

his bad marks—you're going to have them. You're going to demonstrate the flaws in your own presentation. You're going to sound like that individual." (qtd. in Schaaf)

The rest of the band chimed in, discussing how most jazz musicians don't like to play with singers. One instrumentalist said he had to be dragged to play with a singer unless she was really good. So Ruby decided that to be "really good," she would need to sound like a horn— she would learn to scat—and began listening to Miles Davis, Cannonball Adderley, Sonny Stitt, and Gene Ammons. She even listened to the melodic playing of bass players like Donald Bailey.

Her new focus paid off. She recalls how the first time she really tried singing in her own voice was one night at the Red Fox. "In the midst of the song, I was scatting and singing, and I forgot about the microphone and I said, oh, my goodness, that is really me! The people out in front applauded and I was so joyous. I said, I got a sound!" (qtd. in Schaaf). In her scatting, Ruby found her own identity as a singer.

I remember hearing Ruby scat once in 2004 at a small, intimate jam she had organized at Xando's, on 31st and Charles St. She had hired four of her favorite sidemen—Andy Ennis on tenor, Charlie Etzel on piano, Eric Kennedy on drums, Max Murray on bass. On "Take the 'A' Train," Ruby, after singing the head, launched into an exuberant vocal improvisation. Not a foot or a hand or a head in the room was still. She can be heard and seen scatting on this same tune in a video made in at the WEAA studio in March of 2007 with Seth Kibel on tenor saxophone and Sean Lane on keyboard ("Ruby Glover"). She gives the standard new life, seeming, as she sings, to be carried back to her old days on Pennsylvania Avenue. That lady could swing!

On Pennsylvania Avenue

Called by Alvin Kirby Brunson "The Little Giant of Pennsylvania Avenue," the diminutive singer became an important figure in Baltimore's jazz heyday, when the 23 blocks of Pennsylvania Avenue, stretching southward from Fulton Avenue, were home to a number of lively jazz spots. One was Gamby's, the first place on "The Avenue" where Ruby sang, having won a two-week engagement in an "open stage" contest. (In fact, in a similar contest, her daughter Ina won a long engagement at Gamby's.) From Gamby's, Ruby moved to other clubs such as Phil's, and the popular Club Tijuana, where she was a regular. She also sang at the Red Fox, after Ethel Ennis, who had reigned there for some 10 years, headed for Europe with Benny Goodman (Schoettler). "[Pennsylvania Avenue] was just swinging all the time, all the time," Glover told a *Sun* reporter in 2002. "The glamor. The gorgeous feeling. The energy!" (qtd. in Schoettler). Ruby loved her home city. "I was born a black Alice in Wonderland. I love the city 100 percent. She's always been wonderful to me" (qtd. in Sweeney).

She continued singing in various clubs on The Avenue until its demise following the riots of 1968. During those years, she performed locally and traveled worldwide (Anthony), sharing the stage with many of the prominent jazz musicians of Baltimore and the region, including Keter Betts, Andy Ennis, Doug Cane, Vernon Wolst, Charles Covington, Carlos Johnson, Sir Thomas Hurley, Fuzzy Kane, Whit Williams, Charlie Etzel, Dennis Chambers, Gaynell Colburn, Moe Daniels, Dave Ross, and Mickey Fields (Pryor-Trusty), and even with greats such as Art Blakey, Sonny Stitt, Billie Holiday, Miles Davis, and John Coltrane (Shapiro). As the years went by, Ruby's voice became more raspy, but as Charles Simmons remembers, "In the early days, she sounded like Sarah Vaughan, very melodic and always in tune. She could scat like Ella Fitzgerald and talk her way through a song like Carmen McRae" (qtd. in Himes).

Even after Pennsylvania Avenue was no longer jazz central, Ruby continued performing in a wide range of venues throughout Baltimore, including the Hippodrome Theatre and the Lyric Opera House. She also sang at two inauguration ceremonies, for Presidents Jimmy Carter and Bill Clinton, and is featured in the Jazz exhibit of the Smithsonian Museum, in the Reginald E. Lewis Museum of Maryland African-American History and Culture, and in the African-American Fundamentals of Jazz History (Anthony). Her late performances included "A Royal Night at The Senator" (April 2000) to raise funds for a monument memorializing the famed Royal Theatre, a focal point of the Pennsylvania Avenue jazz scene, and a 2004 concert to celebrate the 40th anniversary of the Left Bank Jazz Society, in which Ruby was recognized for her 50 years of outstanding service in the Baltimore jazz community.

A video posted online in December, 2008 at a coffeehouse in Odenton shows why she had become a local legend. She sings a duet on "They Can't Take That away from Me," with a young man named Chris Haley (Marvincomet); the performance is evidence of Ruby's delight in using voice and gesture to tell a story with a song, and also evidence of her great charm as a performer and her love of nurturing younger singers. Singing with this man at least 40 years her junior, she was as flirtatious as a girl—but tastefully so. Warmth, charm, good taste, and generosity were Ruby's hallmarks as a performer and as a person.

Teacher, Organizer, Preservationist, Muse, Mother, Friend

Ruby Glover became known as Baltimore's "Godmother of Jazz." It's not hard to see why, for she was not only a singer; she was also a teacher, organizer, and supporter of the music's preservation. For 30 years she was an administrator at Johns Hopkins University hospital and is remembered by one local fan for her help with Dunbar High School's Health Professional Careers program (Stella). She was a volunteer at the Waxter Center for Senior Citizens and advocated for the arts in the Baltimore schools. In the years before her death, she lectured as Professor of Jazz History and Jazz Appreciation at Sojourner-Douglass College, and taught jazz vocal performance at Towson University. She had a passion for jazz history, and led tours of Pennsylvania Avenue. Ruby Glover was dedicated to keeping jazz alive and well in her beloved city and elsewhere. She said to Peabody interviewer Elizabeth Schaaf:

> In the deepest part of my heart, I don't believe Dizzy [Gillespie] and Charlie Parker and all the ones that went on before thought that the music would ever die. To them it was always going to live. And it only lives through the people who perceive it as a valuable talent and treasure and those who do something about giving it on. It is now ours to keep.

Ethel Ennis says that while everyone else called Ruby Baltimore's "Godmother of Jazz," she (Ethel) called Ruby "the 'Guard Mother of Jazz,' because she was always there to protect it and nourish it. And jazz in Baltimore needed that protection" (qtd. in Himes).

Ruby mentored many up-and-coming jazz singers and helped establish and stage the annual Billie Holiday Vocal Competition for many years. Along with Camay Murphy (daughter of Cab Calloway), she worked through the Jazz Heritage Foundation to promote the careers of notables such as trumpeter Dontae Winslow, and saxophonists Antonio Hart and Gary Bartz. Because she recognized the importance of her own early influences, she was always eager to encourage aspiring young performers: "The minute I hear a developing talent with an electric something inside of them that drives them to want to be better, it's like they press my button," she confided to Schaaf. "You know, I want to get to know this baby [a new talent], and I want to encourage, I want to open a door." She established Jazz Sweets, Inc. to assist in nurturing local talent, and many a performer today can point to some encouragement or some influence that he or she received from Ruby Glover.

Many, many people experienced Ruby Glover as a warm-hearted, caring friend. For example, when guitarist O'Donel Levy suffered a massive stroke, Ruby visited him in four different hospitals and made encouraging calls to his wife (Stella). A former student mentioned how Ruby provided similar support after he had lost a child (HeavyHeart). In the time that I knew her, I too experienced the caring warmth that she seemed to extend to everyone around her.

Married twice, Ruby raised five children on her own, including two step-children. Her youngest son, Aaron Perkins (now an arson detective with the Baltimore City Police Department) shares fond remembrances of his mother in an interview on WBAL conducted shortly after her death (WBALTV). He talks about how she always loved to look good—and in the video, she is shown smartly attired in a bright red jacket and a perky black beret. He says that musicians loved her because she not only taught them about music, but about life—she would say, you learn about life from your successes and your failures.

Above all, however, Ruby Glover was about music. As she movingly speaks in an interview on Peabody's *Sounds & Stories*:

> [Music] has no color. It embraces people, all forms of life, all hues, all nationalities. The music has one spirit and that spirit is so driven and so electrifying when the music is playing. It drives people to either stand up and either shake hands with their neighbor or laugh about a particular person who's on stage. Music excites an individual, and just for the sake of it, they get so overwhelmed. It's like being in a different kind of church, where instead of shouting out loud, because they do some of that, they would embrace whomever was with them, or they would throw their hands up and close their eyes and they'd dance to it in some form or fashion. (qtd. in Schaaf)

Ruby died doing what she loved. On October 20th, 2007, she was performing in a benefit concert for the House of Ruth (a battered women's shelter) at the Creative Alliance in East Baltimore. The house was packed with an enthusiastic audience. After singing two numbers, Ruby became confused, then collapsed, the victim of a stroke. The next day, at Johns Hopkins Bayview Medical Center, Ruby Glover died while surrounded by family and friends softly singing "This Little Light of Mine." She was not quite 78 years old (Shapiro).

Ethel Ennis: Baltimore's First Lady of Jazz
Early Life and Performances, 1932-54

Ethel Ennis was born on November 28, 1932 in Baltimore to Andrew and Arrabell ("Bell") Ennis, both South Carolina natives. Ethel spent most of her childhood and youth living in an entirely black community. When she was nine, the family moved to the Gilmore

Projects, where she attended Booker T. Washington Middle School and the old Frederick Douglass High School.

Ethel's father was a lover of music, a singer and harmonica player. But he worked long hours as a barber and was rarely at home. Much of Ethel's upbringing was handled by her mother and maternal grandmother Elizabeth Small, called Honey. Both women were very religious and quite strict in their approach to childrearing. As a high school girl, Ethel was not allowed to participate in any extra-curricular activities and required to come straight home after school. The life of the Ennis women centered on church, and Honey's ambition for young Ethel was primarily that she learn to be a "lady." This influence remained with Ethel for the rest of her life.

In Bell's eyes, being a "lady" included being able to play the piano, and she started Ethel with lessons at age seven.[1] The lessons continued into her teens, even though Ethel was not fond of playing the piano—she would have preferred to be a ballerina. However, she complied with her mother's wishes and developed her keyboard skills well enough to earn a little money playing for the Sunday school in the local Methodist church.

When Ethel was 15, a friend invited her to join the Abe Riley Quartet. Riley, who played bass, piano, drums and trumpet, thought that having a female in the otherwise all-male group would be a draw. At the time, Ethel didn't know any jazz technique, and it was a challenge to make the transition from playing churchy "popcorn" chords to performing in bebop style. The only music approved in the Ennis home was religious and classical. But Ethel had been surreptitiously familiarizing herself with blues and R&B, despite her grandmother's disapproval—mainly by listening through the floor when the downstairs neighbor, Miss Gertrude, held her lively parties. The Riley group played in tame venues such as local VFW and Fellowship halls, and Ethel earned the grand sum of $2.50 per night. Her mother and grandmother were not concerned about her playing with the group, because grown-up chaperones would be present, and the rehearsals were held right across the street from the Ennis's home.

But Honey might have worried when she heard Ethel's first vocal performance. At one of the group's routine gigs, an audience member offered a big tip if Ethel could sing "In the Dark." Although Ethel had never had vocal training, let alone sung in public, she answered that she could sing it—and sing it she did, having learned the song from Miss Gertrude's parties. The lyrics of this Lillian Green song describe an experience that this sheltered 15-year-old girl was supposed to know nothing about. Nevertheless, the performance was enthusiastically received, and it occurred to Ethel that she could have a life as a vocalist as well as a piano player.[2]

Also during her teens, Ethel made her first recording, of a couple of tunes written by a friend, William Everhart, in a local Baltimore studio. Later, Ethel and William recorded a rock 'n' roll tune called "Little Boy" that was afterwards recorded by five nationally recognized artists, including Little Richard.

After graduating from high school in 1950, Ethel continued her musical activity and joined the local musicians' union—but covered her bases by also enrolling in the Cortez W. Peters Business College (from which she graduated in two years and where she won a shorthand award). By day she learned shorthand; by night she played piano and sang in local clubs—including The Flamingo and the Oasis, two strip clubs on the infamous "Block." Certainly Honey and Bell were worried—but they had thoroughly trained Ethel as a "lady," and when she played gigs at these "devil's dens," she would retire between sets to do crossword puzzles in some safe corner of the premises to avoid exposure to the steamy performances on stage.

As her reputation spread, she began working with other local musicians. After the Oasis, she played regularly with an R&B group called The Tilters, which performed six nights a week at Gamby's on Pennsylvania Avenue. They also had gigs at a white strip club on Pulaski Highway.[3] Ethel recalls how the white truck drivers would hoot, holler and call her insulting names. Once, when the band, upstairs on a break, caught wind of the lewd commentary, they came rushing downstairs to her defense, and a brawl was only narrowly avoided. This was not the only dive she played in during those early years. But the lady-like Ethel glided through these dens of iniquity untouched— although she did acknowledge that in them she learned a lot about the ways of the world.

The Red Fox and Beyond

The Tilters broke up in 1951, and soon Ethel teamed up with bassist Monty Poulson. The duo played in various clubs in and around Baltimore and Annapolis, as well as out-of-state on the Eastern seaboard.

Then, in 1954, Ethel came to the attention of George Fox, the owner of the Red Fox, a popular club on Pennsylvania Avenue. One of the few integrated clubs in the city, the Red Fox welcomed a wide range of humanity, both black and white, straight and gay. Impressed with the young singer, Fox booked her as a regular and became her devoted promoter for the next three years. He also arranged her first recording deals with Jubilee and Capitol Records. Her debut album, *Lullabies for Losers* (1955), was to bring her important attention.

With Fox's help, Ethel was getting bookings in clubs all up and down the East Coast. In 1956, she performed at the famous Apollo Theatre in Harlem, where all the great singers—including Sarah Vaughan, Ella Fitzgerald, and Billie Holiday—had performed. The regular performers called it "The Workhouse" because the theater offered five shows a day, seven nights a week. As Ethel recalls, "You see yourself going on and on. Go on, go off, go on, go off" (qtd. in Schaaf). Apollo audiences were demanding. In her first show, Ethel sang one of her cool jazz ballads—but it was just as coolly received. Owner Frank Schiffman, who knew his audience, persuaded her to follow with a sizzling R&B tune called "You Gotta Drive, Daddy, Drive." With it she scored a solid hit.

She continued to gain attention. One jazz fan listening to *Lullabies for Losers* on the radio phoned the station because he thought he was hearing a new Sarah Vaughan release. A Baltimore *Sun* reporter called her singing "robust, fluent, sweet, and hot" (Catling, qtd. in Kravetz 32). Even Billie Holiday took notice. One day in New York, after listening to the album with Ethel's friend Shery Baker, Billie asked, "Who is this bitch from Baltimore?" Upon hearing his answer, Billie phoned a surprised Ethel and told her, "You're a musician's musician. You don't fake. Keep on singing that way . . . one day you'll be famous" (qtd. in Kravetz 27).

This period also brought changes in Ethel's personal life. Her mother and father separated, and Ethel, her mother, and brother moved out of the Gilmore Projects to Whittier Avenue. Ethel was taking more responsibility for the support of the family and also began her two-year courtship with a young attorney named Jacques ("Jack") Leeds, whom she had met at the Red Fox. Leeds became her first husband in 1957.

A Musician's Musician

Among Ethel's musical influences were singer-piano players Hadda Brooks, Nellie Lutcher, Camille Howard, and Rose Murphy (Schaaf). She also admired Doris Day and Peggy Lee, and of course Ella, Sarah Vaughan, and Lady Day. Ethel became famous for her impersonations of these famous singers, but she developed her own style. She was also known for her onstage sense of humor and for her very slow, feeling renditions of standard ballads, sung in a voice of velvety smoothness and clarity. In 1964, a Chicago *Sun Times* critic described her as "a smoldering jazz contralto with phrasing that leaps, lifts, or melts into a lovely dying fall" (qtd. in Kravetz 53). Another reviewer called her singing "all honey and flame and seduction" (HWF). As she developed her singing style, she also developed her stage presence, eventually being persuaded to leave the piano and perform strictly as a vocalist. Her engaging performance style can be seen in an early video of a youthful Ethel Ennis, sexy but still every bit the lady, singing "I've Got that Feeling."[4]

The Benny Goodman Band and the 1960s

It was while recording her second album, *Change of Scenery*, with Capitol, that Ethel made the connections that led to her a successful audition for Benny Goodman's 18-man "all-stars" band which was to appear at the Brussels World Fair and then tour Europe. The tour was one of several organized by the US State Department as "jazz diplomacy." After a month of intensive rehearsals in New York, Ethel and the band headed for its first stop in Stockholm, and then, for the next four weeks, performed in sixteen cities in eight countries, ending at Brussels on May 25th, 1958. Everywhere they appeared, Ethel Ennis was a huge success. Baltimoreans were filled with pride at the spectacular rise of one of their own, and fully expected Ethel's career to continue its path toward the highest peaks of stardom.

But instead of remaining in New York, Ethel chose to keep Baltimore as her home base. For one thing, that's where her husband had his own career. But she also was feeling the stress of touring and of trying to conform to the image of a star. She enjoyed singing, but all the other trappings of life as an entertainer left her cold. She preferred to just be herself, plain and simple. She says, "I was taught by my grandmother: Don't go against your grain for gain" (qtd. in McCabe). The performing life was also taking its toll on her marriage, as Ethel was often away from home, and as her husband became resentful of her fame.

Although she didn't climb the ladder to the highest altitudes of musical stardom, she did continue to shine brightly in the lesser constellations. Throughout the late 1950s and into the 1960s, she performed in Baltimore and in New York, Philadelphia, Boston, and Los Angeles, as well as holding a month-long gig at the Astor in London. She appeared with jazz greats Louis Armstrong, Miles Davis, Count Basie, and Cab Calloway, and was a huge hit at the 1964 Newport Jazz Festival and the 1965 Monterey Jazz Festival. In 1965, she began appearing on the Arthur Godfrey show, where she continued to appear until the show went off the air in 1973, and she also kept busy recording, mainly with RCA.

But by 1966, she had reached a crisis point. She kept resisting the efforts of her agent, Gerry Purcell, to propel her to stardom, and as she stood in front of her audiences, she felt that she didn't have that nameless "something" that they craved. Purcell was frustrated: "Every time she was about ready to crack through, she would just as quickly go back in her shell" (qtd. in Kravetz 66). He guessed rightly that she was not willing to achieve stardom at the expense of a happy personal life. She canceled her New York contract with Purcell, ending her recording prospects with RCA. She still had a booking arrangement with a more easy-going agent, John Powell, but the break with Purcell was a watershed in her career. She had developed asthma, and her marriage was on the rocks; eventually the marriage dissolved, with divorce finalized in May 1965. Even the Red Fox had passed its peak years as the neighborhood of Pennsylvania Avenue was in decline.

A New Love

Back in Baltimore, Ethel slowed her pace and tried to get recentered. One night as she performed at the Red Fox, a young *Sun* reporter named Earl Arnett happened to drop in after his midnight shift. He had seen Ethel perform at the club in 1963 and was surprised to find her still there. Arnett began to frequent the club, and the relationship soon blossomed into a romance that led to marriage in August of 1967 in Aspen, Colorado. At the time, neither one knew that Maryland had a law against miscegenation—although the law was changed later that same year. This law did not make it easier for the parents of the couple to accept the marriage.

But Ethel had found her soulmate—Earl wasn't interested in show business, never thought he'd marry an entertainer, and wasn't concerned about whether Ethel became a star or not. He was a perfect match in spite of the fact that he was eight years her junior, and white. After being married to "Satan's right-hand man" (as she calls her former husband, in an interview for the National Visionary Leadership Project), Ethel found Earl a welcome contrast. "He was so nice! . . . He's just a gentle man—he was so wonderful! And listen—forty years later, he's still OK with me!" (Poussaint).

Performing for Presidents

Ethel's career again took a sudden upward turn in 1972. The songstress was not aware of it, but Vice President Spiro Agnew was a fan of hers, and it took Ethel quite by surprise when he called to invite her to entertain at the State Governor's Ball, along with Danny Thomas and Frank Sinatra. Then Agnew invited her to sing the National Anthem at the Republican Convention in Florida. Although she was a registered Democrat, Ethel agreed. The performance took a surprising turn: because the big band that was supposed to accompany her was set up at the other end of the large hall, Ethel sang the anthem a cappella. But her rendition received an overwhelmingly positive response, leading to an invitation to sing it again at Richard Nixon's inauguration the next January. Again she hesitated about singing for Republicans, but her friends told her, "You'll be singing it for the people." So she agreed, and spent the next months thinking about how she would make the song especially meaningful. Rejecting the hearty pub-song approach that the song traditionally invites, she instead thought about how America was suffering the travails of the Vietnam War. When Inauguration Day came, the US Marine Corps band was ready to accompany her, but she told them she'd do it alone. As the program was ending, people began to leave, but as "O, say can you see" floated across the hall, people stopped and turned to listen, and then stood in rapt attention as Ethel sang the song like a mother singing a lullaby to comfort a sick child. Like her first, her second performance of the anthem brought raves; fan mail poured in to her house. One fan wrote, "I was crying. She sang for all of America" (qtd. in Kravetz 86). Ethel is credited with being the first to perform the anthem a cappella. Later she performed at the White House for President Jimmy Carter, singing her own composition, "Hey You" ("Tour de Force"), and performed at other White House functions as well as at various McGovern-Shriver events in 1972 (Gelormine).

At Home in Baltimore, 1972–Present

In the ensuing years, Ethel focused on Baltimore, sometimes performing out of state on both coasts, but mostly staying close to home. In 1972, after a disappointing relationship with BASF, which produced the album *Ten Sides of Ethel Ennis*, she and Earl decided to form ENE Productions. There were several other noteworthy episodes during these years. In 1974, she played a costumed character called

"Ethel Earphone" in a children's television show called *Book, Look, and Listen*, produced by the Maryland Department of Educational Television. In 1976, she again sang the national anthem at a Bicentennial celebration at Fort McHenry in Baltimore. In 1977, her brother Andy, the tenor saxophonist, returned to Baltimore after years of playing on the road, and he and Ethel began performing together. ENE Productions produced its first album in 1980, called simply *Ethel*, a live recording in Annapolis at the King of France Tavern where Ethel had been performing with guitarist O'Donel Levy and keyboardist Charles Covington. Also in 1980, she was a highlight at the African-American Heritage Festival (part of the Baltimore Showcase of Nations) with her renditions of "Motherless Child" and "God Bless the Child." The following year, she headlined at Baltimore's first ever Artscape Street Festival.

In 1982, Earl and Ethel were appointed by Governor William Donald Schaefer as Cultural Ambassadors of the City of Baltimore, which led, in 1987, to Ethel's participation in the first annual International Music Festival in Baltimore's sister city, Xiamen, in China, where she sang a Chinese folk song—in Chinese. In 1984, the couple opened their own jazz club, Ethel's Place, where performers of national stature regularly appeared, until the club was sold to Blues Alley in 1988. That year, Ethel began performing in the jazz series at Montpelier Cultural Arts Center, in Laurel, Maryland, and continued appearing there almost annually.

Since then, she has continued to perform as far away as Turkey (Ankara International Music Festival, 1996 and '97) and Italy (Saluzzo Festival, 2003), as well as throughout the Maryland region. Her credits in 2009 include performances for the Creative Alliance (Baltimore) and for the 81st anniversary of Prince Theatre (Chestertown, MD). She also continues to perform with the Great American Music Ensemble on National Public Radio, at festivals, and in the Kennedy Center in Washington.

Nearly a Star

As Ethel's career progressed, observers and critics often expressed their certainty that she was headed for greatness—and their puzzlement that she never achieved the level of success and national recognition of a singer like Nancy Wilson. Why did Ethel Ennis not achieve the pinnacle of stardom that her fans expected and hoped for? Geoffrey Himes says that "while the Baltimorean's unconventional looks are quite striking, they were not easy to market in 1964." Her biographer, Sallie Kravetz, offers several complex explanations. She writes that "[Ethel] just wasn't ready or willing to meet the demands of the business. She was lacking the awareness, wisdom, and confidence that would eventually be hers with the passing of years" (70). Kravetz also explains that during the late 1950s and early '60s, when Ethel was doing most of her touring and performing, the popularity of jazz was fading and the era of swing giving way to rock 'n' roll and R&B, so Ethel was just a few years too late to have a clear path to the top as a jazz singer (57-58). Kravetz also points to the influence of Ethel's first husband, her mother, and her grandmother, which "kept Ethel from truly opening up and letting loose with everything she had" (58). Kravetz also points to Ethel's "fear of success" (70), at least on the terms that "success" was available to her. And to some extent, it was just plain stubbornness that caused Ethel to resist others' efforts to mold her into stardom (82).

But in recent years, Ethel has explained the path of her life as a conscious choice. In an interview with Rene Poussaint for the National Visionary Leadership Project, Ethel says, "I've heard people [such as Kravetz] say, 'Oh, she's afraid of success!' [But] "I just don't like the [entertainment] business. I like to live my life normally." She wanted to explore different paths to gain the experiences that would enable her to sing the songs with authenticity. In that interview, she says that the recording companies put her in a pigeonhole called "jazz," because she didn't sing the songs note-for-note as written. They wanted pop and Broadway tunes, because they were easier to market. Yet she felt that they weren't interested in the real Ethel Ennis, in what she personally had to bring to the songs. Only much later did she begin to look inside herself to find out who she really was. She explains, "I have lived another kind of life, instead of being stunted in the so-called entertainment market. I don't find that fulfilling" (qtd. in McCabe).

"Soft Power"

Through early years of performing, Ethel was learning about "real life." That meant learning about the ways of men; as an entertainer, she was on more than one occasion approached by a man with dishonorable intentions. But this rather shy, reserved young lady who had been taught well by her mother and grandmother managed to maintain her distance and pass unaffected through the seamier side of the musical world, never falling into any questionable or self-destructive activities. She also learned, through several unfortunate experiences, about the kinds of skullduggery practiced in the recording industry, a major factor in her final decision to forgo the climb to stardom. The girl who had grown up sheltered in an entirely black neighborhood also learned about the indignities faced by black entertainers performing for white audiences. These racial experiences caused her, as she reached her mature years, to develop a determination to work for peace and commonality between the races. And all of the experiences fertilized her development as a mature singer with an authentic story to tell in her songs.

After her break with Gerry Purcell and her marriage to Earl Arnett, Ethel began to develop a concept she called "soft power"—a power within, which she explains as "the spiritual energy we all possess to change ourselves and the world around us." Music, she believes, is not only a medium for entertainment, but also a way to "inform and inspire" (qtd. in Delmarva Town Crier). She has been using her "soft power" concept ever since to help promote harmony and good will between the races and among all the people of her native city. As for her return to Baltimore as her home base, she says, "This is where I live, and you gotta live somewhere—and I believe you can bloom where you're planted. . . . But it's nice to just be quiet and find who you are, and then you have much more to give." When Poussaint asks her what is special about Baltimore, she answers, "I think Baltimore will become a leading city for the nation, I really do. There's a lot here–and I think I'm going to do my best work here in Baltimore. And I've got a lot more to do."

Conclusion

Of course, Baltimore was blessed with a number of other popular jazz singers in days gone by. In her book, African-American Entertainment in Baltimore, Rosa Pryor-Trusty mentions or pictures Brenda Alford (48), Damita Jo (53), Jody Myers (62), Judd Watkins (62), "Lady" Rebecca Anderson (63), Nikki Cooper (65), Shirley Fields (71), and "Tiny" Tim Harris (75) as singers who performed in Baltimore's clubs, although not all are Baltimore-born. Other Baltimore vocalists she mentions in a 2007 article in the Baltimore Afro-American are Ruby Dawson, Liz Figueroa, Cathy Dorsey, and Earlene Reed. But Baltimore natives Ethel Ennis and Ruby Glover were the most well-known. Baltimore owes its gratitude to these two great "queens" of jazz who have given so much talent and love to the city.

NOTES

1 Ethel's first piano teacher was her mother, but this plan proved to be a struggle, so Bell hired Mrs. Lovey Husketh, a public school music teacher who was well regarded in Baltimore. The Lovey E. Husketh Music Guild of the National Association of Colored Musicians was named for her (Baltimore *Afro-American*, 23 Feb. 1957).

2 Ethel tells the story of singing "In the Dark" on the Kojo Nnamdi Show on WAMU 88.5, in a show titled "Ethel Ennis: Renaissance Woman." She also sings a couple measures of the song on the show. And Kojo also plays a clip of Ethel giving an earthy rendition of "Honeysuckle Rose."

3 Sherrie's Show Bar & Lounge, where Ethel played in her post-high school days, is still there on Pulaski Highway, as a mid-grade strip club, now featuring both white and black dancers.

4 Ethel singing "I've Got That Feeling" can be seen at http://www.youtube.com/watch?v=Rt6wHi64pk8&feature=related. The video was made for Scopitone, a forerunner of music videos, a sort of video jukebox that didn't ever take off (Kravetz 59-60). The club in which the performance takes place is not identified.

Press photograph of Ethel Ennis.

CREDIT: Courtesy of Hildner Productions.

Works Cited and Consulted

A good deal of the material about Ethel Ennis in this chapter comes from the biography by Sallie Kravetz, a close confidante of Ethel who worked closely with her for nearly ten years on various projects: photographs, a video documentary, a concert production, and as a member of her production company, ENE (The Afro–American, Dec. 29, 1984).

Ankeny, Jason. Ethel Ennis Biography. All Music.com. Web. 2 March 2010.

Anthony, Jocelyn. "Baltimore Jazz Icon Dies While on Stage." 26 Nov. 2007. The 501.com. Web. 2 March 2010.

Catling, Patrick Skene. "Baltimorean to be Vocalist with Goodman in Brussels." The Baltimore *Sun* 26 March, 1958.

Brunson, Alvin Kirby. "Jazz Singer Ruby Glover—The Little Giant of Pennsylvania Avenue—Passes." Qtd. in *Chicken Bones: A Journal for Literary and Artistic African American Themes*, Baltimore Index Page. Web. 2 March 2010.

College of Notre Dame. "College of Notre Dame Celebrates Women's History Month." 26 Feb. 2003. Web. 2 March 2010.

Collins, George. "Miss Ruby Glover Blends Three Lives." 19 August, 1961. Baltimore *Afro-American*. Web. 23 April 2010, *http://news.google.com*

"Ennis Performs for Prince Theatre's 81st Anniversary." *Delmarva Town Crier* 14 Oct. 2009. Web. 2 March 2010.

"Ethel Ennis." Accessed 2 March 2010, Billy Taylor's Jazz at the Kennedy Center. *NPR.org. Web. 2 March 2010.*

"Ethel Ennis at Douglass High." *A Panoramic Photo Blog.* Web. 2 March 2010.

"Ethel Ennis: Change of Scenery (1957)/Have You Forgotten (1958)." Review. Blog. 19 Sept. 2009. *Soulful Divas. Web. 2 March 2010.*

"Ethel Ennis: Biography." *All About Jazz.com.* Web. 2 March 2010.

"Ethel Ennis." *JazzUSA Women in Jazz. Web. 2 March 2010.*

"Ethel Ennis: Renaissance Woman." Audio Interview. *Kojo Nnamdi Show.* WAMU 88.5. Web. 2 March 2010.

"Ethel Llewellyn Ennis." *Maryland Women's Hall of Fame.* Online Exhibits. Museum Online. Maryland State Archives, 2001. Web. 2 March 2010.

Gelormine, Phil. "Ethel Ennis: A New Star." *Billboard Magazine* 24 March 1973: 15. Online. Google Books. Web. 2 March 2010.

Greenfield, Phil. "Concert is Alive with Love." Maestro. Baltimore *Sun*. Web. 2 March 2010.

HeavyHeart. Comments. "Jazz Singer Dies After Onstage Stroke." *Topix.com*. Web. 2 March 2010.

Himes, Geoffrey. "Room to Bloom: Determination Powers Ethel Ennis' Drive To Do What She Wants No Matter What." Baltimore *City Paper* 24 Aug. 2009. Web. 2 March 2010.

---. "Ruby Glover 1929-2007." Mobtown Beat. Baltimore *City Paper* 31 Oct. 2007. Web. 2 March 2010.

HWF. Review. *This is Ethel Ennis*. "On the Record." *The Negro Digest* Dec. 1964: 42. Online. Google Books. Web. 2 March 2010.

"I've Got That Feeling." Video. Scopitones. *YouTube. Web. 2 Mar. 2010.*

Jenkins, Willard. *Ennis, Anyone? Live at Montpelier*. Album Review. "The Independent Ear." *Open Sky Jazz. Web. 2 Mar. 2010.*

---. *If Women Ruled the World*. Album Review. March 1999. *JazzTimes.com*. Web. 2 Mar. 2010.

Kravetz, Sallie. *Ethel Ennis: The Reluctant Jazz Star*. Baltimore: Gateway, 1984. Print.

Marvincomet. "They Can't Take That Away From Me." Video. *YouTube*. Dec. 2008. Web. 2 Mar. 2010.

McCabe, Bret. "Against the Grain: Ethel Ennis Cuts Her Own Path Through Her Life and Music." Baltimore *City Paper* 14 Oct. 2009. Web. 2 Mar. 2010.

Miller, Dean. "Ethel Ennis Releases the Power, Polish of Jazz." *The Spokesman* 12 Aug. 1990. Web. 2 Mar. 2010.

Peters, Ida. "Ethel Ennis: Doing Things Her Own Way with Soft Power." 6 Dec. 1980. *Baltimore Afro-American. Web. 2 Mar. 2010.*

Poussaint, Renee. Interview with Ethel Ennis. Visionary Videos. 2002-2009. *NVLP's Oral History Archive*. National Visionary Leadership Project (NVLP). Web. 2 Mar. 2010.

Pryor-Trusty, Rosa and Tonya Taliaferro. *African-American Entertainment in Baltimore*. Charleston, SC: Arcadia Publishing, 2003

Pryor-Trusty, Rosa. "Ruby Glover, Baltimore's Sweet, Sweet Godmother of Jazz." *Afro-American* 22 October 2007. Qtd. in *Chicken Bones: A Journal for Literary and Artistic African American Themes*. Baltimore Index Page. "Jazz Singer Ruby Glover—The Little Giant of Pennsylvania Avenue—Passes Over," by Alvin Kirby Brunson. Web. 2 Mar. 2010.

"Ruby Glover." Video. MySpace.com. Web. 2 Mar. 2010.

"Ruby Inez Jackson Glover." Abc2news.com . Web. 2 Mar. 2010.

Schaaf, Elizabeth. Interview with Ethel Ennis. *Sounds & Stories: The Musical Life of Baltimore's African-American Community*. Peabody Institute of Johns Hopkins University. Web. 2 Mar. 2010.

---. Interview with Ruby Glover. *Sounds & Stories: The Musical Life of Baltimore's African-American Community*. Peabody Institute of Johns Hopkins University. Web. 2 Mar. 2010.

Schoettler, Carl. "Where Jazz Still Echoes." Baltimore *Sun* 8 Dec. 2002. Web. 2 Mar. 2010.

Shapiro, Stephanie. "Jazz Singer Dies After Stroke Onstage." Baltimore *Sun* 22 Oct. 2007. Web. 2 March 2010.

Stella. Comments. "Jazz Singer Dies After Onstage Stroke." *Topix.com*. 4 Mar. 2010. Web.

Sweeney, Gary. *The Midnight Palace Forum. Web. 2 Mar. 2010.*

Thomas, Martha. "Ruby Glover's Baltimore: The Late Jazz Great in Her Own Voice." 14 March 2008. *SmartWoman online. Web. 2 Mar. 2010.*

"Tour de Force by Leading Female Jazz Singer." *If Women Ruled the World*. Album Review by Customer. Amazon.com. Web. 2 Mar. 2010.

Walker, Miranda. "Lady's Day: Competition Honors Billie Holiday's Legacy By Helping Her Successors." [2000]. Baltimore City *Paper* [2000]. Web. 2 Mar. 2010.

WBALTV.com 11 TV Hill. 28 Oct. 2007. Web. 2 Mar. 2010.

Zandler, Richard. *Ennis Anyone?* Album Liner Notes. Recordings. Montpelier Cultural Arts Center. Prince George's County Dept. of Recreation and Parks. Web. 2 Mar. 2010.

Ruby Glover Discography

In an obituary article by Alvin Kirby Brunson, there is brief mention of a 2000 recording of "God Bless the Child." In the Elizabeth Schaaf interview for Sounds and Stories, *Ruby mentions recording in her youth for Columbia Records. An article by Jocelyn Anthony in* The 501 *(an online newspaper of Towson University) reports Ruby's son Aaron Perkins saying that in the summer of 2007, Ruby was "in the studio and recorded several tracks that should be released next year"; however, no further information could be obtained about these recordings. In a 1961 interview with George Collins, Ruby was asked if she had made any recordings, and she answered, "No, only dubs. You know, cutting tapes to be used as background music. In a telephone conversation on March 4, 2010, Ruby's stepson Aaron Perkins told this writer that the family has some reel-to-reel tapes of Ruby's singing, as well as some "vinyls" from the 1950s. I've found no evidence of recordings of Ruby Glover's performances in the records of Peabody Institute, nor in the catalog of the University of Maryland Performing Arts Library, nor in WorldCat, a catalog of all materials held in libraries worldwide, nor in the Library of Congress Catalog, nor in the collections of the Reginald Lewis Museum, nor in an online discography of Capital Records.*

:::::

Ethel Ennis Discography

Lullabies for Losers. Jubilee, JLP1021, 1955.
  Features pianist Hank Jones and drummer Kenny Clarke.

Change of Scenery. Capitol T941, 1957.

Have You Forgotten? Capitol T 1078, 1/1/58.

This Is Ethel Ennis. RCA. Re-released 2007 by POKER.

Ethel Ennis Sings. Jubilee, JGM5024, 1963.

Once Again. RCA, 1964. Re-release, Cloud 9 Records, 2004.

Eyes for You. RCA, 1964.

Once Again, Ethel Ennis. RCA, 1964

My Kind of Waltztime. RCA, 1965

Ten Sides of Ethel Ennis. BASF, 1973. *God Bless the Child.* RCA. Camden Re-issues, 1973 and 1980. *Ethel: Live at King of France Tavern.* ENE Productions, 1980.

Ethel Ennis. Hildner Productions, 1993. Recorded at Skyline Studios, New York from July 17-19, 1993.

Ethel Ennis (vocals), Marc Copland, Stefan Scaggiari (piano), Drew Gress (bass), Paul Hildner (drums). This is an album of ballads, sung by Ethel with a wistful and worldly-wise attitude. Her voice whispers, croons, pauses to reflect, and is always sensitive to each nuance of emotion.

If Women Ruled the World. Savoy Jazz, 1998.

This album covers 12 pop and jazz songs written by women—including Ethel's own "Hey You." On this song, Ethel begins with a few measures of bluesy humming to a guitar accompaniment, then shares a reflection in spoken word: "You know, many years ago, I asked myself, 'Ethel, are you doin' what you want to do?' And guess what? The answer is still—yes!" She goes on to ask the listener, "Are you doin' what you really want to do?" Ethel gives a spunky, assertive rendition of the title song (by Joan Armatrading) claiming that under the rule of women, the world would be a more peaceful place to live, while Ingrid Jensen's trumpet provides a sassy contrapuntal commentary. Ethel's buttery-smooth voice and tasty jazz styling make this album a rich listening experience. It features Jensen on trumpet and Jane Ira Bloom on saxophone. Pianist Marc Copeland is credited with the arrangements. Other personnel include guitarist John Abercrombie, bassist Drew Gress, and drummers Dennis Chambers and Billy Hart.

Women of Substance. Savoy Jazz, 2003.

This collection of female Jazz vocals from 1945 to 2002 includes one track of Ethel Ennis, singing "God Bless the Child."

Change of Scenery/Have You Forgotten? EMI Music Distribution, 1999.

Ennis Anyone? (Live at Montpelier Cultural Arts Center). Jazzmount, 2005.

Personnel: Stef Scaggiari, piano; Ryan Diehl, drums; Mark Russell, bass. Winner of Washington Area Music Association Award for Best Jazz Recording of 2005. Reviewer Willard Jenkins of Open Sky Jazz writes: "This . . . warm voice of vast experience delivers a 12-track program of largely standards with great aplomb and abundant good humor. Who else could successfully pull off a lyric about an exterminator's visit ("Mr. Roachman Blues")? Great humor is one of [Ethel Ennis's] hallmarks; dig the classy intro monologue to her beautiful reading of "Everything Must Change."

Benny Goodman Yale University Archives, Vol. 2: 1957-1964 CDs (2009). Nimbus Records, 2009.

Includes Ethel on some tracks.

Hank Levy

"Hank can take a group of average music students and turn them into a really great band. I think one of the greatest assets he has as a motivator is the fact that he's so excited about the music himself. They see him up there becoming the music."

7 Giving Jazz a "Kick In The Rear End"
by Bob Jacobson

After touring briefly with a nationally-known big band, saxophonist Hank Levy returned to Baltimore in 1953. Following the path of many a jazz performer before and since, he then worked full-time at a non-musical job, happy to perform, compose and arrange as sidelines. But a dozen years later Levy would emerge as a key figure in the movement to take jazz in a new direction. Then he would become a pioneer in college-level jazz education, enriching the jazz scene in Baltimore and beyond for decades to come.

Henry Levy began singing, dancing and playing the accordion in amateur shows at downtown Baltimore's Hippodrome Theater at age six or seven and wrote his first composition at age ten or twelve. At City College High School his Dixieland band, The Collegians, was known for his arrangement of "The Dipsy Doodle." Levy also led the seven-piece Henry Levy Dance Band and ten-piece Melodiers. With most professional musicians serving in World War II, Levy became a tenor sax player in a big band led by trumpeter Ken Hanna. In 1942, Hanna began writing arrangements for Stan Kenton's popular California-based big band. Levy had the thrill of playing Hanna's charts before they were sent to Kenton.

Graduating from high school in 1945, Levy then spent three years in the service, including study at the Navy School of Music, followed by attendance at College of William and Mary, Peabody Conservatory and Catholic University. On a 1953 visit to Ken Hanna in California, the two went to a Stan Kenton rehearsal. Kenton did Levy the favor of playing some of his arrangements, seemed encouraging but said they weren't for him. Kenton felt that his composers and arrangers needed to spend time with the band, getting to know the players' musical personalities. When baritone saxophonist Bob Gioga gave his notice during the rehearsal, Ken Hanna recommended Levy for the vacant position. Levy had never played baritone sax and had five minutes to prepare. Four decades later he remembered his feelings at that moment with characteristic humor. Naming band members Lee Konitz, Maynard Ferguson, Conte Condoli, Bill Holman and Frank Rosolino, among others, Levy said, "I tell you, I was about to soil my Pampers!" (Reese 6) Nevertheless, he passed the test, then set out on the road. The band had only three days off in six months. Levy missed his girlfriend back home and his family wanted him to help run their business. Just before the band left for Europe, Levy gave his notice. But the connection between Levy and Kenton was far from severed. Over a decade later it would have a profound impact on the shape of jazz.

From the 1950s to late '60s Levy helped run the Independent Beef Company. Started by his grandfather in 1888, it had grown into a large store of five departments on Baltimore's "Antique Row." A 1962 newspaper article, "Champagne Connoisseur Has Taste for Jazz," indicates the niche Levy carved out, describing a wine-buying trip to France. Throughout all his years at the store, however, he was playing, composing, and arranging for one or another "kicks band," playing primarily for enjoyment and their own musical development. Then in 1959 his friend from the Kenton band, guitarist Sal Salvador, asked

Levy to write for him. Two Levy arrangements appeared on Salvador's 1960 album, *The Beat for a New Generation.*

From its inception through the 1940s, jazz had been written and played almost exclusively in 2/4 or 4/4 time (two or four beats to the bar). Waltz time, 3/4, was considered an "odd meter." Fats Waller's "Jitterbug Waltz" was one of the few exceptions. In the 1950s a handful of waltzes entered the jazz repertoire and drummer Max Roach began experimenting with other odd meters. The meter barrier was shattered in 1959 with the immense popularity of Dave Brubeck's album *Time Out*, including Paul Desmond's chart-topping "Take Five" in 5/4 time and other tunes in 6/4, 7/4 and 9/8. Shortly thereafter Hank Levy began listening to odd meters in the music of Dvorak, Stravinsky and Bartok. He was impressed with Johnny Richards's big band pieces in 5/4 and 7/4 on Stan Kenton's 1962 album *Adventures in Time*. Around 1964 or '65, Levy tried his hand at writing an arrangement of the jazz standard "Speak Low" in 5/4 for his kicks band. Recalling this experience, Levy said, "It just sounded so abnormal. It was terrible. . . . They couldn't do it. And I couldn't either. It just threw me for a loop" (Arganian 176). But Levy persisted. The band started playing Levy's odd meter charts in Baltimore clubs, including the Mardi Gras.

Levy believed jazz needed "a kick in the rear end," warned that big band jazz was in danger of stagnation, and referred to the "shackles" of traditional time signatures. He told Kenton biographer Lillian Arganian, "What's great about these odd meters is that you can't use the usual licks . . . the clichés. They don't fit. It forces you to create. And that's good. Jazz needs that kind of thing" (177).

In 1965, Levy learned from Glenn Stuart, a member of his kicks band, about someone on the West Coast experimenting along similar lines. Stuart had moved to California to play lead trumpet for Don Ellis's new band. Ellis's experience as a jazz trumpeter covered a wide range, from the big bands of Charlie Barnet and Maynard Ferguson to recordings with Charles Mingus, Eric Dolphy, and George Russell. His interest in odd meters began while doing graduate work in ethnomusicology at UCLA, where he had studied with Indian sitar and tabla player Harihar Rao. Together they formed the Hindustani Jazz Sextet, opening for the Grateful Dead and Big Brother and the Holding Company at the Fillmore West. Stuart encouraged Levy to send charts to Ellis for his emerging big band. Levy's "Passacaglia and Fugue" (actually in 3/4 and 4/4) was on the program when Ellis's band created a sensation at the 1966 Monterey Jazz Festival and also appeared the next year on the album *Live at Monterey*. Ellis, whom Levy described later as "beyond creative" and "very experimental," encouraged Levy to branch out. "When I got with Don, I knew damn well if I wanted to stay with that band, I was going to have to lose some of my inhibitions. 'Cause I was an inhibited writer, really, at one time, and Don was the one who helped me over that. He would say, 'Gotta stick your neck out, every time you put a note on paper,'" Levy said two decades later (176). Ten Levy pieces in odd meters would appear on seven more Don Ellis albums, and "Chain Reaction," from Ellis's album *Connection*, was chosen for the *Smithsonian Collection of Classic Jazz*.

In 1968 Levy was still working in his family's market, but that would soon change. Towson State College, in suburban Baltimore, needed to fill a vacant position: jazz ensemble director. The college's clarinet instructors recommended Levy. According to Dr. Joseph

Briscuso, the teaching load of 12 contact hours sounded good to Levy. Working up to 16 hours per day in the market, Levy thought this meant hours per day. In fact the offer was for 12 hours per week. Briscuso says, "He thought he'd died and gone to heaven" (Briscuso). Dr. Gil Brundgart, chair of the Music Department at that time, adds, "Hank was so eager to get out of the family business. At Thanksgiving he was up to his eyeballs in hams" (Brundgart). Levy soon sold the business. At Towson he was designated Visiting Guest Lecturer but was required to finish his college degree, which he did within two years. Levy then became a full-time educator, leading as many as five jazz ensembles and teaching composition.

Within a year, Levy took the Towson big band to the Intercollegiate Jazz Festival's Eastern competition at Quinnipiac College in Connecticut. They didn't win, but their performance of Levy's odd meter pieces attracted the interest of honored guest Stan Kenton, an early advocate of jazz education for youth (Kenton had conducted clinics for high school and college students since 1959). Already a fan of Don Ellis, Kenton wanted to move his band into music that was "new, fresh and exciting" (Arganian 180). He invited Levy to bring odd-meter material to his band's rehearsal in Boston. "I spent a week in Boston. Those odd meters are hard to get into, especially for the professional musician who is ingrained in 4/4," Levy told Kenton biographer William Lee. "We did two three-hour rehearsals and didn't get past introductions. I was petrified in front of the band, and the band was infuriated that they couldn't just cut the charts down. Finally, in desperation, I played tapes of the Towson College band to demonstrate. I felt like hell doing it, but it was really my last chance" (Lee 266).

One of Kenton's trumpeters, Mike Vax, remembers,

> The first tune we tried was "Chiapas," and we sounded like a junior high school band. About the only one who felt comfortable with it at all was John Van Ohlen, and he was 'weird enough' to have made a trip to India. . . .We were such neophytes that at one point I played a figure completely backwards and the whole band followed me. . . . Hank was a great teacher and got us clapping rhythmic figures and we actually performed "Chiapas" that night. . . . Hank's charts never got easier, but we did get more used to playing them, and I for one really enjoyed the challenge of 'Time' music. Willie (Maiden, baritone saxophone) kept grumbling and rewriting his charts in 4/4, but he too sounded great on them (Vax.)

Levy credits Kenton's support as crucial to this transformation. "I'm sure if it had been anyone but Stan, I wouldn't have lasted ten minutes. He knew what he liked and whatever it took to get it, Stan stuck with it" (Lee 266). The band's initial resistance to odd meters was later immortalized in their Band Prayer, a parody on The Lord's Prayer, which read in part, "Lead us not into time changes, but deliver us from Levy." Ultimately, 15 of Levy's odd meter composition/arrangements would appear on Kenton albums, contributing significantly to the sound of the Kenton band in the '70s.

Levy continued using Towson State College's jazz ensembles as his odd-meter laboratory. With a repertoire of Levy's unusually-metered composition/arrangements, the ensembles had a unique, exciting sound, enabling them to win the Intercollegiate Festival's Eastern competition each year from 1970 to 1972. Pioneering jazz educator Clem DeRosa, one of the judges, says, "If you closed your eyes, you forgot that they were college students, because the performance was always magnificent" (A HEAD OF TIME). Drummer Dave Gimbel remembers that "People would go totally nuts. It was a completely different kind of thing." After three consecutive wins, Towson was invited to play but not compete. One year they played behind Dizzy Gillespie on Chico O'Farrill's suite, "Three Afro-Cuban Moods." Another year they backed trombonist Bill Watrous. Alumnus Ray Disney remembers, "He told us we did just as professional a job as his own band could have done." Towson's jazz ensemble was the only college band invited to play for the opening of the Kennedy Center in 1971. That same year they played Levy's "Opus for Overextended Jazz Ensemble" with the Baltimore Symphony Orchestra. In 1972 the ensemble recorded its first album, a double LP of Levy's odd-meter originals. Stan Kenton was so enthusiastic about the band that he financed and sold the album through his own company, Creative World. One of the album's trumpeters, Gil Rathel, later with Don Ellis's band, recalls Levy's proudly playing the album for Ellis's musicians. Pianist Milcho Leviev's response was, "This is not a college band. This is just great music" (Rathel). In 1975 the National Association for Jazz Education included Towson on its compilation of seven college bands, *Project One*. The jazz ensemble's second album, *2+2=5*, was sold as a play-along album in the Music Minus One series.

Towson State College was becoming nationally known, not only through the jazz ensemble's achievements, but from Levy's teaching in Stan Kenton's summer clinics and his pieces on Kenton's and Don Ellis's albums. In a "right place, right time" moment, Levy was traveling with Kenton's band just when its leader was looking for a site for his Eastern clinic. Towson, boasting a new Center for the Arts, was chosen, and hosted Kenton clinics throughout the '70s. Ellery Eskelin, today an internationally-known saxophonist and band leader, was one of the clinic's students from age 13. He recalls,

> Hank was on the faculty for the workshops so I got to see him in action for a number of years before I actually enrolled at Towson. He was always inspiring and related very well to us young musicians. He had a great positive energy that was infectious. I liked the fact that Hank wrote all his own music for the Towson band. As such, the band had a sound of its own. That experience was responsible for me choosing to go to Towson in 1977 (Eskelin).

Baltimore saxophonist Greg Thompkins says that he attended so many Towson Jazz Ensemble concerts while in high school in Anne Arundel County that Ellery Eskelin thinks they went to college together (Thompkins). Jim McFalls, currently director of jazz ensembles at Towson, remembers being brought to a Towson rehearsal in 1974 from southeastern Pennsylvania by his high school music teacher. "I was blown away by the level of musicians, stunned" (McFalls). Dr. David Marchand remembers that Levy frequently guest-conducted high school bands, adding to the influx of students to Towson. Students transferred to Towson from Morgan State, Peabody Conservatory, jazz powerhouse North Texas State, and several other colleges. Levy, called into the office of the Dean of Fine Arts, was told, "Hank, we don't want to become known as a jazz college." Levy's response? "I'm sorry, you're too late" (A Head of Time).

In 1977, Don Ellis told an interviewer, "I think today, at least in the U.S. . . . .every young musician coming up is very familiar with all odd time signatures and expects to be doing music that utilizes them. In fact, I would say that in ninety-nine percent of all the college and high school situations they are playing music that uses odd time signatures." No doubt this is an over-estimate, but odd meters were being played all over the country at both high school and college levels. For example, our editor, Mark Osteen, played six Hank Levy charts in the University of Montana Jazz Workshop, from 1973-76. The trend was fueled by the inclusion of dozens of Levy tunes on Ellis and Kenton albums, the *Music Minus One* album and the appearance of Don Ellis's *New Rhythm Book* in 1972 and Hank Levy's *The Time Revolution* in 1973. The latter, published by Stan Kenton's Creative World, includes etudes and seven of Levy's tunes.

Throughout the '70s Levy developed great ensembles, recording an album with the top band every year. In his teaching style Levy managed to combine a relaxed approach with high expectations. Drummer Steve Ashcraft, who today leads the Hank Levy Legacy Band, remembers, "He was not the kind of teacher that would say 'Do it this way or get out.' He would give you a chance to read it over and he pretty much relied on your own musicianship to be able to put it together and to make it sound musical" (Ashcraft). Ellery Eskelin recalls a frequent Levy exhortation: "You're playing too pretty. You have to go out and roll around in the gutter" (Eskelin). Trombonist Bernie Robier, who had actually gone AWOL from his Army base north of Baltimore to hear Levy's band at the Mardi Gras in the mid-'60s, adds,

> You don't become comfortable with Hank's odd meter writing at first sitting. It doesn't happen in a week. It doesn't happen in a month. But Hank had a way of making you feel extremely comfortable. There was only that pressure you put on yourself. He expected a lot from you but because of the respect that everyone had for Hank, that was nothing compared to what you ultimately began to expect of yourself (Robier).

Jim McFalls says that Levy "wouldn't tolerate anything less than what he wanted the charts to sound like. That's why they were so good. He didn't accept anything less than a professional level. His ensembles were incredibly musical." Bill Warfield adds, "Hank can take a group of average music students and turn them into a really great band. I think one of the greatest assets he has as a motivator is the fact that he's so excited about the music himself. They see him up there becoming the music."

Saxophonist Brad Collins recounts Levy's emphasis on work within each section of the band, with older sax players teaching odd meter songs in the practice rooms. "He would encourage more experienced players to bring new players along," citing his older section mates— Glenn Cashman, Ellery Eskelin, Jay Davidson and Joe Colliano. "I always wanted to be like these guys. They challenged me to learn, day in, day out" (Collins). Soon Collins became a mentor to Greg Thompkins.

Many alumni feel that Levy and Towson provided unique experiences in their musical development. While Levy was criticized by some faculty members for disproportionate attention to his own music in the college's ensembles, trombonist and future Grammy winner Douglas Purviance sees that as a plus, "because it was just such beautiful music and cutting edge stuff." Trumpeter Bill Warfield, future big band leader and composer, concurs. "Being in the band was a composition lesson. Hank brought in first drafts. You got to see his process, how he worked with every instrument, a very Kenton-like style," and adds that Levy demonstrated a sense of drama in his compositions. Warfield also had the experience of Levy's writing the piece "Stillness Runs Deep" to highlight his soloing ability. "That's very special, for someone with a national reputation to write a special piece of music for a college student," he recalls, adding that he wouldn't have had this experience with any other band (Warfield). Though previous student albums included only Levy's pieces, the 1979 album included a composition by bass student Drew Gress, who had come to Towson specifically because of Levy's writing. Towson provided other unique opportunities by hosting the Eastern Trombone Workshop (co-founded by faculty member John Melick) and the Single Reed Clinic. Saxophonist Glenn Cashman, who succeeded Levy in the '90s, remembers "having my then idol Phil Woods bring me to the front of the stage to trade fours with him without prior notice." He also remembers that "playing the Supersax charts with Frank Rosolino was a thrill. Those experiences with jazz legends were very important at the time."

Levy inspired tremendous devotion. Beyond the three or four hours of ensemble practice on weekdays, students added rehearsals at 9:30 a.m. on Sundays. Guitarist Brian Kooken remembers practicing eight hours per day to record "Night Scheme" on one of the ensemble's albums (Kooken). Alumni and fellow faculty also speak warmly about Levy on the personal level, with descriptors like "one of the guys," "absolutely unpretentious," "humble," "a second father," and "a class guy." Many became his friend. Drew Gress says, "I think it's really cool, like an intergenerational thing. You don't get to call someone who's twenty-five or thirty years your elder a friend very often, certainly not at a young age" (Gress). Many alumni remember Levy joining them at the Left Bank Jazz Society's concerts at The Famous Ballroom. Several would also be drawn into Levy's passion for golf.

A 1978 *News American* article, "Towson Jazzman Levy All Smiles," profiles a truly contented man, with one exception: "While proud of Towson's music program, Levy said he would like the school to begin more specialized jazz courses". Many students were saying the same thing. "Something had to be done to provide an outlet for these kids," says Dr. David Marchand, who became chairman of the Music Department in 1979. Greg Hatza was brought in to lead smaller ensembles, develop a piano course and other curricula. Some faculty opposed development of the jazz program, but in 1983 a degree program in jazz and commercial studies was established.

Levy's music would be dealt a double blow with the deaths of his two main collaborators, Don Ellis, in 1978, and Stan Kenton, in 1979. Without their concerts, clinics and recordings, the visibility of Levy's work dimmed. Jazz educator and historian Jeff Sultanof, who remembers seeing Levy selling his own charts at the International Association for Jazz Education conference, says that within five years few college bands were playing his music (Sultanof). With chronic heart problems, Levy retired from Towson in 1991 but still led an alumni big band. In 1997 he rehearsed the Army's Jazz Ambassadors for their album *The Legacy of Hank Levy*. In 2001 the Hank Levy Alumni Band performed and recorded a tribute concert at Levy's assisted living residence. Later that year they played "Quintessence" and "A Time for Love" at his funeral.

What is Hank Levy's legacy? In Dick Slade's documentary on Levy, A HEAD OF TIME, *Ahead of Time*, Maynard Ferguson says, "Hank Levy, the guy that should have been Duke Ellington, Count Basie, Stan Kenton, Maynard Ferguson. He really should have been one of us but he was so dedicated to music education and was fantastic at it." Levy had been invited by Lalo Schifrin to write music in Hollywood but preferred to stay at Towson. One result of that commitment is the impressive numbers of jazz musicians currently active in the Baltimore area who studied at the school. Many of Levy's students also went on to the big bands of Stan Kenton, Don Ellis, and the military. Bill Warfield and Glenn Cashman are among the alumni now working in jazz education at the university level (Warfield at Lehigh, Cashman at Colgate); Ellery Eskelin, Drew Gress, and Douglas Purviance are all renowned jazz performers.

Another aspect of Hank Levy's legacy is the breadth and quality of his compositions and arrangements—at least 118 for big bands and at least 40 arrangements of jazz standards. Regarding his work in odd meters, Levy once said, "I wanted to write a blues in 5 or 7 that sounded like the blues in 4, or to write a bossa nova in 9 but make it sound like it was in the traditional form" (*A HEAD OF TIME*). This he certainly achieved. Pianist Milcho Leviev, referring to Levy's 5/4 piece "Simplogic," remembers, "He had made it to sound like in 4/4, like an ordinary Count Basie type of thing" (A Head of Time). In the same documentary, trombonist MSG Lew Chapman of the Jazz Ambassadors says, "I never knew 13/8 could groove so hard." Pianist Rich Collier comments, "Fellow composers always said they wished they could write counterpoint the way he did. He was a great harmonic and contrapuntal writer; some beautiful melodies too" (Collier). To Bill Warfield, "His writing sounds just as fresh now as it did in 1968" (Warfield). Jim McFalls says, "The entire body of work of Hank Levy, they're all pristine, they're all great charts . . . some epic stuff too."

The Baltimore-based Hank Levy Legacy Band, mostly non-alumni, perpetuates his music, as does the Don Junker Band in the Washington, D.C. suburbs. Most teachers who had contact with Hank include his charts in their students' concerts. Levy's "Opus for Overextended Jazz Ensemble" has been performed by the symphony at Lehigh University. Levy's music has been used in several European films. HankLevyJazz, LLC also promotes his legacy.

Trumpeter Greg Reese, commenting on Levy, Ellis and Kenton, says, "Their work allowed people to see odd times as not so odd. Players are used to hearing and playing it now" (Reese). Bob Curnow, former Kenton arranger who sells Levy's charts through Sierra Music, talks about how odd meter music was "in the air" in the early 1970s, speculating that this may be the source of odd meter compositions by Pat Metheny and Lyle Mays, both in college then (Curnow). The list of artists working in odd meters today is substantial, though the number applying it to big bands is still rather small (e.g., Maria Schneider and Bob Mintzer).

Asked to identify jazz trends in the 2000s for the January, 2010 issue of *DownBeat*, saxophonist Eric Alexander says, "People are getting a kick out of playing alternative time signatures other than 4/4 and 3/4—that is all college musicians want to do." Hank Levy's music is just waiting to be rediscovered.

NOTES

The author would like to thank those quoted above, and Anthony Agostinelli, Lillian Arganian, Jim Dilts, Bill Kalkman, Stewart Levy of HankLevyJazz, LLC, and Dick and Ruth Slade.

Works Cited

A HEAD OF TIME... Ahead of Time. Dir. Dick Slade. Audio Visual Artists, 1999. DVD.

Arganian, Lillian. *Stan Kenton: The Man and His Music*. East Lansing: Artistry P, 1989. Print.

Ashcraft, Steve. Telephone interview. 8 Feb. 2010.

Briscuso, Joseph. Telephone interview. 28 Jan. 2010.

Brundgart, Gil. Telephone interview. 28 Jan. 2010.

Cashman, Glenn. "Re.: Hank Levy." Message to the author, 29 Jan. 2010. E-mail.

Collier, Rich. Telephone interview. 5 Feb. 2010.

Collins, Brad. Telephone interview. 2 Feb. 2010.

Curnow, Bob. Telephone interview. 8 Feb. 2010.

Disney, Ray. Telephone interview. 7 Feb. 2010.

Eskelin, Ellery. "Re.: Hank Levy." Message to the author, 25 Nov. 2009. E-mail.

Gimbel, Dave. Telephone interview. 21 Feb. 2010.

Gress, Drew. Telephone interview. 29 Jan. 2010.

Kooken, Brian. Telephone interview. 2 Feb. 2010.

Lee, William. *Stan Kenton: Artistry in Rhythm*. Los Angeles: Creative P of Los Angeles. 1980. Print.

Marchand, David. Telephone interview. 18 Feb. 2010.

McFalls, Jim. Personal interview. 2 Dec. 2009.

Purviance, Douglas. Telephone interview. 19 Feb. 2010.

Rathel, Gil. Telephone interview. 23 Feb. 2010.

Reese, Greg. Liner notes. *The Legacy of Hank Levy*. U.S. Army Field Band, 1997. CD.

Robier, Bernie. Telephone interview. 8 Feb. 2010.

Sultanof, Jeff. "Re.: Hank Levy." Message to the author, 24 Feb. 2010. E-mail.

Thompkins, Greg. Telephone interview. 4 Jan. 2010.

"Towson Jazzman Levy All Smiles." *News American*. 9 April 1978, n. pag. Print.

Vax, Mike. The Network xxvi: n. pg. Web. Spring/Summer 2002.

Warfield, Bill. Telephone interview. 4 Feb. 2010.

DISCOGRAPHY

All albums are CD unless noted otherwise.

AS A PLAYER (with Stan Kenton, 1953)

Retrospective, 4 discs, Blue Note, 1992.

23 Degrees North, 82 Degrees West, Vipers Nest Gold, 1996.

Chris Connor, *All About Ronnie*, Giants of Jazz, 1998.

1950s Birdland Broadcasts, Jazz Band, 1998.

AS COMPOSER and/or ARRANGER:

STAN KENTON
(All have from one to four Levy composition/arrangements)

Live at Redlands University, Creative World, 2006 (originally 1970).

Tunes & Topics 1 (2 discs),Tantara, 2000 (originally 1971).

Live at Brigham Young University, Creative World, 2005 (originally 1971).

Sound of Kenton (2 discs), Hitchcock, 1999 (originally 1971).

Clearwater 72, Hitchcock, 2002 (originally 1972).

Live at Butler University, Creative World, 2005 (originally 1972).
    Includes Levy's "Samba Siete," "Indra," "Fringe Benefit," "Blues, Betwixt and Between," plus Ken Hanna's "Beeline East."

British Tour, Magic, 1998 (originally 1973).

Live at the London Hilton, vol. 1, Status, 1995 (originally 1973).

Live at the London Hilton, vol. 2, Status, 1994 (originally 1973).

Live at Carthage College, vol. 1, Magic, 1994 (originally 1974).

Cologne Concert, vol. 2, Magic, 2000 (originally 1976).

Journey Into Capricorn, Creative World, 2005 (originally 1976).
    Includes "Pegasus," "90 Degrees Celsius" and "Journey Into Capricorn"; Kenton's last studio recording, with Towson alumnus Douglass Purviance on bass trombone.

DON ELLIS (all have one or two Levy pieces)

Live at Monterey, EMD/Blue Note, 1998 (originally 1966).

Live in 3 2/3 /4 Time, Pacific Jazz, 2000 (originally 1967).
   Live at Pacific Jazz Festival and Shelly's Manne-Hole; high-spirited performances in a great variety of styles, meters and moods; includes "Bossa Nueva Nova" and "Thetis"; Glenn Stuart is on seven tracks.

Electric Bath, Columbia/Legacy, 1998 (originally 1967).

Shock Treatment, Koch Jazz, 2001 (originally 1968).

Don Ellis at Fillmore (2-LP). 1970.

Tears of Joy (2 discs), Wounded Bird, 2005 (originally 1970).

Connection, Wounded Bird, 2005 (originally 1972).
   Towson alumnus Gil Rathel plays trumpet and flugelhorn. Levy's "Chain Reaction," from this album, also appears on the Smithsonian Folkways 1996 CD Big Band Renaissance: Evolution of the Jazz Orchestra, *third volume in a five-volume set. Many consider it Levy's best piece and it was his personal favorite.*

Soaring (LP), PAUSA 1973; BASF, 1974.

TOWSON JAZZ ENSEMBLE

   The student big bands directed by Hank Levy made albums nearly every year from 1972 to 1991. Most are out of print. All Towson Jazz Ensemble albums since Levy's retirement in 1991 have at least one Levy arrangement.

Towson State College Jazz Ensemble (also known as "the yellow album") (double LP), 1972.
   All twelve tracks are Levy composition/arrangements, all in odd meters.

2 +2=5, Music Minus One, 1975.

With the Old Man in Mind, Towson University, 2001.
   Seven Levy composition/arrangements, including "A Rock Odyssey," "Abovo," "Thetis," and "Pegasus"; plus three Levy arrangements of jazz standards ("Green Dolphin Street," "Billie's Bounce," and "Little Girl Blue"); directed by Ron Diehl.

HANK LEVY ALUMNI BAND

Hank at Home, Sonority Records, 2001.
   Live album including seven Levy arrangements of standards and three Levy compositions/arrangements; produced by Towson alumnus Ray Disney.

An "Odd Time" Was Had By All (2 discs), Sonority, 2005.

OTHERS
(One or two Levy charts unless noted otherwise)

Sal Salvador, *The Beat for This Generation* (LP), Decca, 1960.

Stan Kenton Alumni Band, *50th Anniversary Celebration, Back to Balboa*, (5 discs), Mama, 1995.
   Two Levy originals, two arrangements of standards.

U.S. Army Jazz Ambassadors, *The Legacy of Hank Levy*, U.S. Army Field Band, 1997 (re-issued in 2007).
   Eight Levy originals, including "Whiplash," "Latintensity," "Chiapas," "Passacaglia and Fugue," and "Chain Reaction"; arrangements of "On Green Dolphin Street" and "A Time for Love," and a rare Levy composition with vocal ("Alone"). Levy himself rehearsed the band for this recording.

Chicago Metropolitan Jazz Orchestra, *Live & Screamin'*, Lakeshore Jazz, 1998.

Al Patacca, *The Best of the Al Patacca Orchestra* (2 discs), Sonority, 2005.
   Thirty-one tracks include five Levy composition/arrangements and 12 Levy arrangements of standards; personnel includes many Towson alumni; Patacca played trumpet with Buddy Rich, Don Ellis and Louie Bellson.

Mike Vax Big Band, *Next Stop: Live...On the Road*, Summit, 2005.

John Blount, *Better Days Ahead*, Sea Breeze, 2007.

Gary Bartz

*"'For me he was just a local saxophonist; I didn't
know he was one of the greatest players in the
world'"*

8 Blues Chronicles
by Geoffrey Himes

Gary Bartz's career is a story of great promise, great risk, tragic fall, long silence, and redemption.

He arrived with great fanfare as one of the brightest young saxophone voices of the late '60s, picking up poll awards while he apprenticed with Max Roach, Art Blakey, and Miles Davis. He then gambled on an ambitious fusion of jazz, African music, R&B, political commentary, vocals, and electric instruments on his solo albums in the '70s. Those records cost him the critical capital he had accumulated and failed to bring him the commercial payoff he desired. Bitterly, he retreated into a long period of silence for most of the '80s until he finally reemerged as a mainstream jazz player with a richer, more mature version of the saxophone voice that had attracted such acclaim in the first place.

The roots of Bartz's story can be found in his Baltimore childhood. Though he left for New York when he was 17, the saxophonist regularly returns to his hometown (though "not often enough, according to my mother," he says) (Bartz 2002). For it was in Maryland that he first forged his love affair with jazz—and like many romances, this one brought as much pain and disappointment as joy and triumph.

On a chilled sunny day in February, 2002, Bartz returns once more to Baltimore. He pulls over to the curb in the 1200 block of Pennsylvania Avenue in his black Jeep SUV. The 61-year-old jazz musician sits in the front seat, wearing gold-rimmed glasses, a black velvet blazer over a white T-shirt, and a frizzy salt-and-pepper ponytail. When I stare out the window, I see housing projects, schools and take-out soul-food joints, but Bartz sees something different.

"Right there," he says, pointing at Furman Templeton Elementary School, "is where the Royal Theatre was. It was a big, beautiful theater with red velvet curtains, a fancy proscenium arch and a balcony. It was very exciting when I was a kid. I'd go down after school and I might see three complete shows before I left. One of my favorites was Louis Jordan because he was so funny and because he played the alto saxophone" (Bartz 2002).

He points at a bar called the Royal Casino and adds, "That used to be the Club Casino when it had live jazz. That's where I met Max Roach when I was 14. Max knew my parents, because my mother would often have the musicians over to the house for dinner, so he told me, 'If you ever come to New York, look me up.' Three years later I did, and he took care of me up there" (Bartz 2002).

Bartz eventually joined Roach's band. The Baltimore saxophonist also played with Miles Davis, Art Blakey, Charles Mingus, and McCoy Tyner between 1962 and 1973 before emerging as a bandleader himself. Over the course of 34 albums under his own name, he has established himself as one of the most distinctive voices on the alto and soprano saxophones that jazz has ever known. The music has taken him all over the world, but it all started in the patch of Baltimore between Coppin State University and Druid Hill Park.

Pennsylvania Avenue used to be the center of African-American culture in Baltimore. In a stretch of just a few blocks, theaters, nightclubs, restaurants, churches, political clubs, haberdasheries, barber shops, and beauty salons catered to the tastes of black Maryland. Today the only sign of the remarkable music, dance, politics, and religion that once flourished here is the statue of Billie Holiday that stands in front of the Upton Courts housing project.

Bartz points at the housing project and says, "That's where the Comedy Club was. That was the biggest nightclub on the strip. The first time I heard Miles Davis, he was playing there. I sat in with Sonny Stitt there when I was 14. . . . It's sad to see Pennsylvania Avenue now," he laments. "We didn't realize it was culture, because we weren't taught that what we did was culture. Culture was what other people did. Just because it was in these little dives doesn't mean it wasn't valuable. When I went to Paris, I found the little dive where Edith Piaf was discovered and it's like a shrine. So why doesn't America preserve the little dives where jazz musicians were discovered?" (Bartz 2002).

Bartz has a love-hate relationship with Baltimore. On the one hand, it's the place where he fell in love with music, where he's had some of his best musical experiences, where he grew up, and where his mother and sister still live. On the other hand, he has never forgiven the city for the racism he experienced as a youngster or for the indifference the city has often shown to its greatest cultural achievement: jazz.

The saxophonist has similar feelings about the music industry. While he treasures his favorite records, he resents how the musicians who made them were usually treated like indentured servants who rarely saw the fruits of their labors. These conflicted feelings are manifested in Bartz's playing. At times his saxophone has the warm, romantic tone of Lester Young or Cannonball Adderley, a sound that caresses a melody the way one lover might another. At other times,

Bartz's horn grows as raspy and dissonant as John Coltrane's or Ornette Coleman's, lashing out at an unjust world. Bartz makes this shift not only within the same set but also within the same song, moving from tender to torrential so naturally that they seem two sides of the same coin.

Which they are. If one is to make emotionally honest music, one must be as open about one's anger as one's affection. Never trust a musician who only gives you half the picture. Bartz has always been a passionate player, asserting his themes and variations with a rhythmic boldness. And in the years since he made his recording comeback, he has pared away the extra notes and filled his solos with strategic pauses that leave the crucial notes in stark relief.

Bartz makes a left off Pennsylvania and drives down Fulton Avenue, where his mother Elizabeth and his sister Tora still live next-door to one another. The pink-formstone rowhouses with metal awnings prompt more memories. "My father's youngest brother, Uncle Leon, would go to New York and come back with the slickest clothes and latest records," Bartz recalls. "Everyone called him 'Sharp.' One day when I was six, he brought back a Charlie Parker record, and when I heard it I said, 'Whatever that person is doing, I want to do it, too.' Every Christmas from then on, I tried to convince my parents to get me a saxophone, and finally when I was 11, they rented me one."

"I could hear a record or band on stage, and I could play what I heard on the saxophone. We had to learn by ear, because there were no schools then for this kind of music. When people said, 'Oh, he's a natural,' they meant he could hear really well. I was a natural" (Bartz 2002).

Bartz looks out at a group of young men leaning against a boarded-up store and at an older woman struggling to carry groceries home.

"Cyrus Chestnut once asked me where I grew up," Bartz says of the Baltimore-born pianist, "and when I said, 'Pennsylvania and Fulton,' he said, 'Oh, my Lord.' It's a tough place now and it was a tough place then."

"We were the third black family to move into the neighborhood, so we saw the whole white flight. Druid Hill Park was two blocks away, and it had black tennis courts and white tennis courts, a black swimming pool and a white swimming pool. It was a very degrading system, and I was very outspoken, so I got into a lot of trouble. I was in one of the first desegregated classes at City College, and they scheduled the prom for Carlin's Drive-In, which didn't allow blacks. So I couldn't go to my own prom. A scuffle broke out over that one" (Bartz 2002).

He drives around his old neighborhood and comes to Pennsylvania and Baker, the site of the Tijuana Club, where Charlie Parker played just before his death. "I was too young to get in," Bartz notes, "so I stood outside and listened. Around the corner was the Peyton Place, where I saw Coltrane and Miles. Don't get me wrong; this neighborhood had its good points—great people and great music."

"One day I was at the Royal Theatre, and I saw this young kid walk up to the band and replace the pianist. I was only 14 at the time and this kid was only two years older than me, but he sounded so good. That gave me hope that maybe I could do it too. I found out his name was Albert Dailey, and later we lived together in New York. He's one of the greatest pianists I've ever heard."

"I cut my teeth as a musician at the Comedy Club. I used to sit in with Sonny Stitt, and that was an eye-opener, because he had no mercy on me. He showed me that if I was going to play this music, I was going to have to be serious about it. He let me know I had to keep my nose to the grindstone. That's how you learn this music, by being on the bandstand with your betters and watching how they handle solos, how they react to the audience." Further down on Fulton is the former office of the Black Musicians Union. Bartz nods at the building and comments, "But it was all segregated here when I was growing up. That's why I couldn't wait to get out" (Bartz 2002).

He was 17 when he moved to New York in 1958. "I wanted to be a world-class musician," Bartz explains, "and New York was where you had to go. In the 1800s you had to go to Vienna; in the 1900s, you had to go to New York. I enrolled in Juilliard, because I knew I didn't know my harmony and theory and I wanted to learn it. I gained an appreciation of classical music, but when I talked to my teachers about advanced jazz harmonies, they had no idea what I was talking about."

"But I loved New York. On Saturdays I would go to Birdland. On Sundays, I would visit Max Roach and Abbey Lincoln at their house on the Upper West Side. I'd play chess with Max all day, and Abbey would make us dinner. On Mondays, I'd go to Count Basie's club in Harlem. It was a great time" (Bartz 2002).

In 1960, Bartz's father Floyd bought a club, The North End Lounge, in East Baltimore at the corner of Gay Street and North Avenue. On the day I interview him, Gary Bartz drives there to discover that the boarded-up storefront has a "For Sale" sign on it. But he can still see the nightclub as it was in the early '60s, with dressed-up couples at the small tables, the single men lined up against the bar, the waitresses carrying trays of cocktails and pretzels, and on the bandstand, the likes of Lou Donaldson, Jack McDuff and George Benson.

"I started going back and forth between New York and Baltimore," he recounts, "so I could play in the house band at the North End as much as possible. Having a house gig is important, because it allows you to try things out without worrying about losing your job. Every entertainer from Frank Sinatra to Coleman Hawkins will admit you need a place to be bad without worrying about your job security."

"My dad did the booking, and he got to know all the musicians. In 1965, he found out that [saxophonist] John Gilmore was leaving Art Blakey & the Jazz Messengers to go back to Sun Ra after Art's gig at the North End. So my dad called me in New York and told me to come down so I could sit in. I did, and Lee Morgan, who was the straw boss in the band, liked me and convinced Art to hire me" (Bartz 2002).

Bartz had already played with the Charles Mingus Workshop and the Max Roach Band, but the saxophone chair in the Jazz Messengers—a slot previously occupied by Wayne Shorter, Jackie McLean, James Moody, Hank Mobley, Benny Golson and Lou Donaldson—solidified Bartz's reputation in the jazz world. In 1968, he joined McCoy Tyner's band. And in 1970, he got the call every jazz musician of his generation dreamed of.

"The phone rang," Bartz remembers, "and someone said, 'This is Miles. I'd like you to join my band.' I didn't think it was him, because all the musicians I knew were always imitating that raspy voice of his. So I said, 'Who is this, really? Is that you, Jack?' He started getting mad, so I figured out it really was him."

"Miles had just gone electric, and people either loved it or hated it; there was no middle ground. I liked it, because the musicians were so great. The band I joined included Miles, Keith Jarrett, Chick Corea, Dave Holland, Jack DeJohnette, and Airto Moreira. It was like being in the Super Bowl."

"Miles was a very caring bandleader," Bartz adds. "Once I stayed in L.A. after a tour and partied till I had spent all my money. I called Miles and he sent me the money so I could come home. If you were in his band, you were part of his family and always had a job. Art wasn't like that. Every time another sax player walked into the club, Art would say, 'How'd you like to join the Messengers?' and he'd say it loud enough to make sure you overheard" (Bartz 2002).

Bartz appeared on Miles Davis's *Live-Evil* album, but by 1973 he was ready to move on. The young saxophonist had released nine albums under his own name, and his combo, was doing well enough that he could support himself as a bandleader, which was his ultimate ambition.

His first two albums for Milestone, 1968's *Libra* with Albert Dailey, and 1969's *Another World* with Pharoah Sanders, were adventurous, rewarding projects in the John Coltrane/McCoy Tyner mode. But then Bartz made a fateful decision. Spurred on by his anger over the racism of his childhood and intoxicated by the Afrocentric cultural vanguard of Harlem in the early '70s, he tried to forge a fusion not just of rock and jazz as his employer Miles Davis had, but of African percussion, R&B vocals, jazz improvisation and political commentary. He formed a new band, the NTU Troop, as the vehicle for this ambitious project.

Unfortunately, Bartz lacked the skills to pull it off. He was a brilliant instrumentalist and improviser, but he wasn't much of a lyricist or vocalist—nor did he exercise much judgment over other people's vocals and lyrics. His knowledge of and love for R&B was deep, but his

194

understanding of African music was not. The instrumental passages on his nine NTU Troop albums for Milestone and Prestige suggest that this might have been one of the most adventurous, satisfying fusion bands of the day, but an awkward vocal section always comes along to ruin the mood. The hybrid music Bartz had in mind was a noble goal but his execution was not equal to his ambition.

Frustrated by the virulent attacks from jazz critics and by the lack of response from the record-buying public, he decided to shift gears again in 1975. He had known Norman Connors, a Philadelphia jazz drummer, since the mid-'60s. Connors had played with everyone from Archie Shepp to Pharoah Sanders, but in 1974 shifted from jazz to R&B, crafting soul ballads swaddled in synths and strings and sparked by the occasional short jazz solo—several of them played by Bartz. When the drummer broke through on the R&B charts (five top-30 singles between 1975 and 1977), Bartz was seduced by his stardom. This world was an entirely different world from the realm of smoky clubs, long car rides, and goateed record collectors; this was a world of concert halls, limousines and party girls. Convinced he could replicate the Connors formula of easygoing grooves, lush arrangements and guest singers, Bartz signed with Blue Note/Capitol Records and released 1977's *Music Is My Sanctuary* and 1978's *Love Affair*.

The results were disastrous. Not only did he alienate his former jazz fans with this middle-of-the-road soul music, but he also struck out with R&B radio. For the broad-minded fan, the problem was not the shift from jazz to soul so much as the tepid quality of the R&B. Years later, however, Bartz refuses to apologize for those records and fiercely defends his collaborations with Connors.

"I stand behind what I did," he says, a bit testily. "I love watching people dance and have a good time. R&B is as valid a part of African-American music as jazz. Backing up Phyllis Hyman on 'Betcha by Golly Wow' gave me the only gold record of my career, and she'll always be my favorite vocalist. No one put any restrictions on those solos I played" (Bartz 2002).

When I push him a bit, though, he does admit, "Yeah, money was a part of it. Someone once asked Marlon Brando, 'How can a great actor like you do a movie like Superman?' He said, 'I can make $3 million in two days and that can subsidize the work I really want to do.' But I still think those Capitol albums are valid music" (Bartz 2002).

Nonetheless, their commercial failure so soured Bartz on the record business that he didn't record again for another 10 years. "I'd put my heart and soul into a record," he explains, "and when I'd turn it in, the label would love it. But when they put it out, that was the last I'd hear about it. In an industry that can move 400,000 units in a week, do you expect me to believe they can only sell three a week of mine? Hell, I can sell 100 a night off the bandstand."

"I asked myself, 'How can they stay in business operating that way?' Then I realized they can take a tax loss on the record today and then 20 years down the line they'll make their money back, because jazz records always sell over time. A jazz record is like a certificate of deposit. So I asked myself, 'Do I want to give them any more of my material that I can't touch for 35 years?' No. I didn't want to be part of a business where the musicians are worth more when they're dead than when they're alive" (Bartz 1999).

As he says this, Bartz turns away from the old North End Lounge and the nearby stone archway to the Baltimore Cemetery. He drives west across North Avenue, stops to pay a bow-tied Nation of Islam peddler for some bean pies ("You can't get these in New Jersey," he notes), and then south on Maryland Avenue to Franklin Street and the former site of the Jazz Closet (Bartz 2002).

The building's bulging bay windows are covered with whitewashed plywood, but in the '80s, it was Baltimore's most important jazz venue. Owner Henry Baker, who ran a chain of beauty salons, kept the musical quality high by hiring Bartz to lead the house band. For the saxophonist, it was the perfect situation, providing him a steady gig out of the music-biz spotlight but allowing him to make the occasional trip to jazz festivals in Europe, Japan, and North America.

The house band featured Bob Butta on keyboards, Steve Williams on drums, and Geoff Harper on bass, with occasional cameos from friends of Bartz such as Woody Shaw. Butta, still an active performer in town, claims that Bartz's return to his hometown transformed the jazz scene in Baltimore.

"Baltimore was a Sonny Stitt town in those days, which was fine," Butta recalls, "but Gary moved the city out of bebop and into the modern era. Gary was a giant icon out of Baltimore, and he came back. He brought Baltimore music up to a New York recording level. And he did it without criticizing anyone; he shaped the music around each musician's ability and brought out that talent to its fullest. He had played with everybody—Art Blakey, Miles Davis, McCoy Tyner—and to bring those elements back to Baltimore was the greatest musical experience any of us had ever had."

"His knowledge of music is 80% street and 20% college. He's 100% self-confident. He knows who he is—that he's a heavy motherfucker—and there's never a doubt about it. His playing came out of Coltrane, especially on soprano. He approached the alto like Coltrane approached the tenor; he got these elongated lines on it, and the lines had a tenor quality. He transcended the bebop approach to the alto and moved it into Coltrane territory" (Bartz).

If Bartz brought New York's standards to Baltimore, the local musicians reinjected the gospel-soul of Baltimore jazz into Bartz's playing. It was a reminder that the musicians who chose to remain in Maryland were no less talented for having avoided the spotlight of Manhattan. It was a reminder of how much he himself had learned from older musicians such as pianist Albert Dailey and saxophonist Mickey Fields and of his own responsibility to pass that knowledge on to younger musicians such as saxophonist Antonio Hart and trumpeter Dontae Winslow.

"The greatest pianist I ever played with was Albert," Bartz declares, "and he's from Baltimore. Most people never heard of him, which is a sin, because he was a great musician. He taught me a lot, and Mickey taught me a lot. I've done the same for Antonio and Dontae. It's a continuum. We're all links in the chain. By coming around me, these younger players become links in the chain. The industry wants to break the links, because then they have better control, but we won't let it happen" (Bartz 2002).

"I don't know why those guys stayed in Baltimore," Hart says, "but it was great for me, because I was learning directly from a master. When Gary came back to Baltimore for several years, it was a priceless experience. For me he was just a local saxophonist; I didn't know he was one of the greatest players in the world."

"Baltimore for me is a real place, it's not sugar-coated. In fact there are still some old people there who will let you know if you're not really playing the heart. Maybe they weren't from the higher echelon of people who had a lot of money, but they were real and they wanted to hear someone tell them a story. When you heard a great artist like Gary Bartz at the Closet or Mickey Fields at the Sportsman's, you heard a story" (Hart).

These players share more than just geography; they share a subtle musical quality as well. Maryland is a border state, butting up against the Mason-Dixon Line, and is neither fully Northern nor fully Southern. Baltimore's jazz musicians have used that to their advantage, combining the more cerebral, experimental approach of New York and Philadelphia with the more emotional, crowd-pleasing attitude of Florida, Georgia, and the Carolinas. Baltimore horn men are known for their ability to shift easily from a complicated harmonic variation to a fat-toned, sensual blues run.

"There's a certain kind of emotion that comes from the players I've known in Baltimore," claims native son Hart, "older cats like Gary Bartz and Gary Thomas, even a young brother like Tim Green, all have that down-home, gospel feeling. Baltimore, being somewhat southern compared to New York, seems to maintain that feeling of blues. Unlike some R&B or church musicians, these guys know all the chords and have all the technique, but they combine that with blues and gospel. Baltimore has always been a very soulful place; we have a lot of churches. Most of us grew up in that tradition. Listen to Gary Bartz; the church element is still there" (Hart).

The years at the Closet restored Bartz's enthusiasm for jazz, and he began to record again in 1988 for a series of small, independent labels such as SteepleChase, Candid, Timeless and Challenge. Then in 1995, he signed with a major label, Atlantic Records, and released two of the finest recordings of his career.

The Red and Orange Poems features an all-star band (bassist Dave Holland, trumpeter Eddie Henderson, pianist Mulgrew Miller, et al.) and a stash of superb compositions that Bartz had been saving for such an occasion. The 1996 follow-up, *Blues Chronicles: Tales of Life*, showcases some of Baltimore's finest musicians—trumpeter Tom Williams, pianist George Colligan, pianist Cyrus Chestnut, and drummer Dennis Chambers. The unorthodox material ranges from a Cole Porter standard to a Bob Marley reggae number, from a tribute to Art Blakey to a tribute to Marvin Gaye, from rap interludes to the street cries of a Baltimore arabber.

"I went into the Atlantic contract knowing what I was getting into," he notes. "I got a budget that enabled me to hire the musicians and I wanted, and I got an advance that enabled me to buy a house and start a record label" (Bartz 1999).

The house is on an acre and a half in Wenonah, New Jersey, just outside Philadelphia, and the record label is OYO. So far the label has released three Gary Bartz albums, *Soulstice: Live @ the Jazz Standard, Vol. 1; Soprano Stories*; and *Mae Velha: Live @ the Jazz Standard Vol. 2*.

"OYO stands for two things," he explains. "For one, it's a tribe in Nigeria. For another, it stands for 'Own Your Own,' which is a crucial concept. Most musicians don't own their music; Duke never owned his own music; Miles never did. I never got a penny off of selling records. I was never in the record business before; I was just working for people who were in the record business. Now that I own a record label, I'm finally in the record business."

"Record labels are like plantations during slavery. When you sign a contract with a label, you can't do the things you want to do unless you fight for it, and sometimes not even then. I don't like being treated like that, I don't like feeling like a slave. I don't like have to ask the massa for permission if I want to record with someone else" (Bartz 1999).

As Bartz drops me off after our tour of Baltimore jazz history, his ambivalence about his hometown reemerges. Parked on 39th Street, he speaks warmly of the Baltimore musicians who have helped to show him the way, and he speaks just as warmly of younger hometown players that he's been able to help. But he seems exasperated that he has received more recognition in Europe than in America and more in New York than in Baltimore.

"I used to take it personally," he admits, "until I saw that Miles went through the same thing. When I worked with Miles, we never played in St. Louis or East St. Louis. I asked him about it once, and he said, 'I'll never play my hometown; they don't appreciate me.' It's the same for everyone. The people who saw you grow up as a snotty-nosed kid will never take you seriously" (Bartz 1999).

Works Cited and Consulted

Bartz, Gary. Interview by Geoffrey Himes. 8 July 1999.

---. Interview by Geoffrey Himes. 9 Feb. 2002.

Bennett, Karen. "Gary Bartz and Antonio Hart." *Musician* July 1994: 58. Print.

Butta, Bob. Interview by Geoffrey Himes. 28 Mar. 2002.

Davis, Natalie. "Gary Bartz: The Jazzman Testifies." *Maryland Music* April 1994: 26-27. Print.

Dilts, James D. "Giant Steps: Hometown Jazz Hero Gary Bartz Strides Back Into the Limelight." Baltimore *City Paper* 15 Jan. 1997: 18-20. Print.

Giddins, Gary. "The Middle Passage: Gary Bartz Escapes the Doldrums." *Village Voice* 12 Nov. 1991: 34. Print.

Hart, Antonio. Interview by Geoffrey Himes. 12 July 2004.

Himes, Geoffrey. "Bartz: Hooking Up His Own 'Live' Wire." *Columbia Flier* 5 April 2000: 5. Print.

---. "Gary Bartz: Owning Up to His Art." *Lifetimes* 14 July 1999: 6. Print.

---. "Hot Chestnut, Yummy 'Gumbo'." Washington *Post* 31 May 1996. Print.

---. "Kind of Blue: Legendary Saxophonist Gary Bartz Reflects on the History of Jazz in His Hometown." *Baltimore Magazine* June 2002: 50-55. Print.

---. "Return of the Prodigal Saxophonist: Gary Bartz Crosses Back Over to Jazz." Washington *Post* 1 Mar. 1995: 5. Print.

---. "Sax and the City." Baltimore *City Paper* 21 July 2004: 19-20. Print.

---. "Stunning 'Tales' from Saxman Bartz." Washington *Post* 13 Sept. 1996: 6. Print.

Macnie, Jim."Between Legends & Lions: A Look at Jazz Musicians Happily Stuck in the Middle." *DownBeat* Jul. 1995: 26-31. Print.

Nahigian, Alan, and Ed Enright. "Take Back the Music." *DownBeat* Sept. 1998: 24-27. Print.

Discography

Gary Bartz, *Libra*. Milestone MSP 9006, 1967.

 Bartz had already apprenticed in the bands of Max Roach and Art Blakey before recording this, his first album as a leader. It sounds very much like a Blakey record—Billy Higgins's muscular drumming dominates the soundscape and Bartz's alto sax duels with Jimmy Owens's trumpet—but the young bandleader already has a distinctive soloing voice and everyone (including bassist Richard Davis and pianist Albert Dailey) plays well.

Gary Bartz, *Another Earth*. Milestone MSP 9018, 1968.

 Bartz declares his independence from the hard-bop formula by beginning this album with the 23-minute, three-part title suite about life on a planet much like ours. The music boasts rippling African flavors with bursts of dissonance, both elements given rambunctious authority by Pharoah Sanders's tenor sax and Charles Tolliver's trumpet. The rhythm section (pianist Stanley Cowell, bassist Reggie Workman, and drummer Freddie Waits) backs the horns with an energy as elastic as it is unfaltering. The other four tracks continue the cosmic theme (Kurt Weill's "Lost in the Stars," an unaccompanied sax/bass duet, joins quartet versions of Bartz's "Dark Nebula," "UFO" and "Perihelion and Aphelion") in more conventional arrangements.

Gary Bartz NTU Troop, *Home*. Milestone MSP 9027, 1970.

 This first album under the NTU Troop banner has little to do with the projects that followed: it's a concert date recorded at Baltimore's Famous Ballroom in 1969 featuring a lineup that included Albert Dailey, trumpeter Woody Shaw, and drummer Rashied Ali. These musicians are as comfortable playing outside as inside, and Bartz's four extended compositions (plus an Ellington encore) give them plenty of platforms for both. Alternately muscular and melodic, angry and lyrical, this record ended the first phase of Bartz's career before he headed into the desert.

Gary Bartz NTU Troop, *Harlem Bush Music/Taifa*. Milestone MS 9031, 1971.

 You have to admire Bartz's ambition in incorporating vocals, R&B elements, and African flavors into his work. You don't have to admire the results, however. In moving into areas outside his area of expertise, Bartz loses quality control and proves a poor lyricist, vocalist and arranger. Also, vocalist Andy Bey was still struggling with pitch, phrasing and tone.

Gary Bartz NTU Troop, *Harlem Bush Music/Uhuru*. Milestone MSP 9032, 1971.

 Taken from the same 1970 session as the above album, this disc reflects similar ambition and similar problems. It's marginally better because bassist Ron Carter provides a steadying hand. The 18-minute "Blue (A Folk Tale)" features brilliant alto sax work and excruciating vocals.

Gary Bartz NTU Troop, *Slingerella: A Ghetto Fairy Tale*. Prestige P 10083, 1972. Unreviewed.

Gary Bartz NTU Troop, *Juju Street Songs*. Prestige P 10057, 1972.
This album opens with a 10-minute version of Michael Jackson's recent hit, "I Wanna Be Where You Are," with Bartz abstracting and extending the melody over Bey's Rhodes piano. Less successful is Bey's overly embellished vocal version of Stevie Wonder's "Black Maybe." Two Bartz compositions, "African Suite" and "Teheran," are more memorable for their exotic motifs and percussion than for their themes and solos.

Gary Bartz NTU Troop, *Follow, the Medicine Man*. Prestige P 10068, 1972.
This album begins with two hard-bop numbers marred by sloppy vocals, followed by a lovely ballad version of the Stylistics' "Betcha By Golly Wow" and a burning funk instrumental, Bartz's "Dr. Follow's Dance." The album finishes with an embarrassing R&B song, the group-written "Standin' on the Corner," and a respectable jazz song, written and sung by Bey. Bartz is to be commended for his ambitious mixing of elements, but seems unable to distinguish the successes from the failures.

Gary Bartz NTU Troop, *Standin' On the Corner*. Prestige, 1972. Unreviewed.

Gary Bartz NTU Troop, *I've Known Rivers and Other Bodies*. Prestige P 66001, 1973.
Shortly before this album was recorded live at Switzerland's Montreux Jazz Festival on July 7th, 1973, Bartz had replaced Bey with keyboardist Hubert Eaves, which, happily, shifts the emphasis from vocals to instrumental solos. Yet it also means that Bartz handles all the singing, resulting in thin, flat vocals that spoil more than one track. Some of the solos are stunning, however, especially on the Coltrane tribute, "Jujuman," "Sifa Zote," the churchy "Bertha Baptist", and the soprano-laced groover "Mama's Soul." The 17-year-old drummer Howard King sounds as precocious and energetic as the young Tony Williams.

Gary Bartz NTU Troop, *Dr. Follow's Dance* Prestige. 1973. Unreviewed.

Gary Bartz. Lee Konitz. Charlie Mariano. Jackie McLean. *Altissimo*. West Wind 2019, 1974. Unreviewed.

Gary Bartz, *Juju Man*. Catalyst CAT-7610, 1976.
Bartz drops the NTU Troop label for this straight-ahead quartet session, but still allows his own singing to mar an otherwise impressive tribute to John Coltrane on the title cut. He also allows Syreeta Wright to over-sing "My Funny Valentine." Nonetheless, his solid rhythm section (pianist Charles Mims, bassist Curtis Robertson, and drummer Howard King) provides a terrific springboard for Bartz's most adventurous, satisfying studio solos in eight years.

Gary Bartz, *Music Is My Sanctuary*. Blue Note 80733, 1977.

This cannot in good faith be described as a jazz album, even though it charted at #26 on Billboard's jazz chart. It is an R&B record, with the rhythm section playing disco grooves, a choir of background singers cooing sweetly, and Bartz playing simple melodies over the beat. There's nothing wrong with making an R&B record, but this isn't a very good one. The play-it-safe polish of these simple charts and anonymous vocals lacks the personality and risk-taking of contemporary albums by Stevie Wonder, Marvin Gaye, or Earth, Wind & Fire.

Gary Bartz, *Love Song*. VJ International, 1978. Unreviewed.

Gary Bartz, *Love Affair*. Capitol 11789, 1978.

The rhythms and harmonies are so panderingly inoffensive that this is better described as easy-listening background music than as R&B. Not even the incongruous tagging on of Coltrane's "Giant Steps" at the end can salvage it.

Gary Bartz, *Bartz*. Arista AB 4263, 1980.

The best-selling record Bartz ever released, this album reached #71 on the R&B charts. The saxophonist turned over most of the production choices to James Mtume, who had been producing hits for Stephanie Mills, Phyllis Hyman and Roberta Flack and he gave Bartz the funkiest grooves of his R&B period. He didn't, however, give Bartz much room to play jazz solos or unfurl his own personality.

Gary Bartz Quartet, *Monsoon*. SteepleChase SCCD-31234, 1988.

This Danish session marks Bartz's return to mainstream, acoustic jazz. Backed by the muscular rhythm section of drummer Billy Hart, bassist Clint Houston and pianist Butch Lacy, Bartz sounds as lyrical on the ballads and as inventive on the barnburners as he ever has. Especially impressive are the knotty staccato accents and liberating geysers of notes on Sonny Rollins's "Strode Rode" and the tension-and-release on Bartz's title track as he jousts with Hart.

Gary Bartz. *Reflections Of Monk—The Final Frontier*. SteepleChase SCCD-31248, 1988.

Bartz is joined by trumpeter Eddie Henderson and drummer Billy Hart, and two underrated Baltimore players—pianist Bob Butta and bassist Geoff Harper. Monk's compositions are, of course, marvelous, and the solos are often impressive. But the disc sounds more like an impromptu blowing session than a thought-out project, and Bartz can't fully suppress his old habit of adding bland female background vocals.

Gary Bartz Quintet, *West 42ⁿᵈ Street*. Candid CCD 79049, 1990.

Recorded live at Birdland in 1990, the date finds Bartz leading an all-star combo (pianist John Hicks, drummer Al Foster, bassist Ray Drummond, and trumpeter Claudio Roditi) through four lengthy standards and one original (the bright-themed hard-bop number "Cousins"). It's astonishing to hear Bartz come up with one idea after another on the fly, even at the ferocious pace of "Speak Low" and the title track. But it's just as impressive to hear him search for the right romantic tone on the ballad "It's Easy To Remember."

The Reunion Legacy Band, *The Legacy*. Early Bird EBCD-102, 1991.

When they were young, unknown jazz musicians, Bartz, Tolliver, trombonist Grachan Moncur, and bassist Mickey Bass used to commute from New York to Baltimore to play at the North End Lounge. That quartet reunites here with Hicks and Hart to update the sound of Art Blakey's Jazz Messengers (where Bartz, Bass, and Hicks all served apprenticeships). The result is a solid, old-fashioned blowing session in the style of the '60s Blue Note albums.

Gary Bartz with the Candid All Stars. *There Goes the Neighborhood*. Candid CCD79506, 1991.

This spectacular disc, recorded during a 1990 show at Birdland, erased all doubts about Bartz's comeback. The Candid All Stars—pianist Kenny Barron, bassist Ben Drummond, and drummer Ben Riley—live up to their name with a robust, tumbling momentum that pushes Bartz into some of the most exuberant alto playing of his life. The album's title is explained by the ferociously fast lead-off Bartz composition, "Racism." The origins of his horn's braying, praying tone are explained by his nod to John Coltrane on "Impressions." Through two Tadd Dameron numbers, a Barron original and two show tunes, the energy and invention never flag.

Gary Bartz: *Shadows*. Timeless SJP 379, 1991. Unreviewed.

Leon Thomas & Gary Bartz, *Precious Energy: Live at Ethel's*. Mapleshade 56942, 1993.

This session, recorded live at Ethel's Place in 1987, seems promising, for Bartz and the gifted avant-garde vocalist Thomas are joined by trumpeter Eddie Henderson and pianist Bob Butta. But the band sounds under-rehearsed and each member tends to meander off in different directions. Thomas dominates and relies too heavily on recycled shtick.

Gary Bartz. *Episode One Children of Harlem*. Challenge CHR 70001, 1994.

This concept album examines different aspects of Harlem: popular culture ("Amos and Andy Theme"), traditional culture ("Tap Dancer"), storefront churches ("Ezekiel Saw the Wheel"), romance ("Crazy She Calls Me"), Spanish Harlem ("Tico Tico") and growing up ("Children of Harlem"). Bartz, a 15-year Harlem resident, is joined by two Harlem products—pianist Larry Willis and Ben Riley—as well as another longtime resident, bassist Buster Williams.

Gary Bartz, *The Red and Orange Poems*. Atlantic 82720-2, 1994.

For his major-label comeback, Bartz assembled an all-star sextet featuring bassist Dave Holland, pianist Mulgrew Miller along with Eddie Henderson. The key is Holland, who brings a sense of urgency to the proceedings as he roams freely and melodically through the changes. Bartz responds not by playing a million notes but by mixing rests and sustained notes into his speedy passages, to create a dramatic, push-and-pull tension that gives the music its personality. Though he's an alto player, Bartz's twin poles have long been Sonny Rollins and John Coltrane—which may account for Bartz's unusually thick, throaty sound. There's more Rollins and less Coltrane here than on the Baltimorean's more adventurous small-label outings. You can hear the echo of Rollins's calypso pieces in Bartz's lilting treatment of South African rhythms on "Soulmates," and Rollins's emphasis on melody in Bartz's patient variations and brisk asides on the Gershwin ballad, "But Not For Me."

Gary Bartz. *Alto Memories*. Verve Records, 1995. Unreviewed.

Gary Bartz, *The Blues Chronicles: Tales of Life*. Atlantic 82893-2, 1996.

Ostensibly a concept album that explores the blues in all its manifestations, it isn't so strict about the premise that Bartz can't find room for a lovely soprano sax reading of "Miss Otis Regrets." Bartz freely treats Bob Marley's "Lively Up Yourself," and Bartz's own soul vamp, inexplicably titled "Gangsta Jazz," evolves seamlessly from punchy horn riffs to Coltranesque alto solos. Bartz's "And He Called Himself a Messenger," a tribute to Art Blakey, is catchy hard-bop, while "One Million Blues" is a gut-bucket blues. Vocals are supplied on four numbers by vocalese pioneer Jon Hendricks, young rappers Nezkar Keith and Ransom, and an actual street vendor, Maatkara Ali. What holds this diverse material together is the forceful, joyful shout of Bartz's vigorously self-assertive horn. His vibrant attack is reinforced by fellow Baltimoreans Cyrus Chestnut and George Colligan, trumpeter Tom Williams, and drummer Dennis Chambers.

Gary Bartz NTU Troop, *Juju Street Songs*. Prestige PRCD-24181-2, 1997.

This is the remastered CD reissue of all five tracks on Juju Street Songs *and six of the seven tracks on* Follow, the Medicine Man.

Gary Bartz, *Libra/Another Earth*. Milestone MCD-47077-2, 1998.

This CD reissue collects seven of the eight tracks from Libra *and all five tracks from* Another Earth.

Gary Bartz Quartet, *Soulstice: Live @ the Jazz Standard Vol. 1*. OYO 1002-1, 1999.

Recorded during one hot set at a Manhattan nightclub on May 8th, 1998, this album finds Bartz switching between alto and soprano sax and backed by pianist Barney McAll, bassist Kenny Davis and drummer Greg Bandy. The quartet charges through five compositions (two Bartz originals, standards by Billy Strayhorn and Walter Davis, and a Gershwin show tune) and nearly an hour of high-level improvisation. In the liner notes, Bartz credits his approach to his time in Miles Davis's band, and there's a similar, restless curiosity in the way Bartz attacks these numbers, stabbing repeatedly at the harmonies, slicing them up this way and that. And because this is a working road band, the four players are well attuned to each other. Hence, the rhythm section is always right there with the leader as the music keeps building through this 56-minute medley.

Gary Bartz, *Soprano Stories*. OYO 1001-1, 2001.

Bartz has often complained that he has gotten pressure from record companies and promoters to stick to the alto, which he's best known for, although he has also played soprano sax since the '60s. Recording for his own label, he can play whatever he wants, and on this session he showcases his soprano playing exclusively. Even if you prefer the warmer tone of his alto, Bartz remains as imaginative and hot-blooded on either horn. Here he's joined by Greg Bandy, bassist James King, and alternating pianists John Hicks and George Cables.

Gary Bartz Peter Leitch. *The Montreal Concert*. DSM 3037, 2001.

This album is unlike anything else in Bartz's oeuvre—and not just because saxophone/guitar duos are a rarity in anyone's catalogue. Leitch—an old-school bop guitarist who has recorded with Oscar Peterson, John Hicks, and Kenny Barron—establishes a relaxed minimalism, and Bartz responds with some of the most restrained and lyrical playing of his career. Recorded during a concert in Canada, the session features three medleys that stretch beyond 15 minutes but never seem padded. Leitch frames both the rhythm and the harmony with his economical chord strokes and leaves most solo space to his guest. Bartz responds with marvelous inventions that never push and never run out of ideas.

Gary Bartz NTU Troop, *Harlem Bus Music*. Milestone MCD-47101-2, 2004.

This remastered CD reissue collects six of the seven tracks from Harlem Bus Music/Taifa *and all five tracks from* Harlem Bus Music/Uhuru.

Gary Bartz Quartet, *Mae Velha: Live @ the Jazz Standard Vol. 2*. OYO 1002-1, 2005.

Like Soulstice, *this live recording powers through several compositions in an hour-long medley that never takes a breath. This time, though, Bartz returns to his fusion phase, blowing over funk rhythms accented by electric guitar, Fender Rhodes and conga drums. The results are more satisfying than they were in the '70s because the improvising is as vigorous as the grooves, which never settle into predictable patterns. Except for brief intrusions by Bartz's vocals, the playing by the leader, guitarist Paul Bollenbeck, keyboardist Barney McAll, bassist James King, drummer Greg Bandy, and percussionist Danny Robins is as inventive as it is muscular. This is what Bartz's first attempt at fusion should have sounded like.*

Cyrus Chestnut

"'Before you hear any flash and dash from me, I'm going to find that groove.'"

9 Soul Food
by Geoffrey Himes

The Bethany Baptist Church—a boxy, brick building in the middle of a grim Southwest Baltimore housing project—an unlikely place to find one of the world's greatest jazz musicians. But on many Sundays of the year, one can find Cyrus Chestnut sitting in the front pew, accompanying the choir on an electric piano.

Chestnut would not have become the musician he has become—recording with Wynton Marsalis, Joe Lovano, Betty Carter, Roy Hargrove, Kathleen Battle, Michael Brecker and the like—if he had not grown up playing in Baltimore churches just like this one. In an era when technically dazzling young pianists who sound like Bill Evans or Herbie Hancock are a dime a dozen, Chestnut's Baptist roots give his playing an earthiness and an emotional punch that separate him from the pack.

On a Sunday in March, 2001, soggy white plastic bags were caught in a cyclone fence in the gray, drizzling rain on the street outside the Bethany church. An old white refrigerator stood by the curb, the victim of an eviction and a reminder of the poverty that still stalks this forgotten Westport neighborhood between the Mount Auburn Cemetery and the old Montgomery Ward building.

Inside the church, though, the blond pews were filled with a stubborn optimism. The ushers wore starchy white uniforms with red berets and white gloves. The children were freshly scrubbed and dressed up as if for a school picture. The men dressed in dark suits, and the women in extravagant hats with all the swoops and curves of spaceships from a 1950s sci-fi movie.

Chestnut, very short and very round, wore a dark blue suit and rectangular, gold-framed glasses. He joined the organist and drummer to provide the music for the opening processional, the choir hymns, the offertory collection, and all the bridging music in between. About an hour into the service, the pianist finally got a chance for his own solo.

He began with a Bach quotation, dissolved that in a jazzy flourish, and introduced the melody from the old spiritual, "Swing Low, Sweet Chariot." The hymn began slowly and solemnly, but gradually gathered momentum. Soon all manner of embellishments and harmony notes were swarming around the melody like moths around a lamp. Chestnut took the melody on further and further tangents from the familiar tune, but always came home to remind the congregation of the original melody before taking off again.

For all its virtuoso dazzle, however, the tune had a story to tell. It is a hymn about death, and Chestnut captured the sadness of losing a loved one in his reluctant, bluesy opening. But gently, wordlessly, he transformed those same blues chords into a confident celebration of the heavenly paradise promised to all good Christians. After all, that's where the chariot of the song wants to take us.

By the end his right hand was trilling triplets over a stomping march beat in the left hand. It was a stunning performance—and as incongruous in this small church as it would be for Ry Cooder to take just one solo during a night-long blues jam. The churchgoers gave Chestnut a standing ovation, but soon they sat down and the pastor proceeded with the birth announcements.

The next day Chestnut sits in the over-stuffed armchair of a brick rowhouse near Baltimore's Herring Run Park. Though the pianist is based in the Bronx, he returns often to his hometown.

"When I played 'Swing Low, Sweet Chariot' yesterday," he explains, "I used that Erroll Garner thing of playing a lot of different quotes in the introduction before I settled on the main theme. . . . For some reason, I wound up playing the ending faster than I usually do, but it always changes. If you heard me play it today, it would be different than it was yesterday and next week it would be different again. I always keep myself open to any last-minute inspiration, because I thrive in the realm of spontaneity. I'm not a play-it-safe guy on stage—sometimes you fall on your face, but then you just turn up the burners and get out of the mess you've created" (Chestnut 2001).

A similar solo version of "Swing Low, Sweet Chariot" was included on his 2001 album, *Soul Food*. So is a sextet version of "Brother Hawky Hawk," an original tune that takes its cue from the offertory procession at Bethany Baptist Church or at Mount Calvary Church, Chestnut's childhood church in Baltimore. For this number, Chestnut enhanced his usual trio format with saxophonist James Carter, trombonist Wycliffe Gordon, and trumpeter Marcus Printup.

"That takes me back to the processions," he says, "to the ushers, the tapping of the feet, the clapping of the hands, the shaking of the tambourines, a certain time and place." He smiles broadly at the memory. "Everyone on this record had a similar church background" (Chestnut 2001).

"The church that really connected with me musically," says Carter, "was my Aunt Campbell's Church of God in Christ on the East

Side of Detroit. On Sunday mornings, at 11 o'clock on the nose, the organ would sweep by, the drums would start that groove and you'd get this holy-roller sensation as the choir marched up the aisle, singing 'Peace Be Still.' That music has always been there in my playing. . . . . Cyrus has this same down-home quality, but with the kind of chordal densities and rhythmic spacing that really makes you think. You can be soulful with just block chords, but to be soulful and have extended harmonies at the same time is something else again. That's something he and I share" (Chestnut 2001).

Is it any different playing "Swing Low, Sweet Chariot," rather than, say, George Gershwin's "Summertime" (which appeared on the 1998 album Cyrus Chestnut)?

"As long as there is a theme, there can always be variations," Chestnut insists, "whether it is a jazz standard, a pop song, or a gospel hymn. I'm like a minister giving his sermon. He will state his theme; he'll improvise variations on that theme; he'll take it to a high point, and then he'll make his closing statement. I'm doing the same thing at the piano. That's why I still like playing in church, because church is all about telling stories. That's why it is called inspirational music. You want as much facility with your instrument as you can get, but if you develop technique just for technique's sake, that's what you become—a technician. Those who fall into theoretical concepts end up playing those concepts rather than telling a story about life. That's what I want to do—tell a story about life" (Chestnut 2001).

Here Chestnut touches on the crisis confronting modern jazz. Never before has jazz enjoyed as many technically accomplished musicians as it has in the post-1980 era—thanks to the acceptance of jazz as an academic discipline at high schools and colleges country-wide. But never before have jazz musicians seemed to have so little to say; hence, too many young players seek to recreate the glories of 1950s jazz rather than forge a new language of their own.

Ever since Charlie Parker and Dizzy Gillespie transformed jazz from a dance music into an art music, the genre has increasingly become an insular world created by intellectuals for intellectuals—"America's classical music," as it is so often labeled. That nickname was meant to boost the status of jazz, but it is also a symptom of the music's alienation from its populist roots.

Those roots lie in the blues and gospel, the essential emotional counterpart to jazz's cerebral side. Traditional gospel shares the cathartic confessions and ecstatic exclamations of the blues. But gospel also possesses an institutional infrastructure and a devotion to spiritual concerns that might make it a better bet to heal the emotional/intellectual divide afflicting jazz.

"Yes, you have to use your intelligence in your music," Chestnut argues, "but you also have to use your emotions and your spirit, because that's just as important a part of who you are. Betty Carter always told us, 'We're not playing for ourselves; we're playing to connect with other people. But we want to win them over with skill—no gimmicks or tricks, just good music.' It would be easy to put on a clown suit and get over, but it would be a hollow victory" (Chestnut 2001).

The gospel influence has a long if often ignored history in jazz. Duke Ellington attempted fusing jazz and gospel in the middle of his career with "Come Sunday," an effort that culminated in the ambitious, large-scale "Sacred Concerts." Ellington's heirs, Charles Mingus and

Wynton Marsalis, followed his example in works such as the former's "Wednesday Night Prayer Meeting" and the latter's "In This House, On This Morning." And John Coltrane's most beloved piece, "A Love Supreme," is essentially an album-long prayer, as is Pharoah Sanders's "The Creator Has a Master Plan." Mainstream pianists such as Ray Bryant and Gene Harris have conspicuously drawn from gospel sources, and so have avant-gardists such as Don Pullen and Dave Burrell.

But no one has given this jazz-gospel fusion the priority or the virtuosity that Chestnut has. The pianist recognizes that the two-fold nature of the religious experience—gut-wrenching in its emotions and airily abstract in its spiritual concepts—make it uniquely qualified to restore the visceral impact of jazz without sacrificing the music's intellectual complexity.

"Some people try to theorize everything until they lose the enjoyment," he told *DownBeat* magazine in 1997. "Before you go and analyze it, just put the CD on; listen to it and react to it. Then if you want to figure out what kind of motif is being played, what kind of rhythmic figure, that's fine" (Eig 29).

"Cyrus never left the church," jazz singer Jon Hendricks said in the same story, "and if he's smart he never will. The church is the origin of the music. The nearer you are to the origin, it stands to reason you're going to have a firmer grasp on the music. For example, Milt Jackson's music is sanctified, and his parents went to a sanctified church. Bags can strike a groove better than anybody, and that's the sanctified church thing. Look at Ray Charles. Change the lyrics back before he made them secular and you've got the sound of the sanctified choirs swinging themselves into bad health. That's what you hear in Cyrus.

He's not going to disappear because he's deeply rooted in the music."

Cyrus Chestnut was born in Baltimore on January 17th, 1963, just 15 months after Wynton Marsalis, just seven months before Marcus Roberts, old enough in other words to be lumped in with the "Young Lions" movement that burst upon the jazz scene in the 1980s. Chestnut recorded with such "Young Lions" as Marsalis, Roy Hargrove, and Tim Warfield, but the pianist soon distinguished himself as something very different indeed.

His 2001 disc, *Soul Food*, for instance, sounds at first like yet another misguided attempt to pretend that it is still 1959—get some famous friends together and play hard-bop over blues and swing riffs. On subsequent listenings, however, that first impression evaporates. The music sounds too fresh, too elemental to wear the retro-jazz suit. The pianist and his friends (Carter, Gordon, Gary Bartz, Marcus Printup, Lewis Nash, and Christian McBride) aren't imitating their favorite Art Blakey and Horace Silver records. There is nothing second-hand about this music.

Instead Chestnut, who wrote nine of the eleven tunes, draws on his own first-hand experiences with blues, gospel, R&B, and classical music. When he lends a classical feel to "Cerebral Thoughts," he is not imitating Bill Evans; Chestnut is offering a jazz interpretation of his years of lessons at the Peabody Conservatory in Baltimore.

When he builds "Welllllll!" around an R&B riff, he is not imitating Jimmy Smith; he is filtering his own experiences in high school funk bands and recent collaborations with Isaac Hayes. When he brings a hand-clapping gospel feel to "Brother Hawky Hawk," he is not imitating Charles Mingus; he is borrowing from the church services he plays almost every Sunday.

Chestnut is not imitating the giants from the '50s; he is merely practicing the same sort of alchemy. He, too, is taking his personal experiences with all kinds of music—especially inner-city, street-corner musics far from Berklee or Lincoln Center—and transforming them into jazz. If any musician is to unite jazz's airy present with its earthy past, it would be someone like Chestnut, who studied not only at the Peabody Conservatory and the Berklee School of Music, but also at Mount Calvary Baptist Church on Milton Avenue near the east-side Baltimore Cemetery.

"I got a great musical education at Mount Calvary," Chestnut claims. "I had instruction in ear training, arrangement, and improvisation. They didn't call it that, but that's what it was. It wasn't until I went to an official music school that I realized how much I had already learned in church. In church, someone would start singing without ever telling you what key the song was in. I'd just have to listen and start playing along. That was my ear training. I had to take the basic chord progressions of gospel and adapt them to fit the song. That was arrangement. But nothing was set in stone, and you were always changing things around to fit the moment. That was improvisation" (Himes 2001).

When Chestnut was growing up in Govans, Mount Calvary was his family's church. It was a small, brick building, not unlike the Bethany Baptist Church. Chestnut's mother, Flossie, who worked for social services, was the choir director, and his father, McDonald, a postal worker, was the church pianist. McDonald also played piano at home and, by the time Cyrus was five, the young boy was imitating his daddy at the keyboard.

"I loved gospel," he remembers, "but I listened to all kinds of music. My mother had old 45s by Sam Cooke, Little Richard, and Jackie Wilson, and I would listen to AM radio stations like WSID, WEBB and WWIN. . . . If I heard something with a good groove, I'd just listen to it. It might be country, an old waltz, or something very funky; I didn't care. When I was in the fourth grade at Northwood Elementary School, we went to see the Baltimore Symphony play Mussorgsky's *Pictures at an Exhibition*. I thought even that was cool. I liked the Charlie Brown cartoons on television because the music pulled me in. I didn't know that music was jazz, but I did know I liked the groove" (Chestnut 2001).

In 2000, Chestnut paid tribute to that childhood experience by releasing the album *Cyrus Chestnut & Friends: A Charlie Brown Christmas* (Atlantic). The friends include Manhattan Transfer, Vanessa Williams, Brian McKnight, Kenny Garrett, Pat Martino, Wallace Roney, Christian McBride, Michael Brecker, and Steve Gadd. The music mixes traditional Christmas fare, Vince Guaraldi's jazz instrumentals for the Charlie Brown Christmas special, and a Chestnut original called "Me and Charlie Brown." It is the pianist's most pop-oriented recording and reflects his ambitions to build bridges between jazz and the broader public.

Chestnut didn't realize that it was jazz he loved until 1972. "When I was nine," he recalls, "I got a $2 allowance each week. I went down to the Woolworth's at the Alameda Shopping Center and saw they had a $1.99 record bin, which was just the right price for my allowance. I found this one album with a very colorful cover with a man playing the piano. I liked the way it looked, so I bought it, took it home and listened to it over and over" (Chestnut 2001).

The album was *Thelonious Monk's Greatest Hits* on Columbia Records. It was a near-perfect example of how a pianist could twist music into strange new harmonies and angular rhythms and yet never lose a strong sense of melody and groove. In a sense, Chestnut has been following that model ever since. That same year Chestnut got his first paying job as a musician, playing piano for the Israel Baptist Church in Baltimore. That same year he started taking classical lessons at Peabody Prep. In 1976, his family moved out to Harford County, and Chestnut wound up in the North Harford High School Jazz Band.

"Moving to the suburbs was a big adjustment," he concedes. "I had never gone to school on a school bus, and I had never been the only black kid on a bus. But music was always my friend; I was known as the guy who could play piano. After high school, I was thinking of going to Towson State, but when I looked at the program at the Berklee School of Music and saw Oscar Peterson, Monty Alexander, and Ray Brown on the faculty, I knew this was a real jazz school. So that's where I went" (Chestnut 2001).

"I remember the day that Betty Carter was at Berklee to do a master class and Cyrus played with her," jazz singer Carla Cook told *DownBeat* in 2006. "Betty asked for a student to play piano with her, and the whole auditorium immediately started chanting 'Cyrus! Cyrus!' He was the obvious choice, and I can still recall how nervous he was walking down the aisle to the stage. But he did a great job and everybody cheered" (Perkins 51).

That's not how he remembers it. "Before Betty came, I was talking a whole bunch of junk about how I was going to sit in with her and show her what I could do, not realizing what was about to happen,"

Chestnut says in the same story. "So when I got up on stage, she said, 'Let's do "Body and Soul,"' and I was happy because I knew it. But she changed keys on me and it freaked me out. Somehow I got through it; everyone cheered, and I figured I'd go see her afterward backstage and get my butt whipping."

"I told her I was sorry, but she just gave me a hug, which made me even madder. I walked back to the dorm and just before I got there, the whole song opened up to me. I stopped in my tracks, walked back to the auditorium and the piano and played it in the right key. I vowed from then on never to take anything for granted musically and to make it up to her someday" (Perkins 52).

While he was in high school, too young to drink and without a car, Chestnut hadn't connected with Baltimore's local jazz scene. But when he started returning home from college in Boston, he discovered just how much music was going on in his hometown.

"I started playing Fender Rhodes and synthesizer in Phases, a band led by Kim Waters and his brothers," Chestnut remembers. "I started sitting in at clubs like the Sportsman's Lounge, the Gentleman 10, Club 2300, the Haven, the Bird Cage, and the Sphinx Club. I used to work on the Harbor cruises—the *Bay Lady* and the *Lady Baltimore*— and after I'd get off, I'd go see organist Dave Ross and his trio. They would groove so hard that when they asked me to play, I had to say, 'Oh, no, that's holy ground up there; I can't touch that.'"

"I asked Dave how he could groove like that all night long. He put his hand on my shoulder and said, 'The first thing I do is search for a groove, and once I find it, I hang onto it for dear life.' I've always remembered that. Before you hear any flash and dash from me, I'm going to find that groove. . . . You can always tell musicians who come from Baltimore," he added, "because they have a different kind of groove—they're straight-out funky."

"Musicians here like Charles Covington and Mickey Fields were major-league talents. Mickey might have taken it easy if he was flirting with the ladies, but if someone from out of town came through the door, especially if it was a real big name, Mickey would stand up straight, turn up the heat on his saxophone and blow them off the stage. One time I was walking around at Artscape and I heard these melodies that were so intense that I had to find out where they were coming from. I followed the sound all the way to the other side of the festival, where I found Charles playing the piano. He has a harmonic capacity like no one else. I don't know why he and Mickey never made it big" (Chestnut 2001).

Unlike Covington and Fields, Chestnut was ready, willing and able to tour as a sideman with other musicians. After graduating from Berklee in 1985, Chestnut worked a steady succession of jobs with the likes of Wynton Marsalis, Branford Marsalis, Jon Hendricks, Terence Blanchard, and Donald Harrison. But it wasn't until 1991 that he landed the job he wanted the most—pianist for singer Betty Carter who, along with Art Blakey, had maintained one of the top finishing schools in jazz for young musicians.

The pianists who graduated from her group include Benny Green, Stephen Scott, John Hicks, Geri Allen, and Mulgrew Miller. Chestnut can be heard playing with her on the 1992 album, *It's Not About the Melody* (Verve).

"Dealing with Betty meant always being on your toes," he explains, "because you never knew what she might do next. She would always throw you a curveball, and you would have to go with her wherever she led. You had to shift gears on a moment's notice. Fortunately, I was used to that from church because a lot of singers there will change keys or tempos whenever the spirit moves them and you have to identify what they're doing and go there.

"Betty always told me that jazz is about finding out who you are. Even back in the days of Jelly Roll Morton, when things were tough for blacks, a jazz musician could always be himself on the bandstand. No one ever got lynched for playing a sharp ninth chord. The United States is built on the philosophy that people can be who they really are, and jazz is one place where that philosophy is realized" (Chestnut 2001).

While he was with Carter, Chestnut recorded three albums under his own name for the Japanese label Alfa: *The Nutman Speaks, The Nutman Speaks Again,* and *Another Direction,* reissued in the U.S. by Evidence. They capture a young pianist of considerable skills still looking for his own voice. He had found it by the time he left Carter and released his first American album for Atlantic in 1994.

The title was *Revelation,* and that's just what it was. At 31, Chestnut was too old to be a "young lion," but his delayed arrival meant he burst on the American scene as an already-mature talent. Backed by his bandmates in the Carter group—bassist Christopher Thomas and drummer Clarence Penn—Chestnut was more than just another fast-fingered pianist; he was a storyteller at the keyboard.

223

"I've never been in a situation where someone told me to play like another person, and I'm not about to start now. Betty Carter used to tell me, 'I don't need to hear Miles Davis's "If I Were a Bell"; I was there when it happened. I've heard it a thousand times; I don't need to hear it the 1,001st time. I want to hear what you have to say.' Betty told me that when I was done with her, I would be ready to go out on my own. And she was right" (Chestnut 2001).

Revelation was number one not only in the *Village Voice* Critics Poll but also on the Gavin jazz-radio chart. Suddenly Chestnut was a figure to be reckoned with, and the invitations for festivals and recording sessions came flooding in. One of the most unusual came from opera star Kathleen Battle, who was preparing a crossover album of spirituals, *So Many Stars*, with jazz figures such as James Carter, Christian McBride, and Grover Washington, Jr.

"This was a high-cotton studio session," Chestnut points out. "I had never been in a room with so many stars, and they had one of the best Hamburg Steinways I've ever played in my life. The producer, Robert Sadin, told me he wanted me to play like Thomas Whitfield meets Herbie Hancock. Now I knew Thomas Whitfield, the great gospel pianist, and I knew Herbie Hancock, the great jazz pianist, but I had never thought about putting them together.

"But I tried it, and I got it all working at once. I came out of that session and said, 'Wow, this can really work.' It was like a door had opened for me and all I had to do was step through. I had never wanted to be a re-creator of other people's music; I had always wanted to create something that was all my own. I had never wanted to wear a lot of different hats—the jazz hat, the gospel hat, the classical hat—I wanted to take them all apart and sew them into one big hat. And this showed me how" (Chestnut 2001).

Chestnut dealt with his gospel background explicitly on the 1995 solo-piano album, *Blessed Quietness: A Collection of Hymns, Spirituals and Carols* (Atlantic). But even more impressive is a trilogy of Atlantic albums that integrate the storytelling gospel musician with the virtuoso classical musician, the playful blues musician with the composing-on-the-run jazz musician: 1995's *The Dark Before the Dawn*, 1996's *Earth Stories*, and 1998's *Cyrus Chestnut*.

During this period, he was living in the Bronx, but returning to Baltimore regularly to see family and play for hometown crowds. Typical was his concert at Baltimore's Frederick Douglass High School on April 4th, 1996. Playing with the same rhythm section he used on *Earth Stories* (bassist Steve Kirby and drummer Alvester Garnett), Chestnut attacked the same tunes with even more fervor than he had in the studio. Wearing a dark blue suit and gold tie, Chestnut began an uptempo medley of "Whoopi" and "East of the Sun and West of the Moon" with whispery arpeggios but built to a key-rattling climax that had the pianist raising his right hand above his head before he brought it crashing down like a gospel shout on the piano keys. Best of all was the solo-piano version of "Gomez," which was so joyful that Chestnut seemed to be dancing while sitting on his piano bench. He was at the peak of his powers and on top of the jazz world. But he soon found the rug pulled out from under him.

"Shortly after *Soul Food*, the whole Atlantic jazz division was just shut down," Chestnut explains. "So I moved to Warner Bros. and released *You Are My Sunshine*, but then it came out that the Warner jazz division was also shutting down. Things got a little crazy around then. The anxiety of not being able to do what you believe you were put on earth to do is very wearing. Plus there's an economic impact. So it was a time of change for me. I was trying to figure out who I was and what I was going to do next. When you find yourself repeating the same motifs or licks, that sets off a warning bell inside that was installed by Miss Betty. You can never repeat yourself; you have to keep pushing for something new. If you're cooking and things start tasting the same, you put different ingredients into the pot and stir" (Chestnut 2001).

The early 2000s were a period of experimentation for the pianist, who tried anything that might jar him out of his comfortable habits. He collaborated with R&B icon Isaac Hayes; he tried his hand at Latin rhythms; he even made an album interpreting the songs of the indie-rock band Pavement. Through his restless curiosity he was able to avoid the creative stall that musicians often experience in their 40s.

"A few years ago," he recalled in 2006, "I was playing a benefit concert for WBGO-FM at the Blue Note Cafe in New York, and I saw someone coming up to the bandstand. I said to myself, 'That looks like Isaac Hayes; I hope I remember how to play "Shaft."' It was Isaac, but he said he wanted to do 'The Shadow of Your Smile.' It went so well that we did a concert together in St. Louis" (Chestnut 2006).

Hayes and Chestnut brought their show to Baltimore's Meyerhoff Symphony Hall on May 10th, 2002. "What I remember about those Isaac Hayes concerts," Chestnut recalls, "is they weren't limited to just R&B or jazz. I had to find a way to be myself and use both elements. We were free to try things, and boy, Isaac was so open to what we were doing."

Chestnut had to go even further out of his comfort zone for the album *Gold Sounds*, jazz interpretations of songs by the lo-fi, indie-rock band Pavement. The project was the brainchild of Brown Brothers Records, a new label in Manhattan run by fans of both indie rock and modern jazz, who commissioned Chestnut, James Carter, drummer Ali Jackson, and bassist Reginald Veal for the project.

"I'd never heard of Pavement," Chestnut admits, "and when I heard their records, to be honest, I said, 'I don't know what I can do with this.' If I flipped the radio dial and heard that, I'd keep flipping. But rather than put it away, I listened to it again, because it was important that I understand what they were up to. I heard some real melody in there; I heard some elements that were conventional and some that were unconventional. In a lot of instances you couldn't say, 'Oh, I know where it's going to go next.' It reminded me of the early blues guys who changed chords whenever they felt like it.

"Mostly I gravitated to the feeling of a song like 'Welcome to My World.'" Chestnut explains. "Rather than play the notes, we tried to play the feeling. If you listen to James, he plays the songs the way the singer sang them. I grabbed hold of the unconventional elements in each song and developed them. The success of this record was due to none of us having a history with Pavement, so we didn't play the songs Pavement's way. That had been done; it didn't need to be done again" (Chestnut 2006).

When Pavement perform the song, "Here," on the 1992 album, *Slanted & Enchanted*, the guitar, bass and drums stumble along at a reluctant tempo, and singer Stephen Malkmus warbles in his strangled tenor, "I was dressed for success, but success it never comes." But there was something about the way the chord changes kept descending

227

further and further, even as the lovely melody kept climbing that gave the song its irresistible drama.

It is that drama the *Gold Sounds* quartet seizes upon. Chestnut opens "Here" with an unaccompanied piano intro that heightens the vertigo of Malkmus's descending chords. Only after Jackson and Veal have joined in does Carter finally enter with Malkmus's vocal melody, now delivered by a soprano sax. Carter has a lot more control over his instrument than Malkmus, of course, but he projects the same feeling of irrepressible hope struggling against crushing reality. It is a welcome reunion for Chestnut and Carter.

"Our common denominator is that we both love to play," Carter argues. "We both have a down-home quality that's indicative of a communal good time." (Carter 2001)

"A lot of invention is going to happen when you get minds like that together," Chestnut adds. "We sketched out where Pavement was coming from and said, 'Why don't we put this kind of groove to it?' But once the tape started rolling and we started playing, our instincts took over and we were throwing all kinds of surprises in. Pavement was being themselves when they recorded these songs, so we thought we should be ourselves when we recorded them" (Chestnut 2001).

All this experimentation paid off on Chestnut's comeback album, 2006's *Genuine Chestnut*. Here conga drummer Steven Kroon adds a new Latin tinge to Chestnut's grooves, while guitarist Russell Malone strengthens the pianist's ties to pop music on tunes such as Fats Domino's "I'm Walkin'" and Bread's "If."

"When I was in the ninth grade at North Hartford High School," Chestnut remembers, "my English teacher, Brenda Sherard, was getting married, and she wanted me to play 'If' for the ceremony. I'd never heard it, so I . . . learned it and played it. I didn't even hear the Bread version till after the wedding. When I got out of Berklee, I was on the road with Byrd Pressley, an R&B singer, and he did it as part of his show. Later, on one gig when I was playing 'Polka Dots and Moonbeams,' I started hearing this melody for 'If,' so I segued into it and then went back and forth between the two songs. It was seamless.

"Now it's evolved so the vamp borrows from Earth, Wind & Fire's 'That's the Way of the World.' I didn't sit down and say, 'This is what I'm going to do. It just occurred to me onstage one night. Rather than wait till I could sit down and work on it, I went for it right there in the moment—just like Betty Carter. I like to listen to all kinds of music, because there might be something in there that might become part of me, that might take me to my next phase. If I lock myself into one genre, I deprive myself of possibilities. I always like to see connections between genres" (Chestnut 2006).

Chestnut's own compositions address the doubts and struggles of those years after Atlantic and Warner Bros. shut down their jazz departments. Nowhere is this more obvious than on the gospel-flavored "Through the Valley," a brooding number full of lament, introspection and revival.

"That song is literally about going through difficult times," Chestnut told *DownBeat* in 2006. "I wrote it when I was at a low point, and it took me a long time to work on it without feeling down. It was a rough period musically, but eventually I realized that the piece wasn't about staying in the valley—it was about continuing to move and continuing the path to get through the valley. That's what I'm doing on everything I'm playing on this record" (Perkins 51).

After starring in films, guesting on big-budget recording sessions, and playing at jazz festivals all over the world, it might seem strange that Chestnut would still make his way to an unimposing church in a down-and-out Baltimore neighborhood once or twice a month to donate his time for a small Sunday service. But he doesn't see it that way.

"It's a give-and-take situation," he insists. "I get so much from church that I'm glad to give something back. Anytime I can be a blessing to someone else, I want to come through. And I still get a lot from church, not just spiritually, but also musically. When I make a recording, I'm trying to be the best Cyrus Chestnut I can be, and part of that is Cyrus Chestnut the gospel musician, and I don't want to lose touch with that."

"Betty always told me that jazz is about finding out who you are. And it was in her band that I started to figure out who Cyrus Chestnut was and what he had to say. Why is there a gospel influence in my music? Because I grew up in the church. Why is there a classical influence in my music? Because I took lessons at Peabody. I learned to be as honest as I could in my playing and to bring everything I am to the music" (Chestnut 2001).

Works Cited and Consulted

Unless another source is specifically cited, all facts come from the author's interviews with Cyrus Chestnut and/or from the information on his officially released recordings.

Chestnut, Cyrus. Interview by Geoffrey Himes. 4 Mar. 2001.

---. Interview by Geoffrey Himes. 5 Mar. 2001.

---. Interview by Geoffrey Himes. 31 Aug. 2001.

---. Interview by Geoffrey Himes. 10 Feb. 2006.

Carter, James. Interview by Geoffrey Himes. 6 Sep.2001.

Eig, Jonathan. "Cyrus Chestnut: For the Love of God." *DownBeat* Mar. 1997: 28-30. Print.

Giddins, Gary. "Tremolos and Elegies." *Village Voice* 8 Feb. 1994: 80. Print.

Himes, Geoffrey. "Artscape Will Be a Homecoming of Sorts for Talented Chestnut." *Columbia Flier* 18 July 1996: 52. Print.

---. "Carter's School of Jazz." Washington *Post* 5 Feb. 1995: G11-12. Print.

---. "CD Marks Ennis' New Beginning." *Columbia Flier* 2 June 1994: 69. Print.

--- "Cyrus Chestnut: Cyrus Chestnut ." Washington *Post* 15 Jan. 1999: 6. Print.

--- "Cyrus Chestnut: 'Soul Food.'" Washington *Post* 22 Feb. 2002: 6. Print.

--- "Cyrus Chestnut: 'Spirit in the Dark.'" Sonic.net 18 Oct. 2001. Web.

--- "Cyrus Chestnut: 'You Are My Sunshine'." Washington *Post* 26 Sep. 2003: 6. Print.

--- "Fight This Generation." Baltimore *City Paper* 4 Jan. 2006: 28. Print.

--- "Hot Chestnut, Yummy 'Gumbo'." Washington *Post* 31 May 1996: 6. Print.

--- "Jazz Hymns, Catholic Tastes." *Jazz Times* Jan./Feb. 2002: 67-72. Print.

--- "Nonstandard Fare: Jazz Is Reinventing Itself by Doing What It Has Always Done: Borrowing from Pop." *Jazz Times* July/Aug. 2006: 71-136. Print.

---. "Piano, Man." Baltimore *City Paper* 9 Dec. 2009: 41. Print.

--- "Sweet Inspiration: Cyrus Chestnut Looks Back to Gospel To Find the Future of Jazz." Baltimore *City Paper* 11 Apr. 2001: 18-25. Print.

Milkowski, Bill. "Cyrus Chestnut: Realizing the Vision." *Jazz Times* Jan./Feb. 1999: 45-47. Print.

Perkins, Terry. "Survival Mode: Cyrus Chestnut Leans on His Inspiration." *DownBeat* Mar. 2006: 51-52. Print.

Discography

Cyrus Chestnut Trio. *Nut.* Alfa/Evidence ECD 22135-2, 1992.

This two-CD set combines Chestnut's first two albums under his own name: The Nutman Speaks *and* The Nutman Speaks Again. *Originally released separately on the Japanese label Alfa, both were recorded at the same New York session in January, 1992, with bassist Christian McBride and drummer Carl Allen. The eight tracks on each album feature the mix of jazz standards, gospel numbers, and original compositions that would define Chestnut's career. Already a dazzling keyboardist, he hasn't yet found the musical identity that makes his subsequent work so thrilling.*

Cyrus Chestnut Trio. *Another Direction.* Alfa/Evidence ECD 22152-2, 1993.

Recorded 14 months after the first two with the same terrific rhythm section, this disc won a Swing Journal Gold Disc Award and anticipates the pianist's astonishing breakthrough the following year. It features four show tunes, an Ellington medley, and three Chestnut originals, with Chestnut's playful agility already evident.

Cyrus Chestnut. *Revelation.* Atlantic Jazz 82518-2, 1994.

On his first album as a leader for a U.S. label, Chestnut works with bassist Chris Thomas and drummer Clarence Penn, displaying not only dazzling dexterity but also a mature vision that insists virtuosity is but a means to his all-embracing vision—that his music could embrace all harmonies, influences, personal experiences, and emotions from the gut-bucket to the sublime. Here he shows enough composing, arranging, and playing chops to include the listener in that vision as well.

Cyrus Chestnut. *The Dark Before the Dawn.* Atlantic Jazz 82719-2, 1995.

Chestnut makes it clear he can play bop at the terrifying speed of a Bud Powell (as he proves on "Kattin") and swing with a sassy swagger (as he proves on "Call Me Later"). His gospel roots surface on the unaccompanied version of the old hymn, "It Is Well," but also in the way he accents certain passages with hammering block chords and imitates the soaring cadenzas of gospel soloists with dizzying right-hand runs. His blues phrasing translates bawdy exuberance into rhythms which make his solos jump.

Cyrus Chestnut. *Blessed Quietness: A Collection of Hymns, Spirituals and Carols.* Atlantic 82948-2, 1996.

Chestnut rearranges a dozen traditional tunes—including three Christmas carols, eight spirituals from the black church and "Amazing Grace"—with an ear for understated minimalism. Though played with exquisite sensitivity, the arrangements often seem too understated and quiet.

Cyrus Chestnut. *Earth Stories*. Atlantic Jazz 82876-2. 1996.

Earth Stories *marks the maturation of Chestnut the composer to the level of Chestnut the soloist; each of the nine originals boasts an irresistibly catchy theme and a dramatic structure that suits his emotional playing. The climactic blues riff on "Grandma's Blues," for example, is not played respectfully, but banged out with the earthy emphasis he associates with his grandmother. "Cooldaddy's Perspective" employs three horns to honk out its raucous R&B riff, while the stride-influenced "Nutman's Invention #1" and the ragtime-influenced "Gomez" are piano treatments. The other eight tunes display Chestnut's rare rapport with bassist Steve Kirby and drummer Alvester Garnett.*

Cyrus Chestnut. *Cyrus Chestnut*. Atlantic 83140-2. 1998.

On Chestnut's all-star project, he set aside his touring trio to record with such big names as saxophonists Joe Lovano and James Carter, drummers Billy Higgins and Lewis Nash, bassist Ron Carter, and R&B singer Anita Baker. Baker's two songs are underwhelming, but everything else sparkles, especially when Higgins ties knots into the rhythms of Chestnut's best compositions and dares everyone else to untangle them. The three soloists joust with great drama, and it all climaxes with a nearly nine-minute version of Chestnut's exciting "Sharp," as the pianist pushes the horns to greater and greater heights.

Cyrus Chestnut & Friends. *A Charlie Brown Christmas*. Atlantic 83366-2, 2000.

Chestnut zeroes in on the songs from the "Peanuts" holiday TV special with numerous special guests, including Manhattan Transfer, Vanessa Williams, Kenny Garrett, Pat Martino, Wallace Roney, Christian McBride, and Michael Brecker. The music mixes traditional Christmas fare, Vince Guaraldi's jazz instrumentals, and a Chestnut original called "Me and Charlie Brown." It is Chestnut's's most pop-oriented, marketable and least interesting recording.

Cyrus Chestnut. *Soul Food*. Atlantic Jazz 83490-2, 2001.

Though modeled on mid-century Blue Note sessions in which a pianist gathered his favorite soloists to tackle bebop numbers rooted in blues and gospel, Chestnut's album sounds like the real thing rather than a young-lion imitation, because he draws not from old records but from the same church services, R&B shows, and cutting contests that inspired Horace Silver and Herbie Hancock. This same sense of immediacy and vibrancy is shared by guest soloists James Carter, Gary Bartz, Wycliffe Gordon, Marcus Printup, and Stefon Harris, and by the rhythm section of Christian McBride and Lewis Nash. Whether it is the finger-snapping swagger of "Welllllll!" or the tender romance of "In the Underground," each tune boasts two or three ear-grabbing melodies that the artists carefully develop.

Cyrus Chestnut. *You Are My Sunshine*. Warner Bros. 48445-2, 2003.

This disc features hymns associated with James Cleveland, Richard Smallwood, Albertina Walker, the Pilgrim Travelers, Thomas Dorsey, and Tennessee Ernie Ford, but it is in no way a gospel project, but rather a very good jazz piano-trio recording. Chestnut treats these hymns the same way he treats his five originals, and the album's standards—as raw material for improvisation. Though he can sprint through sixteenth notes with Art Tatum-like ease, he prefers to shape the numbers with pauses and patient tempos so that each subtle shift proves more telling. He may add an R&B groove to Cole Porter's "It's All Right with Me" or a New Orleans syncopation to Dorsey's "Precious Lord," but Chestnut aims to evoke the moment of epiphany that links the best jazz to the best gospel. With the sympathetic help of bassist Michael Hawkins and drummer Neal Smith, he usually succeeds.

James Carter, Cyrus Chestnut, Ali Jackson, Reginald Veal. *Gold Sounds*. Brown Brothers BBR-CD1, 2005.

Gold Sounds is the brainchild of Brown Brothers Records, a new label run by fans of both indie rock and modern jazz. Pavement seems an unlikely choice, for their songs always seem to be falling apart. Yet they have real melody and drama, and that is what this all-star quartet grabs hold of. Translating the catchy guitar riffs to the keyboard, Chestnut fleshes them out with more ambitious harmonies. James Carter not only recreates Stephen Malkmus's vocals on the tenor and soprano saxophones but also translates Pavement's lo-fi amplifier noise into howls and honks. Drummer Jackson and bassist Veal make the rock rhythms both more emphatic and more elastic. The result proves that new, left-field repertoire can jolt jazz musicians out of old habits and into new discoveries.

Cyrus Chestnut. *Genuine Chestnut*. Telarc CD-83634, 2006.

Chestnut expands the trio format to include conga drummer Steven Kroon on eight of the 11 tracks and guitarist Russell Malone on three. Kroon allows Chestnut to explore Afro-Cuban rhythms on his originals "El Numero Tres" and "Baby Girl's Strut," and the pianist's command of syncopation adapts easily to the Latin dialect. Malone provides the necessary sonic fingerprint as Chestnut scratches his rock'n'roll itch on Fats Domino's "I'm Walkin'" and Bread's "If." This project reveals new facets of Chestnut's jazz virtuosity.

Cyrus Chestnut. *Cyrus Plays Elvis*. Koch KOC-CD-4238, 2007.

It sounds like a gimmick, but this album of 10 instrumental arrangements of songs recorded by Elvis Presley (plus an original composition dedicated to Presley) works. Presley and his early songwriters adapted blues and gospel by adding pop melodies and jittery rhythms. Chestnut transforms these rhythms to a more elastic boogie-woogie, but digs into the King of Rock 'n' Roll's blues roots as if stepping into the shoes of Albert Ammons and Meade Lux Lewis. The original tunes dart in and out of view between Chestnut's digressions; the result is the bluesiest album of his career.

Cyrus Chestnut. *Spirit*. JLP 0901002, 2009.

    Chestnut's piano is the only thing heard on the 14 tracks, but the record provides a fascinating dialogue between two distinct voices: his right hand and his left. On "Wade in the Water," for example, each hand pursues a different melody with different phrasing, as if two musicians were playing a duet. The right hand seems light and happy, as if basking in the joys of Christian faith, while the left seems to strain every muscle as it wrestles with temptation and sin. Yet somehow the hands mesh to form grand, unexpected chords. Chestnut also tackles hymn-like numbers from the pop world (Bill Withers's "Lean on Me" and Paul Simon's "Bridge Over Troubled Water") and from the jazz world (Duke Ellington's "Come Sunday," Chris Potter's "All in All" and Horace Silver's "Peace"). Able to find the gospel in any music, Chestnut invents a new, ear-grabbing bass figure for the Withers number and adds strutting stride piano to the Ellington.

III. LEGACIES

Passing The Axe

"There was a time in Baltimore when 'saxophonist' was a profession."

10 The Baltimore Saxophone Tradition
by Eliot Caroom

Baltimore was a thriving jazz city in the 1940s and '50s, with plenty of clubs and gigs. Over the years, Baltimore's jazz sax scene shrank, but its sax fraternity was bound together by some of the country's toughest crowds—and the fellowship of some of the world's best players.

WHIT

According to Whit Williams, a teacher and sax player who lived in Baltimore through the last half of the twentieth century, there was a time in Baltimore when "saxophonist" was a profession. Sometimes it was in combination with schoolteacher, professor or another day job, but at other times a bread-winning job by itself.

"There were so many clubs with people working," Williams remembers of the city when he first arrived in 1954. "On Baltimore Street, there were guys who raised their families and paid for them to go to college, playing music on Baltimore Street, right here in Baltimore."

Williams wasn't born in Baltimore, but arrived during its heyday for jazz musicians and for sax players. A native of Raleigh, North Carolina, Whit Williams got turned on to jazz by a neighbor in his home state who stunned him by playing effortless bop. Williams saw Charlie Parker and Dizzy Gillespie play, and even met them, before moving north.

He moved to Baltimore after serving in the Army, service which included 57 successful jumps from airplanes in the 82nd Airborne Division's Triple-Nickel (5-5-5) Battalion, the first group of black paratroopers in the world. He remembers being one of the first three blacks in the Army band. After he came to Baltimore, Whit got his start as a substitute at the legendary Royal Theatre, amidst a thriving club scene on Baltimore Street and Pennsylvania Avenue.

During the '40s, '50s, and '60s, almost one million Baltimoreans were voracious consumers of jazz. The biggest national acts came through town, drawn by a healthy population of about 950,000 at Baltimore's high mark in 1950 (Hayward and Shivers 275). Williams recalls a week when saxophone legends rubbed shoulders in his new home: Sonny Stitt finished a tour at the Comedy Club on lower Pennsylvania Avenue and Charlie Parker followed him two days later, playing up the street at the Tijuana. Bud Powell and Thelonious Monk also stayed in Baltimore for a week in the late '50s, hanging out in a house with Williams and other local players.

GARY

Gary Bartz, one of Charm City's biggest names and most talented exports, is a Baltimore native who worked with a list of greats including Max Roach and McCoy Tyner. He remembers growing up in Baltimore during the '40s and '50s and being drawn to the saxophone first by a national artist heard from afar who made a mark on every saxophonist: Charlie Parker. "I was six years old when I heard Charlie Parker," Bartz recalls. "When I heard Charlie Parker, I knew that's what I wanted to do."

Baltimore had ample opportunities in the early '50s to see the big national acts, and Bartz's dad took him when he was in his early teens. "I was always going to the Theatre, to the Royal Theatre," Bartz says. "I saw Louis Jordan, I saw Jimmy Reed . . . I saw Jackie Wilson . . . James Brown, Little Richard, you know, Chuck Berry, people like that." After five years of begging his parents, 11-year-old Bartz got his own saxophone and started taking lessons and playing in school. However, he really began learning one afternoon when his dad took him to see Sonny Stitt at a Comedy Club matinée. "I didn't know [my father] had the horn in the trunk of the car," Bartz remembers. "He went up to Sonny Stitt—I didn't know none of this— and said, 'My son plays alto, he'd like to play.' So Sonny Stitt announces on stage, 'we have this young man.' I said, 'Oh my lord, why would he do that?' Sonny Stitt took me through all the keys on the blues: at the time I didn't know one key from the other, so it didn't matter."

Bartz also met Max Roach in Baltimore, with whom he later played his first professional gig.

ANDY

Before he was one of Baltimore's top sax players, Andy Ennis was born into a musical household, with a mother who gave lessons, and a sister, Ethel, who would become Baltimore's best-known singer in the years after Sarah Vaughan.

Ennis grew up listening to horn players like Tex Beneke and Ray Noble on the radio, and picked up the saxophone in his teens. The young horn player ventured into a jazz scene complete with intimidating venues and rough-and-tumble audiences.

He remembers Smith's Hotel on Druid Hill Avenue near Eutaw Street, across from the old *Afro-American* newspaper building. The bar was called Bucket of Blood, and on Ennis's first visit with his high school friends, a broom flew out the door along with the sounds of a wild brawl:

"I said, 'I don't know if I want to go in this place,'" and his friend replied, "'Oh, they do this all the time.'"

The music of the day was mostly bop, according to Ennis, because big bands started falling apart following the end of World War II. Even though the bands were small combos, there were a variety of venues in Baltimore for the music.

"At that time there was at least 30 different small places, clubs, actually, they were bars," Ennis remembers. "They called them lounges."

Out of numerous nights in the lounges, one stands out in Andy's mind after many decades. It's the night he first saw Mickey Fields, Baltimore's greatest saxophone player (according to virtually all of Fields's surviving peers). "I'll never forget that," recalls Ennis. His sister, Ethel, was singing with Mickey and his brother Kenny Fields in one of Mickey's classic groups, the Seven Tilters, at a club called Sherrie's Showbar on Pulaski Highway. She would sing in between the Tilters' sets. Ethel knew her little brother wanted to play saxophone, so she knew he should see Mickey.

"You want to play saxophone, don't you?" she said, as she got ready for work, putting her eyelashes on. "You've got to hear this guy Mickey play." "'I can't go,'" Andy said.

"C'mon, c'mon, c'mon! We ain't going to tell Momma—just put your coat on," Ethel said, and he threw a coat on over his pajamas. He got into the car and his sister sneaked him into the back of Sherrie's to his first Mickey Fields show.

"He was walking the bar, blowing the horn, walking the bar, blowing the horn, dah dah dah, dah dah dah dah," Andy recalls, glowing with the memory. "I really wanted to play saxophone when I heard Mickey Fields."

Andy remembers Mickey Fields as one of the best, referring to him the same way most people who heard him do—the word they use is "monster."

"Mickey had a rough sound. He had a hardcore sound. It wasn't really sweet like Lester Young," Ennis says. "He had a straight tenor sound. . . . To me, he always had a hard sound, and believe me, he played hard, too."

GARY

Bartz also knew Mickey Fields. He knew him not only as a hard player, but also as a good man.

"I met him when I was really young," explains Bartz. "My horn got stolen one time when I was working at The Closet in Baltimore, and he gave me, he didn't lend me, he gave me his [horn]. He said, 'I've got an alto laying around here, use that.' . . . [H]e was just a good friend music-wise and otherwise."

But Bartz was influenced by records and national touring artists, along with local greats like Mickey and Ray Kitts, the sax player at the time in the house band at the Royal Theatre.

"When he would stand up and play and take his solo, it was just . . . I was just fascinated," Bartz said of Kitts.

Whit Williams was a mentor to Bartz as well, one of many he had in Baltimore.

"I learned a lot from Whit," Bartz says. "I learned a lot from Mickey. I learned a lot from everybody."

WHIT

Despite the thriving scene, Williams, born 300 miles south of Baltimore, found the city's racial climate to be worse than Raleigh's in many ways.

"In terms of where you could play, and all that, [Raleigh] was nothing like it was here in Baltimore—Baltimore was like back in the 1700s or something," Williams recalls, referring to the city's segregated venues. The segregation in Baltimore wasn't just in clubs. "In Raleigh, my mother, she could go any place on Federal Street—this is the main street in Raleigh—and try on a dress. Well, . . . in 1955, after I'd been here about a year, my mother came up to Baltimore. I obviously wanted to do something for my mother, so I wanted to take her downtown to Hecht-May to try on a dress, and she couldn't try on a dress. That was right here in Baltimore," says Williams. Williams was a member of the city's association of jazz-lovers, first called the Interracial Jazz Society, and later the Left Bank Jazz Society, a group that promoted jazz. Some members were players, some were fans, and black and white alike they were bound by their love for the music.

GARY

Gary Bartz joined the society while still in his teens. He saw great shows that the group promoted—Wilbur Ware, Harold Ousley, and others at the YMCA on Madison Avenue, before Left Bank started producing shows at the Famous Ballroom. There were parties with records, there were concerts, there were jam sessions. Then the name changed from "Interracial Jazz Society" to "Left Bank" as the organization moved beyond the jams to book bigger out-of-town acts.

"So many musicians said, 'Oh, what an ugly name,'" recalls Bartz. "Musicians coming from the North, they were saying, '"Interracial Jazz Society", what kind of a name is that for [a group]?'"

The ugly name came from an ugly truth that Bartz couldn't tolerate. Bartz left Baltimore before reaching legal adulthood, and remembers his departure as an easy choice. "I left Baltimore . . . in 1958, [and] I couldn't wait to get out of there," explains Bartz. "Baltimore was a segregated city when I grew up and it was a very hateful place to me. . . . I didn't like the vibe, . . . I had to get out of there."

He had visited New York and been enticed by the great jazz of the tail end of the bebop era, which saw the arrival of Freddie Hubbard and McCoy Tyner. But in addition to that, New York's racial climate was far better in Bartz's eyes.

"If I'd stayed in Baltimore, I don't know what I would have done," Bartz says. "It was not a good place, believe me. Racism is not a good deal."

He came back to work at The Closet for two and a half years in the 1980s, and between 1960 and '65 he commuted and played weekends at a nightclub that his parents ran. But those were just visits. Bartz's home was beyond Baltimore.

Gary Bartz found great success in New York, but many of Baltimore's sax stars stayed. Despite the city's racism and small size compared with the looming jazz metropolis of New York, there was camaraderie to the scene, bred in part by tough crowds—crowds who booed and who cared. That is something that even after 50 years, Bartz remembers well.

"Music was very important in Baltimore," says Bartz. "That's why the audiences were so hard, because they knew what was good or not. . . . That's the way it should be. I want a hard audience. It raises your game. . . . [Entertainers] everywhere said, 'Boy, we're going to Baltimore, we gotta be up on our stuff' . . . just like when you come to New York, you gotta be up on your stuff."

Baltimore pianist, former horn player, and Howard University professor Reppard Stone had a more concise way of putting it.

"They called it TOBA," Stone said in 2002. "Tough on black asses. . . . Baltimore had the worst audiences. If you weren't good, they'd throw things on the stage at you and boo you and that kind of thing. So it was like, make Baltimore the last stop" (Baker and Stone). But the audiences booed because they cared. And the pressure of the tough crowds created camaraderie among sax players who wanted it.

ANDY

Ennis, who appreciated the hard tone Mickey had, also came under the wing of a more lyrical player.

"Jimmy Harrell had a sound, it was unbelievable. When he played a ballad, it was so sweet," remembers Ennis.

Ennis worked at the Red Fox on Pennsylvania and Fulton in a combo with his high school friends, and Harrell worked across the street at a place called The Crossroads. Harrell, like Fields and most other Baltimore players, played standards such as "Cherokee," and blues like "Red Top"—songs that the audience knew. Harrell worked with big bands at the Royal Theatre, the city's premier venue, and also on Baltimore Street, called "The Block." Harrell pushed the younger, less confident man toward bigger gigs.

"I was about 17 or 18 then," Ennis says. "He would say, 'Look, you want the Theatre or The Block?' And I was scaaa-rred of the theatre, so I [always] said, 'The Block.'"

"I need a uniform," was the excuse Ennis would give, but Harrell finally told him, "'Wear mine.'"

That got Ennis's foot in the door with Tracy McCleary's house band at the Royal Theatre, the first big band he played with, which backed big out-of-town performers like Sam Cooke and Barbara Mason. Eventually Ennis found himself in the same spot as Fields, Williams, and Bartz: facing the choice of whether to stay home or go out into the wide world beyond Baltimore.

After he was drafted into the Army in 1961, Ennis played in the military band, and like Williams, served as a rifleman. When he left the Army in 1963, he started touring with the Bill Doggett band, traveling the country for about two years.

Ennis's big band experience with the Army, and at the Royal, put him in good stead when he was auditioning for one of the biggest names in the country at that time, Ray Charles. With a strange chart—"Zig Zag"—in front of him, Ennis suddenly saw a man in sunglasses walk in.

"That's Ray! Now I'm trying to watch the music, watching him, you know?! He walked straight to me! And put his ear down in the bell of my horn! I was reading this music for the first time," recalls Ennis.

A Royal Theatre lesson saved him.

"Even if you're wrong, play it. How are you going to know if you don't hear it?" Ennis asks. "That's what got me through. I learned from Jimmy Harrell in the Tracy McCleary Royal Theatre band. No matter what it is, don't stop, keep playing, don't stop, keep playing. Play anything—just keep going." It was good enough to win Ennis the gig, and about a decade on the road with "The Genius," from 1968 through '77. Ennis toured, but he eventually chose to stay in Baltimore. It was a choice not every sax great made, but one that Baltimore's best faced.

Staying meant playing the clubs, dealing with the tough crowds, and enjoying the fellowship of world-class players. Often it also meant working another job. Going could mean constant touring, or the intensely competitive and happening world of New York, jostling for gigs and attention from record companies in the mecca of jazz.

Recording was unusual in Baltimore during the '50s, '60s, and '70s outside of tapes that the Left Bank Jazz Society made at their shows, which were mostly of national acts. Shows were what earned money for players, sax and otherwise.

WHIT

"Most of the music I heard guys play was from the standard repertory," Whit Williams recalls. "There were guys who'd write songs, but a lot of times they wouldn't play them out on gigs."

"If you were able to record, then everybody knew your name," Williams says. "But there were so many monster, terrific, fantastic players right here in Baltimore who never even made any recordings."

"During that particular time," says Williams, "the emphasis was not on recording. . . . It was on getting a gig."

Since the listening tastes of the Baltimore public ran mainly to standards and followed national jazz trends, the city was no exception to a craze that swept over the jazz-listening public in the '60s and '70s. Hammond B-3 organs dropped like 400-pound anvils on the corners of stages around Baltimore (Nelson).

ANDY

The B-3 was a fad that Ennis looked on with mixed feelings. "Jimmy Smith caused a lot of problems, and when I saw problems, everybody wanted to put the piano down and get this great big Hammond B-3 with Leslie speakers, ohhh mannn, everybody was saying, 'What is all this furniture coming up on the bandstand for?'" Ennis recalls.

There were winners and losers with the organ fad—bass players, obviously, didn't approve. But many sax players, including Fields, thrived in the thick aural environment an organ generated. The B-3 era was good to Mickey, Ennis explains. At that time, he worked at the Bird Cage with organist Dennis Fisher, with Ennis, and with an organ player named Charlie Covington.

In 1977, at the peak of the organ era, Mickey was caught on tape in a show at the Famous Ballroom featuring Fields and organist Richard "Groove" Holmes. It would be his single full-length recording—*The Astonishing Mickey Fields*—and the recording, on the Groove Merchant label, was of Holmes's gig, in fact. Mickey sat in on the gig because Holmes's group included Gene Evans on guitar and George "Mousey" Randall on drums—two out of the Seven Tilters.

"'Hey, buddy, sit in with us,'" is how Ennis remembers the Famous Ballroom gig starting, "and [Mickey] was like a fish in water." The record shows a saxophonist at home leading an organ-fueled bop ensemble—cutting up standards like "Straight No Chaser," and blowing with facility and power in jams like "Left Bank Cookout," in which Mickey trades unbelievable licks with "Groove" Holmes. That night's gig, along with a few other hard-to-find EPs, is how the world continues to know and love Fields after his passing. If that single album defines Mickey, it also serves as a clear high-water mark for Baltimore jazz in the time of B-3.

Even if B-3 jazz put some bass players and pianists out of work in the '70s, it was better than other nationally-led, locally embraced movements away from jazz and toward rock over several decades—and, in the '70s, the sharp veer into disco.

Disco, the next big move in popular music, also leached the jazz audience in Baltimore and beyond. But changing tastes weren't the only problem for Baltimore jazz, or for Baltimore, in the late 1960s and 1970s.

The city convulsed with riots after the death of Martin Luther King, Jr. in 1968, and its population had begun a long and steady decline, dropping by 50,000 people from 1950-1970. In the next 20 years, the population would fall three times faster to 736,000, from its apex of about a million (Hayward and Shivers 275). The Royal Theatre held its last big jazz show in 1965, featuring Count Basie. Smaller venues around Pennsylvania Avenue, the lounges and bars, also struggled from the late '60s on.

"I don't know which died first, Pennsylvania Avenue or the Royal Theatre," says McCleary, the Royal's bandleader, in an interview years later (Schaaf). No matter which died first, the '70s and '80s saw further attrition of Baltimore's jazz venues and listeners.

CRAIG

By the 1980s, jazz competed not with disco, but with rock and a newcomer, rap. But while other kids his age were listening to Wu-Tang or Public Enemy, Craig Alston had Wynton Marsalis's *Black Codes (From the Underground)* playing through his headphones as he walked the streets of Baltimore.

Baltimore in the 1980s was smaller than it had been in earlier decades, and so was the jazz scene. Yet some things were the same. Baltimore's sax contingent was still supportive and tight-knit— and players still grew their ears on records and national artists, but honed their chops in the clubs.

Like Gary Bartz, Andy Ennis, and Whit Williams, Alston was inspired by national greats. Wynton Marsalis was big in the 1980s, and his example of a young black man who had mastered both classical and jazz inspired Alston, who still remembers watching him on Charles Kuralt's show.

Craig enrolled in Morgan State's music education program in 1993, but it wasn't a jazz program.

"That was a period where there was a lot of jazz in the streets and the clubs but jazz pedagogy was still kind of a new, foreign thing," remembers Alston. "Towson had it. University of Maryland was working on it. Peabody didn't get it 'til the late '90s."

An education in the clubs was necessary. One night, Craig's friend and Baltimore trumpet player Dontae Winslow invited him to the Balkan Blazers on Druid Hill Lake Drive.

"I got Mickey Fields playing," Winslow said, and Craig, not knowing any better, just said, "OK, cool."

"I see this kind of old dude walkin' around, with his hands all swollen, and he doesn't say a lot," Craig says. "He picks up this horn and starts playing, and I was like, 'Goddamn. Who is this dude?' His sound was huge."

Winslow invited Alston to sit in on blues.

"I played next to Mickey, and I got discouraged," Alston says of that first meeting. "So I told Mickey, 'Man, I'm about to quit.'"

"'If you quit, I'm going to whip your ass,'" Alston remembers Mickey responding. "He told everybody that, that was Mickey's nature. He was like, 'Boy, you need to come to the Sportsman's tomorrow night.'" That was Mickey's Monday night gig. Along with the camaraderie and the tough crowds, Mickey was still on the scene, and still a magnet to young players with a reed between their lips. That was even after he was stricken with arthritis—and had learned how to play with his swollen hands.

"Mickey was in there killing. . . . [W]hat's scary about him, was he was so good he could pace," Alston says. "He could kind of compartmentalize and put his playing on levels. He would never really play that much better than the next best person on stage. . . . [H]e would never try to dwarf me. . . . To me that's complete mastery," Alston concludes. "He was one of the best I've ever seen."

"Mickey could play the entire history and the entire range of the horn. He could play bluesy. I've heard him sound just like Sonny

Stitt, but then I've heard him sound like Dexter. I've heard him sound like Stanley Turrentine, but I've also heard him sound like 'Trane [Coltrane]. . . . This dude knew a crapload of tunes. He knew everything in every key."

"This dude was monstrous."

To hear Alston tell it, Mickey was still the same player Andy Ennis saw in the '40s—awe-inspiring, intimidating, and afterwards, always approachable.

ANDY

By that time, Andy Ennis, back home after nearly a decade on the road with Ray Charles, was himself a role model.

In the 1980s, Andy and Mickey Fields mentored the young players coming through the club scene. Ennis remembers Alston as a sax player with early promise who, like Mickey, wouldn't leave the city. "Me and Mickey, we used to put him in what we called a 'cradle,'" Ennis recalls. "I would get on one side, and Mickey on the other side, and Craig Alston in the middle. . . . We used to have a good time, and let him play all he wanted, just blow, blow, blow," Ennis says. "And then after we blow, he'd look at us as if to get our approval, and we'd say, 'All right, you're good.'"

Craig, for his part, remembers the attention of his elders modestly: "I spent probably about a good 2 or 3,000 times just killing people's ears, you know?"

It wasn't just Alston in the "cradle" at the Sportsman's Lounge, recalls Ennis. Gary Thomas was there, too, and Antonio Hart, a memorable talent who attended the Baltimore School for the Arts with Jada Pinkett Smith before moving north to New York to apply his talents.

ELLERY

Another young horn player who learned from the greatest generation of Baltimore jazz was Ellery Eskelin, who enrolled in Hank Levy's Towson jazz program early in its development. In the late '70s, the program was a music teachers' college, says Eskelin, and Levy's innovative arrangements for Stan Kenton and Don Ellis were a draw for students, but didn't constitute a jazz program.

"The reason we all went there was because of Hank, but . . . the music department was all about music education," Eskelin says. "They tolerated the fact that Hank had a jazz band."

According to Eskelin, Levy was an incredible talent at arranging, but wasn't a teacher of improvisation.

"When it came time to play a solo, it was like, 'Well you've got to go out and roll around in the gutter, you're playing too pretty.' That was about the extent of it, you know?" Ellery says.

Luckily for Alston and Eskelin, Mickey, Andy and many others were still holding court in the remaining clubs of the day.

"There was still a lot going on," Eskelin recalls. "When we came of age . . . we could go to these clubs and go hang out with somebody like Mickey Fields who was completely generous with his time and spirit and would let us guys come up on stage."

Like Craig Alston, years after Mickey's death in 1995, Ellery Eskelin still has a vivid memory of hearing him play (Himes).

"There was one night in particular that I'll never forget," says Eskelin. "I think it was at the 20 Grand Club he was playing. . . . I walked in, and I'm standing at the door in the back of the club and I'm listening to this sound coming out of his horn. It was particularly huge that night, and it had nothing to do with amplification."

With nothing extraordinary about the sound system, Fields burned his playing deep into Eskelin's mind. Telling the experience, Eskelin rushes his words one after another to recall the night:

"His sound that night was so enormous and so raw it bordered on Albert Ayler to my ears. . . . [T]imbrally it was all over the place, he was getting so much out of the horn, and it was so massive that it sounded like Albert Ayler playing bebop. . . . I was completely knocked out, I was astonished and I still remember it to this day, and I'm sure it had a big impact on me and how I try to play."

When Eskelin sat in with Mickey, he got lessons from the master— and from Baltimore's discriminating crowds.

"I remember the first time I sat in at the Bird Cage with Mickey. Tom McCormick and I sat in," Eskelin says. "Tom did a good job and I thought I did too but a guy came up to me later and said I needed to slow down. It was usually more general things like that. Old school in a way."

Like Gary Bartz and many others, Ellery moved to New York at a young age and stayed. But not before he'd established early chops in Baltimore.

Baltimore jazz, and its saxophone legacy, lost some players and fans, like the genre. But common refrains over the years tell of a real tradition.

CRAIG

"It's a hard place to make it," Craig Alston observes. "If people in Baltimore like you, there's a good chance that everyone else in the rest of the world will like you. Baltimore audiences are real tough. They're not taking no bullshit. . . . If you can't play, they will boo you. They will let you know you suck."

While those audiences may be TOBA, as Reppard Stone remembers, the musicians continue to support one another. That includes Stone himself, who chose Craig Alston as an artist to promote when he started working with a new local jazz label.

GARY

"As far as a Baltimore sound. Hmmm." He contemplates the question, but doesn't commit. "I don't know. You can say a lot of great musicians came out of Baltimore. . . . I don't think it was a sound, I think it was just—music was very important in Baltimore. That's why the audiences were so hard, because they knew what was good or not."

ANDY

Baltimore's jazz scene has shrunk and shrunk more. But the city's best know the story isn't over.

"Jazz will survive," Ennis predicts, thinking about the business, the audience, and the music itself. "You just hope that you will survive—because it will beat you up. Jazz is hardcore."

Acknowledgments

It was an honor learning Baltimore jazz history, and thanks go to all the sources who shared their time. Thanks also go to Eliot's family, as well as to Barry Glassman, who had long encouraged a piece on Mickey Fields's legacy; to Mark Osteen, for invaluable confidence; to Bob Jacobson, for patient newsletter help; and to Camay Calloway Murphy, whose passion for Baltimore jazz is truly special.

Works Cited

Alston, Craig. Personal interview. 7 Nov. 2009.

Baker, Henry and Reppard Stone. *Sounds and Stories*. "Oral History: Transcript. Interview No. SAS8.20.02." Interview by Elizabeth Schaaf. 20 Aug. 2002. Web.

Bartz, Gary. Personal interview. 2 Dec. 2009.

Ennis, Andrew. Personal interview. 14 Nov. 2009.

Eskelin, Ellery. Personal interview. 22 Nov. 2009.

Hayward, Mary Ellen, and Shivers, Frank R. *The Architecture of Baltimore: an Illustrated History*. Baltimore: Johns Hopkins University P, 2004. 275. Print.

Himes, Geoffrey. "Sax and the City." www.citypaper.com. 21 July 2004. Web. 14 Jan. 2010.

Nelson, Glen E. "History of the Hammond B-3 Organ." www.theatreorgans.com.N.p. n.d. Web. 14 Jan. 2010.

Pryor, Rosa. Personal interview. 7 Nov. 2009.

Schaaf, Elizabeth. "Oral History: Transcript. Interview No. SAS8.20.02." Johns Hopkins University. N.d. Web.

Schaaf, Elizabeth. "Royal Theatre." *Maryland Online Encyclopedia*. N.d. Web. 14 Jan. 2010.

Williams, Whit. Personal interview. 14 Nov. 2009.

Discography

Bartz, Gary. *See Chapter Eight for complete discography.*

Charles, Ray. *My Kind Of Jazz.* Perf. Andy Ennis (tenor saxophone) feat. on "Booty Butt." Rec. Tangerine, April 1970. Record. iTunes and Amazon.com. *http://itunes.apple.com/us/album/my-kind-of-jazz/id310043337*
Andy Ennis toured with Ray Charles for nearly a decade, and his horn work can be found on 1970's My Kind of Jazz. "Booty Butt," a jam between Ray and Ennis, got its name from "a nickname [Ray] like[d] to call certain people," according to Ray Charles's website, which says the instrumental track made it to #31 on the Pop Charts.

Doggett, Bill. *Wow!* Perf. Andy Ennis (tenor saxophone). Polygram Records,1965. LP, CD, iTunes and Amazon.com. *http://www.amazon.com/Wow/dp/B000V698BK*

Eskelin, Ellery. *The Sun Died.* Soul Note, 1996. CD. *http://home.earthlink.net/~eskelin/order.html*

Eskelin, Ellery. *One Great Day.* hatOLOGY, 1996. CD. *http://www.hathut.com/home.html*

Eskelin, Ellery. *Vanishing Point.* hatOLOGY, 2000. CD. *http://www.hathut.com/home.html*
After leaving Baltimore, Ellery Eskelin found great success playing in a variety of settings, most often small groups, sometimes with accordion. The music is challenging, exemplified by his 2000 album Vanishing Point, *in which Eskelin improvised compositions with a group of string musicians and vibraphonist Matt Moran, earning a perplexed but appreciative review from* All About Jazz.

Eskelin, Ellery. *Ten.* hatOLOGY, 2004. CD. *http://www.hathut.com/home.html*

Eskelin, Ellery. *Every So Often.* Prime Source, 2008. CD.

Fertile Ground. *Seasons Change.* Perf. Craig Alston (tenor/baritone saxophone). Blackout Studios, 2002. CD.

Fertile Ground. *Black Is...* Perf. Craig Alston (tenor/baritone saxophone). Blackout Studios, 2004. CD.

Fields, Mickey. *The Astonishing Mickey Fields*. Perf. ("Straight, No Chaser," "Lover Man," "Left Bank Cook-out."): Mickey Fields (tenor saxophone), Richard "Groove" Holmes (organ), George Freeman (guitar), Billy Jackson (drums); ("Little Green Apples," "Light My Fire"): Mickey Fields (tenor saxophone), Calvin Vaughn (organ), Don Bowie (drums). Edmar, 1977. LP.
The Astonishing Mickey Fields, *like other Fields recordings, has the same cache among Baltimore jazz fans as a rare Grateful Dead gem has for Deadheads. Copies are gingerly offered to novice listeners, and emigrant jazz artists have carried it to jazz radio stations in other cities to stump DJs who can't seem to guess the identity of the mysterious phenom. The 1977 recording shows Mickey in his element at a show in the Famous Ballroom featuring Fields and organist Richard "Groove" Holmes. The best bet for finding a Mickey Fields recording, barring future reissues, is searching virtual used record stacks on the internet.*

Fields, Mickey. *Mickey and his Mice*. Perf. Mickey Fields (tenor saxophone), Eddie Drennon (arrangements). Marti, 1970. LP.

Fields, Mickey. "Little Green Apples/Light My Fire". Edmar. 45rpm Record.

Fields, Mickey. Video.
http://vids.myspace.com/index.cfm?fuseaction=vids.individual &VideoID=29738495

Fields, Mickey. Video.
http://vids.myspace.com/index.cfm?fuseaction=vids. individual&videoid=29738495

Williams, Whit. *The Whit Williams "Now's the Time Big Band" featuring Slide Hampton and Jimmy Heath*. MAMA Records, 2008. CD.
Whit Williams spent most of his career performing, teaching and mentoring young musicians. But in 2008 he released this full-length album with old friends Jimmy Heath on tenor sax and Slide Hampton on trombone. The album, featuring mostly work written by Hampton, also showcases young talent whom Whit helped rear, including tenor sax player Gary Thomas, head of the Peabody Institute's jazz program.

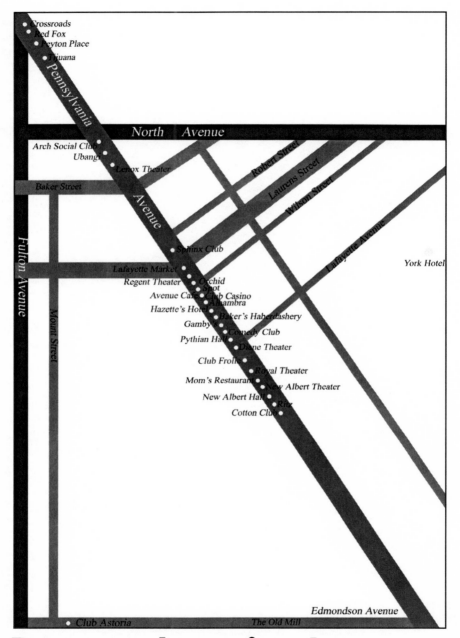

Pennsylvania Avenue

"If you were in West Baltimore, an African American, you functioned . . . on Pennsylvania Avenue. . . . That's where the work was, and that's where the musicians played."

11 Making The Scene
by Mary Zajac

Billie Holiday stands on the corner of Lafayette and Pennsylvania Avenues. Shoulders thrown back, mouth open, a signature gardenia tucked behind her ear, she dominates this brick-enclosed corner (now known as Billie Holiday Plaza) as if it were the stage of the Club Tijuana. Although the man on the corner waiting for the number seven bus looks at sculptor James Earl Reid's rendering of her and asks, "Who's that?," the words on the granite pedestal beneath the folds of her gown acknowledge her as "'Lady Day' . . . a socially relevant artist who served suffering as well as beauty through her songs."

Across the street, on the southeast corner of the intersection, The Royal Theatre Marquee Monument stands tall in the shadow of the Providence Baptist Church. Two pillars bear the silhouettes of horn players, keyboarders, and vocalists, but the theater's vintage marquee offers a vague "We support you" instead of its classic promise of "Always a good show." It is all that remains of the Royal Theatre, demolished in 1971 and perhaps the most iconic of the many entertainment venues that made this street thrum with music in the first half of the twentieth century. Still, there's more of the Royal than there is of The Comedy Club, which once stood at 1528 Pennsylvania Avenue, now the site of the Woodford Street Apartments. Or of the Sphinx Club at 2115, the memory of which is captured in Donald Tyson-Bey's (aka "Doc Toonz") spectacular black and gold mural one block south, where the image of a vintage cruiser, all fins and whitewalls, is parked in front of the club's curved block windows where "cocktails" are advertised in neon letters.

The distance along Pennsylvania Avenue from North Avenue, where paint flakes from the ornate frieze of the Arch Social Club ("Celebrating Black Men Together for Over 90 Years" reads the banner hanging across the face of the building), southwest to Lafayette Avenue is only a dozen or so blocks, now filled with the commerce of everyday urban life. Dollar stores and liquor stores, Chinese food takeouts and nail salons share the street with Wireless World and Penn Health Center. But the concentration of musical history here is enormous.

Pennsylvania Avenue is where singer Ruby Glover first met Miles Davis, where bassist Montell Augustus Poulson met Ella Fitzgerald and took her back to his mother's house to "throw on the feedbag" (Poulson), where a very young Louisa Lara sang for Lionel Hampton at the Royal and won a singing contest, where Ethel Ennis sang regularly at the Red Fox, where white folks flocked to hear jazz music, but where black folks often felt confined.

Although jazz musicians performed at the Club Orleans and other venues on Baltimore's east side, as well as in the burlesque houses of The Block, Pennsylvania Avenue remained the locus of Baltimore's rich African-American music scene from the 1920s to the early 1960s in concert houses like the Royal Theatre, the Comedy Club, and the Club Tijuana, and private clubs like the Sphinx Club or the Arch Social Club. Nat "King" Cole performed on The Avenue. So did Duke Ellington, Sarah Vaughan, and Dinah Washington. And when folks like to say that anyone who was anyone in black entertainment (as well as a handful of white jazz artists like Gerry Mulligan and Louie

Bellson) played on Pennsylvania Avenue, that accounting, however vague, isn't wrong.

"If you were in west Baltimore, an African American," reports Dr. Reppard Stone, a pianist and faculty emeritus of Howard University, in a 2002 interview, "you functioned either on Pennsylvania Avenue or on Fremont Avenue. That's where the work was, and that's where the musicians played" (Stone).

The turn of the century marked Pennsylvania Avenue's beginnings as a hub for Baltimore's African-American community. And as white Baltimoreans moved outward from the city into new suburbs, African-Americans, restricted by where they could live and shop, settled and claimed the area of West Baltimore around what soon became known as simply "The Avenue."

The Avenue was where you ate, shopped, worked, where you went to the movies, went to have a drink, or to see a show. This is where, in its heyday, you could find the Lafayette Market in the 1700 block; the Charm Center, a fashionable dress shop for African American women (who were not allowed to shop in Baltimore's downtown department stores) at 1811; and the Penn Hotel, at 1631, an overnight refuge for black entertainers performing in Baltimore (who were not allowed to stay in "white" hotels) as part of the Chitlin' Circuit[1] before moving on to places like Carr's Beach, a historically African-American beach and concert venue just south of Annapolis. As former *Afro-American* journalist James E. "Biddy" Wood, Sr. puts it baldly, "We had to make our own [places] because we weren't welcome anywhere else."

In a 2010 interview, Wood, who also managed musical talent like Gregory and Maurice Hines, The Four Tops, and his late wife, singer Damita Jo, in the late 1960s, admonishes us not to "glorify" The Avenue and its history under Jim Crow law, a point fair taken. Yet the denigrating challenges of segregated life also allowed tight communities to blossom and flourish, and Pennsylvania Avenue was no exception.

Perhaps what is most striking in the remembrances of those who attended shows and, later, performed on The Avenue, is the accessibility of the artists, and the amount of networking, mentoring, and in many cases, inspiration that occurred on these city blocks. Jam sessions could occur in unlikely places—from someone's home to Henry Baker's haberdashery shop—and often a youngster's first introduction to live music was seeing a big name performer at the Royal. "The best in black entertainment came through here," recalls Stone. "That was really a help for us young guys—to give us incentive to go on and do things."

In a 1996 interview, trumpeter Roy McCoy remembers Louis Armstrong's Royal performance that served as an early inspiration for him to take up the trumpet. "[I] saw Louis Armstrong playing his horn," McCoy recalls. "It was just shining and the notes were just coming out and I thought, 'This is what I'm going to do'"(McCoy). He subsequently saved up enough money selling newspapers to put down $2 on a $14 pawn shop trumpet, and years later, around 1942, McCoy got the chance to play with his inspiration when he was called in at the last minute to replace a trumpeter in Armstrong's band during a performance at the Royal: "So I'm sitting up behind Louis Armstrong and he's playing notes that I used to be up front listening to. That was really exciting."

Not only did West Baltimoreans get to see or play alongside big name performers, they also got to spend time with them outside the concert houses. Musician James Crockett reminisces how at the Royal, it was "a common thing to see them [the musicians] because they were in the Black community" (Crockett).

Meeting musicians was easy for fans. According to Crockett, "You'd just walk up to them and you'd say to them: may I have your autograph? And he would say yes. And you would say where's your home? And he would tell you. And you'd say how long have you been playing so and so and so and so. He said, well, I've been practicing for a number of years, and I started out when I was seven years old" (Crockett).

Later, as musicians became more popular and media coverage increased, approaching the musicians became more difficult. "[W]hen the bobbie soxers started going, coming out, then there would be a crowd," says Crockett, "and it became a problem then getting close to the musicians."

"But during those days, nobody had a bodyguard, so [even then] you could get close to the musicians. You could talk to them; you could hug them; you could shake their hands. And they were there for you."

The fans, in turn, were there for the musicians, putting them up in their own houses when (white) hotels wouldn't take them, making them meals, and even showing them the city, something James Crockett recalls doing for Billy "Mr. B" Eckstine, Count Basie, Ella Fitzgerald, and Pearl Bailey (Crockett).

Saxophonist Donald Smith also had the opportunity to spend time with one of his idols, Miles Davis. Smith recalls a night in the early 1950s before "Miles really hit it." Davis and drummer Max Roach had just played a late gig on Pennsylvania Avenue (most likely at the Comedy Club), but neither was ready for the night to end, so Smith and a buddy took Miles and Max to the Adams Club, a small jazz room on the second floor of a building in Turners Station, the African-American community on the far southeastern part of Baltimore County, near Dundalk. "We got there around five a.m.," Smith remembers, "and Max took over for the drummer." It was late (or early, depending on your point of view), "but when Miles came in," says Smith, "a lot of those folks who were ready to leave stayed and some of them even called friends."

The tight-knit community—both geographical and cultural—encouraged these kinds of relationships between musicians and their fans. And as Biddy Wood explains, especially when traveling in heavily segregated cities, "[musicians] needed to be befriended too."

Although segregation also prevented African Americans from attending shows in Baltimore's white music venues and movie theaters like the Hippodrome, white fans were not restricted from visiting The Avenue's concert houses, and audiences on Pennsylvania were often mixed. By all reports, folks got along, though an item in a 1934 "Nite Clubbing" column of the *Afro-American* reported that "the majority of my nite club fans are shooting in complaints about mixed races in certain clubs, one in particular is said to be duplicating the famous Cotton Club, ringside tables for ofays [a derogative term for whites] only. Dangerous stuff, lid might blow off any minute" ("Nite Clubbing" 9).

But in Gil Sandler's *Small Town Baltimore*, white jazz fans Al Patacca and Sigmund "Siggy" Shapiro offer only positive experiences of

Pennsylvania Avenue. "It didn't matter if you were black or white, The Avenue clubs were where the true jazz buffs went," says Patacca, who was a trumpet player in the Royal's house band under the direction of Tracy McCleary (qtd. in Sandler 183). A Saturday night, recalls Patacca, would see Pennsylvania Avenue with "people wall-to-wall inside, curb-to-curb outside, well-dressed and orderly, all come to hear good jazz. It was high-tone, and elegant" (qtd. in Sandler 183). Adds Shapiro: "People who liked jazz didn't care about color, they cared about jazz" (qtd. in Sandler 183, emphasis in the original).

Pianist Jimmy Wells, who is African American, concurs as he explains, in a 2002 interview, what he calls the "mystery" of Pennsylvania Avenue: "It didn't matter what color you was, you was always welcome on Pennsylvania Avenue. You could walk up and down that street any time, any time, day or night, two, or three o'clock in the morning, man. No problem. The white folks could come to all the clubs up there, Tijuana, Comedy Club, Candy's, Trolley Bar, Avenue Bar, right on up there to Fulton Avenue where the Red Fox was. Any of those clubs, c'mon" (Wells).

It was only after the riots, he adds, that whites weren't welcome on The Avenue, because then, says Wells, "you know, the hate was up" (Wells).

Some clubs, like the Club Tijuana, came to be identified with white patronage, although the artists who performed there were both black and white. In an interview with the *Sun*'s Carl Schoettler in 2002, Ruby Glover recalls the Tijuana as "a real, real hip avenue bar and a beautiful place to go [and hear] jazz. The Tijuana offered you an opportunity to see the giants, and touch them and be in the midst of them."

And plenty of giants played there in the 1950s—from Miles Davis and John Coltrane to Chet Baker, Art Farmer, Ben Webster, and vocalist Chris Connor. Henry Baker specifically recalls bringing Charlie Parker there in 1952, and Baker's friend, Reppard Stone, remembers putting Parker up in his apartment for the duration of his run, so that he didn't have to take the train back to New York at night (Stone also recalls putting up Charles Mingus) (Baker and Stone).

"[Dave] Brubeck used to come to the Tijuana," remembers Donald Smith, who describes the club as "a real nice cozy club on the upper part of Pennsylvania [Avenue]." "At the Tijuana, you could have Lester Young, Dave Brubeck, Carmen McCrae," continues Smith. "They were big then." Smith remembers that Billie Holiday was at the Club Tijuana in 1957 "cause I stood in line to see her" (Smith).

The Sphinx Club, on the other hand, served as a private club for the city's black elite. Founded in 1946 at 2115 Pennsylvania Avenue by Charlie Tilghman (who later founded Super Pride markets), the Sphinx Club offered an occasion when the women wore furs and fancy jewelry and members mixed with entertainers such as Sam Cooke, who played the club or other venues on The Avenue.

"The Sphinx Club wasn't a jazz club," Donald Smith explains. "It was supposed to be a membership club, but I went there all the time."

The Sphinx featured mostly local musicians, but Ruby Glover remembered that, as a performer, "you could always sing when you went in [the Sphinx Club] because they kept a house band, Chico Johnson and his organ trio and Earlene Reed, singing in there. And whomever was down The Avenue performing, after the clubs closed that's where you went. Put on a good show in there. If you were a musician all you had to do is ring the bell. They'd tell you, 'Hey, come on in here, give us a little song'" (qtd. in Schoettler).

Scores of other clubs lined the sides of Pennsylvania Avenue and drew the music fans in. There was Gamby's, where Lester Young and James Moody played. There was the Casino that hosted Max Roach and Miles Davis, and The Avenue Bar where local groups performed. Ethel Ennis had a long-standing engagement at the Red Fox, and at Skateland, girls danced on roller skates as musicians like Stan Getz, Gene Ammons, and Sonny Stitt blew their horns.

Clubs were within walking distance of each other, so that folks didn't have to move their cars to go from one performance to another. And a night out could be as affordable as you wanted it to be because there often wasn't a fee to get into any clubs.

"You could walk in and people would be having dinner," says Donald Smith. "All the clubs would serve food—you're talking about seafood, you're talking about chicken, some even served soul food" (Smith).

But arguably the largest draw on The Avenue was the Royal Theatre at 1300 Pennsylvania Avenue. A major stop on the Chitlin' Circuit, the Royal drew the starriest names, the most elaborate shows, the largest crowds.

A classic black-and-white photo taken circa 1949 captures the Royal's vibe. "Always a good show," reads the marquee, and though it's not dark yet, the lights under the marquee glow like tiny white globes, and men in suits and hats gather on the steps. A street sign in the foreground of the photo admonishes "No parking during theatre hours," and the line of cars that skirts the curb suggests that the show—no matter how good—hasn't yet begun. But soon, a line of well-dressed folks—many who will have taken the 21 trolley to get here— will stretch around the theatre, ready to enter the carpeted lobby, hand a ticket to a uniformed usher, find a seat and stare in anticipation at the heavily curtained stage until the show begins.

"The Royal," sighs Donald Smith, "that's where all the stage shows came in. All the big bands. Lionel Hampton, Cab Calloway, Duke Ellington, Earl Hines, Billy Eckstine."

The Royal offered a seemingly never-ending cycle of movies and stage shows. Smith recalls how as teenagers in the late '40s and early '50s, he and his brother used to go to The Avenue as soon as their father would "release" them: "You could go in the Royal about one o'clock in the daytime to see a movie. After the movie the stage show would come on. Nat "King" Cole. Then maybe a band. They always had some kind of comedian. You'd have a tap dancer or Moms Mabley. Then Lionel Hampton comes in with his band. Or the Ink Spots, then the Mills Brothers" (Smith).

The shows would go on all day with the adults coming out later in the day, all dressed up for an evening out. You'd go to a show, then maybe out to dinner at Mom's across the street for soul food. "Once you hit Pennsylvania Avenue, you knew everyone," Smith explains. "People would sort of look for you, and someone would say, 'I just saw your brother; he was going up The Avenue'" (Smith).

The Royal opened at 1300 Pennsylvania Avenue in 1921 originally as the Douglas Theater, but became the Royal in 1926. The largest of The Avenue's venues, it doubled as both a movie theater and a concert venue with seats for 1,400 guests. Fats Waller was the first to perform on the theater's raised stage after the 1926 name change, and he was followed by scores of others, including Dinah Washington, Cab Calloway, Count Basie, Duke Ellington, Ella Fitzgerald, and Billie Holiday. Pearl Bailey got her start as a chorus girl at the Royal, which also boasted performances from comedians like Redd Foxx, Jackie "Moms" Mabley in her inimitable housedress, and Edward "Slappy" White. The 1930s saw performers as diverse as personality Stepin Fetchit, composer/pianist Eubie Blake, dancer Bill "Bojangles" Robinson, and blues belter Bessie Smith. In 1931, the *Afro-American* advertised tickets to see opera star Marian Anderson (prices were from 50 cents to one dollar and were on sale "at all colored drug stores, Y.M.C.A, and the theatre" (Display Ad 37). Later that year, the paper lauded Louis Armstrong, "who will give away 100 bags of coal to early patrons from the steps of the Royal Theatre Saturday morning" (22). (Patrons were also advised to buy tickets early for his midnight show.)

In the 1940s performers like the Ink Spots, Fletcher Henderson, and Duke Ellington's band with a young Ben Webster all played the Royal, and a 1941 item from the *Afro-American* reported in January that "Jimmie Lunceford and his band are playing to tremendous crowds" (13). In 1959, the pianist Red Garland even got married (to former showgirl Marie Adams) on the stage of the Royal, "after their first song in the first show," reported the *Afro-American* (5).

White bands, including those of Louis Prima and Tommy Dorsey, played the Royal too, and later, the stage would be home to early rhythm and blues acts like the Orioles, Little Anthony & the Imperials, and the Supremes. "If you weren't good," the Orioles' Albert "Diz" Russell told the *Sun*'s Gil Sandler in 1996, "you didn't play at the Royal, because the crowds would boo you right off the stage" (qtd. in Sandler 1996).

The Royal was also a place for aspiring performers to see (and maybe even receive a souvenir from) their musical idols. Ethel Ennis remembers getting Ella Fitzgerald's autograph at the Royal (Ennis), and Jimmy Wells recalls the time when he got a piece of one of Lionel Hampton's mallets: "I used to stand up in front of the band, and I was really fascinated with him [Hampton], man, getting over that instrument, man. So one night he was really hot, man, this particular time I went, and one of those balls on the mallet—the mallet actually almost broke in half. The ball jumped off the stick, the shaft, you know. And I picked it up and I kept it. I wouldn't give it back to him, man. And it was just something about that. I can't explain why, you know, but I was fascinated watching him playing that instrument. And this big band, 17 pieces behind him, backing him up, and he's just wailing away, man, you know. That's how, that was number one of my interests, how I got involved" (Wells).

Hampton was a tremendously popular performer, recalls Wells, and the audience would explode during his performances, dancing in the aisles of the sold-out balcony or floor level. But despite a bevy of guest performers, the Royal also boasted an ace house band, first under the direction of Rivers Chambers and then "The Royal Men of Rhythm," under the direction of Tracy McCleary, who performed at the theater between 1949 and 1968.

In a 1996 interview, McCleary remembers some of the less well-known acts who played the Royal, like the all-girl band he conducted from a small platform in the wings (he refused to conduct the band in drag), and a European duo in which a woman played violin while doing a handstand from a man's shoulders ("One of the most fantastic acts of my life," he recalled. "They could play!") (McCleary).

But McCleary also remembers the last show at the Royal, a female impersonator group known as "The Jewel Box Review." "The theater had been dark for about a year preceding this show," recalls McCleary, "and so the house was packed for what patrons knew would be only a two-week run—and probably the last show to play the Royal" (qtd. in Sandler 1994).

The Comedy Club, at 1528 Pennsylvania Avenue, was another hot venue. Even in 1934, the year of its birth, the *Afro-American*'s "Nite Clubbing column" enthused, "Ike Dixon's Comedy Club is still the mecca for this end as evidenced by the crowds here. When other places fall flat they send out a scout to see what Ike is doing. I caught the place three quarters full and caught a scout from another place tell his boss there were about ten persons there. . . . When you want to find out where the gang hangs out try here" (9). By December, 1934, the enthusiasm was sustained when the column noted that the club was "still holding its own with The Avenue's smartest floor show" during the week of December 1st, and by December 8th, still "remain[ed] the swanky spot on The Avenue" (9, 8).

Proprietor Ike Dixon, a former bandleader, opened the nightclub when he retired from the road, and the small room with its endless mirrors and oval-shaped bar lined with chrome-legged barstools was a popular hangout for musicians as well as for fans who came to see performances nightly on the club's small stage. Sammy Davis, Jr. played the Comedy Club, as did Dizzy Gillespie, Dinah Washington, Della Reese, and Jimmy Wells (in a group called Jerry and the Tomcats). Reppard Stone remembers how he "sat at the piano one day in there, and Miles Davis came in. And he wanted to know what I was doing, and I told him that I was writing. He was fascinated, and he stayed there for quite some time and watched me working. He talked and that kind of thing, and I was just elated. That here I was in the Comedy Club—that's what it was called, you know—talking with Miles Davis. That just wiped me out" (Stone).

Donald Smith also remembers Davis's performances at the Comedy Club; he saw him there at least three times in the late 1950s. But Smith also remembers another favorite performance when Cannonball Adderley played the club with a band that included his brother, Nat. That was the best, he recalls.

One of the most moving stories circulating around the Comedy Club was when Ruby Glover met Billie Holiday, not long before Holiday's death in 1959. Holiday had just been released from the hospital, recalls Glover in a 2002 interview, and was very frail both in her dressing room and later on stage. As Glover remembers, Holiday said,

"'You're a singer,' and I said, 'I try at it.' She said, 'I'm told by Albert [Dailey] that you're very good.' I said, 'Thank you and thanks to my musician brother, I get better.' She said, 'Do you drink or smoke?' I said, 'No, I don't drink or smoke.' And she said, 'You work in the clubs?' And I said, 'Yes.' She said, 'You're a family person, too?' I said yes, like that. She said, 'Well, never do as I do because,' she says, 'I didn't have a family life. But be as great as you can be for yourself, and never forget that you have to live within the walls of who you are, even in the midst of a crowd. You still have to be you.' I never forgot that. I took her hand and I shook her hand and she said, 'Don't go home.'" (Glover)

Glover stayed for Holiday's performance where she recalls that Holiday was "as beautiful as ever, but she was very ill, and you could see that" (Glover).

Dixon himself passed away in January of 1953, and the club closed in 1964 as The Avenue began to change and lose its audience, both black and white, due to a variety of circumstances. Little by little, the Chitlin' Circuit waned as black musicians could perform for larger, mixed audiences in venues like Baltimore's Civic Center, and rock 'n' roll and rhythm and blues replaced jazz as black America's popular music. The riots in 1968 further destabilized the area, and subsequent years saw Baltimore residents, again, both black and white, move out of the city and into suburban neighborhoods. In 1971, the Royal, which had been the symbol of Pennsylvania Avenue's heyday, was demolished, and names like Gamby's, the Spot Bar, the Red Fox, Bam-Boo Lounge, Ubangi, Alhambra, and Club Tijuana, soon became confined to memory.

And yet the Pennsylvania Avenue legacy persists—in clubs, like the Caton Castle or the Haven, that survive in other parts of the city, in the patrons who still seek out and listen to jazz, and in the artists who constantly blend the past and the present in their performances. It's impossible to name another concentration of musical talent in any genre or in any other Baltimore neighborhood equal to what Pennsylvania Avenue had, and the richness of the experience shaped countless musicians and music lovers alike.

In 2004, the Pennsylvania Avenue Redevelopment Collective, under the leadership of George Gilliam, erected the Royal Theatre Marquee Monument. Billie Holiday Plaza was re-dedicated in 2009, and despite the passing of local Pennsylvania Avenue historian and tour leader Alvin Brunson in 2008, a website promoting the Pennsylvania Avenue Heritage Trail remains active. A man waiting for the number seven bus has a chance now to stop and look closely around him to get a glimpse of what and who were once near this spot and to hear the heartbeat of American jazz as it pumped through the Pennsylvania Avenue artery.

NOTES

[1] The Chitlin' Circuit refers to the circuit of theaters and nightclubs throughout the eastern and southern parts of the country where African Americans could safely perform before predominantly African-American audiences during the era of segration in the United States. It included such notable venues as the Cotton Club and the Apollo Theater in New York City, the Regal Theater in Chicago, and the Royal Theatre in Baltimore.

Works Cited

Baker, Henry and Reppard Stone. Interview by Elizabeth Schaaf. *Sounds & Stories*. Interview No. SAS8.20.02. Web.

Crockett, James. Interview by Daniel Thomas Davis. *Sounds & Stories*. Interview No. SAS4.10.02. Web.

Display Ad 37. Baltimore *Afro-American*. 7 Feb. 1931. Print.

Ennis, Ethel. Interview by Elizabeth Schaaf. *Sounds & Stories*. Interview No. SAS08.07.02. Web.

Glover, Ruby. Interview by Elizabeth Schaaf. *Sounds & Stories*. Interview No. SAS08.28.02. Web.

Hilson, Robert, Jr. "Sphinx Club is a relic of joyous times on 'the Avenue.'" Baltimore *Sun*. 13 Feb. 1992. Print.

"Louis Armstrong to Give Away Coal." Baltimore *Afro-American*. 12 Dec. 1931: 22. Print.

"Lunceford Band and Reote at Royal Theatre." Baltimore *Afro-American*. 4 Jan. 1941: 13. Print.

McCleary, Tracy. Interview by Elizabeth Schaaf. *Sounds and Stories*. Interview No. SAS8.12.96. Web.

McCoy, Roy. Interview by Elizabeth Schaaf. *Sounds & Stories*. Interview No. SAS8.12.96. Web.

"Nite Clubbing in Baltimore." Baltimore *Afro-American*. 4 Aug. 1934: 9. Print.

"Nite Clubbing in Baltimore." Baltimore *Afro-American*. 1 Dec. 1934: 9. Print.

"Nite Clubbing in Baltimore." Baltimore *Afro-American*. 8 Dec. 1934: 8. Print.

Pryor-Trusty, Rosa and Tonya Taliaferro. *African-American Entertainment in Baltimore*. Charleston, SC: Arcadia, 2003. Print.

"Red Garland takes a bride on stage of Royal Theatre," Baltimore *Afro-American*, 24 Oct. 1959: 5. Print.

Sandler, Gilbert. "Baltimore Glimpses." Baltimore *Sun*. 22 Feb. 1994. Print.

---. *Small Town Baltimore*. Baltimore: Johns Hopkins UP, 2002. Print.

---. "A Sprig of Rosemary for three Baltimore Theatres." Baltimore *Sun*. 16 Apr. 1996. Print.

Schoettler, Carl. "Where Jazz Still Echoes." Baltimore *Sun*. 8 Dec. 2002. Print.

Smith, Donald. Telephone interview. 3 Mar. 2010.

Wells, Jimmy. Interview by Tony DePaolis. *Sounds & Stories*. Interview No. SAS4.02.02. Web.

Wood, James E. "Biddy," Sr. Telephone interview. 18 Feb. 2010.

FAMOUS BALLROOM

1717 N. CHARLES STREET

NEW HOME OF THE

LEFT BANK JAZZ SOCIETY, Inc.

Jazz's Longest Running Show

"The LBJS . . . brought the music back to the people; it brought the fun back into the music; and it provided a space where the artists and audience could connect in an intimate atmosphere."

12 The Left Bank Jazz Society
by Cathleen Carris

The date is May 7th, 1967, and the place is the Famous Ballroom
on North Charles Street, where no one has any idea that they are
witnessing the last live performance of world–renowned saxophonist
John Coltrane, who will die of liver cancer in just two months (*Baltimore
Jazz Scene* 1968, 80). The audience is an eclectic array of races, ages,
and styles: there are professors from the Peabody Conservatory of
Music, college students of all colors, members of the militant Black
Panther organization, and middle-aged women dressed in their Sunday
best. Yet the only tension in the air is in the sound of the music, and
the only words exchanged during the performance are, "shhhh," the
audience hushed under the weight of the extreme intensity emanating
from the stage. Coltrane, accompanied by the other members of his
quintet—Pharoah Sanders, tenor sax, Alice Coltrane, piano, Donald
Garrett, bass, and Rashied Ali, drums—begins with "Resolution," a
section from his spiritual suite, *A Love Supreme*. Only at the end of
the first set, which lasts two hours, is the spell broken by the group's
rendition of "My Favorite Things," as Sanders plays the piccolo against
Coltrane's soprano sax. "The ringing brilliance of both instruments
enhanced their piercing high notes and rushing arpeggios. The
surprise of the afternoon came when Coltrane began to chant against
the piccolo, beating his chest. The crowd went wild," noted one writer
in attendance (Stanier 4).

The concert is as much a social experience as a musical one. Several patrons have been here all afternoon, having arrived three or four hours before the five o'clock start time, just to make sure they could claim their favorite table, and to get a head start on the drinking and feasting. The round tables are lined with picnic baskets and paper bags teeming with fried chicken and potato salad. If you forgot to pack a meal, Chef Willis is on hand with a full supply of barbecue and collard greens, and Miss Gladys with her famous pies. But despite the diverse make-up of the crowd and the free flow of alcohol, there are no heated arguments or drunken brawls: in other words, none of the unpleasant incidents often endemic to the night club scene. In fact, "There's a certain camaraderie," according to 41-year-old Social Security worker Johnny Mathews, quoted in a 1979 Baltimore *Sun* article: "This is a special place for jazz friendships. People are interested in the same thing" (Dawson "And All That Jazz").

The party responsible for this four-hour Sunday concert, and over 40 others like it in 1967 alone, is the Left Bank Jazz Society (LBJS), the nation's longest running nonprofit jazz organization, "dedicated to the promotion of jazz as an art form without restrictions of race, creed and color, which the music exemplifies" (*LBJS Constitution*).

While Baltimore has a rich history of showcasing both local and national jazz greats, the city has also experienced hard times of low turn-out and fleeing musicians. The heyday of Pennsylvania Avenue in the first half of the twentieth century, where both blacks and whites frequented the theaters and night clubs, was followed in the 1960s by a resounding declaration that jazz was dead, and an exodus of white patrons. National jazz critic Don Buday sums up this sad state in a

1966 *Sounds and Fury* article, writing not only that "the talent pool is bone dry," but also that "unlike any other city of its size, jazz is without a home in Baltimore"(35). In an earlier article written for *The Count*, Buday blames the audience for an almost nonexistent jazz scene, criticizing the atmosphere at the clubs that do feature jazz, and the majority of self-proclaimed jazz fans who think themselves too "cool" to listen to live music—"the same cat who appears hipper than hip, who knocks the sounds he hears on the radio" ("Memo"). Concerned jazz aficionados threw the city a musical lifeline with the formation of the Left Bank Jazz Society. It was a "breath of new life," according to Buday, founded by unselfish jazz fans who brought about "the most activity seen in Baltimore since the mid-50's" ("Memo").

The charter members of the LBJS met one evening in 1964 on the second floor of a bar in South Baltimore, at the corner of Fremont Avenue and Washington Boulevard. In attendance were Benny Kearse, Vernon Welsh, Phil Harris, Charles Simmons, Joseph Simmons, Eugene Simmons, Gilbert Rawlings, Earl Hayes, Benjamin Kimbers, Otts Bethel, John O. Thompson, Ray Pino, Glen McGill, James Dunn, Harold Bell, Robert Brice, Charles Brice, and Lionel Wilson (Kearse 3). Kearse was elected president, Harris, vice president, Wilson, secretary, Joseph Simmons, financial secretary, Charles Simmons, business manager, and Kimbers, treasurer. Jamal Simmons and Lionel Wilson were partners in managing this room, furnished with tables covered in red-checkered tablecloth and seating about 40-45 people, where they met to play jazz records. Wilson, who had spent time in Paris during his stint in the military, was trying to re-create the ambience of the places he had frequented there, where patrons gathered to listen to jazz records (hence the name—The Parisian Left Bank Room). The first concerts, featuring local musicians, were held in this room, which the society very quickly outgrew. So they moved to the Al-Ho Club on Franklintown and Frederick Roads, which held about 100 people (Pryor-Trusty 111-113). Soon the Al-Ho proved too small as well, and the Left Bank moved to the Madison Club on Madison and Chester streets, although the group maintained its headquarters at its previous location. After two fires and a temporary stint at the Crystal Ballroom on North Avenue, the LBJS moved to the Famous Ballroom on North Charles Street in December of 1966, where it stayed for the next 18 years.

Several Baltimoreans offered their own theories for why jazz found itself struggling so much in the 1960s. In the 1950s, local jazz organizations had formed in order to increase promotion and awareness. By 1958, the Modern Jazz Club of the Madison Avenue Branch YWCA was sponsoring workshops about this very topic: "What's Stopping the Promotion of Jazz in Baltimore?" was the question for one panel led by Leo Hunt, former president of the Interracial Jazz Society (IJS), and a future member of the LBJS (Morten 20). Another local publication, Walter Carr's *Nightlifer*, which chronicled Baltimore's clubs and theaters and also offered brief editorials on issues of importance to the African-American community, drew similar conclusions. Carr firmly believed that the LBJS resuscitated the city's dying jazz culture: "From the very beginning of the society's weekly concerts," he wrote in 1965, "the capacity and near-capacity audiences served only to prove that the people were actually starved for the cultural art form known as modern jazz" (*Baltimore Jazz Scene* 1966, 7).

Baltimore *Sun* Reporter John Goodspeed believed that the musicians themselves were the problem—their self-important attitude and detached demeanor made it difficult for fans to make an effort to support them. "Since 1940," he writes, "when the 'modern' harmony and broken rhythms of cool jazz took the field, serious jazzmen have come within a flatted fifth of playing themselves into a corner, out of communication with the public and out of work" (6). The LBJS, according to Goodspeed, was vital to jazz's resurrection because it brought the music back to the people; it brought the fun back into the music; and it provided a space where the artists and audience could connect in an intimate atmosphere. "They [the LBJS] are proving . . . something that badly needs proving in the modern era; that jazz is still a people's music" (6).

Before the LBJS, Benny Kearse had spent over 10 years trying to establish a lasting jazz organization in Baltimore. Many newspaper and magazine articles cite one of his earliest attempts, The Interracial Jazz Society, as the predecessor to the Left Bank. Kearse and other Left Bank members, including Vernon Welsh, were also involved with the IJS. There is some disagreement over the date of the group's inception: a *City Paper* article in 2000 places the foundation in 1954, the same year of the Supreme Court ruling in *Brown vs. the Board of Ed. of Topeka, Kansas* which outlawed segregation in public venues (Dilts). Other Baltimore *Sun* articles—most of them obituaries for deceased IJS members—place the group's beginnings in the late 1940s. In any case, it disbanded in 1958, followed by another short-lived enterprise called the Modern Jazz Society (of which Kearse served as president).

The Interracial Jazz Society, by its very name, sought to make a strong statement against segregation in addition to promoting jazz. The group made its home at Club Tijuana, located at 2674 Pennsylvania Avenue, where it held modern jazz sessions every Saturday from 3 to 7 p.m. During these four hours, patrons were entertained by the likes of local artists Mickey Fields and Albert Dailey, the latter of whom went on to enjoy national and international acclaim, as well as by some of the best-known jazz artists of the era: John Coltrane, Julian "Cannonball" Adderley, and Miles Davis. At this point, the IJS modern jazz sessions were part of a lively musical nightlife in which jazz was one of the main attractions. In March of 1957, the IJS was commended by the Baltimore *Afro-American* for its efforts in bringing jazz into the Baltimore Museum of Art, and therefore confirming the high level of culture and respectability it believed that jazz had achieved ("Strolling the Avenue").

How Did They Do It!?!

Sun reporter James Dilts wondered the same thing after a year of watching the Left Bank bring in some of the biggest names in jazz, from Baltimore-born alto saxophonist Gary Bartz to legendary bebop trumpeter Dizzy Gillespie. According to the laws of jazz economics, it is difficult for anyone to survive even a few years, let alone 40, while presenting only jazz artists to his/her audience. "Many a night club owner has discovered the difficulty of consistently putting modern jazz musicians before audiences at a profit," writes Dilts. No other Baltimore enterprise before or since has matched the success and longevity experienced by the LBJS. The secret, Dilts discovered, combined several elements: the savvy and hardworking entertainment committee, the unique opportunity offered by the intimate and less stressful atmosphere of the Left Bank concerts, and the chance for musicians to augment their weekly salaries. Sunday was a day off for most musicians, and those who found themselves in D.C., New York, or Philadelphia were more than happy to come and play for the Baltimore crowds at a fraction of their usual fee, especially when given the freedom to play whatever they wanted to play. "The difference between the success of this society and the failure of many purely commercial ventures," Dilts explains, "is a lot of hard work on the part of the aggressive and knowledgeable members." In short, the LBJS thrived because its members were "interested more in the sound of the music than in the cash register."

Several of these members were well connected in the professional jazz community. According to founding member Jamal Mubdi-Bey (formerly Jamal Simmons), one of the early key players was Ray Pino, a former club owner from Brooklyn, New York, who had stayed well connected with the Big Apple's jazz community. Pino, who had also belonged to the Interracial Jazz Society, was most likely responsible for many of the out-of-town stars that this earlier group was able to bring to Club Tijuana. After only a year of operation, everyone knew the Left Bank name, and savvy agents were soliciting Left Bank officers to give their artists a chance to make it in Baltimore (Promotion Packets).

According to John Fowler, a former LBJS president, musicians were drawn to the Famous Ballroom by the highly attentive and appreciative audience—and by the food. In the words of former member Michael Binsky, "Even the guy who cooked the chicken at the Famous was famous." As Jack Ellis wrote, reporting for the Baltimore *News American*, "There are so few jazz clubs anywhere in the country that serious jazzists, like aficionados, will go to the ends of the earth to find a receptive audience" (8). Time and again, visiting artists had the same reaction, and the same desire to return for repeat performances. On February 27th, 1966 for example, while renovations were underway to repair the damages caused by the fire at the Madison Club, Charles Lloyd and his Quartet played a concert at the Crystal Ballroom on North Avenue, after which Lloyd told Ellis, "I've never played before a more appreciative and more responsive audience. I'm in this business just to turn people on, and man, that's exactly what happens in Baltimore" (Ellis 8).

Being a jazz artist is just about as lucrative as owning a jazz club. There are exceptions to the rule—big names like Duke Ellington and Dizzy Gillespie, or Stan Kenton and his big band. But, as Fowler recalls, about 70 percent of artists struggled to get by. "You had to really, really love the music to be a musician," says Fowler, as he recalls the players who would show up with holes in their shoes, mismatched suits, or with their instrument cases held shut with rope. At the Left Bank, not only did they receive the highest levels of appreciation, but they also got a free meal and some free booze. "You come off the stage, and it's like, 'Hey man, come to my table. Have a meal, have a drink!'" Fowler recalls.

One of the Society's biggest sponsors was the National Brewing Company, which made possible, among many other things, the publication of a monthly LBJS newsletter sent to 4,000 patrons on the organization's mailing list, containing news concerning jazz in Baltimore (Kearse 1). In an article from the 1977 Yearbook, Kearse expresses tremendous gratitude for the company's generous contributions: "In the early days when we were struggling to make jazz go, National came to our rescue. They underwrote several concerts, and are big contributors to our yearbook" (Case). In fact, judging from a sampling of unofficial financial reports for the 1973 concert season, the organization made money from its concerts more often than not. Maynard Ferguson, for example, drew in over $3,300 at the door, leaving the Left Bank with a profit of over $1,000 for that concert. At this point, general admission was set at $4. The organization also made money with Art Blakey, Richard "Groove" Holmes, Stanley Turrentine, Elvin Jones, and Horace Silver, a list that clearly indicates Baltimore's enthusiasm for the hard bop style.

Community Connections—Music as Art, Education, and Rehabilitation

From its beginnings, the Left Bank Jazz Society was concerned with improving the quality of life in the Baltimore community in ways that involved more than just providing exposure to great musical talent. Fundraising for community improvement initiatives was one of the first ways in which the Left Bank made a contribution. Proceeds from their concerts helped fund projects like the construction of the new Provident Hospital, the Morgan State College ROTC Fund, and Project Survival, an affiliate of the Community Action Agency which sponsored an Inner-City Basketball League and programs for pre-schoolers and the elderly ("Left Bank Jazz Society has concert" 7).

The LBJS also instituted a lecture series at 27 colleges and other educational institutions in the Baltimore area, and held a number of summer concert series for the Neighborhood Youth Corps. In 1972, for example, during July and August, the Left Bank held concerts every Monday and Thursday evening featuring a different ensemble, including names like the Mickey Fields Quintet, Frank Foster's Big Band, the Jimmy Wells Quintet, and the Vernon Wolst Quintet. Up to a thousand children attended these concerts, which were held at Southwestern High School ("A Summer Educational").

Perhaps the most unlikely initiative was a chapter of the LBJS created in conjunction with the inhabitants of Maryland State Correctional facilities. Along with all the out-of-state mail that the society had received from other jazz aficionados seeking advice on how to maintain a successful arts organization, Kearse and company began getting letters from the inmates of the Maryland Penitentiary, the oldest of the state's correctional institutions, located at 954 Forrest Street in Baltimore. At first the writers just asked for records, but soon many of the LBJS members began bringing local jazz groups into the prison. On January 31st, 1969, LBJS #954 was founded at the Penitentiary as an extension of the Douglas Farmer Project. A few years earlier, Farmer, one of the inmates at the Penitentiary who served as #954's first president, had made it his mission to bring some sort of entertainment to the facility. The #954 chapter had a social mission as well, producing its own publication, called *Jazzbo*, where members discussed not only music but also the social situation and hardships faced by the inmates and their families, both during incarceration and after their release. "At present, our purpose is to provide each and every resident here, with a sense of civic and social awareness through music" (*"Left Bank Jazz Society #954"* 43). After a visit to the Penitentiary in 1969, Baltimore *Sun* reporter Earl Arnett writes, "The men in Chapter 954 have found strength in jazz and affirmation of their existence while in society's cage" ("Left Bank Chapter Liberated").

In this setting, as in other Left Bank events, bringing people together in a community was a top priority. Musical performances at the Penitentiary, for example, included the instrumental talents not only of outside visitors, but of the inmates themselves and even some of the guards. At one particular banquet described in the Left Bank's 1971 Yearbook, "The trumpeter was one of the guards. The bongos were inmates of the institution. The piano, the castanets and the drums were manned by friends from the free world outside" ("Jazz and Sartorial Splendor" 23). Professional jazz artists also often made an appearance at these gatherings, brought in with the help of the original LBJS, and often funded by grants from the National Endowment for the Arts. One of the most frequent visitors was jazz vocalist and local legend Ruby Glover.

The LBJS #954 strove to implement a number of programs in addition to live jazz performances in order to educate its members and provide them with a social forum. In 1969, the #954 chapter organized the Eastern Conference of Jazz Societies, a program which ran for at least three years. The third annual conference took place in the Thomas B. Turner Auditorium of Johns Hopkins University, and featured live musical performances by Count Basie, the Towson State College Orchestra, African Jazz Ensemble, and the Mickey Fields and Buck Hill Quintet. In attendance were over 200 people from jazz societies based in New York, New Jersey, Philadelphia, and Washington, D.C. Speakers included Dr. Donald Byrd, not only an extremely talented and well-educated jazz musician and composer, but also a pioneer in the formation of higher-level jazz education; Dr. Elliot Galkin, faculty member and future director of Baltimore's Peabody Institute, one of the oldest music schools in the country; and Walter Carter, a Loyola College (now Loyola University Maryland) sociology instructor who gave the keynote address ("3rd Annual Eastern Conference of Jazz Societies" Program).

News of the new Left Bank chapter soon spread to another penal institution, the House of Corrections in Jessup, MD, where the inmates decided to form another chapter, LBJS #534. This group lasted about five years and made a profound impact on the incarcerated community. Some of its members even formed their own jazz workshop combo. Working in prisons, however, was not without its risks, and John Fowler recalls one time when Left Bank members of the parent organization found themselves in the middle of a small riot. No one was hurt, but the #534 did suspend its activities for a few months. For the most part, however, the prison inmates were on their best behavior, not wanting to spoil the banquets and the concerts brought about by the Left Bank and its chapters. In fact, when Maj. Forrest R. Clingenpeel, one of the chief prison guards, was asked his thoughts about the jazz organization and its effects on prisoners' behavior, he responded very positively, even though the group's gatherings meant more work for the guards ("Jazz and Sartorial Splendor", 23).

Race Relations

The LBJS formed a few months before President Lyndon B. Johnson signed into law the Civil Rights Act, which extended voting rights for African Americans and outlawed racial segregation in the workplace, education, and at all public venues. This landmark piece of legislation was just one of the many manifestations of a society mobilized for change. Nonetheless, Baltimore remained notorious for the racial discrimination that often drove off its best talent. The Left Bank, therefore, did face obstacles throughout its run as a society that brought together people of different races, economic statuses, and social standings. There was one concert in particular at which visiting musician Jackie McLean was thoroughly outraged upon being refused service at the North Inn, located down the block from the Crystal Ballroom at North Avenue and St. Paul Street. He stopped in the middle of the concert "to deliver an emotional condemnation against segregated taverns in Baltimore" ("Jazz artist calls boycott").

Incidents like this were rare, however, in part because many of the musicians took the train into Penn Station, just a few blocks away from the Famous, and took it out again right after the concert. Fowler did run into trouble when trying to make accommodations for some of the black artists at the Baltimore Motel, on the corner of Howard and Guilford Avenues. According to Fowler, the motel needed some convincing, but in the end it all worked out. Their hesitance resulted not just from the color of the musicians, but from the very fact that they were jazz musicians from New York City, and according to the stereotype, every jazz musician was a drug addict.

In order to gauge the progressive atmosphere of the Left Bank concerts, one only needs to listen to the impressions made on the audience itself. In a 1975 Baltimore *Sun* article, one patron from Silver Spring remarks, "I've never seen a place like this and I've listened to jazz all over the world. . . . I've never seen an act of violence. The atmosphere and the camaraderie are a real phenomenon" (Dawson). Dr. Louis Cheslock, a Peabody professor, came to the Famous Ballroom for the first time on April 23rd, 1972 to see Duke Ellington perform a week before the jazz legend's 73rd birthday. According to *Sun* reporter Earl Arnett, Cheslock was stunned both by the performance and the crowd: "He was struck by the friendly atmosphere at the Left Bank, the uninhibited way in which black and white people enjoyed the concert together, talking, sharing drinks, laughing. The music seemed to break down artificial barriers and create new communication out of shared feeling and appreciation" ("Duke Ellington pre-birthday concert" 40).

A Nation of Jazz Buffs in Awe

In 1966, the Baltimore *Afro-American* published a story about the newly formed LBJS, applauding its efforts and noting the national recognition it had already achieved. Nonetheless, the *Afro* writer appears quite surprised that the group "has managed to survive for nearly two years now" (Baltimore Afro-American). During the LBJS tenure, many more societies came and went. Even the success of the various LBJS chapters—in D.C., the Maryland Penitentiary, and the House of Corrections—pales in comparison to the more than 40-year run of its parent organization.

Some of the LBJS's greatest admirers were right next door in

Washington, D.C. They convinced the Baltimoreans to help them found a new chapter in the nation's capital. The founders included Charles Johnson, Joseph Boozer, Peter Smith, Charles R. Willis, Chester Butler, Leon Johnson, George Johnson, James Ingram, Jr., and Billy Best, Sr. They first met at 3221 Eli Pl., SE on January 2nd, 1967 (Matthews 19), and created a group that lasted for about five years. Most of their concerts took place at the Smithsonian.

But the Left Bank name reached farther than just the capital, and Baltimore became once again an icon for jazz buffs across the nation. Not only was it recognized for the caliber of its concerts and the size of its audience in national magazines such as *DownBeat* and *Sounds and Fury*, but it also received attention as a model community organization that brought together people from all walks of life. In St. Louis, MO, for example, Buddy Lonesome dedicated his column, "Hellbox," in the St. Louis *Argus* to a discussion of the merits of jazz music and a story about how the LBJS was making Baltimore a better place. "Jazz is basically the stimulus of the young adult. It reflects the modern day idiom of progression and relativity to an excellence that no other musical effort can achieve." Indeed, most of the original members of the Left Bank were young adults, and they were certainly committed to progress and excellence. Lonesome urges his readers to emulate the LBJS and to use the promotion of jazz to revitalize his own community. He wrote this column at a time when the Left Bank had been in operation for little more than a year, but the philosophy he extols continued to guide the organization throughout its extensive run.

Years after the Left Bank had left the Famous Ballroom, rumors still floated around about the phenomenal performances that took place there and about their recording by founding member and frequent emcee Vernon Welsh. For many years, even outside of Baltimore, the story of Welsh's tapes was the stuff of urban legend. According to James Dilts, Welsh recorded about 350 shows between 1965 and 1980. In 2000, the tapes were bought by record producer Joel Dorn of the Label M record company in New York, after they had been stored for many years in the Morgan State University library. Dorn has since reissued a small number of these gems as CDs. He was amazed by the collection: as he told Dilts, "The Left Bank Jazz Society tapes comprise one of the most extensive 'live' collections I've ever run across. Its value is that it covers a great many of the major names in jazz when they were at the height of their powers. The recordings [some of which are listed below] open a window to that magical time and place." The tapes are the tangible relics of a tremendous legacy, capturing 18 years of elite musical performances.

After they left the Famous Ballroom, it became difficult for the Left Bank to maintain its audience. Both the reduced space and the changed atmosphere affected attendance. Chef Willis was gone; Miss Gladys the cake lady was gone; and jazz itself began to lose the great wealth of musicians that it had enjoyed in the '60s and '70s. Even so, the Left Bank continued to hold weekly concerts throughout the rest of the '80s, and more sporadically throughout the '90s, alternating at first between Moreco's, at 5425 Reisterstown Road, and the Omni International Hotel at 101 West Fayette Street, moving to Coppin State University in 1987, and later in the '90s to Teamsters Union Hall at 6000 Erdman Ave. The LBJS even started a new tradition in the late 1980s—jazz cruises between Baltimore and Annapolis. Each boat ride hosted over 400 people, and was almost always sold out ("Left Bank Jazz Society cruises" 10). Audience members could bring their own food, just as they had done at the Famous, and bushels of steamed crabs were waiting at their Annapolis destination. There would be two bands, one on the lower deck and one on the middle deck, and it was never hard to secure a group for the whole day. "It got to the point where the bands would fight over who would get the gig," Fowler explains with a laugh.

The Left Bank Jazz Society ushered in a new era of jazz in Baltimore that differed largely from the glitz and the glamour of Pennsylvania Avenue in its heyday. This group of jazz fans and concerned community members became more important than the club owners and even the musicians themselves in keeping jazz alive in the city, in exposing it to a diverse cross-section of the population, in garnering attention and respect for modern jazz as an art form and, lastly, in providing a friendly environment for the evolution of integration. The Left Bank included musicians, both locally and nationally recognized, in the community they had created, supporting their endeavors, treating them with respect, and celebrating with them. "Nobody ever left town without their money," proudly states Fowler. Thus, in 1983, over 500 people attended an LBJS benefit concert for the children of the late saxophonist Sonny Stitt, a frequent performer at the Famous Ballroom (Dawson "Sonny Stitt" 32). For local musicians, the LBJS also offered an opportunity to sit in and play with some of jazz's biggest stars.

In 1968, Al Rutledge hailed the LBJS as "the official curator" of the history of modern jazz (*The Baltimore Jazz Scene* 1968). More than that, its members created a vibrant and vital community out of an atmosphere lacking solidarity and plagued by indifference. The 1960s was a decade of immense social and political change, charged by the civil rights movement and an activist culture. Young people all over the country organized themselves and fought for what was important to them. In Baltimore, the members of the Left Bank found in jazz an expression of the freedom that the country's African-American population was fighting for. The world of jazz was one of the first places where blacks and whites could come together. Integration, which had started on Pennsylvania Avenue, was threatened by the turbulence of the 1960s, especially the riots of April, 1968. On April 7th of that year, the Yearbook lists "No Concert—Disorder in the City" (82). But two short weeks later, while the rest of Baltimore continued on a path toward racial polarization, the Left Bank was once again holding concerts for its interracial audience. Baltimore's nightlife was a key factor in the evolution of integration, whether it was an active goal for the members of the Interracial Jazz Society, or a simply an effect of the commitment to good music and community-building on the part of the Left Bank Jazz Society.

NOTES

Special thanks to Desiree Collins, who generously welcomed me into her home to review the materials recovered from the late Benny Kearse's estate.

Works Cited

Arnett, Earl. "Duke Ellington prebirthday Concert Inspires Audience at Left Bank Jazz Society." Baltimore *Sun* 26 Apr. 1972. Rpt in *The Baltimore Jazz Scene* 1964-1975. 40. Print. Benny Kearse Collection of Desiree Collins, Maryland. 18 August 2009, 40-41.

—. "Left Bank Chapter 'Liberated' By Music." Benny Kearse Collection. Walter P. Carter Community Library/Reference Room. Sojourner-Douglass College, Maryland. 24 Sept. 2009. Print.

Baltimore *Afro-American*. 20 Feb. 1966. Benny Kearse Collection of Desiree Collins, Maryland. 26 August 2009.

Binsky, Michael. Personal Interview. 17 Jan. 2009.

Buday, Don. "The Four Hour Renaissance." *Sounds and Fury 1966*: 34-36. Benny Kearse Collection. Walter P. Carter Community Library/Reference Room. Sojourner-Douglass College, Maryland. 24 Sept. 2009. Print.

—. "Memo to the Ballamere Hip." *The Count* 1.1 (1965). Benny Kearse Collection. Walter P. Carter Community Library/Reference Room. Sojourner-Douglass College, Maryland.

Carr, Walter. *Baltimore Jazz Scene* 1966: The Left Bank Jazz Society, Inc., 7. Benny Kearse Collection of Desiree Collins, Maryland. 26 August 2009. Print.

Case, Paul F. "Jazz in Baltimore: 'It's there folks, all you got to do is dig it!'" *Baltimore Jazz Scene* 1977: The Left Bank Jazz Society, Inc. Benny Kearse Collection. Walter P. Carter Community Library/Reference Room. Sojourner-Douglass College. Print.

Dawson, Jack. "And All That Jazz!" Baltimore *Sun* 25 Mar. 1979: Vertical Files Jazz Music-Baltimore. Enoch Pratt Free Library. Print.

—. "Sony Stitt." Baltimore *Sun*, 2 Dec. 1983. Rpt in *Baltimore Jazz Scene 1990: The Left Bank Jazz Society Inc.*, 32. Collection of John Fowler, Maryland. 25 Jan. 2010.

Dilts, James D. "Bringing the Top Jazzmen to Baltimore." Baltimore *Sun.* 28 Nov. 1965. Vertical Files Jazz Music-Baltimore. Enoch Pratt Free Library, Baltimore. Print.

—"The Closet Tapes: A Treasure Trove of Classic Live Recordings Revives Baltimore's Premier Jazz." Baltimore *City Paper*. 10 Apr. 2000. Web.

Ellis, Jack. "Concerts For Jazz Buffs." The Baltimore *News American*. Reprinted in *Baltimore Jazz Scene* 1966: The Left Bank Jazz Society, Inc., 8. Collection of Desiree Collins, Maryland. 18 Aug. 2009. Print.

Fowler, John. Personal Interview. 17 Jan. 2010.

Goodspeed, John. "Concert by the Left Bank Jazz Society." Baltimore Evening *Sun*. Rpt in *Baltimore Jazz Scene* 1966: The Left Bank Jazz Society, Inc. Collection of Desiree Collins, Maryland. 18 Aug. 2009. Print.

"Jazz artist calls boycott of taverns that refuse service to all." Baltimore *Afro-American*. 23 Apr. 1966: 25. Benny Kearse Collection. Walter P. Carter Community Library/Reference Room. Sojourner-Douglass College. Print.

"Jazz and Sartorial Splendor Mix at the State Penitentiary." *Baltimore Jazz Scene* 1971: The Left Bank Jazz Society Inc. Collection of Desiree Collins, Maryland. 18 Aug. 2009. Print.

Kearse, Benny. "History of the Left Bank Jazz Society, Inc." *Baltimore Jazz Scene* 1967: The Left Bank Jazz Society Inc. 3. Benny Kearse Collection. Walter P. Carter Community Library/Reference Room. Sojourner-Douglass College. Print.

"Left Bank Jazz Society #954." *Baltimore Jazz Scene* 1971: The Left Bank Jazz Society Inc. Collection of Desiree Collins, Maryland. 18 Aug. 2009. Print.

Left Bank Jazz Society Constitution. Benny Kearse Collection of Desiree Collins, Maryland. 26 Aug. 2009. Print.

"Left Bank Jazz Society cruises to Annapolis in style." Baltimore *Afro-American*. 5 Sep. 1987: 10. Google.com Newspapers. Web. 25 Jan. 2010.

Lonesome, Buddy. "Hellbox." St. Louis Argus. Benny Kearse Collection. Walter P. Carter Community Library/Reference Room. Sojourner-Douglass College. Print.

Matthews, Bob. "Left Bank Jazz Society: In the Groove." Metropolitan Magazine (March 1980). Vertical Files Jazz Music-Baltimore. Enoch Pratt Free Library. Print.

Morten, Baker E. "YWCA jazz club has 2nd workshop." Baltimore *Afro-American*. 20 Dec. 1958. Google.com Newspapers. Web. 28 Nov. 2009.

Mubdi-Bey, Jamal. Personal Interview. 13 Jan. 2010.

Promotion Packets. Benny Kearse Collection of Desiree Collins, Maryland. 26 Aug. 2009.

Pryor-Trusty, Rosa, and Tonya Taliaferro. *African–American Entertainment in Baltimore*. Charleston, SC: Arcadia, 2003. Print.

Rhoden, Bill. "'Jam Session City'": Non-progressive Baltimore still gives jazz a chance." Baltimore *Sun*. 21 April 1978. Vertical Files Jazz Music-Baltimore. Enoch Pratt Free Library. Print.

Rutledge, Al. *The Baltimore Jazz Scene* 1968. Benny Kearse Collection of Desiree Collins, Maryland. 26 Aug. 2009. Print.

Stanier, Carole. "Every Man Should Have a Jazz He Can Call His Own." *The Baltimore Jazz Scene* 1968: The Left Bank Jazz Society Inc. 4. TS. Benny Kearse Collection. Sojourner-Douglass College Library. 16 October 2009. Print.

"Strolling the Avenue." Baltimore *Afro-American*. 2 March 1957: 21. Google.com Newspapers. Web. 10 February 2010.

"A Summer Educational and Cultural Jazz Concert Series." Flyer. Benny Kearse Collection of Desiree Collins, Maryland. 26 Aug. 2009. Print.

"3rd Annual Eastern Conference of Jazz Societies." Program. Benny Kearse Collection of Desiree Collins, Maryland. 26 Aug. 2009. Print.

Discography

The following were recorded live at the Famous Ballroom by Vernon Welsh. They are a must-have for any jazz collection: the performers feed off the uniquely attuned and responsive audience, whose cheers, applause, and passionate outbursts are caught on tape. Musicians could play their hearts out, unrestricted by the time constraints of a recording studio. One would be hard-pressed to find another venue like the Famous. In the words of Jimmy Heath, describing his first show there: "The atmosphere on this date was hip, with integrated, enthusiastic crowds . . . in a cabaret, party atmosphere. We felt like giving all our appreciation. Folks would clap or holler out your name in the middle of your solo when they got your message or felt your groove" (Jam Gems).

Hubbard, Freddie and Jimmy Heath. *Jam Gems.* Recorded live, 13 June 1965. Label M, 2000.
  Freddie Hubbard, trumpet; Jimmy Heath, tenor saxophone; Wilbur Little, bass; Bertell Knox, drums; Gus Simms, piano.

Hubbard, Freddie. *Fastball.* Recorded live, 23 April 1967. Hyena Records, 2005.
  Freddie Hubbard, trumpet; Benny Maupin, tenor saxophone; Kenny Barron, piano; Freddie Waits, drums. Hubbard really lets loose on this date, and has a great time joking with the audience in between numbers.

Cohn, Al and Zoot Sims. *Easy as Pie.* Recorded live, 27 Oct. 1968. Label M, 2000.
  Al Cohn, saxophone; Zoot Sims, saxophone; Dave Frishberg, piano; Victor Sproles, bass; Donald McDonald, drums.

Gordon, Dexter. *L.T.D.* Recorded live, 4 May 1969. Prestige Records, 2001.
  Dexter Gordon, tenor saxophone; Bobby Timmons, piano; Victor Gaskin, bass; Percy Brice, drums. Gordon shows off every facet of his repertoire. Timmons really takes off on his solo during Duke Ellington's "In a Sentimental Mood." It's a true jam session, as Gordon picked up this rhythm section out of New York, and played with them for the first time on this night.

Gordon, Dexter. *XXL.* Recorded live, 4 May 1969. Prestige Records, 2002.
  Dexter Gordon, tenor sax; Bobby Timmons, piano; Victor Gaskin, bass; Percy Brice, drums. These tracks were recorded on the same night as those on the previous album, all of them marathon numbers—the longest piece is a 24-minute long rendition of Thelonius Monk's "Rhythm-a-ing."

Stitt, Sonny. *Just the Way It Was*. Recorded live, 23 Apr. 1971. Hyena Records, 2005.

Sonny Stitt, saxophone; Don Patterson, organ; Billy James, drums. Stitt played with the likes of Dizzy Gillespie and Miles Davis, and was influenced early on by Charlie Parker and Lester Young. He was one of the first to play the electric saxophone, as he does here.

Walton, Cedar. *Three Sundays in the Seventies*. Recorded live, 5 Sep. 1971, 27 Feb. 1972, 3 Feb. 1974. Label M, 2000.

Cedar Walton, piano; Clifford Jordan, tenor saxophone; Bill Hardman, trumpet; Sam Jones, bass; Herbie Lewis, bass; Billy Higgins, drums; Etta Jones, vocals. The 1971 performance featured Walton leading a trio with Lewis and Higgins. These three were joined by Jordan and Hardman in 1974, while Etta Jones lent her vocals to the 1972 show. Tracks include two of Walton's own compositions, "Plexus" and "I'm Not So Sure."

Ammons, Gene, and Sonny Stitt. *God Bless Jug and Sonny*. Recorded live, 24 June 1973. Prestige Records, 2001.

Gene Ammons, tenor saxophone; Sonny Stitt, tenor and alto saxophone; Cedar Walton, piano; Sam Jones, bass; Billy Higgins, drums; Etta Jones, vocals. Captured here are some great be-bop duels between Ammons and Stitt.

Ammons, Gene, and Sonny Stitt. *Left Bank Encores*. Recorded live, 24 June 1973. Prestige Records, 2001.

Gene Ammons, tenor saxophone; Sonny Stitt, tenor saxophone; Cedar Walton, piano; Sam Jones, bass; Billy Higgins, drums. More great battles between Jug and Stitt.

Getz, Stan. *My Foolish Heart*. Recorded live, 20 May 1975. Label M, 2000.

Stan Getz, tenor saxophone; Richie Beirach, piano; Dave Holland, double bass; Jack DeJohnette, drums. Getz made his name with the Woody Herman orchestra in the late 1940s, but he became most famous for his bossa nova period in the early '60s. Getz's lyrical sound is complemented by DeJohnette, who rocks out with several unconventional solos.

Hard Times
for Hard Bop

*"In many ways, the fate of jazz music's future in
Baltimore remains undecided, as it rides a
rollercoaster of successes complicated by roadblocks."*

13 Charm City's New Jazz Scene
by Andrew Zaleski

"How do we get the word out, and how do we get people in the clubs to hear local music?"

Barry Glassman sounds a little dejected. Roughly 40 minutes into talking about the jazz scene in Baltimore, he sighs this rhetorical plea, seemingly exhorting the music gods to help him see the light. For Glassman, one of the co-founders of the Baltimore Jazz Alliance, revitalizing Baltimore's aged—and aging—jazz scene has been a central concern since he moved here in the late 1980s.

"What surprised me about Baltimore is I kept running across world-class musicians who could play with anyone, anywhere," says Glassman. "But after living in New York [City], I was quite dismayed that there was so little jazz visible to the public."

Indeed, in many respects, Glassman showed up well after jazz had enjoyed its heyday in Baltimore. The vibrant Pennsylvania Avenue jazz scene of the 1950s and 1960s, one that thrived on performances at venues like the Royal Theatre and the Comedy Club, had faded by the late '70s. While jazz survived through other outlets and in other clubs during the next 20 years, the music's presence in Baltimore had gradually deteriorated by the end of the '80s. By 1990, a city that had been home to some of the most famous American jazz musicians—drummer Chick Webb, jazz vocalists Billie Holiday and Cab Calloway—and had showcased the likes of Miles Davis, Philly Joe Jones, and John

Coltrane, was seeing once-bustling clubs close or stop featuring jazz for good; national musicians passing on opportunities to play in Baltimore; and a river of jazz music and musicianship dry up, either to relocate to places like New York City, or to disappear entirely.

And then came the '90s.

For the past 20 years, jazz has struggled to maintain a foothold in Baltimore. While it exists in small pockets around the city, kept alive by nonprofit groups, colleges and universities, and what few dedicated clubs that remain, the scene lacks a central focus. Pennsylvania Avenue has come and gone. The revered Left Bank Jazz Society, which fueled jazz's legacy for a good two decades beginning in 1964, stopped promoting back in 1998.

Some jazzers still in the area hold their own hypotheses as to why jazz seems to have fallen off the grid of Baltimore's music scene. But, irrespective of any single reason for the decay of Charm City's jazz scene, the genre's survival in Baltimore faces a crossroads heading into the coming decade: eke out a following by continuing to promote shows at the clubs that remain, spreading the word about the musicians still powering through bop and blues; or institutionalize itself entirely— become America's "classical music," as many are prone to call it —and keep time by relying on grants and funding from nonprofits.

::::::

"You want a wing?"

I'm sitting with 75-year-old Eleanor Janey and her husband, Arthur Hoffman, at the Caton Castle jazz club. A long, stucco-walled corridor leads to the club's entrance, where a faint glow from the stage combined with the dirty yellow from the bar lights illuminate the joint. In some ways, the place is a throwback to the jazz haunts of Pennsylvania Avenue in the '50s: white tablecloths draped over round tables; a small, rectangular, wooden dance floor in the front; vertical mirrors the height of the wall serving as the backdrop to a stage too small to fit an entire band.

Situated just beyond the intersection of West Baltimore Street and Hilton Avenue, the Castle is not 15 minutes from the tourist-attracting Inner Harbor. But driving to the West Baltimore jazz joint will take one past rows of boarded up houses and the occasional blinking blue "Police Watch" light. As organist Greg Hatza notes in a 2007 article by Mary Zajac, it's the type of neighborhood "that people aren't happy about venturing into" (2).

Nonetheless, on the second Saturday in January, 2010, I find myself seated before a white tablecloth, reporter's pen in hand, sipping a Coke while Arthur digs into his platter of fish and fries. Eleanor has ordered the chicken wings.

Warren Wolf's quartet is the entertainment for the evening. His fingers deftly maneuver left and right across the piano keys, soaring through Miles Davis and John Coltrane standards. My jaw begins to drop as John Lamkin, III transitions into his drum solo. He's playing a triplet groove between his toms and his snare drum, and his hands are barely even moving.

"Get it, John! Yeah!" Applause cuts through the timbre of Lamkin's drums. Wolf responds, his fingers dancing along keys of black and white.

"Yeah, Warren!"

As shouts from the audience punctuate the solos, the crowd's volume creates the illusion that the place is packed. It's not. About 25 patrons are scattered among the various tables. A group of three college-aged people sits at one table. Minus the musicians in Wolf's quartet, and a student from Johns Hopkins's Peabody Institute guest-playing with him, everyone else is well over the age of 40.

Midway through the band's first break, Eleanor motions for Ron Scott, the owner of the Castle, to join her and Arthur. Black loafers, black mock turtleneck, black driver's cap, and gray pants: Ron looks like a jazz club owner.

"Hey, Ron, what were some of those venues in the '90s? The ones still doin' music?"

Scott sits, leans heavily with his hand on his right leg, and then slowly begins compiling a list. There was the Sportsman's Lounge, which stopped presenting live jazz in earnest about 15 years ago. The Bird Cage on East North Avenue—now just a neighborhood bar—used to be the follow-up spot to the Sportsman's. Every Monday, it was jazz at Sportsman's until midnight, and then everyone would shift to the Bird Cage for another two hours, according to Eleanor. After the Bird Cage came Club 2300, but that has since closed. The Short Stop on Washington Boulevard. Harry's Corner at the intersection of Chase and Maryland. Gordon's, which had jazz every Wednesday and Thursday. Buddie's Pub, closed in 2002. The Closet, on Franklin Street, which was called that because "that's what you were in when you went in there," says Eleanor.

Many of the venues Scott ticks off were big jazz joints prior to the '90s; once the decade began, some were still offering music, but due either to new ownership or a diminishing audience, many closed down or adopted newer entertainment throughout the week, keeping jazz going only one night each week (the Caton Castle typically runs shows solely on Saturday nights; bigger acts garner both a Saturday and Sunday night show). Eventually his speech slows to a crawl, and the steady stream of venue names hits a dam.

"In the '90s, not too many places [were] doing music," says Scott. "That's why it's so hard [to remember]."

Indeed, Baltimore jazz in the '90s faced a dry period, one that was equal parts puzzling and frustrating.

"It just got strange in the '90s. I don't really know what it was—it's hard to explain what happened."

For saxophonist Craig Alston, labeling the jazz scene as "strange" is as close as he can come to a tidy explanation of how music and musical tastes changed beginning in 1990. Alston himself got his start in 1993, when he was a music education major at Morgan State University. Playing first with Morgan State's jazz ensemble, Alston branched out into the city's jazz scene, hitting up clubs like the Sportsman's and the Wall Street Lounge. At that point, some of Baltimore's more famed jazz musicians, guys like Mickey Fields and Andy Ennis, were still gigging.

"The biggest thing," says Alston, "is back then, [there were] a lot more places to play, and it was in the streets. Now, we have a whole bunch of jazz in schools, but no clubs. Kids learn all this theory, but they have nowhere to apply it, to learn how to respond or interact with the music."

When Alston was first exploring Baltimore's jazz culture, he could attend jam sessions to work on his chops. "You could sit there and

313

someone like Dennis Chambers would be there," says Alston, and that became the way he learned group dynamics, all-too important in jazz, which is utterly dependent upon each musician not only playing the right notes, but also listening to the notes that the other musicians are playing. "At the Sportsman [sic], if I'm messin' up, they'd tell me to get off the stage." That would be Alston's cue to work on his chops some more, take another listen to the tunes, and return the following week to jam again.

But as venues closed down or changed ownership throughout the decade, the opportunities for gigs and jam sessions—and the part-entertainment, part-educational experience they offered—dried up. Thus the '90s became the decade in which Baltimore lost a widespread, dedicated jazz-listening audience.

Alston cites a generational shift as the culprit: "The nightlife just kind of changed. A whole younger crowd came out and they didn't know how to listen to [jazz] or appreciate it. I guess people just didn't see the relevance of live music."

To temper this flow of audiences from where the jazz was, and to work on publicizing performances, Barry Glassman, prior to his BJA days, had worked independently in the mid-'90s to compile an online jazz calendar, cataloging the various Baltimore gigs and disseminating the information so people knew where and when to find the music.

"It was a labor of love," says Glassman, "but I had to enter everything manually and by myself," a tall order for just one person. But in Glassman's endeavors lay the second part of the problem for jazz, not only in the '90s, but also in today's Baltimore: publicity. Hence Glassman's ire, when it comes to publicizing the city's jazz scene, is directed mainly at Baltimore's print media.

"I blame the *Sun* more than anybody. The biggest problem is just putting the word out, but the Baltimore scene would be so much more vibrant if they just had a jazz writer every week. Right now, it's sort of a vicious cycle—we can't get out of the starting blocks."

But describing precisely where and how jazz fell off the scene in the '90s involves, at best, an amalgamation of causes and pitfalls and, at worst, deals in pure speculation.

Certainly, a lack of venues coupled with minuscule publicity— combined with a general musical culture in the '90s that was not only younger, but also more attuned to the sounds of hip-hop and rock music—did not help increase the popularity or influence of jazz in the '90s, despite its history in Baltimore.

"There's a lot of art and culture in Baltimore," says Alston. "But people don't know how to support it. The problem with Baltimore is that, when you start something, people support it for the first two months, and then the support drops off."

Or the support is sporadic. On January 2nd, merely one Saturday before a crowd of 25 trickled into the Caton Castle to catch Warren Wolf, more than 95 paying customers had streamed into the Castle to catch drummer Lee Pearson and his group. And according to Ron Scott, that number does not even include the patrons relegated to standing room. But even an audience of 95 for one night pales in comparison to the audiences Baltimore's former jazz scene used to bring out.

As the '90s ended, the challenge for purveyors and performers of jazz became not only to discover a means by which they could have more venues available, but how to create more visibility for a jazz culture that, however diminished, still remained in Baltimore City.

The formation of the Baltimore Jazz Alliance provided one solution. Pooling his list of contacts, Glassman, looking to arrange a meeting of jazz musicians, venue owners, and fellow fans, e-mailed more than 40 individuals to begin discussing how to resurrect Baltimore's lagging jazz scene.

"It was a lot of bitchin' and moanin,' a lot of venting, but the point initially was to bring people together to talk about the state of jazz in Baltimore," says Mark Osteen, a professor of English at Loyola University Maryland and a saxophonist with Cold Spring Jazz Quartet.

After some preliminary meetings, the larger crowd had been whittled down to a core membership, a steering committee composed of Cheryl Goodman, Osteen, Glassman, Bob Jacobson, Camay Calloway Murphy, Bob Brinkman (the manager of Harry's Impressions, where the group met originally), Nancy Haragan (of the Greater Baltimore Cultural Alliance), Marianne Matheny-Katz, Tom Saunders, Larry Williams, Earl Wilson, Rhonda Robinson, George Spicka, and Darryl Harper. Naming themselves the Baltimore Jazz Alliance and electing Harper as president, the BJA immediately set out with a five-point plan: create new audiences in Baltimore for jazz; improve communication among members of the city's jazz community; gain more media coverage of jazz gigs and events; encourage and promote visibility for Baltimore jazz; and assist jazz musicians in acquiring gigs.

The BJA's ambitious initial plan proved difficult to implement during the first few years of the group's existence. A membership drive in 2003 failed to bring a larger contingent of supporters. Incorporating in 2004, the BJA countered by winning two grants, each worth $1,500, from the Greater Baltimore Cultural Alliance and the Baltimore Office of Promotion and the Arts (BOPA), which were then used in part to hire Eliot Caroom, who developed a monthly newsletter for the group. By 2005, the Alliance had begun jazz programming around the city, first co-sponsoring a composers' showcase that drew a crowd of more than 100 in October of that year, and then—with the help of a $4,000 grant from BOPA—presenting a Baltimore Youth Jazz Congress in April, 2006, at which six high school and middle school jazz bands performed.

"The school shows weren't well attended, but they established us as being interested in education," says Osteen. With that foothold, the BJA, this time with a $2,800 dollar grant from BOPA, used the Eubie Blake Center to present "Pre-Cool Jazz," with more than 50 kids participating to learn some jazz history, gain exposure to musical instruments, and hear performances. More recently, the Alliance released two Baltimore *Jazzscapes* CDs—compilations of current Baltimore artists—as well as the *Baltimore Real Book*, which features more than 50 original jazz compositions from 18 Baltimore jazz musicians.

But even with its current membership of more than 150 people, the Baltimore Jazz Alliance has provided more of an eager nudge than a permanent fix when it comes to revitalizing the city's decaying jazz culture.

"The problem with Baltimore is it's always been a great incubator for jazz, but it's hard to make a living," says Geoffrey Himes, long-time journalist and jazz critic in Baltimore.

Only four jazz venues now call Baltimore home: An die Musik in Mount Vernon, the New Haven Lounge in the Northwood Shopping Center, the Wine Cellar on Water Street, in the basement of Velleggia's Italian Restaurant, and the Caton Castle. Even at these venues, actual jazz music takes a back seat most nights, with the Caton Castle presenting music only on Saturdays and both An die Musik and the Haven dedicating only a few nights each week strictly to jazz.

"The jazz in town now is incidental music at restaurants or bars," says BJA vice president Bob Jacobson. "There aren't a whole lot of places we'd call jazz clubs."

Indeed, one of the main difficulties involved in owning a jazz club in Baltimore today is the perpetual problem of economics. Offering only jazz would force places like the Haven to close (though the club used to provide jazz exclusively, the Haven now supplements its jazz performances with DJ, reggae, and blues music on other nights), since a diminished jazz-listening public does not bring in enough money through food and drink sales. At the same time, in order to bring out the jazz musicians for performances, venue owners need the money to pay them. To this extent, then, venue owners have been forced to adopt a strategy they strayed away from for many years—charging their audiences a cover fee, a tactic that tends to be more a hindrance than a saving grace.

"The problem is, you can charge a cover . . . but if people aren't willing to pay it, you go out of business," says Himes. What transpires is the consistent frustration jazzers like Alston experience in trying to advance their music in Baltimore: people stop coming to shows.

Vernard Gray, a transplant from D.C. and founder of the nonprofit Be Mo Jazz (begun in March 2008), initially tried his luck at piecing together shows at various venues around Baltimore. A series of performances he arranged at The Teavolve Café in Harbor East at first drew consistent crowds of around 40 people, with a starting cover charge of $7. Over time, though, Gray's crowds dwindled, and the people who attended the shows in the beginning eventually stopped coming.

"It's just one of those things you just can't put your finger on," says Gray. "I've seen people turn right around at the door at Teavolve if they have to pay a cover."

Various jazz clubs in nearby Washington, D.C., regularly charge covers. Patrons of Twins Jazz in D.C. are used to paying a cover of anywhere between $10 and $30. Blues Alley mandates that all patrons purchase at least $10 of food and drinks in addition to paying the price for a ticket and a $2 surcharge. For jazz in D.C., one expects to pay a cover charge.

But not in Baltimore.

"People tend to scoff at $5 or $10 cover charges," says Todd Marcus, a bass clarinetist who has been on the Baltimore scene since the late '90s.

A vicious cycle becomes established, then, making it difficult for jazz and jazz musicians to survive, let alone thrive. Musicians cannot work for free, but with a limited number of consistent venues, the lack of a large-scale, committed audience, and a uniquely Baltimorean aversion to paying cover charges, it appears as though Baltimore jazzers must consistently swim against the current to promote and perform their music.

Compounding the funding issue is a lack of community among Baltimore's jazz musicians. Jazz music and the musicians themselves are independent by nature. Indeed, the jazz aesthetic fosters a freelance mentality. Solo-oriented, the music places an emphasis upon individuals, not the collective. (Rock bands are known by band names; jazz groups are known by the fronting musician: Dizzy Gillespie, Cab Calloway, Miles Davis, and so on.)

Transferring that freelance mentality to the economics of the jazz world illustrates two of musicians' most pressing concerns: what shows can I get in on, and how much will those shows pay me? Though not exactly cutthroat, this mentality creates disjointedness not only among musicians, keeping individual groups segmented, but also among the various venues and audience members.

"In Baltimore, venues are first gathering places, and then you add the jazz to it," says Gray. "It's really about social groups coming together."

Recalling his teenage years, Gray remembers coming up from D.C. to Baltimore's Pennsylvania Avenue scene in the 1950s, hopping from joint to joint.

"It was people gathered in there that were always in there."

This sense of community is largely absent today. Add to this the lack of community among jazz musicians, and the situation becomes troublesome, says Gray.

"The musicians need to get their act together. There are some talented musicians in this town, but I defy you to name 10 groups of three, four, or five people that rehearse together and have a group identity. It ain't happenin'.'"

Marcus, who regularly rehearses with his larger, nine-piece band as well as with his smaller group, started his jazz tenure in Baltimore trying to facilitate jam sessions across the city, which were once the way that musicians would connect, network, and form a tight-knit group. But without the jam session, suggests Marcus, that broader sense of togetherness is missing, a particular problem for a city with a history of economic and racial segregation.

"Jazz was a big social force that brought people across racial lines," says Marcus. "What's lost without the jam session is that people aren't willing to leave their circles."

From a personal perspective, Marcus also thinks the sub-par attendance of Baltimore jazzers at other musicians' shows hurts the city's jazz culture.

"To be truthful, I'm disappointed in the poor representation of my colleagues at shows. Musicians are a little shortsighted in coming and showing support—a greater sense of community is missing."

Though the BJA was created to address these problems of community, they have struggled to change this ingrained individualist ethos.

And in addition to issues of division and apathy, a generational component also fuels jazz's decay in Baltimore.

"We need to reach out to young kids to keep jazz alive," says Henry Wong, owner of An die Musik. "People [are] looking at music nowadays as individuals; it lost the whole meaning of being a culture."

Presenting free jazz concerts to inner-city schools is one avenue Wong is exploring to try to develop and inculcate interest in jazz to a newer, younger generation of listeners.

To be sure, efforts abound in Baltimore by people working to maintain jazz in unconventional ways. Along with the BJA, Wong's An die Musik and Gray's Be Mo Jazz are both nonprofit enterprises, as is the Chamber Jazz Society, which holds jazz concerts periodically at the

Baltimore Museum of Art. The advantage here is that such groups can seek out grants and donations, while places like the Caton Castle have to rely on an unpredictable business cycle.

Marianne Matheny-Katz's Jazzway 6004 provides an innovative approach to staging jazz concerts. Matheny-Katz holds the shows in her home, offering patrons a concert and a meal. However, her venue, which might host a show once every month, only holds a maximum of 60 people—ideal for an intimate setting, but too small to accommodate listeners en masse.

"What we don't have," says Glassman, "is a white tablecloth jazz club, where you can go for fine dining, good service, and a regional act rather than a local act."

But even if such a place came into being, as Gray and Marcus both acknowledge, the communal aspect of Baltimore's jazz scene could remain absent. The people who attend shows at the BMA, or at An die Musik, or at Jazzway, are not necessarily the same people who would head to the Caton Castle on Saturday nights; this fact highlights subconscious divisions that persist in Baltimore's broader jazz community, which effectively turn the broader jazz community into a number of mini-communities, each with its own identity rather than a larger group identity.

The uncomfortable undertone in this dynamic argues for an authenticity—in the music and the listening experience—which functions by implicitly accusing some jazzers and venues of being exclusionary or fake. And the accusatory tone travels both ways: from black jazzers to white jazzers, and vice versa.

"The problems are obvious," says Himes. "The solutions are not so obvious."

One viable solution seems to exist in education. Programs at the Peabody Institute, Towson University, and Loyola University essentially perform jazz upkeep, maintaining the presence of the music and keeping jazz musicians like Gary Thomas and Mike Formanek in Baltimore. And that is why younger musicians seek to promote jazz not only at colleges and universities, but also at the elementary and high school level, something Alston has done in recent years through a program at the Eubie Blake Center, where he runs a summer program for three to four weeks that teaches kids the foundations of jazz music.

"Baltimore musically is being felt all around the world," says Alston. "I've been places where they go, 'You're from Baltimore—you must be able to play.' I just try to encourage the youth, try to give them advice on where to go to school to study."

Indeed, in Baltimore's institutions of higher learning the cultivation—and survival—of jazz appears most promising.

"European classical music has been institutionalized for hundreds of years. Jazz will go the way of classical music," says Marcus, citing the example of the Lincoln Center in New York City.

Himes agrees, noting the difficulty in trying to make ticket sales pay for expenses, such as a venue's utility costs, food, drinks, promotion, as well as musicians, and to bring in enough money to court regional and national acts. Ultimately, he sees jazz becoming America's classical music, not only in name, but also in terms of its business model.

"Jazz increasingly needs grants to stay alive," says Himes.

Optimism, however, remains.

"I really think there's gonna be another resurgence, a renaissance," declares Alston.

Signs of a renaissance certainly exist, especially compared to jazz's state in the '90s. Over the past few years, jazz music has regained a place at Baltimore's annual Artscape festival, thanks in large part to the efforts of the Baltimore Jazz Alliance. Marcus also cites the passion of young up-and-comers along the city's North Avenue strip, where men and women approach jazz with a rock-music mentality, seeking out and performing shows for the experience and the love of the music, not for the paycheck.

In many ways, the fate of jazz music's future in Baltimore remains undecided, as it rides a rollercoaster of successes complicated by roadblocks. But the jazz is alive, supported and promoted by pockets of enthusiasts around town.

"I think Baltimore is gonna have some energy, but it's gonna take another two years or so," says Gray. He pauses for a bit, his breathing sounding a little short over the receiver of my phone. It feels like he is trying to decide how believable his sentiments are, whether he is tricking himself into a false state of security. After about another minute he clears his throat, and then his voice cuts confidently through the stiff silence.

"It's gonna take another two years or so. . . . But you can feel it. There's a potential for a whole lot of stuff to happen."

Works Cited

Alston, Craig. Personal interview. 29 Dec. 2009.

Glassman, Barry. Personal interview. 18 Dec. 2009.

Gray, Vernard. Personal interview. 4 Jan. 2010.

Himes, Geoff. Personal interview. 5 Jan. 2010.

Hoffman, Arthur. Personal interview. 9 Jan. 2010.

Jacobson, Bob. Personal interview. 17 Dec. 2009.

Janey, Eleanor. Personal interview. 4 Jan. 2010.

Janey, Eleanor. Personal interview. 9 Jan. 2010.

Marcus, Todd. Personal interview. 5 Jan. 2010.

Osteen, Mark. Personal interview. 15 Dec. 2009.

Scott, Ron. Personal interview. 9 Jan. 2010.

Wong, Henry. Personal interview. 28 Jan. 2010.

Zajac, Mary K. "Jazz Sings The Blues." BaltimoreStyle.com Sept./Oct. 2007.
20 Dec. 2009 Web.
Zajac's article provides an excellent general overview of how Baltimore's jazz scene has decayed over the past 20 years. Featuring interviews from musicians, venue owners, and fans, Zajac's piece offers an insightful look into the problems plaguing jazz music in Baltimore. Indeed, many of the issues Zajac cites appear in my article as well, retold to me by some of the same people Zajac spoke with in 2007.

Discography

Al Maniscalco Quartet. *One Blessed Day*. 2006.
    Though he has since moved from Baltimore, tenorist Maniscalco recorded this fine straight-ahead session in Baltimore with local musicians, including bassist Jeff Reed and drummer Eric Kennedy.

Asirvatham, Sandy. *Memoir*. Jazzgrrl. 2007.

Baltimore Jazz Alliance. *Baltimore Jazzscapes*. 2006.

Baltimore Jazz Alliance. *Baltimore Jazzscapes II*. 2009.
    The two Jazzscapes discs compile tracks from a varied group of Baltimore jazz artists, including Anthony Villa, Marianne Matheny-Katz, and George Spicka. The second disc also features Mickey Fields playing "Lover Man," recorded live at the Famous Ballroom in 1977.

Carter, Felicia. *Feather / Step Lightly*. Alberta Records. 2007.
    A double CD, one disc showcases singer Carter's original compositions and the other her renditions of standards.

Cold Spring Jazz Quartet. *Urban Pastoral*. 2008.

Holmes, Joel. *African Skies*. 2009.

Todd Marcus Jazz Orchestra. *In Pursuit of the 9th Man*. HiPNOTIC Records. 2006.
    Debut disc from Marcus's nonet, featuring his intriguing compositions and compelling arrangements. "Harper's Choice" swings moderately, but punchy snare work and a dancing piano, aided by Marcus's distinctive bass clarinet, propel the track to completion. Check out the title track: a vibrant swing and a crafty call-and-response between the horns and the bass clarinet demonstrate Marcus's orchestra's creativity and tidy musicianship.

Wolf, Warren. *Raw*. Wolf Pac. 2008.
    A veritable one-man band, Wolf is not only a phenomenal drummer and a superior vibes player, but also plays a mean piano. This Berklee grad lets loose on Raw, tracking on both the vibraphone and marimba; "427 Mass Ave" is the tune to listen to, with a melodic vibes riff from Wolf kicking off the beat, which then expands and receives accompaniment from a shuffle pattern laid down by drummer Charles Haynes.

IV. APPENDICES

LEFT BANK JAZZ SOCIETY CONCERT LISTING

The following list is a reproduction of the concerts listed in the 1968, 1972, 1979, and 1990 Left Bank Jazz Society Yearbooks. From the end of 1966 until 1984, the weekly Sunday afternoon concerts were held at the Famous Ballroom on North Charles Street, unless otherwise noted.

ALHO CLUB

8/16/64   **DONALD BAILEY**, Bass
Jimmy Wells-vibes; Tom Baldwin-piano; Teddy Hawke-drums

8/24/64   **OTTS BETHEL**, Tenor Sax
Bill Stocksdale-trumpet; Earl Hayes-drums; George Hoffman-bass

8/31/64   **JOE CLARK**, Tenor Sax
Al Cotton-drums; Phil Harris-bass; Jimmy Wells-piano

9/6/64   **MICKEY FIELDS**, Tenor Sax
Donald Bailey-bass; Jimmy Wells-vibes; Bobby Nelson-drums

9/13/64   **DONALD CRISS**, Piano
Luqman Abdul Lateef-tenor sax; Wayne Alston-bass; Gary Wilmore-drums

9/27/64   **DAVE HUBBARD**, Tenor Sax
Lee Jeffers-alto sax; Andrew Rock-bass; Maurice Williams-piano;
Jerome McCardell-drums

10/4/64   **DELORES LYNN**, Singer
Jean Luc Vallet-piano; Joe Clark-tenor sax; Phil Harris-bass;
Earl Hayes-drums

10/11/64   **GARY BARTZ**, Alto Sax
Jean Luc Vallet-piano; Mousy Johnson-trumpet; Bill Henderson-bass;
Gary Wilmore-drums

10/16/64   **BUCK HILL QUARTET AND DELORES LYNN**
Caberet Party, Wilson's Restaurant

10/18/64   **MICKEY FIELDS**, Tenor Sax
Jimmy Wells-piano/vibes; Donald Bailey-bass; Harold White-drums

10/25/64   **MONTY STARK**, Vibes
Prentice Sterling Pointer-bass; Gary Wilmore-drums

11/1/64   **JIM BADALATO**, Tenor Sax
Bill Starksdale-trumpet; Brent Price-drums; George Hoffman-bass;
Tom Garvin-piano

11/8/64   **BUCK HILL**, Tenor Sax
Claude Hubbard-piano; Harold White-drums; Phil Harris-bass

11/15/64   **DONALD CRISS**, Piano
Luqman Abdul Lateef-tenor sax; Mike Seymour-bass; Reggie Glascoe-drums

11/22/64   **DAVE HUBBARD**, Tenor sax
Lee Jeffers-alto sax; Maurice Williams-piano; Jerome McCardell-drums;
Andrew Rock-bass

11/29/64   **MONTY STARK**, Vibes
Prentice Sterling Pointer-bass; Gary Wilmore-drums

12/6/64   **DIZZY GILLESPIE**, Trumpet
James Moody-alto sax; Rudy Collins-drums; Kenny Barron-piano;
Chris White, bass

FAMOUS BALLROOM

12/13/64   **MICKEY FIELDS**, Tenor Sax
Donald Criss-piano; Reggie Glascoe-drums; Mike Seymour-bass

12/20/64   **MICKEY FIELDS**, Tenor Sax
Donald Criss-piano; Reggie Glascoe-drums; Mike Seymour-bass

12/27/64 BUCK CLARKE, Drums
Charles Ables-guitar; Steve Novosel-bass

1/3/65 PAUL BLEY, Piano
Phil Harris-bass; Ben Cerquetti-drums

1/10/65 OTTS BETHEL, Tenor Sax
Bill Stocksdale-trumpet; Bill Henderson-bass; Brent Price-drums;
Jean Luc Vallet-piano;

1/17/65 JIMMY HEATH, Tenor Sax
Donald Bailey-bass; Jimmy Wells-piano/vibes; Teddy Hawke-drums

1/24/65 BUCK CLARKE, Drums
Charles Ables-guitar; David Hubbard-tenor sax; Steve Novosel-bass

1/31/65 REPPARD STONE, Trombone and Piano
Vernon Wolst, Dave Hubbard-tenor sax; Louis Hamlin-trumpet; Phil Harris-
bass; Earl Hayes-drums

2/14/65 JIMMY HEATH, Tenor Sax
Kenny Dorham-trumpet; Donald Bailey-bass; Jimmy Wells-piano;
Teddy Hawke-drums

2/21/65 YUSEF SALIM, Piano
Louis Hamlin-trumpet; Ray Kitz-tenor sax; Whit Williams-baritone
sax; Bill Henderson-bass; Ricky Johnson-drums

2/28/65 FREDDIE HUBBARD, Trumpet
Clifford Jordan-tenor sax; Donald Bailey-bass; Jimmy Wells-piano;
Teddy Hawke-drums

3/7/65 BILL SWINDELL, Tenor Sax
Johnny Burkes-trumpet; Claude Hubbard-piano; Donald Bailey-bass;
Harold White-drums

3/14/65 JIMMY HEATH,Tenor Sax
Pepper Adams-baritone sax; Gus Simms-piano; Bertell Knox-drums;
Wilbur Little-bass

3/21/65 BLUE MITCHELL,Trumpet
Sonny Red-alto sax; Claude Hubbard-piano; Phil Harris-bass;
Harold White-drums

3/28/65 THE JAZZ CRUSADERS
Wayne Henderson, trombone/euphonium; Wilton Felder-tenor/alto sax;
Herbert Lewis-bass; Stix Hooper-drums; Joe Sample-piano

4/4/65 BENNY GOLSON, Tenor Sax
Johnny Coles-trumpet; Donald Bailey-bass; Jimmy Wells-piano;
Teddy Hawke-drums

4/11/65 GRACHAN MONCUR, III, Trombone
Charles Davis-baritone sax; Gary Bartz-alto sax; Gus Simms-piano;
Bertell Knox-drums; Wilbur Little-bass

4/18/65 ARCHIE SHEPP, Tenor Sax
Ted Curson-trumpet; Marion Brown-alto sax; Joe Orange-trombone;
Reggie Johnson-bass; Marvin Patillo-drums; Reppard Stone-piano/trombone;
Dave Hubbard-tenor sax; Louis Hamlin-trumpet; Phil Harris-bass;
Earl Hayes-drums

4/25/65 JIMMY HEATH,Tenor Sax
Pepper Adams-baritone sax; Sonny Red-alto sax; Reggie Workman-bass;
Cedar Walton-piano; Roy Brooks-drums;

MORGAN STATE COLLEGE

5/2/65   **AL COHN**, Tenor Sax
Zoot Sims-tenor sax; Stomp Saunders-drums; Wilbur Little-bass; Gus Simms-piano

5/9/65   **MICKEY FIELDS**, Tenor Sax
Buck Hill-tenor sax; Wilbur Little-bass; Bertell Knox-drums; Gus Simms-piano

5/16/65   **ART TAYLOR**, Drums
Walter Bishop, Jr.-piano; Frank Foster-tenor sax; Eddie Kahn-bass

5/23/65   **HERBIE HANCOCK**, Piano
Ron Carter-bass; Tony Williams-drums; Sam Rivers-tenor sax

5/30/65   **YUSEF LATEEF**, Alto/Flute, Tenor Sax
Reggie Workman-bass; George Arvinitas-piano; James Black-drums

6/6/65   **CLIFFORD JORDAN**, Tenor Sax
J.C. Moses-drums; Ronnie Matthews-piano; Eddie Kahn-bass

6/12/65   **CANNONBALL ADDERLEY**, Alto Sax
Nat Adderley-cornet; Charles Lloyd-tenor sax; Louis Hayes-drums; Sam Jones-bass; Joe Zawinul-piano

LYRIC THEATRE

6/13/65   **JIMMY HEATH**, Tenor Sax
Freddie Hubbard-trumpet; Wilbur Little-bass; Bertell Knox-drums; Gus Simms-piano

6/20/65   **CARMELL JONES**, Trumpet
Grachan Moncur-trombone; Charles Davis-baritone sax; Wilbur Little-bass; Bertell Knox-drums; Ted Carson-piano

6/27/65   **CHARLES LLOYD**, Tenor Sax
Louis Hayes-drums; Sam Jones-bass; Joe Zawinul-piano

7/11/65   **ROY HAYNES**, Drums
Wayne Shorter-tenor sax; Albert Dailey-piano; Larry Ridley-bass

7/18/65   **BILL SWINDELL**, Tenor Sax
Phil Harris-bass; Claude Hubbard-piano; Mousy Johnson-trumpet; Purnell Rice-drums

7/25/65   **BLUE MITCHELL**, Trumpet
Junior Cook-tenor sax; Wilbur Little-bass; Bertell Knox-drums; Ted Carson-piano

8/1/65   **ELLSWORTH GIBSON**, Piano
Buck Hill-tenor sax; Wilbur Little-bass; Bertell Knox-drums

8/8/65   **CLIFFORD JORDAN**, Tenor Sax
Kenny Dorham-trumpet; Phil Harris-bass; Claude Hubbard-piano; Purnell Rice-drums

8/15/65   **CHARLES DAVIS**, Baritone Sax
Bertell Knox-drums; Wilbur Little-bass; Reuben Brown-piano

8/22/65   **JACKIE McLEAN**, Alto Sax
Charles Tolliver-trumpet; Larry Willis-piano; Jack DeJohnette-drums; Wilbur Little-bass

8/29/65 **GRACHAN MONCUR, III**, Trombone
Bill Barron-tenor sax; Butch Warren-bass; Stomp Saunders-drums;
Lennie Grazier-piano

9/5/65 **WYNTON KELLY**, Piano
Paul Chambers-bass; Jimmy Cobb-drums; Wes Montgomery-guitar

9/12/65 **JIMMY HEATH**-Tenor Sax
Mickey Fields-tenor sax; Wilbur Little-bass; Bertell Knox-drums;
Reuben Brown-piano

9/19/65 **SONNY RED**, Alto Sax
Dizzy Reece-trumpet; Barry Harris-piano; Gene Taylor-bass;
Frank Gant-drums

9/26/65 **THE JAZZ CRUSADERS**
Wilton Felder-tenor/alto sax; Wayne Henderson-trombone/euphonium;
Stix Hooper-drums; Joe Sample-piano; Herbert Lewis-bass

10/3/65 **JACKIE BLAKE**, Alto Sax
Louis Hamlin-trumpet, Whit Williams-baritone sax; Dave Hubbard-tenor
sax; Monty Stark-vibes; Reppard Stone-trombone; Phil Harris-bass;
Gary Wilmore-drums

10/10/65 **YUSEF LATEEF**, Tenor/Alto Sax, Flute, Argol and Shannas
Reggie Workman-bass; Hugh Lawson-piano; James Black-drums

10/17/65 **CHARLES LLOYD**, Tenor Sax/Flute
Gabor Szabo-guitar; Albert Stinson-bass; Pete La Roca-drums

10/24/65 **DONALD BYRD**, Trumpet
Jimmy Heath-tenor sax; Duke Pearson-piano; Joe Chambers-drums;
Walter Booker-bass

10/31/65 **DAVE HUBBARD**, Tenor Sax & Flute
Mack Rucks-trumpet; Maurice Williams-piano; Jerome McCardell-drums;
Andrew Rock-bass

11/7/65 **BUCK CLARKE**, Drums
Charles Ables-guitar; Marshall Smith-bass; Dave Hubbard-tenor sax/flute

11/14/65 **FREDDIE HUBBARD**, Trumpet
Joe Henderson-tenor sax; Arthur Harper-bass; Clifford Jarvis-drums;
John Hicks-piano

11/21/65 **ROLAND KIRK**
Horace Parlan-piano; Sonny Brown-drums; Eddie Mathias-bass

11/28/65 **HANK MOBLEY**, Tenor Sax
Johnny Coles-trumpet; Wilbur Little-bass; Bertell Knox-drums;
Reuben Brown-piano

12/5/65 **SHIRLEY HORN**, Piano/Singer
Bernard Sweetney-drums; Marshall Hawkins-bass; Mickey Fields-tenor sax/
flute; Claude Hubbuard-piano; Phil Harris-bass; Purnell Rice-drums

12/12/65 **PEPPER ADAMS**, Baritone Sax
Blue Mitchell-trumpet; Ron Carter-bass; Duke Pearson-piano;
John Dentz-drums

12/19/65 **LUCKY THOMPSON**, Soprano Sax & Tenor Sax
Tommy Flanagan-piano; Walter Perkins-drums; Bob Cranshaw-bass

12/26/65 **GARY WILMORE**, Drums
Harris Teddy Brown-trombone; Phil Harris-bass; Maurice Williams-piano;
Dave Hubbard-tenor sax

| 1/2/66 | **SHIRLEY HORN**, Singer/Piano |

1/2/66 **SHIRLEY HORN**, Singer/Piano
Bernard Sweetney-drums; Marshall Hawkins-bass; Charles Ables-guitar
1/9/66 **WALTER NAMUTH**, Guitar
Mickey Fields-tenor sax; Phil Harris-bass; Claude Hubbard-piano;
Purnell Rice-drums
1/16/66 **TONY SCOTT**, Clarinet
Larry Willis-piano; Victor Sproles-bass; Eddie Marshall-drums;
Joelee Wilson-singer
1/23/66 **BILLY MITCHELL**, Tenor Sax
Donald Bailey-bass; Stomp Saunders-drums; Jimmy Wells-piano

CRYSTAL BALLROOM

2/13/66 **HANK LEVY'S ORCHESTRA**
Margie Schaefer; Gus Cucoras; Tom Garvin-piano; Chuck Regnor-bass;
Larry Wooridge-guitar
2/27/66 **CHARLES LLOYD**, Tenor/Flute
Cecil McBee-bass; Jack DeJohnette-drums; Keith Jarrett-piano
3/6/66 **JIMMY HEATH**, Tenor Sax
Freddie Hubbard-trumpet; Albert Dailey-piano; Walter Booker-bass;
Mickey Roker-drums
3/13/66 **PHIL WOODS**, Alto Sax
Wilbur Little-bass; Bertell Knox-drums; Ruben Brown-piano
3/20/66 **BLUE MITCHELL**, Trumpet
Sonny Red-alto sax; Gene Taylor-bass; John Hicks-piano; Joe Chambers-drums;
3/27/66 **ROLAND KIRK**, Reeds
Lemonk Johnson-piano; Edward Mathias-bass; J. C. Moses-drums
4/3/66 **MEL LEWIS**, Drums
Pepper Adams-baritone sax; Dollar Brand-piano; Donald Moore-bass; Carlos Ward-alto sax; Morris Goldberg-alto sax, clarinet
4/10/66 **HANK MOBLEY**, Tenor Sax
McCoy Tyner-piano; Jack DeJohnette-drums; Eddie Marshall-bass
4/17/66 **JACKIE McCLEAN**, Alto Sax
Clifford Jarvis-drums; Larry Willis-piano; Donald Moore-bass

MADISON CLUB

4/24/66 **LUCKY THOMPSON**, Tenor/Soprano Sax
Hugh Lawson-piano; Walter Perkins-drums; Abdul Malik-bass
5/1/66 **YUSEF SALIM**, Piano
Count Lantz-vibes; Donald Bailey-bass; Purnell Rice-drums; Henry Mays-cello
Bob Smith-violin; Matt Frailing-violin; Bill Haithcock-violin

FAMOUS BALLROOM

5/6/66 **CABARET PARTY featuring LBJ's ALL STARS**
Buster Brown-singer; Baby Lawrence-tap dancer

MADISON CLUB

5/8/66   **ART FARMER**, Trumpet
Jimmy Heath-tenor sax; John Hicks-piano; Mickey Roker-drums;
Walter Booker-bass

5/15/66   **FREDDIE HUBBARD**, Trumpet
Hank Mobley-tenor sax; Philly Joe Jones-drums; Paul Chambers-bass
Ronnie Matthews-piano

5/22/66   **AL COHN**, Tenor Sax
Zoot Sims-tenor sax; Major Holly-bass; Dave Frishberg-piano;
Moosy Alexander-drums

5/29/66   **WALTER NAMUTH**, Guitar
Mickey Fields-tenor sax; Henry T. "Stomp" Saunders-drums;
Paul Chambers-bass; Ronnie Matthews-piano

6/5/66   **McCOY TYNER**, Piano
Joe Henderson-tenor sax; Jack DeJohnette-drums; Herbert Lewis-bass

6/12/66   **ROLAND KIRK**, Misc. Instruments
Eddie Mathias-bass; Bruce Woody-bass; Purnell Rice-drums

6/19/66   **SHIRLEY HORN**, Vocals/Piano
Marshall Hawkins-bass; Bernard Sweetney-drums; Yusef Salim-piano, leader;
Donald Bailey-bass; Purnell Rice-drums; Thomas "Wit" Williams-baritone/
alto sax; Ray Kitz-tenor sax; Louis Hamlin-trumpet

6/26/66   **ELVIN JONES**, Drums
Dollar Brand-piano; Donald Moore-bass; Frank Foster-tenor sax

7/3/66   **JOE LEE WILSON**, Vocals
Phil Harris-bass; Gary Wilmore-drums; Whit Williams-baritone/tenor sax;
Dave Hubbard-tenor sax, flute; Louis Hamlin-trumpet;
Claude Hubbard-piano

7/10/66   **RANDY WESTON**, Piano
Cecil Payne-baritone sax; Ray Copeland-trumpet; Lennie McBrowne-drums;
Bill Wood-bass

7/17/66   **KENNY BURRELL**, Guitar
Martin Rivera-bass; Bill English-drums; Richard Wyands-piano

7/24/66   **THE JAZZ CRUSADERS**
Wayne Henderson-trombone, euphonium; Wilton Felder-tenor/alto sax;
Joe Sample-piano; Stix Hooper-drums; Herbert Lewis-bass

7/31/66   **GRANT GREEN**, Guitar
Harold Vick-tenor sax; John Patton-organ; Hugh Walker-drums

8/7/66   **KETER BETTS**, Bass
Buck Hill-tenor sax; Charles Ables-guitar; Stomp Saunders-drums

8/14/66   **NO CONCERT**
Due to the absence of Freddie Hubbard, Philly Joe Jones, Jymie
Merritt, Tim Spaulding and Ronnie Matthews

8/21/66   **NO CONCERT**
Due to the absence of Andrew Hill, Sam Rivers, Richard Davis, and
Joe Chambers

8/28/66   **WALTER BISHOP, JR.**, Piano
Harold Vick-tenor sax, flute, soprano sax; Lou McIntosh-bass; Dick "Tiny"
Berk-drums

9/4/66   **FREDDIE HUBBARD**, Trumpet
Jim Spaulding-alto sax, flute; Ronnie Matthews-piano; Larry Ridley-bass;
Ray Appleton-drums

9/11/66   **DONALD BAILEY**, Bass
Teddy Hawk-drums; Jimmy Wells-vibes; Henry Levy-baritone sax; Joe Clark-
tenor sax; Claude Hubbard-piano; Stanley Johnson-trumpet;
Freddie Robier-trombone

9/18/66   **BLUE MITCHELL**, Trumpet
Junior Cook-tenor sax; Gene Taylor-bass; Roy Brooks-drums;
Chick Corea-piano

9/25/66   **COLEMAN HAWKINS**, Tenor Sax
Gene Taylor-bass; Roy Brooks-drums; Barry Harris-piano

10/2/66   **ART FARMER**, Trumpet
Jimmy Heath-tenor sax; Albert Dailey-piano; Walter Booker-bass,
Mickey Roker-drums

10/9/66   **JACKIE McLEAN**, Alto Sax
Scotty Hart-bass; Lamont Johnson-piano; Billy Higgins-drums

10/16/66   **FRANK FOSTER**, Tenor Sax
Bill English-drums; Dave Burns-trumpet; Bross Townsend-piano;
Charles White-bass

10/23/66   **SAM RIVERS**, Tenor Sax
Herb Lewis-bass; Steve Ellington-drums; Hal Galper-piano

10/30/66   **JOE LEE WILSON**, Singer
Mickey Fields-tenor sax/flute; Phil Harris-bass; Claude Hubbard-piano;
Purnell Rice-drums

LYRIC THEATRE

11/27/66   **WOODY HERMAN ORCHESTRA**
Chuck Matthews-bass; Bill Byrne-trumpet; Dick Rueddebuch-trumpet;
Lloyd Michaels-trumpet

12/4/66   **HERBIE HANCOCK**, Piano
Ron Carter-bass; Wayne Shorter-tenor sax; Freddie Hubbard-trumpet;
Jack DeJohnette-drums

FAMOUS BALLROOM

12/11/66   **PEPPER ADAMS**, Baritone Sax
Frank Foster-tenor sax; Bobby Timmons-piano; Freddie Waite-drums;
Cecil McBee-bass

12/18/66   **JACKIE McLEAN**, Alto Sax
Scotty Holt-bass; Lamont Johnson-piano; Billy Higgins-drums

1/29/67   **SONNY STITT**, Electric Varitone and Alto/Tenor Sax
Don Patterson-organ; Billy James-drums

2/5/67   **COLEMAN HAWKINS**, Tenor Sax
Barry Harris-piano; Major Holley-bass; Oliver Jackson-drums

2/12/67   **AL COHN**, Tenor Sax
Zoot Sims-tenor sax; Dave Frishberg-piano; Victor Sproles-bass; Steve
Schaefer-drums

2/19/67 **LOU DONALDSON**, Alto Sax
Tommy Turrentine, trumpet; Peck Morrison-bass; Walter Davis, Jr.-piano;
Leo Morris-drums

2/26/67 **WALTER BISHOP, JR.**, Piano
Harold Vick-tenor & soprano sax/flute; Dick "Tiny" Berk-drums;
Reggie Johnson-bass

3/5/67 **BILLY HIGGINS**, Drums
Walter Booker-bass; Dave Hubbard-tenor sax; Claude Hubbard-piano

3/12/67 **BOOKER ERVIN**, Tenor Sax
Lennie McBrowne-drums; Horace Parlan-Piano; Jan Arnett-bass

3/19/67 **KENNY BURRELL**, Guitar
Martin Rivera-bass; Richard Wyands-piano; Bill English-drums

3/26/67 **JIMMY HEATH**, Tenor Sax
Hank Mobley-tenor sax; Mickey Roker-drums; Cedar Walton-piano

4/2/67 **ROLAND KIRK**, Misc.
Ronnie Boykins-bass; Lonnie Smith-piano; Bob Thompson-drums

4/9/67 **GEORGE BENSON**, Guitar
Ronnie Cuber-baritone sax, Lonnie Smith-organ; Marion Booker-drums

4/16/67 **YUSEF Lateef**, Misc. Instruments
Cecil McBee-bass; Hugh Lawson-piano; Roy Brooks-drums

4/23/67 **FREDDIE HUBBARD**, Trumpet
Benn Maupin-tenor sax; Ronnie Matthews-piano; Herbie Lewis-bass;
Freddie Waite-drums

4/30/67 **MILT JACKSON**, Vibes
Jimmy Heath-tenor sax; Cedar Walton-piano; Mickey Roker-drums;
Walter Booker-bass

5/7/67 **JOHN COLTRANE**, Tenor/Soprano Sax
Pharoah Sanders-tenor sax; Alice Coltrane-piano; Donald Garrett-bass;
Rashid Ali-drums

5/14/67 **LONNIE HILLYER**, Trumpet
Barry Harris-piano; Charles McPherson-alto sax; Paul Chambers-bass;
Billy Higgins-drums

5/21/67 **JACKIE McLEAN**, Alto Sax
Lamont Johnson-piano; Scotty Holt-bass; Billy Higgins-drums

5/28/67 **FRANK FOSTER'S BIG BAND**
Frank Foster-reeds; Norris Turney; Ronnie Aprea; Harold Cumberbach-reeds;
Roland Alexander; Russ Andrews; Bennie Green; Calvert Brown; Ashley
Fennell; Vince Prudente-trombone; Martin Banks; Tommy Turrentine;
Jimmy Owens; Blue Mitchell; Steve Furtado-tuba; Major Hulley-bass;
Gene Taylor-piano; Albert Dailey-drums; Elvin Jones

6/4/67 **GEORGE BENSON**, Guitar
Ronnie Cuber-baritone sax; Lonnie Smith-organ; Marion Brown, drums

6/11/67 **BLUE MITCHELL**, Trumpet
Gene Taylor-bass; Junior Cook-tenor sax; John Hicks-piano

6/18/67 **HORACE SILVER**, Piano
Woody Shaw, trumpet; Tyrone Washington-tenor sax; Larry Ridley-bass;
Roger Humphries-drums

6/25/67	**ART BLAKEY**, Drums
	Slide Hampton-trombone; Arthur Harper-tenor sax; Junior Booth-bass; Bill Hardman-trumpet
7/2/67	**JOE LEE WILSON**, Singer
	Charles Williams-piano, Earl May-bass; Jimmy Lovelace, drums; Big Neck Nicholas-tenor sax/vocals
7/9/67	**DON ELLIS BIG BAND**
	Ruben Leon; Joe Rocisan; John Magruder; Ron Starr; Ira Schulman-reeds; Ed Warren; Alan Ray Neopolitan-bass; John Rodby-drums; Alan Estes; Mark Stevens; Steve Bohonon; Chino Valdez
7/16/67	**CLIFFORD JORDAN**, Tenor Sax
	Richard Davis-bass; Lee Morgan-trumpet; Ron Matthews-piano
7/23/67	**EDDIE HENDERSON**, Trumpet
	Joe Clark-tenor sax; Mike Smith-drums; Marshall Hawkins-bass; Vince Genova-piano; Greg Hatza-organ; Bill Murphy-drums; Charles Ables-guitar
7/30/67	**MAX ROACH**, Drums
	Odean Pope-tenor sax; Chas Tolliver-trumpet; Jymie Merritt-bass
8/6/67	**JOE HENDERSON**, Tenor Sax
	Kenny Barron-piano; Herbie Lewis-bass; Louis Hayes-drums
8/13/67	**JIMMY HEATH**, Tenor Sax
	John Blair-violin; Cedar Walton-piano; Walter Booker-bass; Mickey Roker- drums
8/20/67	**CLARK TERRY'S BIG BAND**
8/27/67	**DIZZY GILLESPIE**, Trumpet
	James Moody-alto sax and flute; Mike Longo-piano; Russell George-bass; Candy Finch-drums
9/10/67	**SONNY STITT**, Tenor & Alto Sax
	Don Patterson-organ; Billy James-drums
9/17/67	**CLIFFORD JORDAN**, Tenor Sax
	Charles Davis-baritone sax; Hubert Laws-flute/piccolo; Julian Priester-trombone; Roy Burrows-trumpet; Lonnie Smith-piano; Billy Less-bass; Walter Perkins-drums
9/24/67	**ELVIN JONES**, Drums
	Joe Farrell-tenor sax; Wilbur Little-bass; Billy Green-piano
10/8/67	**REGGIE WORKMAN**, Bass
	Roland Alexander-soprano/tenor sax; Roy Ayers-vibes; Larry Willis-piano; Alvin Queen-drums
10/15/67	**GARY BARTZ**, Alto Sax
	John Hicks-piano; Vincent McEwen-trumpet; Ronald Jackson-Drums; Mickey Bass-bass
10/22/67	**KENNY BURRELL**, Guitar
	Martin Rivera-bass; Richard Wyands-piano; Bill English-drums
10/29/67	**RICHARD "GROOVE" HOLMES**
11/5/67	**LOU DONALDSON**, Alto Sax
	Tommy Turrentine-trumpet; Bill Gardner-organ/piano; Pick Morrison-bass; Howard Hill-drums
11/12/67	**WYNTON KELLY**, Piano
	Jimmy Cobb-drums; Cecil McBee-bass; Hank Mobley-tenor sax

11/19/67 **TOSHIKO AKIYOSHI**, Piano
Lou Tabackin-tenor flute; Lynn Christy-bass; Ronnie Zito-drums

12/3/67 **COUNT BASIE'S BIG BAND**
Count Basie-piano; Al Aarons; Gene Goe; Sonny Cohn;
Reese Rostelle-trumpets; Eric Dixon; Bobby Plater; Marshall Royal; Eddie
"Lockjaw" Davis; Charles Fowlkes-saxes; Keenan-guitar; Freddie
Greene-drums; Rufus Jones-piano; Quinn Williams-vocals

12/10/67 **YUSEF LATEEF**, Misc. Instruments
Hugh Lawson-piano; Cecil McBee-bass; Roy Brooks-drums

1/28/68 **MAX ROACH**, Drums
Odean Pope-tenor sax; Charles Tolliver-trumpet; Stanley Cowell-piano;
Jymie Merritt-bass

2/4/68 **ROLAND KIRK**, Misc. Instruments
Dick Griffin-trombone; Cevera Jeffries-bass; Hank Duncan-drums; Ron
Burton-piano

2/11/68 **MILT JACKSON**, Vibes
Sonny Red-alto sax; Cedar Walton-piano; Bob Cranshaw-bass;
Leo Morris-drums

2/18/68 **JACKIE McLEAN**, Alto Sax
Woody Shaw-trumpet; Lamont Johnson-piano; Roy Brooks-drums;
Scotty Holt-bass

2/25/68 **RUFUS HARLEY**, Bagpipes, Alto/Tenor Sax, Flute
Oliver Collins-piano; James Glenn-bass; Billy Abner-drums

3/3/68 **DIZZY GILLESPIE**, Trumpet
James Moody-alto/tenor sax, flute; Mike Longo-piano; Candy Finch-drums;
Paul West-bass

3/10/68 **WOODY HERMAN ORCHESTRA**
Bill Byrne, Bob Yance, Tommy Nygaard, Bob McGee Roger Perrot-trumpet;
Mel Wanzo, Sam Burgess; Tom Senff-bass; Carl Pruit-piano; Al Dailey-drums;
John Von Older-tenor sax; Joe Alexander; Sal Nistico; Joe Temperley-alto sax-
clarinet; Woody Herman

3/17/68 **CHICAGO ALL STARS**
Clifford Jordan-tenor sax; Hubert Laws-flute/piccolo; Charles Davis-baritone
sax; Julian Priester-trombone; Richard Williams-trumpet; Harold Mabern-
piano; Bill Lee-bass; J.C. Moses-drums; Chief Bey-conga drums

3/24/68 **RICHARD"GROOVE" HOLMES**
Mickey Fields-tenor sax

3/31/68 **JIMMY HEATH**, Tenor Sax
Blue Mitchell-trumpet; Reggie Workman-bass; Chick Corea-piano;
Al Foster-drums

4/21/68 **WYNTON KELLY**, Piano
Paul Chambers-bass; Jimmy Cobb-drums; Joe Henderson-tenor sax

4/28/68 **ELVIN JONES**, Drums
Joe Farrell-misc. instruments; Jimmy Garrison-bass

4/18/71 **CEDAR WALTON**, Piano
Billy Higgins-drums; Herbie Lewis -bass; Claudette Brown-vocals

5/2/71 **CHICO HAMILTON QUARTET**
Chico Hamilton-drums; Victor Gaskins-bass; John Abercrombie-guitar;
Mark Cohen-reeds

5/9/71   **DON ELLIS AND HIS ORCHESTRA**
Fred Seldon-alto sax; Lonnie Shetter-alto sax; Sam Falzone-tenor sax; Jon Clark-baritone sax; Paul Babosian-trumpet; Jack Caudill-trumpet; Bruce Mackay-trumpet; Ken Nelson-french horn; Jim Sawyer-trombone; Kenny Sawhill-bass trombone; Doug Bixby-tubs; Milcho Leviev-piano; Dennis Parker-bass; Ralph Humphrey-drums; Ron Dunn-drum; Lee Pastora-conga; Earl Corry-violin; Al Ebat-violin; Ellen Smith-viola; Cris Ermacoff-cello

5/23/71   **GEORGE COLEMAN QUINTET**
George Coleman-tenor sax; Danny Moore-trumpet/flugel horn; Larry Ridley-bass; Al Dailey-piano; Harold White-drums

5/30/71   **BARRY MILES TRIO**
Barry Miles-piano, Larry Kit-bass; Terry Silverlight-drums

6/6/71   **DIZZY GILLESPIE**, Trumpet
Orin Smith-guitar; Mike Longo-piano; Alex Blake-bass; Mickey Roker-drums

6/13/71   **THE COLLECTIVE BLACK ARTISTS - KENNY DORHAM**, Trumpet;
Joe Gardner-trumpet; Johnny Coles, Jimmy Owens-trumpet

6/20/71   **LEE MORGAN QUINTET**
Lee Morgan-trumpet; Billy Harper-sax tenor; Harold Mabern-piano; Freddy Waits-drums

6/27/71   **DONALD BYRD**, Trumpet
Roger Hogan-tenor sax, Tom Sezniack-piano, Terry Plumeri-bass, Keith Killgore-drums

7/4/71   **ARNOLD STERLING**, Alto Sax
Chester Thomas-drums; Charles Covington-piano; Freddie Williams-bass; Robert Williams-tenor sax

7/11/71   **JAMES MOODY**, Alto Sax, Flute
Bobby Pierce-organ; Roy Brooks-drums; Eddie Jefferson-vocals

7/18/71   **JAMES SPAULDING**, Alto Sax, Flute
Andy Bey-vocal; Absalam Derrick Jenkins-bass; Mychael Vaughters-piano; St Clair V. Burne

7/25/71   **GARY BARTZ**, Alto Sax
Andy Bey-singer; Stanford James-bass; Harold White-drums; Mtume-conga drums

8/1/71   **WILTON FELDER**, Tenor/Alto Sax
Wayne Henderson-trombone/euphonium; Joe Sample-piano; Kent Brinkley-bass; Stix Hooper-drums

8/8/71   **JIMMY HEATH**, Tenor/Soprano Sax, Flute
Curtis Fuller-trombone, Cedar Walton-piano, Sam Jones-bass, Freddie Waits-drums, Mtume-congo drums

8/15/71   **RICHARD "GROOVE" HOLMES BOATRIDE**

8/22/71   **MAX ROACH**, Drums
Billy Harper-tenor sax; Cecil Bridgewater-trumpet; Reggie Workman-bass

8/29/71   **RASHAAN ROLAND KIRK**, various instruments
Richard Wyands-piano; Pete Pearson-bass; Khalil Mhadi-drums; Joe Texidor-soundtree/ tamborine

9/5/71   **ETTA JONES**, vocals, **CEDAR WALTON**, Piano
Herbie Lewis-bass; Sonny Red-tenor/flute; Billy Higgins-drums

9/12/71   **AHMAD JAMAL**, Piano
Jamil Sulieman Nasser-bass; Frank Gant-drums

9/19/71 **WOODY HERMAN**, Clarinet
Alan Broadbent-piano; Peter Marshall-bass; Bill McCullough-drums; Forrest Buchtel-trumpet

9/26/71 **FREDDIE HUBBARD**, Trumpet
Junior Cook-tenor sax; Joe Bonner-piano; Mickey Bass-bass; Harold White-drums

10/3/71 **LEE MORGAN**, Trumpet
Billy Harper-tenor sax; Jymie Merritt-bass; Harold Mabern-piano; Freddie Waits-drums

10/10/71 **BARRY MILES**, Piano
Larry Kit-bass; Terry Silverlight-drums

10/17/71 **MAYNARD FERGUSON**, Trumpet
Martin Drover-trumpet; John Donnelly-trumpet; Bud Parks-trumpet; Mike Bailey-trumpet; Billy Graham-trombone; Derek Wadsworth-tombone; Adrian Drover-trombone; Jeff Daley-sax; Stan Robinson-sax; Bob Sydor-sax; Bob Watson-piano, electric piano; Pete Jackson-bass; Dave Lynane-bass guitar; Randy Jones-drums

10/24/71 **CLARK TERRY**, Trumpet
Don Friedman-piano; Mousy Alexander-drums; Victor Sproles-bass

10/31/71 **THE STUDO BAND OF THE UNITED STATES ARMY FIELD BAND**
Andy Woodard-trumpet; Trumpets: Buz Parker, Gary Daily, Larry Skinner, Jim Ertter, Joe Mosello; Trombones-Dave Hegman, Gary Russell, Brett Stamps, Jim Sochinski, Ted Kramer, Saxes: Terry Cook, Eric Traub, John Potochney, Garry Noonan, Reggie Jackson, Tom Dupin-drums; Tony Schwartz-piano; Jim Boggs-bass

11/7/71 **RED HOLT**, Drums
El Dee Young-bass; Bobby Lyles-piano; William Valentine-vocalist

11/14/71 **THE WORLD'S GREATEST JAZZ BAND**
Bob Haggart-bass; Yank Lawson-trumpet; Eddie Hubble, Vic Dickenson-trombone; Bob Wilber-clarinet/ alto sax

11/21/71 **STAN KENTON**, Piano
John Warster-bass; John Von Ohlen-drums; Ramon Lopez-bongos/congo drums; Saxophones-Quin Davis, Richard Torres, Kim Frizell, Willie Maiden, Chuck Carter, Trumpets-Mike Vax, Dennis Noday, Jay Saunders, Ray Brown, Joe Marcinkiewicz, Trombones-Dick Shearer, Mike Jamieson, Fred Carter, Mike Wallace, Phil Herring

11/28/71 **CARLOS GARNET**, Tenor
Olu Dara-trumpet; Rene McClean-alto/flute; Harry Constants-piano; John Lee-bass; Gerald Brown-drums; Al Morrison-congos; Ayodele, Sheli, Ghannya-vocals

12/5/71 **JIMMY HEATH**, Tenor/Soprano Sax, Flute
Curtis Fuller-trombone; Kenny Barron-piano; Buster Williams-bass; Kuumba Heath-drums

12/12/71 **KENNY BURRELL**, Guitar
Richard Wyands-piano; Major Holley-bass; Bill English-drums

1/23/72 **SONNY STITT**, Tenor/Alto sax
Don Patterson-organ; Irv Bates-drums

1/30/72 **RICHARD "GROOVE" HOLMES**, Organ
Darryl Washington-drums; Jerry Hubbard-guitar;
Kwasi Jayourba-congo drums

2/2/72 **WOODY HERMAN**, Clarinet
Trumpets: John Thomas, Charles Davis, Bill Stapleton, Bob Summers, Bill
Byrne; Trombones: Bobby Burgess, Rick Stepton, Harold Garrett,
Saxes: Frank Tiberi, Steve Lederer, Gregory Herbert, Tom Anastas-baritone
sax; Alex Camp-bass; Alan Broadbent-piano; Joe Labarbera-drums

2/13/72 **STANLEY TURRENTINE**, Tenor sax
Tommy Turrentine-trumpet; Hugh Lawson-piano; Bob Cunningham-bass;
Eddie Moore-drums

2/20/72 **MAYNARD FERGUSON**, Trumpet
Trumpets-Martin Dover, John Donelly, Bud Parks, Mike Bailey; Trombones-
Billy Graham, Norman Fripp, Adrian Drover, Jeff Daley-alto sax;
Bob Cyder-tenor sax; Brian Smith-tenor sax; Bob Watson-baritone sax

2/27/72 **ETTA JONES**, Vocals, **CEDAR WALTON**, Piano
Hank Mobley-tenor sax; Charles Davis-baritone/soprano sax; Sam Jones-
bass; Billy Higgins-drums

3/5/72 **GEORGE BENSON**, Guitar
Dave Hubbard-tenor sax/flute; Lonnie Smith-organ; Art Gore-drums; Mike
Cameron-conga drums

3/12/72 **ELVIN JONES**, Drums
Gene Perla-bass; David Liebman-tenor/soprano sax, flute; Steve Grossman-
tenor/soprano sax; Don Alias-congo drums;
Carlos "Potato" Valdes-congo drums

3/13/72 **THE UNITED STATES NAVAL ACADEMY JAZZ ROCK ENSEMBLE**
Joe Phillips-director; Barry Weinstein, Ed Hayes, Denny Davis, Paul
Schortgen, Ron Dieht, Nels Durrell, Tony Vail, Larry Finnegan, Gordon
Beckwith, Larry Callahan, Steve Enlow, Bob Cady, Hugh Ferguson, Dwayne
McClaeb, Gene Ronsonette, Bob Rumbley, Gene Pelletier-guitar;
Bob Simmons-bass; Garry McPherson-horn; Don Carter-horn; Rex
North-tuba; Larry Shirk-vocals; Jimmy Howard

3/19/72 **LES McCANN**, Piano
Buck Clarke-congo drums; Donald Dean-drums; Jimmy Rowser-bass

3/26/72 **STAN GETZ**, Tenor Sax
Tony Williams-drums; Kenny Barron-piano; Stan Clark-bass

4/2/72 **GENE WALKER**, Alto Sax
Saxophones: Ben Knop-alto sax, Thomas Williams, Ray Kitz-tenor sax, Kellog
Johnson-baritone sax; Roy McCoy, Alan Dean, John Burkes,
William Myers-trumpet; Ed Myers, Fay Carmichael, Robert Strurtevant,
Randy Neilson, Lincoln Ross-trombone; Paul Case-piano; Gary Kerner-bass;
Larry Jendras-guitar; Chester Thompson-drums

4/9/72 **ART BLAKEY AND THE JAZZ MESSENGERS**
Art Blakey-drums; Ramon Morris-tenor sax, Denny Marouse-tenor sax,
Stanley Cowell-piano, Austin Wallace-bass; Bobby Terry-flute

4/16/72 **JEREMY STEIG**, Flute/Piccolo
Steve Kuhn-piano; Stan Clark-bass; Airto Moriera-drums

1/25/76 **BUDDY RICH AND THE BIG BAND MACHINE**
Buddy Rich-drums; Greg Cogan-piano; Ben Brown-bass; Lin Biviano, Bill

Lamb, Toru Okaoshi, Gary Dailey-trumpet; Alex Kaufman, Harold
Clark, Roger Homefield-trombone; Steve Marcus, Bill Blount, Rick
Centalonza, Bob Mintzer, Jan Konopase-saxophone

2/1/76   **FREDDIE HUBBARD QUINTET**
Freddie Hubbard-trumpet/flugelhorn; George Cables-piano; Tony Dumas-
bass; Carl Burnett-drums; Carl Randall-tenor sax, flute

2/8/76   **GERRY MULLIGAN QUINTET**
Gerry Mulligan-baritone sax; David Samuels-vibes; Tom Fay-piano; Frank
Luther-bass; Bill Goodwin-drums

2/15/76   **BETTY CARTER**, Vocals
John Hicks-piano; Walter Booker-bass; Clifford Barbaro-drums

2/22/76   **DUKE ELLINGTON ORCHESTRA**
Willie Singleton, James Bolden, Barry Hall-trumpets; Harold Minerve-alto;
Robert Eldrige-baritone, Richard Ford-tenor, Eddie Alex-alto, Percy Marion-
tenor, saxes; Chuck Connors, Art Barron, Vince Prudente, trombones; Cedric
Lawson-piano; Gerald Wiggins-bass; Rocky White-drums; Edward
Ellington II-guitar; Marsha Frazier-electric piano, flute; Anita Moore-vocals

2/29/76   **MONTY ALEXANDER**, Piano
John Clayton Jr-bass; Jess Hamilton-drums

3/7/76   **GEORGE COLEMAN OCTET**
George Coleman-tenor sax; Harold Vick-tenor sax; Frank Strozier-alto sax;
Mario Revera-baritone sax

3/14/76   **SONNY FORTUNE QUINTET**
Sonny Fortune-alto/soprano sax, flute; Charles Sullivan-trumpet; Wayne
Dockery-bass; Michael Cochrane-piano; Chip Lyles-drums

3/21/76   **DIZZY GILLESPIE QUARTET**
Dizzy Gillespire-trumpet; Al Gafa-guitar; Ben Brown-bass;
Mickey Roker-drums

3/28/76   **WOODY HERMAN AND HIS ORCHESTRA**
Woody Herman-leader/alto sax/clarinet; Jeff Davis, Nelson Hatt,
John Hoffman, Dennis Dotson, Bill Byrne-trumpets; Jim Pugh, Dale
Kirkland, Vaughn Weister-trombone; Frank Tiberi, Pat LaBarbara, Sal
Spicola, John Oslawski-saxopohone; Pat Coil-piano; Kirby Stewart-bass;
Steve Houghton-drums

4/4/76   **GARY BURTON QUINTET**
Gary Burton-vibraphone; Pat Metheny-guitar; Steve Swallow-bass;
Bob Moses-drums

4/11/76   **THE COMMODORES**
Jeff Taylor, Director Steve Griffith, Gary Marcus, Jack Estinbaum, Ron Diehl,
Gary Buckley-saxophones; Bryce Concklin, Robert Rannells, Leland Gause,
Howard Lamb-trombones; Gary Adams, Ron Belanger, David Dodge,
Bob Pomerleau-trumpets; Charles Wilson-piano; Louis Hinds-bass; James
Warren-guitar; Leonard Addy-percussion; Evangeline Bailey,
Robert Drummond-vocalists

4/18/76   **AHMAD JAMAL TRIO**
Ahmad Jamal-piano; Jamil S. Nasser-bass; Frank Grant-drums;

4/25/76   **STAN KENTON AND HIS ORCHESTRA**
Stan Kenton-leader/piano; Terry Layne-alto; Roy Reynolds-tenor;
Dan Salalition-tenor; Chuck Carter –baritone; Greg Smith-baritone; Dick

Shearer, Dave Keim, Mike Eagan, Allan Morrisey, Doug Purviance,
Jay Sollenberger, Dave Kennedy, Steve Campos, Joe Cusano, Tim Hagans,
John Worster-bass; Gary Hobbs-drums; Ramon Lopez-conga

5/2/76 DAVE POCHONET QUINTET-GROOVE HOLMES QUINTET
Dave Pochonet-drums; Paul Quinichette-tenor sax; Taft Jordan-Trumpet;
Red Richards-Piano; Dave Sibley-bass; Groove Holmes-organ; Khalid Moss-
electric piano; Mel Broach-drums; Brenda Jones-vocalist

5/8/76 CHARLES MCPHERSON QUINTET
Charles McPherson-alto sax; Lonnie Hillyer-trumpet; Duke Jordan-piano;
Peck Morrison-bass; Leroy Williams-drums

5/16/76 ART FARMER, Trumpet
George Coleman-tenor sax; Cedar Walton-piano; Sam Jones-bass;
Billy Higgins-drums

5/23/76 ARTHUR PRYSOCK & RED PRYSOCK TRIO
Arthur Prysock-vocals; Red Prysock-tenor sax; Billy Gardiner-organ;
Forrest Fulford-drums

5/30/76 ETTA JONES & HOUSTON PERSON QUARTET
Etta Jones-vocals; Houston Person-tenor sax; Sonny Phillips-organ;
Frankie Jones-drums

6/13/76 ELVIN JONES QUARTET
Elvin Jones-drums; Pat LaBarbera-tenor/soprano sax, flute; Ryo
Kawasaki-guitar; David Williams-bass

6/20/76 PHAROAH SANDERS QUARTET
Pharoah Sanders-tenor sax/percussion; Cedric Lawson-piano/percussion;
Calvin Hill-bass/percussion; Idris Muhammad-drums /percussion

6/27/76 HORACE SILVER QUINTET
Horace Silver-piano; Tom Harrell-trumpet; Bob Berg-tenor sax;
Steve Beskrone-fender bass; Eddie Gladden-drums

7/4/76 NEWPORT JAZZ FESTIVAL CELEBRATION

7/11/76 PHILLY JOE JONES, Drums and leader
Jymie Merritt-bass, Sumi Tonooka-piano; Charles Bowen-soprano/tenor sax;
Wil Letman-trumpet

7/18/76 BARRY MILES QUARTET
Barry Miles-piano; Vic Juris-guitar; Harvey Swartz-bass;
Terry Silverlight-drums

7/25/76 LOUIS HAYES & THE JUNIOR COOK QUINTET
Louis Hayes-drums; Junior Cook-tenor sax; Woody Shaw-trumpet;
Ronnie Matthews-piano; Stafford James-bass

8/1/76 DAVE LIEBMAN & LOOKOUT FARM
Dave Liebman-reeds; Richard Beirach-keyboards; Frank Tusa-acoustic bass;
Jeff Williams-drums

8/8/76 LEON THOMAS, Vocalist
Neal Creque-piano; Mervin Bronson-bass; Greg Bandy-drums; Babatunde-
conga; Sugar Blue-harmonica

8/15/76 JOHN HANDY SEXTET
John Handy III-alto sax; John Handy IV-drums; Michael Hoffman-guitar;
Tom Nickolas-congas and percussion; Rudy Coleman-bass;
George Spencer-piano

8/22/76 ANNUAL BOAT RIDE
Etta Jones-vocals; Houston Person-tenor saxophone; Sonny Phillips-organ;
Frankie Jones-drums

8/29/76 BOBBY HUTCHERSON QUARTET
Bobby Hutcherson-vibes; James Leary-acoustic bass; Eddie Marshall-drums;
Manny Boyd-tenor/soprano sax

9/5/76 SHIRLEY SCOTT TRIO
Shirley Scott-organ; Harold Vick-tenor sax; Idris Muhammad-drums

9/12/76 BETTY CARTER, Vocalist
John Hicks-piano; Dave Holland-bass; Clifford Barbaro-drums

9/19/76 NAT ADDERLEY QUINTET
Nat Adderley-cornet; John Stubblefield-tenor/alto sax, flute, alto flute;
Onaje Allan Gumbs-piano, electric piano; Fernando Gumbs-bass, electric bass;
Buddy Williams-drums

9/26/76 CHARLIE ROUSE QUINTET
Charlie Rouse-tenor sax; Waymon Reed-trumpet; Hugh Lawson-piano; Rufus
Reid-bass; Jual Curtis-drums

10/3/76 ROY BROOKS AND THE ARTISTIC TRUTH FEATURING
EDDIE JEFFERSON
Roy Brooks-drums; Vincent Bowen-tenor sax; Cass Harris-trombone; Ahmed
Abdullah-trumpet

10/10/76 SUN RA AND HIS MYTHSCIENCE COSMO SWING ARKESTRA

10/17/76 ARTHUR PRYSOCK & RED PRYSOCK QUARTET
Arthur Prysock-vocals; Red Prysock-saxophone; Billy Gardner-organ; Forrest
L. Fulford Jr.-drums; Neil Clarke-bongos

10/24/76 DEXTER GORDON QUARTET
Dexter Gordon-tenor sax; Hugh Lawson-piano; Eugene Taylor-bass;
Eddie Moore-drums

10/31/76 WOODY SHAW OCTET
Woody Shaw-trumpet; Frank Foster-tenor sax; Rene McLean-alto/soprano
sax; Clifford Adams-trombone; Ronnie Matthews-piano; Stafford James-bass;
Louis Hayes-drums

11/14/76 LEON THOMAS SEXTET (FULL CIRCLE)
Leon Thomas-leader/vocalist; Neal Creque-piano; Mervin Bronson-bass;
Sadiq Shabazz-drums; Babatunde-percussion; Sugar Blue-harmonica

11/21/76 ARCHIE SHEPP QUINTET
Archie Shepp-tenor sax; Grachan Moncur III-trombone; Art Matthews-piano;
Boots Malehson-bass; Charlie Persip-drums

11/28/76 STAN KENTON AND HIS ORCHESTRA,
Stan Kenton-piano/leader; Tim Hagans, Steve Campos, Jay Sollenberger,
Dave Kennedy, Joe Casano-trumpets; Alan Yank

12/5/76 AHMAD JAMAL TRIO
Ahmad Jamal-acoustic and electric piano; Frank Grant-drums; Jerome
Hunter-bass

12/12/76 ART BLAKEY AND THE JAZZ MESSENGERS
Art Blakey-drums/leader; Dave Schnitter-tenor sax; Frank Gordon-trumpet;
Walter Davis-piano; Cameron Brown-bass

12/19/76 THE ARMY BLUES
Robert Smith, piano/conductor; Dallas Smith-bass; Bruce Baldwin-drums;
David Spadazzi-guitar; Jaques Johnson

1/16/77 SUN RA AND HIS MYTH-SCIENCE COSMOS SWING ARKESTRA.
SUN RA, Piano/organ/ percussion/Sun; Craig Harris-trombone; Vincent
Chancet-french horn; John Gilmore-tenor and clarinet

1/23/77 RAHSAAN ROLAND KIRK AND THE VIBRATION SOCIETY
Rahsaan Roland Kirk-tenor, bass sax/flute/trumpet/strich; Steve Turre-
trombone; Hilton Ruiz-piano; Phil Bowler-bass; Sonny Brown-drums

1/30/77 THAD JONES & THE MEL LEWIS ORCHESTRA
Thad Jones-cornet/flugelhorn; Mel Lewis-drums; Rufus Reid-bass; Harold
Danko-piano; Jerry Dodgion, Eddie Xiques, Gregory Herbert

2/13/77 ETTA JONES, Vocals, and **HOUSTON PERSON**, Tenor Sax
Sonny Phillips-organ; Frankie Jones-drums

2/20/77 PHIL WOODS QUINTET
Phil Woods-alto sax; Mike Melillo-piano; Harry Leahey-guitar; Steve Gilmore-
bass; Bill Goodwin-drums

2/27/77 THE NEW YORK JAZZ QUARTET
Sir Roland Hanna-piano; Greg Herbert-various reed instruments; George
Mraz-bass

3/6/77 SONNY STITT, Alto/ Tenor Sax
Reuben Brown-piano; Steve Novosel-bass; Bertell Knox-drums

3/12/77 THE HEATH BROTHERS (JIMMY AND PERCY)
Jimmy Heath-tenor sax, soprano sax, flute; Percy Heath-tenors sax, soprano
sax, flute, acoustic bass, piccolo bass; Stanley Cowell-piano

3/20/77 WOODY SHAW CONCERT ENSEMBLE
Woody Shaw-trumpet; Carter Jefferson-tenor sax; Rene McLean-soprano and
alto sax; Steve Turre-trombone; Ronnie Matthews-piano

3/27/77 PHAROAH SANDERS GROUP
Pharoah Sanders-tenor sax/various instruments, Luqman Lateef-saxophones;
Munoz-guitar; Khalid-piano; Steve Neil-bass; Steve Turre-trombone

4/3/77 AL COHN, Tenor sax, **AND BARRY HARRIS**, Piano
Hal Dodson-bass; Leroy Williams-drums

4/10/77 BUDDY RICH AND KILLER FORCE
Buddy Rich-drums/leader; Joe Rodriguez, Dean Pratt, Ross Konikoff,
John Marshall-trumpets

4/17/77 SLIDE HAMPTON, Trombone
Kiane Zawadi-trombone; Doug Purviance-trombone; Al Patterson-trombone;
Joe Bonner-piano;

4/24/77 GROOVE HOLMES QUINTET
Groove Holmes-organ; Walt Namuth-guitar; Mickey Fields-sax;
Darryl Washington-drums

5/1/77 BILL HARDMAN/JUNIOR COOK QUINTET
Bill Hardman-trumpet; Junior Cook-tenor sax; Mickey Tucker-piano;
Cameron Brown-bass; Eddie Gladden-drums

5/8/77 DEXTER GORDON QUARTET
Dexter Gordon-tenor sax; George Cables-piano; Rufus Reid-bass;
Billy Hart-drums

5/15/77 DUKE ELLINGTON ORCHESTRA
Duke Ellington-conductor; Barrie Hall, Willie Singelton, James Bolden,
Bobby Rutledge-trumpets

5/22/77 WOODY HERMAN'S YOUNG THUNDERING HERD
Frank Tiberi-leader and sax; Steve Slagle, Joe Lovano, Bruce Johnstone-
saxophones

5/29/77 DON PATTERSON/RICHIE COLE QUARTET
Don Patterson-organ; Richie Cole-alto sax; Vic Juris-guitar;
Eddie Gladden-drums

6/5/77 HORACE SILVER QUARTET
Horace Silver-piano; Larry Schneider-tenor sax; Tom Harrell-trumpet; Chip
Jackson-bass; Eddie Gladden-drums

6/12/77 SUN RA AND HIS MYTH-SCIENCE COSMOS SWING ARKASTRA
SUN RA-piano, organ, moog, Rocksichord, leader; John Gilmore-tenor sax,
clarinet; Marshall Allen-alto sax, oboe, flute; Danny Davis-alto

6/19/77 EARL KLUGH QUARTET
Earl Klugh-guitar; Gary Schunk-keyboards; Burt Myrick-drums;
Hubie Crawford-bass

6/26/77 THE UNITED STATES NAVY BAND, THE COMMODORES
Larry Skinner-director; Conrad Laundry, Jack Eslinbaum, Ron Diehl, Gary
Buckley

7/3/77 DON ELLIS AND HIS ORCHESTRA
Don Ellis-leader; Ann Patterson, Ted Nash, James Coile, Jim Snodgrass-
woodwinds; Glen Stuart, Gil Rathel

7/10/77 STAN GETZ AND HIS QUARTET
Stan Getz-tenor sax; Joanne Brackeen-piano; Mike Richmond-bass;
Billy Hart-drums

7/17/77 CEDAR WALTON QUARTET
Cedar Walton-piano; Bob Berg-tenor sax; Sam Jones-bass; Billy Higgins-
drums

7/24/77 AHMAD JAMAL QUINTET
Ahmad Jamal-piano; Calvin Keyes-guitar; Mike Taylor-bass; Azadeen
Weston-percussion; Reggie Tyler-drums

7/31/77 BLUE MITCHELL/HAROLD LAND QUINTET
Blue Mitchell-trumpet; Harold Land-tenor sax; Marc Cohen-piano; Steve
Novosel-bass; Bernard Sweetney-drums

8/14/77 WARREN CHIASSON QUARTET
Warren Chiasson-vibraphone; Chuck Wayne-guitar; Jack Six-bass;
Sonny Brown-drums

8/21/77 SONNY FORTUNE QUARTET
Sonny Fortune-alto/soprano sax, flute; Tom Browne-trumpet; Charles
Eubanks-piano; Brian Smith-bass; Chip Lyles-drums

8/28/77 ALBERT DAILEY QUARTET
Albert Dailey-piano; Virgil Jones-trumpet; Alex Blake-bass; Adam Nussbaum-
drums; Steve Elson-tenor/soprano sax

9/4/77 WALT DICKERSON TRIO

9/11/77 JOE HENDERSON QUARTET
Joe Henderson-tenor sax; Joanne Brackeen-piano; Ratso Harris-bass;
Danny Spencer-drums

9/18/77 THE HEATH BROTHERS
Jimmy Heath-tenor/soprano sax; Percy Heath-bass; Albert Heath-drums;
Stanley Cowell-piano

9/25/77 BILL HARDMAN/JUNIOR COOK QUARTET
Bill Hardman-trumpet; Junior Cook-tenor sax; Mickey Tucker-piano; Yoshio
"Chin" Suzuki-bass; Eddie Gladden-drums

10/1/77 THE WOODY SHAW CONCERT ENSEMBLE
Woody Shaw-trumpet; Steve Turre-trombone; Carter Jefferson-tenor
and soprano sax; Jimmy Vass-alto sax; Onaje Allan Gumbs-piano;
Clint Houston-bass; Victor Lewis-bass

10/9/77 DEXTER GORDON, Tenor sax
George Cables-piano; Rufus Reid-bass; Victor Lewis-drums

10/16/77 CHARLIE ROUSE QUARTET
Charlie Rouse-tenor sax; Claudio Roditi-trumpet; Hugh Lawson-piano; Bob
Cranshaw-bass; Wilby Fletcher-drums

10/23/77 RAHSAAN ROLAND KIRK AND THE VIBRATION SOCIETY
Rahsaan Roland Kirk-tenor sax, flute, manzello, stritch, nose flute; Hilton
Ruiz-piano; Phil Bowler-bass; Sonny Brown-drums; Steve Turre-trom
bone; Michael Hill-vocalist

10/30/77 CLIFFORD JORDAN QUINTET
Clifford Jordan-tenor sax; Charles Davis-tenor sax; Muhal Richard Abrams-
piano; Bill Lee-bass; Wilbur Campbell-drums

11/6/77 AHMAD JAMAL JAZZ ENSEMBLE
Ahmad Jamal-piano; Selden Newton-percussion; Calvin Keyes-guitar; Mike
Taylor-bass; Wilby Fletcher-drums

11/13/77 BOBBY HUTCHERSON, Vibes
Danny Mixon-piano; Buster Williams-bass; Michael Carvin-drums

11/20/77 ART FARMER QUARTET

11/27/77 TED CURSON, Trumpet/piccolo trumpet/flugelhorn
Nick Brignola-baritone sax, soprano sax; Jim McNeely-piano;
John Burr-bass; Jeff William

12/4/77 DON PATTERSON/RICHIE COLE QUARTET
Don Patterson-organ; Richie Cole-alto sax; Vic Juris-electric guitar;
Bernard Sweetney-drums

12/11/77 CARLOS GARNETT

12/18/77 THAD JONES-MEL LEWIS
SHOW CANCELED, CHET BAKER QUARTET SUBSTITUTED

12/31/77 NEW YEARS EVE JAZZ CABARET
FEATURING HOUSTON PERSON QUINTET
Houston Person-tenor sax; Etta Jones, Vocals; Sonny Phillips-organ; Frankie
Jones-drums; Lawrence Gillian-congas

1/22/78 ART BLAKEY AND THE JAZZ MESSENGERS
Art Blakey-drums; Dennis Irwin-bass; James Williams-piano; Curtis Fuller-
trombone; Dave Schnitter-tenor sax; Bobby Watson-alto sax; Valery
Ponomarev-trumpet

1/29/78 SUN RA AND HIS MYTH SCIENCE COSMOS SWING ARKESTRA
SUN RA-organ, piano, sound intergalactic organ; John Gilmore–tenor sax,
clarinet; Marshall Allen-alto sax, flute, oboe; Danny Davis-alto sax,
flute; Danny Thompson-baritone sax; James Jackson-bassoon, ancient

Egyptian infinity drum; Vincent Chuncer-french horn; Michael Ray-trumpet; Ahmed Abdullah-trumpet; Charles Stephen-trombone; Luqman Ali-drums; Eddie Thomas-drums; Greg Bufford-drums; Henry Dixon-conga drums; Thomas Hunter-drums; June Tyson-vocals, dance; Dancers: Cheryl Banks, Mickey Davidson, Matune Durham

2/5/78   **HANK CRAWFORD**, alto sax
Calvin Newborn-guitar; Charles Green-bass; Billy Kaye-drums; Gary Cardile-percussion, vocals

2/12/78   **JON FADDIS QUINTET**
Jon Faddis-trumpet; Alex Foster-alto/tenor sax, flute; Mike Longo-piano; Paul West-bass; Mel Lewis-drums

2/19/78   **STAN KENTON ORCHESTRA**

2/26/78   **SIR ROLAND HANNA AND THE NEW YORK JAZZ QUARTET**
Sir Roland Hanna-piano; Sam Jones-bass; Grady Tate-drums; Frank Wess-sax, flute

3/5/78   **HOUSTON PERSON**, Tenor sax
Sonny Phillips-organ; Frankie Jones-drums; Etta Jones-vocals

3/12/78   **SONNY STITT QUARTET**

3/19/78   **SAM JONES QUARTET**
Sam Jones-bass; Bob Berg-tenor sax; Terumasa Hino-cornet; Ronnie Matthews-piano; Al Foster-drums

3/26/78   **BARNEY KESSEL/HERB ELLIS QUARTET**
Barney Kessel-guitar; Herb Ellis-guitar; Keter Betts-bass; Bertell Knox-drums

4/2/78   **MILT JACKSON QUARTET**
Milt Jackson-vibes; Reuben Brown-piano; Steve Novosel-bass; Bernard Sweeney-drums; Buck Hill-tenor sax

4/9/78   **LEON THOMAS**, Vocals
Neal Creque-keyboards; Steve Neil-bass; Greg Bandy-drums; Tito Sumpa-conga, percussion

4/16/78   **LOUIS HAYES/FRANK STROZIER QUARTET**
Louis Hayes-drums; Frank Strozier-alto sax, flute; Curtis Fuller-trombone; Harold Mabern-piano; Stafford James-bass

4/23/78   **MONGO SANTAMARIA**, Conga, bongo
Chris Alpert-trumpet; Allen Hoist-baritone/soprano/alto sax, flute; Doug Harris-tenor/soprano sax, flute, piccolo; Bill O'Connell-piano; Lee Smith-bass; Steve Berrios-drums, timbales; Hector Laporte-percussion, vocals

4/30/78   **THE COMMODORES (U.S. NAVY BIG BAND)**
Free Concert

5/7/78   **WOODY SHAW QUINTET**
Woody Shaw-trumpet; Carter Jefferson-tenor/soprano sax; Onaje Allan Gumbs-piano; Clint Houston-bass; Victor Lewis-drums

5/14/78   **THAD JONES/MEL LEWIS ORCHESTRA**
Thad Jones-flugelhorn; Mel Lewis-drums; Harold Danko-piano; Ray Drummond-bass; Saxes: Jerry Dodgion, Dick Oats, Richie Perry, Bob Mintzer, Kenny Berger; Trumpets: Earl Gardner, Larry Moses, Gary Guizio, Frank Gordon; Trombones: Lolly Bienenfeld, John Musca, Lee Robertson, Earl McIntyre

5/21/78 ARTHUR PRYSOCK, Vocals
Red Prysock-tenor sax; Billy Gardner-organ; Forrest Fulford-drums;
Bashiri-conga; The Lorelei-vocals

5/28/78 RED GARLAND TRIO

6/4/78 CLARK TERRY AND HIS JOLLY GIANTS
Clark Terry-trumpet, flugelhorn; Chris Woods-alto sax, flute;
Hilton Ruiz-piano; Victor Sproles-bass; Ed Soph-drums

6/11/78 JIMMY SMITH, Organ
Ray Crawford-guitar; Warren Shad-drums; Holley Maxwell-vocals

6/18/78 YUSEF LATEEF, Tenor/soprano sax, flute, oboe
Khalid Moss-keyboards; Steve Neil-bass; Greg Bandy-drums

6/25/78 HORACE SILVER QUINTET

7/2/78 MICKEY FIELDS QUINTET
Mickey Fields-tenor sax; John Lamkin-trumpet; Charles Covington-piano;
Donald Bailey-bass; Hugh Walker-drums

7/2/78 ALLEN HOUSER QUARTET
Allen Houser-trumpet; Joe Clark-tenor sax; Phil Harris-bass;
Michael Smith-drums

7/9/78 LAURINDO ALMEIDA & THE L.A. 4,
Laurindo Almeida-guitar; Ray Brown-bass; Jeff Hamilton-drums;
Bud Shank-alto sax, flute

7/16/78 DEXTER GORDON QUARTET
Dexter Gordon-tenor sax; George Cables-piano; Rufus Reid-bass;
Eddie Gladden-drums

7/23/78 SUN RA AND THE SUN RA ARKESTRA,
SUN RA-organ, piano; John Gilmore-tenor sax, clarinet; Marshall Allen-alto
sax, flue, oboe; Danny Davis-alto sax, flute; Danny Thompson-baritone sax,
flute; James Jackson-bassoon, oboe, ancient infinity drum; Elo Omo-bass
clarinet, flute; Michael Bey-trumpet; Walter Miller-trumpet; Dale
Williams-guitar; Luqman Ali-drums; Atacka Tune-conga;
Richard Williams-bass; Tuny Bey-bass; William Goffigan-drums;
June Tyson-vocals, dance; Cheryl Banks-dance; Ted Thomas-dance

7/30/78 SAM JONES/TOM HARRELL ORCHESTRA
Sam Jones-bass; Tom Harrell-trumpet; Terumasa Hino-trumpet; Fred Jacobs-
trumpet; Sam Burtis-trombone; Emmett McDonald-trombone; Bob
Mintzer-tenor sax; Harold Vick-tenor sax; Arnie Lawrence-alto sax;
Pat Patrick-baritone sax; Fred Hersch-piano; Keith Copeland-drums

8/6/78 DON PATTERSON QUARTET
Don Patterson-organ; Richie Cole-alto sax; Vic Juris-guitar;
Bernard Sweetney-drums

8/13/78 ART BLAKEY AND THE JAZZ MESSENGERS
Art Blakey-drums; Dave Schnitter-tenor sax; Bobby Watson-alto sax; Valery
Ponomarev-trumpet; James Williams-piano; Dennis Irwin-bass

8/20/78 RAY BRYANT QUARTET
Ray Bryant-piano; Peck Morrison-bass; Jual Curtis-drums;
Charlie Rouse-tenor sax

8/27/78 SAM RIVERS QUARTET
Sam Rivers-tenor/soprano sax, flute, piano; Dave Holland-bass, cello; Joe
Daley-tuba, baritone, horn; Thurman Barker-percussion

9/3/78 **BUCK HILL/ARNOLD STERLING QUINTET**
Buck Hill-tenor sax; Arnold Sterling-alto sax; Reuben Brown-paino;
Dave Wundrow-bass; George "Dude" Brown-drums

9/10/78 **LOU DONALDSON QUINTET**
Lou Donaldson-alto sax; Bill Hardman–trumpet; Mickey Tucker–piano;
Sam Jones–bass; Billy Kay-drums

9/17/78 **JIMMY HEATH,** Tenor Sax
Percy Heath–bass; Stanley Cowell–piano; Keith Copeland–drums

9/24/78 **JOHNNY GRIFFIN QUARTET**
Johnny Griffin-tenor sax; Ronnie Matthews–piano; James Leary–bass;
Eddie Marshall–drums

10/1/78 **SONNY FORTUNE QUINTET**
Sonny Fortune-soprano/alto sax; Richard Nesbitt–trumpet;
Charles Eubanks–piano; Andy McCloud–bass; Billy Hart-drums

10/8/78 **WOODY HERMAN AND HIS YOUNG THUNDERING HERD**
Woody Herman-soprano/alto sax; Dave Lalama–piano; Jay Anderson–bass;
John Riley-drums; Saxes: Frank Tiberi, Billy Ross, Joe Lovano,
Gary Smolyan; Trumpets: Dave Kennedy, Tim Burke, Glen Drews,
Jim Powell, Bill Byrne; Trombones: Birch Johnson, Nelson Hines,
Larry Shunk

10/15/78 **ART ENSEMBLE OF CHICAGO**
Joseph Jarman-alto/tenor sax, piccolo; Roscoe Mitchell-alto/tenor sax;
Lester Bowie-trumpet;

10/22/78 **BARRY HARRIS QUINTET**
Barry Harris-piano; Harold Vick-tenor sax; Tommy Turrentine-trumpet;
Hakim Jamil-bass; Leroy Williams-drums

10/29/78 **EDDIE HARRIS QUARTET**
Eddie Harris-electric sax, reed trumpet, piano; Ronald Muldrow-electric
guitar; Bradley Bobo-electric bass; Terry Thompson-drums

11/5/78 **JIMMY FORREST/AL GREY QUINTET**
Jimmy Forrest-tenor sax; Al Grey-trombone; Howard Whaley-piano; John
Duke-bass; Bobby Durham-drums

11/12/78 **MILT JACKSON QUARTET**
Milt Jackson-vibes; Ronnie Matthews-piano; Ray Drummond-bass;
Al Harewood-drums

11/19/78 **ART FARMER QUARTET**
Art Farmer, flugelhorn; Fred Hersch-piano; Mike Richmond-bass;
Akira Tana-drums

11/26/78 **WOODY SHAW QUINTET**
Carter Jefferson-tenor/soprano sax; Onaje Allan Gumbs-piano; Clint
Houston-bass; Victor Lewis-drums

12/3/78 **MONTY ALEXANDER TRIO**
Monty Alexander-piano; Reggie Johnson-bass; Frank Gant-drums

12/10/78 **RAY BARRETTO AND HIS ORCHESTRA**

12/17/78 **ARTHUR PRYSOCK,** Vocals
Red Prysock-tenor sax; Gene Ludwig–organ; Forrest Fulford-drums; Jackie
and Carol Durden-vocals (The Lorelei)

12/31/78 **NEW YEAR'S EVE CELEBRATION**
HOUSTON PERSON/ETTA JONES QUARTET

1/28/79   **DEXTER GORDON QUARTET**

2/4/79   **DUKE ELLINGTON ORCHESTRA**

2/25/79   **HORACE SILVER**, Piano
John McNeil-trumpet; Larry Schneider-tenor/alto sax, flute; Todd Coolman-bass; Harold White-drums

3/4/79   **EDDIE JEFFERSON**, vocals
Richie Cole-alto sax; Reuben Brown-piano; Lou Hinds-bass; Mike Shephard-drums; Vic Juris-guitar

3/11/79   **HERB ELLIS**, Guitar
Bob Fields-piano; Reggie Johnson-bass; Ronnie Dawson-drums

3/18/79   **PHIL WOODS QUARTET**

3/25/79   **DON CHERRY**, Cornet
Dewey Redman-tenor sax/musette; Charlie Haden-bass; Ed Blackwell-drums

4/1/79   **COMMUNICATION JAZZ TRIO**
Red Mitchell-bass; Tommy Flanagan-piano; Jerry Dodgion-alto sax, flute

4/8/79   **TED CURSON**,Trumpet
Chris Wood, Aman Donelian-piano; Ratso Harris-bass; Jeff Williams-drums

4/15/79   **EARL "FATHA" HINES**, Piano
Jim Cox-bass; Clarence Becton-drums; Eric Schneider-reeds; Marva Josie-vocals

4/22/79   **KETER BETTS**, Bass
Introduces Pieces of a Dream with Terri Lyne Carrington-drums

4/29/79   **JIMMY SMITH**, Organ
H. Ray Crawford-guitar; Clarence Johnston-drums

5/6/79   **EDDIE HARRIS**, Tenor sax
Reuben Brown -piano; Steve Novosel-bass; George "DUDE" Brown-drums

5/13/79   **JOSEPH JARMAN**, Reeds
Lester Bowie-trumpet; Roscoe Mitchell-reeds; Malachi Favors-bass; Don Moye-drums

5/20/79   **WALTER BISHOP, JR.**, Piano
Ricky Ford-tenor sax; Roger Rosenberg-tenor sax; Ronnie Boykin-bass; Michael Carvin-drums

5/27/79   **ARNOLD STERLING**, Alto sax
Arnold Sterling-alto sax; Marvin Cabell-tenor sax, saxcello; Reuben Brown-piano; Reggie Johnson-bass; George "Dude" Brown-drums

6/3/79   **THE APOLLO STOMPERS**
Led by Jaki Byard

6/10/79   **IRA SULLIVAN QUARTET**
Ira Sullivan-trumpet/flugelhorn/tenor/alto/soprano sax/flute; Hilton Ruiz-piano; Victor Venegas-bass; Steve Berrios-drums

6/17/79   **SUN RA ARKESTRA**

6/24/79   **JOHNNY GRIFFIN**, Tenor sax
Ronnie Matthews-piano; Ray Drummond-bass; Idris Muhammad-drums

7/1/79   **CLIFFORD JORDAN QUARTET**
Clifford Jordan-tenor sax; Barry Harris-piano; Philly Joe Jones-drums

7/8/79   **HUGH MASEKELA**, Flugelhorn
Rene McLean-sax, flute; Hotep Gaba Galeta Cecil Bernard-keyboards; Phil Bowler-bass; Toko Motohiko Hino-drums

7/15/79 HEATH BROTHERS QUINTET
Jimmy Heath-tenor/soprano sax, flute; Percy Heath-bass; Stanley Cowell-piano; Tony Purrone-guitar; Keith Copeland-drums

7/22/79 YUSEF LATEEF, Tenor sax, flute, oboe
Khalid Moss-electric piano; Don Pate-bass; Marty Barker-drums

8/5/79 FRANK FOSTER QUINTET

8/12/79 ARTHUR PRYSOCK WITH RED PRYSOCK TRIO

8/19/79 MICKEY FIELDS/CARLOS JOHNSON QUARTET
Shirley Fields-vocals

8/26/79 DUKE ELLINGTON ORCHESTRA
Duke Ellington-conductor; Mulgrew Miller-piano; Gerald Wiggins-bass; Quinten White-drums; Anita Moore-vocals; Trumpets: Barry Hall, John Longo, Yousef Rakha; Saxes: Harold Minerve, Dave Young, Kenneth Garrett, Lisa Pollard, Marvin Holliday; Trombones: Malcolm Taylor, Chuck Connors, Keith Jackson

9/2/79 BUCK HILL, Tenor sax
Kenny Reed-trumpet; Reuben Brown-piano; Reggie Johnson-bass; Bernard Sweetney-drums; Jimmy Wells-vibes; Harold Adams-tenor sax; Marc Cohen-piano; Donald Bailey-bass; Harold White-drums

9/9/79 DON PATTERSON QUARTET
Bootsie Barnes-tenor sax

9/16/79 KETER BETTS, Bass
Buck Hill-tenor sax; Kirk Stuart-piano; Hugh Walker-drums; Curtis Daniel Harmon-percussion, vocals; James Keith Lloyd-keyboards, vocals; Cedric Alexander Napolean-bass, vocals; Barbara Walker-vocals

9/23/79 CARLOS GARNETT AND SOLAR ENERGY
Carlos Garnett-tenor/alto sax, vocals; Kwatei-eletric/acoustic guitar; Winston Daley-piano/synth; Ken Thornhill-bass; Buddy Goddard-drums; Cosa Ross-congas, percussion

9/30/79 ART BLAKEY AND THE JAZZ MESSENGERS
Art Blakey-drums; Dave Schnitter-tenor sax; Bobby Watson-alto sax; Valery Ponomarev-trumpet; Ray Draper-flugelhorn; James Williams-piano; Dennis Irwin-bass

10/7/79 JAMES MOODY QUARTET
James Moody-alto/tenor sax, flute; Mike Longo-piano; Paul West-bass; David Lee-drums

10/14/79 MAX ROACH QUARTET
Max Roach-drums; Odean Pope-tenor sax; Cecil Bridgewater-trumpet; Calvin Hill-bass

10/21/79 JACK McDUFF QUARTET, Organ
Jack McDuff-organ; Ramon Morris-tenor sax; Marc Ribot-guitar; Gerryck King-drums

10/28/79 BOBBY HUTCHERSON, Vibes
George Cables-piano; Heshima Williams-bass; Lawrence Marable-drums

11/4/79 ELVIN JONES AND HIS JAZZ MACHINE
Elvin Jones-drums; Andy McCloud-bass; Marvin Horne-guitar; Art Brown-tenor/soprano sax; Pat LaBarbera-tenor/soprano sax, flute

11/11/79 JOHNNY GRIFFIN, Tenor sax
Ronnie Matthews-piano; Ray Drummond-bass; Idris Muhammad-drums

11/18/79 **BAIRD HERSEY AND THE YEAR OF THE EAR**
Baird Hersey-guitar; Ernie Povencher-bass; Doane Perry-drums; Roger Squitero-percussion; Tim Sessions-trombone; Lee Genesis-vocals; Trumpets: Stanton Davis, Daniel Mott, Mark Harvey; Saxes: John Hagen, Len Detlor, Stan Strickland

11/25/79 **SHIRLEY SCOTT TRIO**

12/2/79 **WOODY SHAW QUINTET**
Woody Shaw-trumpet; Carter Jefferson, tenor sax; Larry Willis-piano; Stafford James-bass; Victor Lewis-drums

12/9/79 **TIM EYERMANN AND EAST COAST OFFERING**
Tim Eyermann-alto/soprano sax, bass flute, clarinet, oboe, piccolo; Dale Carrigan-drums; Jeff Hurwitz-electric keyboards; Wade Matthews-bass

12/31/79 **NEW YEAR'S EVE CELEBRATION**
DON PATTERSON QUARTET WITH BOOTSIE BARNES

1/27/80 **MONGO SANTAMARIA**, Conga, bongo

2/3/80 **SUN RA ARKESTRA**

2/10/80 **GEORGE COLEMAN QUINTET**
George Coleman-tenor sax; Danny Moore-trumpet; Harold Mabern-piano; Clint Houston-bass; Walter Bolden-drums

2/17/80 **GARY BURTON QUARTET**
Gary Burton-vibes; Tiger Okohi-trumpet; Chip Jackson-bass; Mike Hyman-drums

2/24/80 **AHMAD JAMAL TRIO**
Ahmad Jamal-piano; Thomas Palmer-bass; Payton Crossley-drums

3/2/80 **FREDDIE HUBBARD QUARTET**
Freddie Hubbard-trumpet; Billy Childs-piano; Larry Klein-bass; Carl Bernett-drums; Leon Thomas-vocals

3/9/80 **PIECES OF A DREAM**

3/16/80 **HUGH MASEKELA QUARTET**

3/23/80 **HORACE SILVER QUINTET**
Horace Silver-piano; Ron Bridgewater-tenor sax; Barry Ries-trumpet/flugelhorn; Todd Coolman-bass; Harold White-drums

3/30/80 **EDDIE HARRIS QUINTET**
Eddie Harris-electric sax; Reuben Brown-piano; Steve Novosel-bass; Keith Kilgore-drums

4/6/80 **SHIRLEY SCOTT TRIO**
Shirley Scott-organ; Harold Vick-tenor sax; Bobby Durham-drums

4/13/80 **WOODY SHAW QUINTET**
Woody Shaw-trumpet; Carter Jefferson, tenor sax, flute; Larry Willis-piano; Stafford James-bass; Victor Lewis-drums

4/20/80 **JOHNNY GRIFFIN QUARTET**
Johnny Griffin-tenor sax; Ronnie Mathews-piano; Ray Drummond-bass; Kenny Washington-drums

4/27/80 **RED RODNEY/BILLY MITCHELL**, Trumpet, flugelhorn/tenor sax
Gary Dial-piano; Paul Berner-bass; Tom Whaley-drums

5/4/80 **SPECIAL EDITION: JACK DeJOHNETTE**, Drums, electric melodica, acoustic/eletric piano
Chico Freeman-tenor sax, flute, bass clarinet; Arthur Blythe-alto sax; Peter Warren-bass, cello

5/11/80 **DEXTER GORDON,** Tenor sax
Kirk Lightsey-piano; Chuck Metcalf-bass; Eddie Gladden-drums

5/18/80 **CARMEN McRAE,**Vocals
Marshall Otwell-piano; Jay Anderson-bass; Mark Pulice-drums

5/25/80 **MONTY ALEXANDER,** Piano
Gerald Wiggins-bass; Othello Molineaux-steel drums; Frank Gant-drums

6/1/80 **JOANNE BRACKEEN,** Piano
Ratso Harris-bass; Toko Motohiko Hino-drums

6/8/80 **BAIRD HERSEY'S YEAR OF THE EAR**

6/15/80 **CHICO HAMILTON SEXTET,** Drums
George King-alto/soprano sax/flute; Jean-Paul Bourelly-guitar;
Mike Santigo-guitar; Paul Ramsey-bass; Kathleen Adair-vocals

6/22/80 **JIMMY SMITH,** Organ
Larry Fraser-guitar; Kenny Dixon-drums

6/29/80 **BYRON MORRIS AND UNITY**

7/6/80 **OSCAR BROWN JR. AND JEAN PACE**

7/13/80 **JAMES MOODY,** Alto/Tenor Sax, Flute
John Hicks-piano; Calvin Hill-bass; Horace Arnold-drums;
George Johnson-vocals

7/20/80 **KENNY BURRELL,** Guitar
Richard Reid-bass; Sherman Ferguson-drums

7/27/80 **TEDDY WILSON TRIO**

8/3/80 **ROY BROOKS AND THE ARTISTIC TRUTH,** Drums
Marcus Belgrave-trumpet/flugelhorn; Larry Smith-tenor/soprano/alto sax;
Cass Harris-trumpet, flugelhorn; Geri Allen-piano; Mike Taylor-drums;
Saxy Williams-tap dance (sit-in)

8/10/80 **THE CREATIVE ARTISTS MUSIC ENSEMBLE**

8/17/80 **O'DONEL LEVY,** Guitar
David Smith-alto/tenor/soprano sax/flute; Bob Butta-piano; Jeff Andrews-
bass; Kirk Driscall-drums

8/24/80 **EARL "FATHA" HINES,** Piano
Jim Cox-bass; Ed Graham-drums; Eric Schneider alto/tenor sax,clarinet;
Marva Josie-vocals

8/31/80 **LES McCANN LIMITED,** Electric/acoustic piano
Steve Erquiago-guitar; Bobby Bryant-sax; Tony St. James-drums;
Curtis Robertson, Jr-bass

9/7/80 **NAT ADDERLEY,** Cornet
Ricky Ford-tenor sax; Larry Willis-piano; Walter Booker-bass;
Jimmy Cobb-drums

9/14/80 **TIM EYERMANN,** Alto/soprano sax, flute, oboe
Phil McCusker-guitar; Wade Matthews-bass; Bruce Harrison-keyboards;
Robby Magruder-drums

9/21/80 **HEATH BROTHERS QUINTET**
Percy Heath-bass; Jimmy Heath-tenor/soprano sax, flute; Stanley
Cowell-piano; Tony Purrone-guitar; Akira Tana-drums

9/28/80 **LEFT BANK ALL STARS-MICKEY FIELDS,** Tenor sax
Carlos Johnson-alto sax; Andy Ennis-tenor sax; Reppard Stone-piano; Donald
Bailey-bass; Johnny Polite-drums

10/5/80 JOE FARRELL, Tenor sax, Flute
Andy Laverne-piano; Ron McClure-bass; Danny Gottlieb-drums

10/12/80 LOU DONALDSON, Alto sax
Tommy Turrentine-trumpet; Herman Foster-piano; Jeff Fuller-bass; Nat Yarborough-drums

10/19/80 IRA SULLIVAN, Sax, Trumpet, Flute
Reuben Brown-piano; Victor Sproles-bass; Steve Bagby-drums

10/26/80 SUN RA ARKESTRA, Piano
Juribi-bass; Eric Walker-drums; Luqman Ali-durms; Eric Lewis-conga; Damon Choice-vibes; Pharoad Abdullah/Mohamed Santos-bells; Tony Bethel-trombone; June Tyson-vocals; Chandree Washington-dance; Trumpets: Al Evans, Mike Ray; Saxes: Marshall Allen-alto; Danny Thompson-baritone; Noel Scott-baritone/alto; Elo Omoe-bass clarinet; James Jackson-bassoon, drum; John Gilmore-tenor

11/1/80 DEXTER GORDON AND JOHNNY GRIFFIN QUARTET

11/2/80 BIG NICK NICHOLAS QUINTET

11/9/80 JOE LEE WILSON, Vocals
Bill Saxton-tenor sax; Bert Eckoff-piano; Cameron Brown-bass; Art Lewis-drums

11/16/80 BILL HARDMAN/JUNIOR COOK QUINTET
Bill Hardman-trumpet; Junior Cook-tenor sax; Walter Bishop, Jr-piano; Paul Brown-bass; Leroy Williams-drums

11/23/80 PIECES OF A DREAM

11/30/80 JAZZ AMBASSADORS (U.S. Army Field Band)

12/7/80 GARY BARTZ QUARTET, Alto sax
Hilton Felton-piano; Ameen Raheem-bass; William Goffigan-drums

12/14/80 RON SUTTON QUARTET
Ron Sutton, Jr.-alto sax; Charles Wright-guitar; Richard Henderson-bass; Chris Fender-drums

12/21/80 BALTIMORE ALL STARS-ARNOLD STERLING, Alto sax
Harold Adams-tenor sax; Marvin Cabell-tenor sax; Marc Cohen-piano; Donald Bailey-bass; Willie Barber-drums

12/28/80 LEFT BANK ALL STARS-MICKEY FIELDS, Tenor sax
Andy Ennis-tenor sax; Carlos Johnson-alto sax; Charles Covington-piano; Donald Bailey-bass; Johnny Polite-drums

2/1/81 HORACE SILVER, Piano
Barry Ries-trumpet; Ralph Moore-tenor sax; Dennis Irwin-bass; Harold White-drums

2/8/81 ART BLAKEY AND THE JAZZ MESSENGERS
Art Blakey-drums; Billy Pierce-tenor sax; Bobby Watson-alto sax; Wynton Marsalis-trumpet; Charles Fambrough-bass; James Williams-piano

2/15/81 HOUSTON PERSON, Tenor sax
Etta Jones-Vocalist; Rudy Robinson-organ; Frankie Jones-drums; Ralph Dorsey-congas

2/22/81 JACK McDUFF, Organ
Steve Slagle-alto/soprano sax; Jonathan Woods-bass; Gerrick King-drums

3/1/81 CHARLIE ROUSE, Tenor sax
Kenny Barron-piano; Rufus Reed-bass; Ben Riley-drums

3/8/81 EDDIE HARRIS QUINTET

3/15/81 **PEPPER ADAMS QUARTET**, Baritone sax
Ameen Abdul Raheem-bass; William Goffigan-drums

3/22/81 **TOP SHELF -REGGIE WORKMAN**, Bass
Steve McCall-drums; Cecil Bridgewater-trumpet; Arthur Rhames-tenor sax, guitar, piano; Donald Smith-piano

3/29/81 **LOU BENNETT**, Organ
Hugh Walker-drums; Mickey Fields-tenor sax

4/5/81 **WODDY SHAW**, Trumpet
Steve Turre-trombone; Mulgrew Miller-piano; Stafford James-bass; Tony Reedus-drums

4/12/81 **IRENE REID**, Vocals
Bill Phipps-alto/tenor/baritone sax/flute; Bobby Forrester-organ; Calvin Lockhart-guitar; Tootsie Bean-drums

4/19/81 **TED CURSON OCTET**
Ted Curson-trumpet; Nick Brignola-baritone/soprano sax; Ryo Kawasaki-guitar; Montego Joe-percussion; Guillermo Cruz-percussion; Jim McNeely-piano; Hal Dodson-bass; Jukkis Votila-drums

4/26/81 **JAMES MOODY**, Alto/Tenor Sax, Flute
Ronnie Mathews-piano; Ray Drummond-bass; Kenny Washington-drums

5/3/81 **REY SCOTT**, Baritone Sax, Flute
Joe Ford-soprano/alto sax/flute; Gerry Eastman-guitar; Gene Torres-bass; Nasar Abadey-drums; Babafemi Akinlana-congas; Hassan Bakr-percussion, shaker

5/10/81 **ARTHUR PRYSOCK**, Vocals
Red Prysock-tenor sax; Ernie Jones-organ; Steve Fishman-guitar; Don Williams-drums

5/17/81 **THE NEW YORK 4: MICHAL URBANIAK**, Violin
Kenny Barron-piano; Buster Williams-bass; Roy Haynes-drums

5/24/81 **CARMEN McRAE AND HER TRIO**, Vocals
Marshall Otwell-piano; Bob Bowman-bass; Mark Pulice-drums

5/31/81 **CHARLES TOLLIVER**, Trumpet
Albert Dailey-piano; Bob Cunningham-bass; Cliff Barbaro-drums

6/7/81 **WIDESPREAD JAZZ ORCHESTRA: JORDAN SANDKE**, Trumpet
Billy Grey-trumpet/vocals; Tim Atherton-trombone; Mike Hashim-alto sax; Dean Nicyper-tenor sax; David Lillie-baritone sax; Mike Le Donne-piano; Bill Conway-bass; John Ellis-drums

6/14/81 **THE EAST COAST OFFERING**
Tim Eyermann-reeds; Stefan Scaggiari-keyboards; Jay Dulaney-bass; Ralph Fisher-drums

6/21/81 **JIMMY SMITH**, Organ
Herman Riley-tenor/soprano sax,flute; Kenny Dixon-drums

6/28/81 **MELBA LISTON AND COMPANY**

7/12/81 **KALIMA: DERRICK AMIN**, Keyboards
Tony Douglass-drums; Andre Williams-bass guitar; James Tart-guitar; Wesley"Rico" James-percussion; Joe Thomas-woodwinds; Singers: Jeanne Harris, Nadiyah Bilal, Narramin Alif, Sabreen Sharif

9/13/81 **HOUSTON PERSON**, Tenor sax
John Logan-organ; Billy James-drums; Ralph Dorsey-conga; Etta Jones-vocals

9/20/81 **JOHNNY GRIFFIN**, Tenor sax
Ronnie Mathews-piano; Ray Drummond-bass; Kenny Washington-drums

9/27/81 **PIECES OF A DREAM: CURTIS DANIEL HARMON**, Drums
James Keith Lloyd-piano; Cedric Alexander Napoleon-bass; Barbara Walker-vocals; Glen Williams-alto sax

10/4/81 **DAVID SCHNITTER**, Tenor sax
Michael Cochrane-piano; Dennis Irwin-bass; Leo Mitchell-drums; Marti Mabin-vocals

10/11/81 **MONTEGO JOE,** Conga, Percussion
Alan Gerber-piano; Mack Goldsbury-woodwinds; Andrei Strobert-percussion; Jack Scavella-percussion; Rachim Ausar Sahu-bass; Lester Bailey-percussion

10/18/81 **MAYNARD FERGUSON ORCHESTRA,** Trumpet
Dave Ramsey-piano; Paul Rostock-bass; Dave Mancini-drums; Saxes: Eric Traub, Nelson Hill, Dennis DeBlasio; Trombones: Chris Brayman, Steve Weist; Trumpets: Stan Mark, Serg Yow, Dave Trigg, Alan Wise

10/25/81 **RED RODNEY**, Trumpet/Flugelhorn
IRA SULLIVAN, Trumpet, flugelhorn, soprano/alto sax, flute
Gary Dial-piano; Jan Anderson-bass; Jeff Hirshfield-drums

11/1/81 **JIMMY McGRIFF**, Organ
Ken Karsh-guitar; Arnold Sterling-reeds;Vance James-drums; John Franklin, bass, tenor sax, vocals

11/8/81 **SUN RA ARKESTRA**, Keyboard
John Gilmore-tenor sax/clarinet; Marshall Allen-alto sax/flute/dora/steiner; Elo Omo-contra bass, clarinet, flute; Danny Thompson-baritone sax, flute, steiner; James Jackson-ancient Egyptian infinity drum, bassoon, flute; Walter Miller-trumpet; Fred Adams-trumpet; Tyrone Hill-trombone; Carl Le Blanc-guitar; Skeeter McFarland-guitar; Steve Clarke-electric bass; Samaral-drums; Kamu Phillips-percussion; Eric Lewis-percussion; June Tyson-dance, vocals; Pharoah Abdullah and Muhammed Santos-bells, percussion

11/15/81 **HANK CRAWFORD**, Alto Sax/Piano
Calvin Newborn-guitar; Charles Green-bass; Hugh Walker-drums

11/22/81 **BUCK HILL**, Tenor sax
Marc Cohen-piano; Tommy Cecil-bass; Hugh Walker drums

11/29/81 **TOWSON STATE UNIVERSITY ENSEMBLE: HANK LEVY**, Director
Rusty Witt, Guitar; Geoff Harper-bass; John Hall, Adrien Green-drums; Josh Schwarzman-piano; Reeds: Bob Sholl, Mary Pat Hughes, Brad Collins, Barry Crudill; Trumpets: Bill Rowe, Mike Bergland, Vince Ciecbski, Cliff Bigoney, Tom Williams; Trombones: Dan Gottshall, Steve Dekken, Ken Mease, Ted Wilson, Nate Lynch

12/6/81 **LES McCANN AND THE MAGIC BAND**
Les McCann-vocals, keyboards; Tony St. James-drums; Curtis Robertson-bass; Bobby Bryant-sax

12/13/81 **DEXTER GORDON QUARTET**
Dexter Gordon-tenor sax; Kirk Lightsey-piano; Dave Eubanks-bass; Eddie Gladden-drums

1/31/82	**HUGH MASEKELA**, Flugelhorn
	Fred Foss-reeds; Bill Amey-trombone; Hotep Cecil Barnard-piano; Victor Ntoni-bass; Sipho Kunene-drums
2/7/82	**ART BLAKEY AND THE JAZZ MESSENGERS**
2/14/82	**CHICO FREEMAN**, Tenor/soprano sax, alto flute, bass clarinet
	Kenny Barron-piano; Cecil McBee-bass; Ronnie Burrage-drums
2/21/82	**BYRON MORRIS**, Tenor/alto/soprano sax
	Ron Holloway-tenor sax; Clyde Dickerson-tenor sax; Reuben Brown-piano; Steve Novosel-bass; Warren Shad-drums
2/28/82	**JANET LAWSON**, Vocals
	Roger Rosenberg-sax; Bill O'Connell-piano; Ratso Harris-bass; Billy Hart-drums
3/7/82	**HOUSTON PERSON**, Tenor sax
	Jon Logan-organ; Billy James-drums; Ralph Dorsey-percussion; Etta Jones-vocals
3/14/82	**SONNY STITT QUARTET**
3/21/82	**DIZZY GILLESPIE QUARTET**
3/28/82	**THE ORIGINAL HOOFERS**
	Isaiah "Lon" Chaney, Chuck Green, Bernard Manners, Jimmy Slyde, Toes Tiranoff (sit in); Johnny Polite-drums; Charles Covington-piano; Larry Kinling-bass; Mickey Fields-tenor sax;
4/4/82	**DAKOTA STATON**, Vocals
	Bross Townsend-piano; David Jackson-bass; Michael Fox-drums
4/11/82	**FREDDIE HUBBARD**, Trumpet
	Dave Schnitter-tenor sax; Kenny Barron-piano; Clint Houston-bass; Louis Hayes-drums
4/18/82	**JACK McDUFF**, Organ
	Jim Snidero-alto sax; Mitch Stein-guitar; Gerryck King-drums; Roslyn Pratt-vocals
4/25/82	**CHARLIE EARLAND**, Keyboards
	Sheryl Kendrick-backup keyboards, vocals; Terry Kendrick-bass; Michael Tingle-lead guitar, Chico Rouse-drums; Sam Carpenter-guitar; Tommy Labella-tenor/alto sax; Pete Maurer-trombone
5/2/82	**JAMES LLOYD**, Piano
	Cedric Napoleon-bass; Curtis Harmon-tenor sax; Connie Parker-vocals
5/9/82	**HORACE SILVER**, piano
	Ralph Moore-tenor sax; Tom Harrell-trumpet; Richard A. Reid-bass; Michael White-drums
5/16/82	**JAMES MOODY**, alto/tenor sax, flute
	Harold Mabern-piano; Calvin Hill-bass; Victor Jones-drums
5/23/82	**ARNOLD STERLING**, alto sax
	Marc Cohen-piano; Steve Novosel-bass; Bobby Ward-drums
6/6/82	**BILL HARDMAN**, Trumpet, **JUNIOR COOK**, Tenor sax
	Mickey Tucker-piano; Paul Brown-bass; Leroy Williams-drums
6/13/82	**JIMMY HEATH**, Tenor/Soprano sax, Flute
	Percy Heath-bass, baby bass; Stanley Cowell-piano; Tony Purrone-guitar; Akira Tana-drums
6/20/82	**Ballroom closed for summer**

9/19/82   **ART BLAKEY**, Drums
Jean Toussaint-tenor sax; Donald Harrison-alto sax; Terence Blanchard-trumpet; Johnny O'Neal-piano; Charles Fambrough-bass

9/26/82   **CHARLIE ROUSE**, Tenor sax
Kenny Barron-piano; Buster Williams-bass; Ben Riley-drums

10/3/82   **PHILLY JOE JONES**, Drums
Charles Davis-tenor sax; Martin Banks-trumpet; Walter Davis, Jr.-piano; Larry Ridley-bass

10/10/82   **HOUSTON PERSON**, Tenor sax
Jon Logan-organ; Billy James-drums; Ralph Dorsey-conga, percussion; Etta Jones-vocals

10/17/82   **WOODY SHAW**, Trumpet/flugelhorn
Steve Turre-trombone; Mulgrew Miller-piano; Stafford James-bass; Tony Reedus-drums

10/24/82   **JOHNNY GRIFFIN**, Tenor sax
Ronnie Mathews-piano; Curtis Lundy-bass; Kenny Washington-drums

10/31/82   **SUN RA**, Organ/piano
John Gilmore-tenor sax, timbales, clarinet; Marshall Allen-alto sax, flute, kora, oboe; Danny Thompson-alto/baritone sax, flute; Elo Omo-clarient, bass clarinet, contra bass, alto sax; James Jackson-bassoon, flute, ancient Egyptian infinity drum; Walter Miller-trumpet; Ronnie Brown-trumpet; Tyrone Hill-trombone; Radu-bass; Samarie Celestial-drums; June Tyson-vocals

11/7/82   **DEXTER GORDON**, Tenor sax
Kirk Lightsey-piano; David Eubanks-bass; Eddie Gladden-drums

11/14/82   **CLIFFORD JORDAN**, Tenor sax
Barry Harris-piano; Walter Booker-bass; Vernell Fournier-drums

11/21/82   **LOU DONALDSON**, Alto sax
Herman Foster-piano; Jeff Fuller-bass; Nat Yarbrough-drums

11/28/82   **BING MILLER BIG BAND (free concert)**

12/5/82   **BUCK HILL**, Tenor sax
Ron Elliston-piano; Tommy Cecil-bass; Steve Williams-drums

12/12/82   **ARTHUR PRYSOCK REVUE**
RED PRYSOCK QUARTET

12/19/82   **DAVE LIEBMAN**

2/20/83   **DOROTHY DONEGAN**

2/27/83   **NAT ADDERLEY**, Cornet
Sonny Fortune-alto sax; Larry Willis-piano; Walter Booker-bass; Jimmy Cobb-drums

3/6/83   **BOBBY HUTCHERSON**, Vibes
George Cables-piano; Cecil McBee-bass; Marvin Smith-drums

3/13/83   **DEWEY REDMAN**, Tenor sax
Charles Eubanks-piano; Mark Helias-bass; Eddie Moore-drums

3/20/83   **GARY BURTON QUARTET**

3/27/83   **WARREN CHIASSON**, Vibes
Chuck Wayne-guitar; Reggie Johnson-bass; Leroy Williams-drums

4/3/83   **LOUIS HAYES**, Drums
Bobby Watson-alto sax; James Williams-piano; Clint Houston-bass

4/10/83 **ARNOLD STERLING**, Alto sax
Marc Cohen-piano; Joe Jose-bass; Bobby Ward-drums;
Dave Yarborough-alto sax

4/17/83 **JOHNNY GRIFFIN**, Tenor sax
Bernard Wright-piano; Curtis Lundy-bass; Kenny Washington-drums

4/24/84 **ART BLAKEY**, Drums
Jean Toussaint-tenor sax; Terence Blanchard-trumpet;
Donald Harrison-alto sax; Johnny O'Neal-piano; Charles Fambrough-bass

5/1/83 **HOUSTON PERSON**, Tenor sax
Dave Braham-organ; Frankie Jones-drums; Ralph Dorsey-conga/percussion;
Etta Jones-vocals

5/8/83 **ARTHUR PRYSOCK**, Vocals
Red Prysock-tenor sax; Ken Wessel-guitar; Lloyd Wilson-organ;
Don Williams-drums

5/15/83 **NICK BRIGNOLA**, Sax
Bill Dobbins-piano; John Lockwood-bass; Dave Clarro-drums

5/22/83 **THE ORIGINAL HOOFERS**
Lon Chaney, George Hillman, Ralph Brown, Jimmy Slyde;
Johnny Polite-drums; Mickey Fields, tenor sax; Charles Covington-piano;
Larry Kinling-bass

5/29/83 **KETER BETTS**, Bass
O'Donel Levy-guitar; Marc Cohen-piano; Keith Kilgore-drums;
Tony Williams-alto sax

6/5/83 **No concert (Kool Jazz Festival, Washington, D.C.)**

6/12/83 **JOE HENDERSON**, Tenor sax
Fred Hersch-piano; Tommy Cecil-bass; Keith Kilgore-drums

6/19/83 **Ballroom closed for summer**

10/2/83 **ART BLAKEY**, Drums
Donald Harrison-alto sax; Jean Toussaint-tenor sax;
Terence Blanchard-trumpet; Mulgrew Miller-piano; Lonnie Plexico-bass

10/9/83 **RICKY FORD**, Tenor sax
Dave Stewart-piano; Leon Maleson-bass; Victor Jones-drums

10/16/83 **HOUSTON PERSON**, Tenor sax
David Braham-organ; Frankie Jones-drums; Ralph Dorsey-conga;
Etta Jones-vocals

10/23/83 **CURTIS HARMON**, Drums
James Lloyd-piano; Cedric Napoleon-bass; Randy Boland-guitar;
Michelle Becham-vocals

10/30/83 **JAMES MOODY**, Alto/tenor sax, flute
Harold Mabern-piano; Todd Coolman-bass; Eddie Gladden-drums

11/6/83 **LONNIE LISTON SMITH**, Keyboards
Donald Smith-flute, vocals; Premik-sax, flute; Billy Colburn-bass;
Abe Speller-drums; Steve Thornton-percussion

11/13/83 **LOU DONALDSON**, Alto sax
Herman Foster-piano; Jeff Fuller-bass; Victor Jones-drums

11/20/83 **NAT ADDERLEY**, Cornet
Sonny Fortune-alto sax; Larry Willis-piano; Walter Booker-bass;
Jimmy Cobb-drums

11/27/83 **BETTY CARTER AND HER TRIO**
12/4/83 **FREDDIE HUBBARD**, Trumpet, flugelhorn
Billy Pierce-tenor sax; Mulgrew Miller-piano; Charles Fambrough-bass;
Carl Allen-drums
12/11/83 **DIZZY GILLESPIE**, Trumpet
Ed Cherry-guitar; Marcus McLaurine-bass; Ignacio Berroa-drums
12/18/83 **ARNOLD STERLING**, Alto/tenor sax
Marc Cohen-piano; Drew Gress, Steve Novosel-bass; Tony Sweet-drums
2/5/84 **HERBIE MANN**, Alto/ tenor sax, flute
David "Fathead" Newman-alto / tenor sax, flute; O'Donel Levy-guitar;
Frank Gravis-bass; Scott Peaker-drums
2/12/84 **BUCK HILL**, Tenor sax
Elsworth Gibson-piano; Tommy Cecil-bass; George "Dude" Brown-drums
2/19/84 **PIECES OF A DREAM**
2/26/84 **HOUSTON PERSON**
Etta Jones
2/26/84 **CHICO FREEMAN**, Sax
Mark Thompson-piano; Cecil McBee-bass; Freddie Waits-drums
3/4/84 **BILL HARDMAN**, Trumpet
Junior Cook-tenor sax; Mickey Tucker-piano; Andy McCloud-bass;
Leroy Williams-drums
3/11/84 **TRIBUTE TO LESTER YOUNG**
Byron Morris, Ron Holloway, Orrie Hall-sax, Charlie Young-sax;
Dick Hopkins-piano; Steve Novosel-bass; Bertell Knox-drums;
K. Shalong-vocals
3/18/84 **JIMMY HEATH**, Tenor/soprano sax, flute
Percy Heath-bass; Albert "Tootie" Heath-drums; Stanley Cowell-piano
3/23/84 **TRACY McCLEARY AND HIS ROYAL MEN OF RHYTHM**
Tracy McCleary-leader; Charlie Harris-bass; Robert Gardner-drums; William
Mackel, Bill Forrester-guitar; Trombones: Charles Funn, Fredd Webb;
Trumpets: Roy McCoy, Phil White, Joe Day Saxes; Earl Cornell-alto; Calvin
Geary-alto; Aaron Gross-tenor; John Luke-tenor; Bruce Henderson-baritone
This show was a special Friday night dance-cabaret benefit for LBJS
3/25/84 **IRA SULLIVAN**, Alto/tenor/soprano sax, flugelhorn, flute, trumpet
Reuben Brown-piano; Rufus Reid-bass; Steve Bagby-drums
4/1/84 **MALACHI THOMPSON**, Trumpet
Carter Jefferson-tenor sax; Gary Thomas-tenor sax; Hilton Felton-piano;
James King-bass; Nassar Abadey-drums
4/8/84 **WOODY SHAW**, Trumpet
Harold Mabern-piano; Ray Drummond-bass; Terri Lyne Carrington-drums
4/15/84 **CARTER JEFFERSON**, Tenor sax
Danny Mixon-piano; Mickey Bass-bass; Greg Bandy-drums
4/22/84 **ARNOLD STERLING**, Alto sax
Marc Cohen-piano; Steve Novosel-bass; Johnny Polite-drums
4/29/84 **JOHNNY GRIFFIN**, Tenor sax
Harry Pickens-piano; Curtis Lundy-bass; Kenny Washington-drums
5/6/84 **SUN RA ARKESTRA**
Sun Ra-keyboards; John Gilmore-tenor sax, clarinet; Marshall Allen-alto sax,
oboe, flute, Danny Thompson-alto / baritone sax; Elo Omo-alto sax, bass

clarinet; James Jackson-bassoon, flute, ancient Egyptian infinity drum; John Ore-bass; Alan Nelson-drums; Bruce Edwards-guitar; June Tyson-vocals; Trumpets: Morton Banks, Fred Adams, Al Evans, Bucky Thorpe

5/13/84 **JENELLE FISHER AND HER GROUP**
Jenelle Fisher-vocals; Brad Collins-tenor sax; Tim Murphy-piano; Vincent Loving-bass; Ralph Fisher-drums

5/20/84 **ARTHUR PRYSOCK REVUE**
Arthur Prysock-vocals; Red Prysock-tenor sax; Lloyd Wilson-organ; Duck Scott-drums; Doug Cuomo-guitar

6/25/84 **PIECES OF A DREAM AND SHEE**

10/28/84 **BOBBY WATSON**, Sax
Mulgrew Miller-piano; Kenny Washington-drums; Curtis Lundy-bass

11/4/84 **STEVE WILLIAMS**, Drums
Gary Thomas, Charles Young-sax; Reuben Brown-piano; Steve Novosel-bass

11/18/84 **FREEBOP BAND FEATURING MALACHI THOMPSON AND DAVID MURRAY**

11/25/84 **ARNOLD STERLING QUINTET**

12/2/84 **ART BLAKEY AND THE JAZZ MESSENGERS**

12/9/84 **RICHIE COLE QUARTET**

12/16/84 **HOUSTON PERSON QUARTET WITH ETTA JONES**

3/31/85 **MICKEY FIELDS QUARTET**

9/8/85 **HOUSTON PERSON QUARTET WITH ETTA JONES**

9/22/85 **NAT ADDERLEY QUINTET**

10/27/85 **JOHNNY GRIFFIN QUARTET**

11/24/85 **EDDIE "LOCKJAW" DAVIS QUARTET**

2/23/86 **LOU DONALDSON AND JIMMY McGRIFF**

3/23/86 **JIMMY HEATH QUARTET**
Jimmy Heath-reeds; Tony Purrone-guitar; Stafford James-bass; Akira Tana-drums

4/27/86 **HANK CRAWFORD**

6/1/86 **RICHARD "GROOVE" HOLMES AND SIR THOMAS HURLEY AND TINY TIM**

9/7/86 **JACK McDUFF AND THE HEATIN' SYSTEM**

9/21/86 **PHIL WOODS QUINTET**

10/26/86 **JOE SUDLER, BUCK HILL, MICKEY FIELDS**

11/16/86 **HANK CRAWFORD/ JIMMY McGRIFF**

2/22/87 **SUN RA ARKESTRA**

3/22/87 **ARNOLD STERLING, DON PATTERSON, DAVID "FATHEAD" NEWMAN**

4/12/87 **JOHNNY GRIFFIN QUARTET**

4/26/87 **MICHAEL PHILIP MOSSMAN**-Trumpet
Kenny Garrett-alto sax; Ralph Bowen-tenor sax; Bob Hurst-bass Ralph Peterson-piano

6/7/87 **JIMMY McGRIFF, DAVE ROSS**

9/9/87 **ARTHUR PRYSOCK WITH RED PRYSOCK BAND**

9/27/87 **NAT ADDERLEY QUINTET**

10/25/87 **SONNY FORTUNE QUARTET**

11/15/87 **JAMES MOODY QUARTET**

12/13/87 **BOBBY WATSON, CURTIS LUNDY, SLIDE HAMPTON**

2/28/88	TERENCE BLANCHARD/DONALD HARRISON QUINTET
3/27/88	HOUSTON PERSON QUARTET WITH ETTA JONES
4/24/88	OUT OF THE BLUE SEXTET
6/5/88	CARLOS JOHNSON BAND AND THE DENNIS FISHER BAND
9/11/88	JIMMY MCGRIFF/HANK CRAWFORD BAND
9/25/88	VOCALIST TERRI THORNTON WITH REUBEN BROWN TRIO
	Reuben Brown-piano; Keter Betts-bass; Bertell Knox-drums
10/23/88	SHIRLEY SCOTT QUARTET
	Shirley Scott-piano; Benny Nelson-bass; Mickey Roker-drums;
	Bootsie Barnes-tenor sax
10/23/88	MALACHI THOMPSON QUARTET ft. CARTER JEFFERSON
12/11/88	JACK McDUFF MINI BAND
2/26/89	TERENCE BLANCHARD/DONALD HARRISON QUINTET
3/19/89	LOU DONALDSON QUARTET
4/16/89	JOHNNY GRIFFIN QUARTET
6/4/89	SIR THOMAS HURLEY BAND AND THE DAVE ROSS BAND
9/10/89	RICHARD "GROOVE" HOLMES TRIO
9/23/89	AWARDS CEREMONY
	EUBIE BLAKE CULTURAL CENTER
10/22/89	JIMMY SMITH QUARTET AND HOUSTON PERSON QUARTET WITH ETTA JONES
11/19/89	MICKEY FIELDS QUINTET
	Ruby Glover, vocalist; Carlos Johnson Zone One Band; Dennis Fisher Band feat. Jennifer Jones

PHOTOGRAPHS

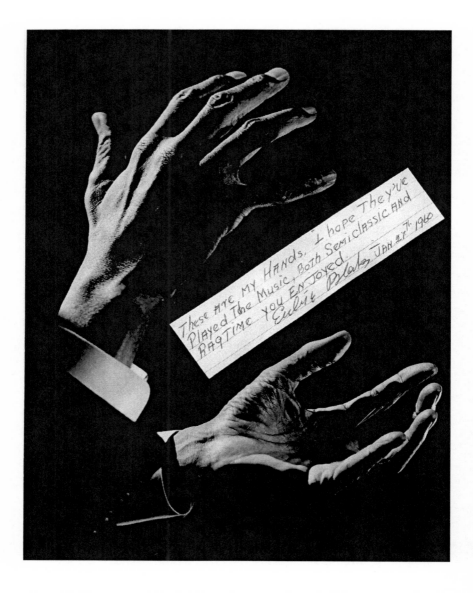

Eubie Blake's hands along with a handwritten note from the famous ragtime artist.

CREDIT: Reproduced by permission of the Maryland Historical Society.

Eubie Blake at the piano in 1968 during his brief retirement.

CREDIT: Reproduced by permission of the Maryland Historical Society.

Chick Webb performing with his big band. Singing are Ella Fitzgerald and Charles Linton.

CREDIT: Courtesy of the Frank Driggs Collection.

CAB CALLOWAY

In spite of the exuberance of his performances, Cab liked to consider himself a professional and took his art very seriously, maintaining an offstage gravitas that tended to extend to his family life as well.

CREDIT: Courtesy of Camay Murphy.

An intimate shot of Calloway backstage at Jordan Hall in Boston, MA. Even as musical trends dramatically changed over the course of his career, Cab managed to remain active through a combination of theatre, film, and bandleading on the side.

CREDIT: Courtesy of Camay Murphy.

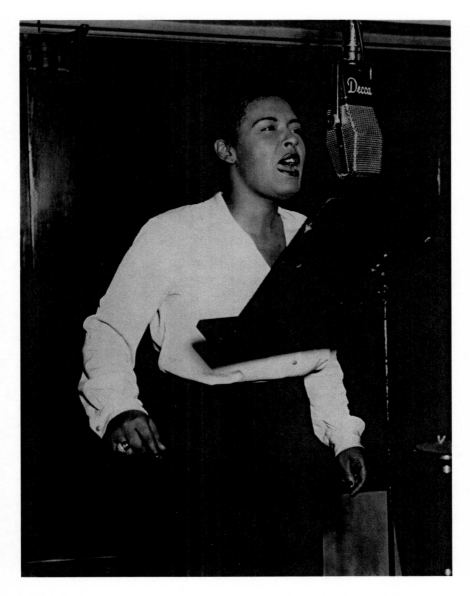

Billie Holiday recording vocals at Decca Studios in New York City.

CREDIT: Courtesy of the Frank Driggs Collection.

Larkins Guest Artist at School Celebration

ELLIS LANE LARKINS

Ellis Lane Larkins, prodigy and pianist, was guest artist at the Negro History Week celebration at School No. 105, East Street near Lexington.

Young Larkins now a junior at

sponsored the program in the school, presented Larkins a black leather zipper music case.

Also a guest was Miss Florence Turner, a student of Mrs. Adah K. Jenkins, who played "Mona-

tributions to civilization by ored people.

Children who participate the program were: Lillia Ma vis, Matthew Goodman, C Redding, Laura Fisher, Th Venerable. Mrs. Orangi

A news clipping containing a photograph of a young Larkins, from February 25th, 1939.

CREDIT: Reprinted by permission of the *Afro-American*.

Hank Levy conducting, 1972.

CREDIT: Courtesy of Towson University archives.

Cyrus Chestnut at the piano.

CREDIT: Copyright Jimmy Katz.

Chestnut discussing a chart with saxophonist James Carter.

CREDIT: Copyright Jimmy Katz.

Mickey Fields with young saxophonist Miriam Kaul.

CREDIT: Courtesy of Jackie Fields.

The outside of the Famous Ballroom taken in 1975. The patrons outside are waiting for the start of a Freddie Hubbard concert.

CREDIT: The Left Bank Jazz Society's *The Baltimore Jazz Scene 1975-1976.*

A crowd inside the Famous Ballroom.

CREDIT: Courtesy of Sojourner-Douglass College

Enjoying music and drinks at the Famous.

CREDIT: Courtesy of Sojourner-Douglass College

A photograph of the Royal Theatre in 1930, where Louis Armstrong had paid for bags of coal to be distributed to the public.

CREDIT: Reproduced by permission of the Maryland Historical Society.

CONTRIBUTORS

Contributors

Matthew Blackburn is a biology and chemistry double major at Loyola University Maryland, class of 2011. An avid fan of jazz, he has played the trumpet for the past twelve years and has been a member of the Loyola Jazz Ensemble for several semesters. He plans to enroll in a graduate program to continue his studies in either organic chemistry or biochemistry, and hopes to eventually enter a research career in one of those fields.

Erin Bowman graduated in May, 2010 from Loyola University Maryland, where she studied history and philosophy. This is her first published piece of writing. She embarked on her first experience with independent research in the summer of 2008, which she spent in Guatemala studying issues of justice in its post-civil war society. Since then, she has continued to explore ideas and experiences that engage her heart and intellect.

Eliot Caroom, who holds a Masters in Journalism from NYU, was the Baltimore Jazz Alliance's first newsletter editor, and employee, beginning in 2004. He produced the Baltimore Youth Jazz Congress and wrote several grants before leaving Baltimore in 2007. For other work by Eliot, see www.EliotCaroom.com.

Cathleen Carris graduated in May, 2010 with a BA in History and Spanish from Loyola University Maryland, where she was a Presidential Scholar, Honors Program student, and Phi Beta Kappa Society inductee. Her interests include travel, immigration advocacy, and Latin American history and literature. She has translated into English two of the speeches given by Peruvian essayist Manuel Gonzalez Prada, from his collection entitled, *Horas de Lucha.*

Benjamin DiFranco is a lifesaver with Nags Head Ocean Rescue, a horticulturist, an entertainer, and an honorary southerner. He is an economics and English major at Loyola University Maryland who has seen the world. He aspires to save the world. You ask what aspect of the world? He answers: all of it.

Liz Fixsen is a frequent contributor to the Baltimore Jazz Alliance Newsletter. She is keyboardist and vocalist with her band, Moonstruck Jazz, with the Glenn Angus trio, and with the DC-based Bob Schwartz Quartet. A resident of Savage, Maryland, Liz is a regular habitue of the jazz clubs and shows in Baltimore and the region. She teaches professional writing at the University of Maryland, College Park and the introductory literature course at Loyola University Maryland. She also writes a weekly column for the *Laurel Gazette.*

Frank J. Graziano is a graduate of Loyola University Maryland, class of 2010. His interests include jazz, writing, Brazilian jiu jitsu, and meditation. This is his first editorial effort and he looks forward to more in the future.

Geoffrey Himes has written about music weekly for the Washington *Post* since 1977 and is currently a senior editor at *Paste Magazine.* He has also written about music for *DownBeat, Jazz Times, Rolling Stone,* the *Oxford American,* the *New York Times,* National Public Radio, the Chicago *Tribune, Baltimore* Magazine, the Baltimore *City Paper,* the Baltimore *Sun,* and other outlets. He has been honored for Music Feature Writing by the Deems Taylor/ASCAP Awards, by the Abell Foundation Awards, and by the Music Journalism Awards. His book on Bruce Springsteen, *Born in the U.S.A.,* was published by Continuum Books in 2005. He is currently working on a book about Emmylou Harris, Rosanne Cash, Rodney Crowell, and Ricky Skaggs for the Country Music Hall of Fame. He has lived in Baltimore since 1974. His stage musical, *A Baltimore Christmas Carol,* premiered at Baltimore's Patterson Theatre in 2004.

Bob Jacobson has been a jazz fan since his pre-teens and has played jazz on saxophone and clarinet since age 16. Since 1995 he's led the small jazz band Sounds Good. His freelance writing on jazz has appeared in *DownBeat* and on the websites AllAboutJazz.com and JazzReview.com. Bob is currently vice-president of Baltimore Jazz Alliance, developed its Jazz for Kids program, works on its newsletter, and has coordinated BJA's community outreach, particularly at Baltimore's annual Artscape festival. Sounds Good appears on both BJA compilation CDs and four of Bob's compositions appear in BJA's the *Baltimore Real Book.*

Jennifer Margaret Nordmark is an undergraduate at Loyola University Maryland studying writing and political science. She was drawn to this project by her love of both jazz and the city of her wonderful alma mater. As a jazz musician herself, she felt a kinship with Eubie Blake early in her research and was honored to have the opportunity to write about his profound musical influence. Jennifer hopes to find herself in law school in the upcoming years, but realizes that the future is as unpredictable as a musician's solo.

Mark Osteen, a professor of English at Loyola University Maryland, is the author or editor of six books and dozens of articles on literature and film. In 2004 he edited a special double issue of *Genre* devoted to jazz and jazz writing. A working musician since 1971, Osteen is president of the Baltimore Jazz Alliance, and produced the organization's two compilation CDs and edited the *Baltimore Real Book.* He is also the saxophonist and singer for Cold Spring Jazz Quartet. His memoir, *One of Us: A Family's Life with Autism,* will be published in Fall, 2010 by the University of Missouri Press.

Katherine R. Rynone, a member of the Loyola University Maryland class of 2010, is currently pursuing her BA in English and was recently selected for membership in Loyola's chapter of Sigma Tau Delta, the International English Honor Society. Katherine has dedicated a significant amount of her academic career to studying French language and public policy. Katherine enjoys traveling, concert going, and spending time with her family in upstate New York.

Mary Zajac has written widely about the local music scene, including articles on Carr's Beach, R & B DJ Willie Bacote, aka "The Moon Man," and the current state of jazz in Baltimore. A columnist for *Style* magazine, she is also the restaurant critic for *Chesapeake Life* and the *City Paper*, a frequent contributor to *Urbanite* magazine, and the co-host, with Jonathan Palevsky, of WBJC's "Word on Wine." Her work has also appeared in *Saveur* and the *New York Times*. A Loyola College graduate, she holds an MA from West Virginia University and a Ph.D. from the University of Illinois at Chicago.

Andrew Zaleski is a student at Loyola University Maryland who graduates in May, 2011 with a bachelor's degree in English. An aspiring writer and journalist, he has published work in several venues, including such magazines as *College, Urbanite*, and *The Big Issue: South Africa*, as well as in the book *Chicken Soup for the Soul: Campus Chronicles*. More recently, at the behest of the print advertising gods, he has begun to dabble in graphic and web design. To contact Andrew, visit www.AndrewZaleski.com.

INDEX

M

N

O

P

Y

The future of publishing...today!

Apprentice House is the country's only campus-based, student-staffed book publishing company. Directed by professors and industry professionals, it is a nonprofit activity of the Communication Department at Loyola University Maryland.

Using state-of-the-art technology and an experiential learning model of education, Apprentice House publishes books in untraditional ways. This dual responsibility as publishers and educators creates an unprecedented collaborative environment among faculty and students, while teaching tomorrow's editors, designers, and marketers.

Outside of class, progress on book projects is carried forth by the AH Book Publishing Club, a co-curricular campus organization supported by Loyola University Maryland's Office of Student Activities.

Student Project Team for *Music At The Crossroads: Lives & Legacies of Baltimore Jazz;*
    Jesse DeFlorio
    Johanna Murphy

Eclectic and provocative, Apprentice House titles intend to entertain as well as spark dialogue on a variety of topics. Financial contributions to sustain the press's work are welcomed. Contributions are tax deductible to the fullest extent allowed by the IRS.

To learn more about Apprentice House books or to obtain submission guidelines, please visit www.ApprenticeHouse.com.

Apprentice House
Communication Department
Loyola University Maryland
4501 N. Charles Street
Baltimore, MD 21210
Ph: 410-617-5265 • Fax: 410-617-5040
info@apprenticehouse.com

Breinigsville, PA USA
24 May 2010
238598BV00001B/1/P